Writing Excel Macros

Writing Excel Macros

Steven Roman

O'REILLY®

Beijing · Cambridge · Farnham · Köln · Paris · Sebastopol · Taipei · Tokyo

Writing Excel Macros
by Steven Roman

Copyright © 1999 Steven Roman. All rights reserved.
Printed in the United States of America.

Published by O'Reilly & Associates, Inc., 101 Morris Street, Sebastopol, CA 95472.

Editor: Ron Petrusha

Production Editor: Clairemarie Fisher O'Leary

Printing History:

      May 1999:   First Edition.

This book is printed on acid-free paper with 85% recycled content, 15% post-consumer waste. O'Reilly & Associates is committed to using paper with the highest recycled content available consistent with high quality.

ISBN: 1-56592-587-4   [7/99]

To Donna

Table of Contents

Preface

As the title suggests, this book is intended for those who want to learn how to program Microsoft Excel Version 8 (for Office 97) and Version 9 (for Office 2000).

We should begin by addressing the question, "Why would anyone want to program Microsoft Excel?" The answer is simple: to get more power out of this formidable application. As you will see, there are many things that you can do at the programming level that you cannot do at the user-interface level—that is, with the menus and dialog boxes of Excel. Chapter 1 provides some concrete examples of this.

This book provides an introduction to programming the Excel object model using Visual Basic for Applications (VBA). However, it is not intended to be an encyclopedia of Excel programming. The goal here is to acquaint you with the main points of Excel programming—enough so that you can continue your education (as we all do) on your own. The goal is that after reading this book you should not need to rely on any source other than the Excel VBA Help file or a good Excel VBA reference book and a nice object browser (such as my Enhanced Object Browser, a coupon for which is included in the back of this book).

It has been my experience that introductory programming books (and, sadly, most trade computer books) tend to do a great deal of handholding. They cover concepts at a very slow pace by padding them heavily with overblown examples and irrelevant anecdotes that only the author could conceivably find amusing, making it difficult to ferret out the facts. Frankly, I find such unprofessionalism incredibly infuriating. In my opinion, it does the reader a great disservice to take perhaps 400 pages of information and pad it with another 600 pages of junk.

There is no doubt in my mind that we need more professionalism from our authors, but it is not easy to find writers who have both the knowledge to write about a subject and the training (or talent) to do so in a pedagogical manner. (I should hasten to add that there are a number of excellent authors in this area—it's just that there are not nearly enough of them.) Moreover, publishers tend to encourage the creation of 1000-plus page tomes because of the general feeling among the publishers that a book must be physically wide enough to stand out on the bookshelf! I shudder to think that this might, in fact, be true. (I am happy to say that O'Reilly has not succumbed to this opinion.)

On the other hand, *Writing Excel Macros* is not a book in which you will find much handholding (nor will you find much handholding in any of my books). The book proceeds at a relatively rapid pace from a general introduction to programming through an examination of the Visual Basic for Applications programming language to an overview of the Excel object model. Given the enormity of the subject, not everything is covered, nor should it be. Nevertheless, the essentials of both the VBA language and the Excel object model are covered so that, when you have finished the book, you will know enough about Excel VBA to begin creating effective working programs.

I have tried to put my experience as a professor (about 20 years) and my experience writing books (about 30 of them) to work here to create a true learning tool for my readers. Hopefully, this is a book that can be read, perhaps more than once, and can also serve as a useful reference.

The Book's Audience

As an introduction to programming in Excel VBA, the book is primarily addressed to two groups of readers:

- Excel users who are not programmers but who would like to be. If you fall into this category, it is probably because you have begun to appreciate the power of Excel and want to take advantage of its more advanced features or just accomplish certain tasks more easily.

- Excel users who are programmers (in virtually any language—Visual Basic, Visual Basic for Applications, BASIC, C, C++, and so on) but who are not familiar with the Excel object model. In this case, you can use *Writing Excel Macros* to brush up on some of the details of the VBA language and learn about the Excel object model and how to program it.

Organization of This Book

Writing Excel Macros consists of 21 chapters that can informally be divided into four parts (excluding the introductory chapter). In addition, there are five appendixes.

Chapter 1, *Introduction*, examines why you might want to learn programming, and provides a few examples of the kinds of problems that can best be solved through programming. Chapter 2, *Preliminaries*, introduces programming and the Visual Basic for Applications language.

Chapters 2 and 4 form the first part of the book. Chapter 3, *The Visual Basic Editor, Part I*, and Chapter 4, *The Visual Basic Editor, Part II*, examine the Visual Basic integrated development environment (IDE), which is the programming environment used to develop Excel VBA applications.

The second part of the book consists of Chapters 5 through 8, which form an introduction to the VBA language, the language component that is common to Microsoft Visual Basic and to many of Microsoft's major applications, including Word, Excel, PowerPoint, and Access, as well as to software from some other publishers. Individual chapters survey VBA's variables, data types, and constants (Chapter 5), functions and subroutines (Chapter 6), intrinsic functions and statements (Chapter 7), and control statements (Chapter 8).

The third part of the book is devoted to some general topics that are needed in order to create usable examples of Excel applications, and to the Excel object model itself. We begin with a discussion of object models in general (Chapter 9). The succeeding chapters discuss just what constitutes an Excel application (Chapter 10), Excel events (Chapter 11), Excel menus and toolbars (Chapter 12), and Excel dialog boxes, both built-in and custom (Chapter 13 and Chapter 14). (Those who have read my book *Learning Word Programming* might notice that these topics came at the end of that book. While I would have preferred this organization here as well, I could not construct meaningful Excel examples without covering this material *before* discussing the Excel object model.)

The last chapters of the book are devoted to the Excel object model itself. This model determines which elements of Excel (workbooks, worksheets, charts, cells, and so on) are accessible through code and how they can be controlled programmatically. Chapter 15 gives an overview of the Excel object model. Subsequent chapters are devoted to taking a closer look at some of the main objects in the Excel object model, such as the Application object (Chapter 16), which represents the Excel application itself; the Workbook object (Chapter 17), which represents an Excel workbook; the Worksheet object (Chapter 18), which represents an Excel worksheet; the Range object (Chapter 19), which represent a collection of cells in a workbook; the PivotTable object (Chapter 20); and the Chart object (Chapter 21). I have tried to include useful examples at the end of most of these chapters.

The appendixes provide a diverse collection of supplementary material, including a discussion of the Shape object, which can be used to add some interesting artwork to Excel sheets, determining what printers are available on a user's system (this is not quite as easy as you might think), and how to program Excel from other applications (such as Word, Access, or PowerPoint). There is also an appendix containing a very brief overview of programming languages that is designed to give you a perspective on where VBA fits into the great scheme of things.

The Book's Text and Sample Code

When reading this book, you will encounter many small programming examples to illustrate the concepts. I prefer to use small coding examples, hopefully just a few lines, to illustrate a point.

Personally, I seem to learn much more quickly and easily by tinkering with and tracing through short program segments than by studying a long, detailed example. The difficulty in tinkering with a long program is that changing a few lines can affect other portions of the code, to the point where the program will no longer run. Then you have to waste time trying to figure out why it won't run.

I encourage you to follow along with the code examples by typing them in yourself. (Nevertheless, if you'd rather save yourself the typing, sample programs are available online; see "Obtaining the Sample Programs" later in this Preface.) Also, I encourage you to experiment—it is definitely the best way to learn. However, to protect yourself, I *strongly* suggest that you use a throw-away workbook for your experimenting.

One final comment about the sample code is worth making, particularly since this book and its coding examples are intended to teach you how to write VBA programs for Microsoft Excel. Generally speaking, there is somewhat of a horse-before-the-cart problem in trying to write about a complicated object model, since it is almost impossible to give examples of one object and its properties and methods without referring to other objects that may not yet have been discussed. Frankly, I don't see any way to avoid this problem completely, so rather than try to rearrange the material in an unnatural way, it seems better to simply proceed in an orderly fashion. Occasionally, we will need to refer to objects that we have not yet discussed, but this should not cause any serious problems, since most of these forward references are fairly obvious.

About the Code

The code in this book has been carefully tested by at least three individuals— myself, my editor Ron Petrusha, and the technical reviewer, Matt Childs. Indeed, I have tested the code on more than one machine (with different operating systems) and at more than one time (at least during the writing of the book and during the final preparation for book production).

Unfortunately, all three of us have run into some deviations from expected behavior (that is, the code doesn't seem to work as advertised, or work at all) as well as some inconsistencies in code behavior (that is, it works differently on different systems or at different times). Indeed, there have been occasions when one of us did not get the same results as the others with the same code and the same data. Moreover, I have personally had trouble on occasion duplicating my own results after a significant span of time!

I suppose that this shouldn't be entirely surprising considering the complexity of a program like Excel and the fallibility of us all, but the number of such peccadilloes has prompted me to add this caveat.

Offhand, I can think of two reasons for this behavior—whether it be real or just apparent—neither of which is by any means an excuse:

- The state of documentation being what it is, there may be additional *unmentioned* requirements or restrictions in order for some code to work properly, or even at all. As an example, nowhere in the vast documentation—at least that I could find—does it say that we cannot use the HasAxis method to put an axis on a chart before we have set the location of the data for that axis! (This seems to me to be putting the cart before the horse, but that is not the issue.) If we try to do so, the resulting error message simply says "Method 'HasAxis' of object '_Chart' has failed." This is not much help in pinpointing the problem. Of course, without being privy to this kind of information from the source, we must resort to experimentation and guesswork. If this does not reveal the situation, it will *appear* that the code simply does not work.

- Computers are not static. Whenever we install a new application, whether it be related to Excel or not, there is a chance that a DLL or other system file will be replaced by a newer file. Sadly, newer files are not always better. This could be the cause, but certainly not the excuse, for inconsistent behavior over time.

The reason that I am bringing this up is to alert you to the fact that you may run into some inconsistencies or deviations from expected behavior as well. I have tried to point out some of these problems when they occur, but you may encounter others. Of course, one of our biggest challenges (yours and mine) is to determine whether it is we who are making the mistake and not the program. I will hasten to add that when I encounter a problem with code behavior, I am usually (but not always) the one who is at fault. In fact, sometimes I must remind myself of my students, who constantly say to me "There is an error in the answers in the back of the textbook." I have learned over 20 years of teaching that 99 percent of the time (but not 100 percent of the time), the error is *not* in the book! Would that the software industry had this good a record!

I hope you enjoy this book. Please feel free to check out my web site at *www. romanpress.com.*

Conventions in this Book

Throughout this book, we have used the following typographic conventions:

`Constant width`

> indicates a language construct such as a language statement, a constant, or an expression. Lines of code also appear in constant width, as do functions and method prototypes.

Italic

> represents intrinsic and application-defined functions, the names of system elements such as directories and files, and Internet resources such as web documents and email addresses. New terms are also italicized when they are first introduced.

`Constant width italic`

> in prototypes or command syntax indicates replaceable parameter names, and in body text indicates variable and parameter names.

Obtaining the Sample Programs

The sample programs presented in the book are available online from the Internet and can be freely downloaded from our web site at *http://www.oreilly.com/ catalog/exlmacro/.*

How to Contact Us

We have tested and verified all the information in this book to the best of our ability, but you may find that features have changed (or even that we have made mistakes!). Please let us know about any errors you find, as well as your suggestions for future editions, by writing to:

> O'Reilly & Associates
> 101 Morris Street
> Sebastopol, CA 95472
> 1-800-998-9938 (in the U.S. or Canada)
> 1-707-829-0515 (international/local)
> 1-707-829-0104 (fax)

You can also send messages electronically. To be put on our mailing list or to request a catalog, send email to:

nuts@oreilly.com

To ask technical questions or comment on the book, send email to:

bookquestions@oreilly.com

Acknowledgments

I would like to express my sincerest thanks to Ron Petrusha, my editor at O'Reilly. As with my other books, Ron has been of considerable help. He is one of the best editors that I have worked with over the last 17 years of book writing.

Katie Gardner and Tara McGoldrick put their considerable organizational skills at work in making sure that this book came out on time and on schedule. I want to thank them for their efforts.

Also thanks to the production staff at O'Reilly & Associates, including Clairemarie Fisher O'Leary, the Production Editor; Edie Freedman for designing another memorable cover; Mike Sierra for Tools support; Robert Romano for illustrations; Ruth Rautenberg for the index; and Sarah Jane Shangraw, John Files, and Jeff Liggett for quality control. Also, I would like to thank Matt Childs for doing an all-important technical review of the book.

1

Introduction

Microsoft Excel is an application of enormous power and flexibility. But despite its powerful feature set, there is a great deal that Excel either does not allow you to do or does not allow you to do easily through its user interface. In these cases, we must turn to Excel programming.

Let me give you two examples that have come up in my consulting practice.

Selecting Special Cells

The Excel user interface does not have a built-in method for selecting worksheet cells based on various criteria. For instance, there is no way to select all cells whose value is between 0 and 100 or all cells that contain a date later than January 1, 1998. There is also no way to select only those cells in a given column that are different from their immediate predecessors. This can be very useful when you have a sorted column and want to extract a set of unique values, as shown in Figure 1-1.

I have been asked many times by clients if Excel provides a way to make such selections. After a few such questions, I decided to write an Excel utility for this purpose. The dialog for this utility is shown in Figure 1-2. With this utility, the user can select a match type (such as number, date, or text) and a match criterion. If required, the user supplies one or two values for the match. This has proven to be an extremely useful utility.

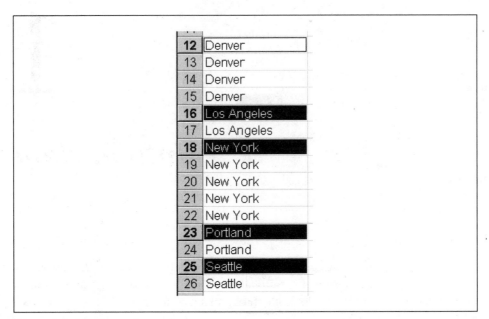

Figure 1-1. Selecting unique values

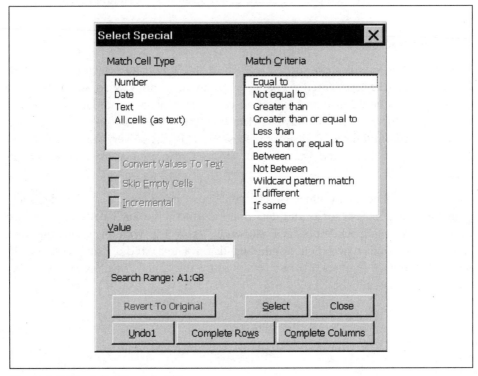

Figure 1-2. The Select Special utility

In this book, we will develop a simpler version of this utility, whose dialog is shown in Figure 1-3. This book will also supply you with the necessary knowledge to enhance this utility to something similar to the utility shown in Figure 1-2.

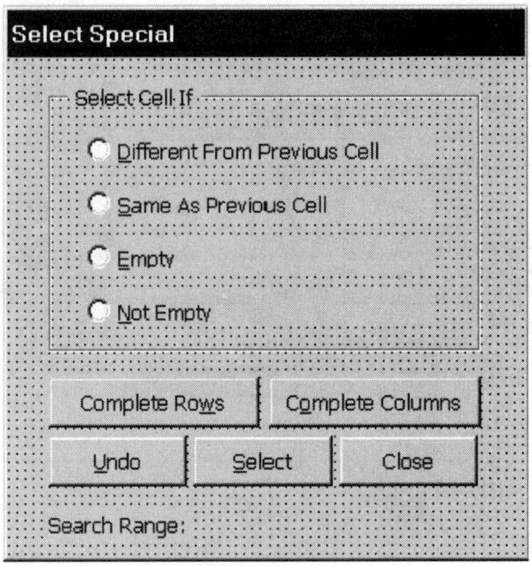

Figure 1-3. Select Special dialog

Setting a Chart's Data Point Labels

As you may know, data labels can be edited individually by clicking twice (pausing in between clicks) on a data label. This places the label in edit mode, as shown in Figure 1-4. Once in edit mode, we can change the text of a data label (which breaks any links) or set a new link to a worksheet cell. Accomplishing the same thing programmatically is also very easy. For instance, the code:

```
ActiveChart.SeriesCollection(1).DataLabels(2).Text = "=MyChartSheet!R12C2"
```

sets the data label for the second data point to the value of cell B12. Note that the formula must be in R1C1 notation. (We will explain the code in Chapter 21, *The Chart Object*, so don't worry about the details now.)

Unfortunately, however, Excel does not provide a simple way to link all of the data labels for a data series with a worksheet range, beyond doing this one data label at a time. In Chapter 21 we will create such a utility, the dialog for which is shown in Figure 1-5. This dialog provides a list of all the data series for the selected chart. The user can select a data series and then define a range to which the data labels will be linked or from which the values will be copied. If the cell

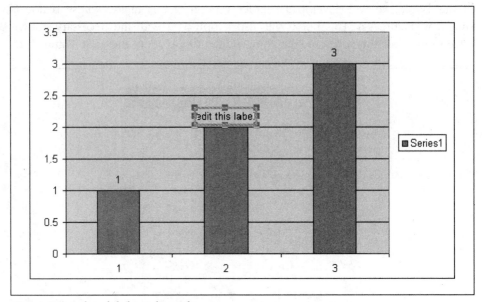

Figure 1-4. A data label in edit mode

values are copied, no link is established, and so changes made to the range are not reflected in the chart. There is also an option to control whether formatting is linked or copied.

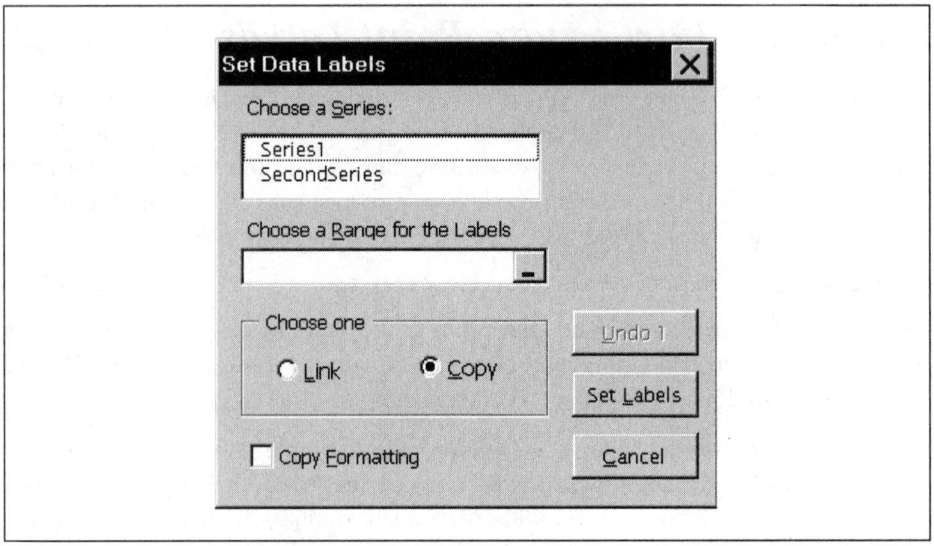

Figure 1-5. Set Data Labels dialog

I hope that these illustrations have convinced you that Excel programming can at times be very useful. Of course, you can do much more mundane things with Excel programs, such as automating the printing of charts, sorting worksheets alphabetically, and so on.

Topics in Learning Excel Programming

In general, the education of an Excel programmer breaks down into a few main categories, as follows.

The Visual Basic Editor

First, you need to learn a bit about the environment in which Excel programming is done. This is the so-called *Visual Basic Editor* or Excel VBA *integrated development environment* (IDE for short). We take care of this in Chapter 3, *The Visual Basic Editor, Part I*, and Chapter 4, *The Visual Basic Editor, Part II*.

The Basics of Programming in VBA

Next, you need to learn a bit about the basics of the programming language that Excel uses. This language is called *Visual Basic for Applications*, or VBA. Actually, VBA is used not only by Microsoft Excel, but also by the other major components in the Microsoft Office application suite: Access, Word, and PowerPoint. Any application that uses VBA in this way is called a *host application* for VBA. (There are also a number of non-Microsoft products that use VBA as their underlying programming language. Among the most notable is Visio, a vector-based drawing program.) It is also used by the standalone programming environment called Visual Basic (or VB).

We will discuss the basics of the VBA programming language in Chapters 5–8.

Object Models and the Excel Object Model

Each VBA host application (Word, Access, Excel, PowerPoint, Visual Basic) supplements the basic VBA language by providing an *object model* to deal with the objects that are particular to that application.

For instance, Excel VBA includes the *Excel object model*, which deals with such objects as workbooks, worksheets, cells, rows, columns, ranges, charts, pivot tables, and so on. On the other hand, the *Word object model* deals with such objects as documents, templates, paragraphs, fonts, headers, tables, and so on. Access VBA includes two object models, the *Access object model* and the *DAO object model*, that allow the programmer to deal with such objects as database tables, queries, forms, and reports. (To learn more about the Word, Access, and DAO object models, see my books *Learning Word Programming* and *Access Database Design and Programming*, also published by O'Reilly.)

Thus, an Excel programmer must be familiar with the general notion of an object model and with the Excel object model in particular. We discuss object models in general in Chapter 9, *Object Models*, and our discussion of the Excel object model takes up most of the remainder of the book.

Incidentally, the Excel object model is quite extensive—a close second to the Word object model in size and complexity, with almost 200 different objects.

Lest you be too discouraged by the size of the Excel object model, I should point out that you only need to be familiar with a handful of objects in order to program meaningfully in Excel VBA. In fact, as we will see, the vast majority of the "action" is related to just seven objects: Application, Range, WorksheetFunction, Workbook, Worksheet, PivotTable, and Chart.

To help you get an overall two-dimensional picture of the Excel object model, as well as detailed local views, I have written special object browser software. (The object browser comes with over a dozen other object models as well.) There is a coupon at the back of the book that you can use to obtain this object browser.

Whether you are interested in Excel programming in order to be more efficient in your own work, or to make money writing Excel programs for others to use, I think you will enjoy the increased sense of power that you get by knowing how to manipulate Excel at the programming level. And because Excel programming involves accessing the Excel object model by using the Visual Basic for Applications programming language—the same programming language used in Microsoft Word, Access, and PowerPoint—after reading this book, you will be half-way to being a Word, Access, and PowerPoint programmer as well!

2

Preliminaries

We begin with some general facts related to programming and programming languages that will help to give the main subject matter of this book some perspective. After all, VBA is just one of many programming languages, and anyone who wants to be a VBA programmer should have some perspective on where VBA fits into the greater scheme of things. Rest assured, however, that we will not dwell on side issues. The purpose of this chapter is to give a very brief overview of programming and programming languages that will be of interest to readers who have not had any programming experience, as well as to those who have.

What Is a Programming Language?

Simply put, a programming language is a very special and very restricted language that is understood by the computer at some level. We can roughly divide programming languages into three groups, based on the purpose of the language:

- Languages designed to manipulate the computer at a low level, that is, to manipulate the operating system (Windows or DOS) or even the hardware itself, are called *low-level languages*. An example is assembly language.

- Languages designed to create standalone applications, such as Microsoft Excel itself, are *high-level languages*. Examples are BASIC, COBOL, FORTRAN, Pascal, C, C++, and Visual Basic.

- Languages that are designed to manipulate an application program, such as Microsoft Excel, are *application-level* languages. Examples are Excel VBA, Word VBA, and PowerPoint VBA.

Those terms are not set in concrete and may be used differently by others. However, no one would disagree with the fact that some languages are intended to be used at a lower level than others.

The computer world is full of programming languages—hundreds of them. In some cases, languages are developed for specific computers. In other cases, languages are developed for specific types of applications. Table 2-1 gives some examples of programming languages and their general purposes.

Table 2-1. Some Programming Languages

Language	General Purpose
ALGOL	An attempt to design a universal language
BASIC	A simple, easy-to-learn language designed for beginners
C, C++	A very powerful languages with excellent speed and control over the computer
COBOL	A language for business programming
FORTRAN	A language for scientific programming and number crunching
Lisp	A language for list processing (used in artificial intelligence)
Pascal	A language to teach students how to program "correctly"
SIMULA	A language for simulating (or modeling) physical phenomena
Smalltalk	A language for object-oriented programming
Visual Basic	A version of BASIC designed for creating Windows applications
Visual C++	A version of C++ designed for creating Windows applications

Programming languages vary quite a bit in their syntax. Some languages are much easier to read than others (as are spoken languages). As a very simple example, Table 2-2 shows some ways that different programming languages assign a value (in this case 5) to a variable named X. Notice the variation even in this simple task.

Table 2-2. Assignment in Various Languages

Language	Assignment Statement
APL	X <- 5
BASIC	LET X = 5 or X = 5
BETA	5 -> X
C, C++	X = 5;
COBOL	MOVE 5 TO X
FORTRAN	X = 5
J	X =. 5
LISP	(SETQ X 5)
Pascal	X := 5
Visual Basic	X = 5

If you're interested in how Visual Basic compares with some of the other major programming languages, Appendix F, *High-Level and Low-Level Languages*, contains a short description of several languages, along with some programming examples.

Programming Style

The issue of what constitutes good programming style is, of course, subjective; just as is the issue of what constitutes good writing style. Probably the best way to learn good programming style is to learn by example, and to always keep the issue somewhere in the front of your mind while programming.

This is not the place to enter into a detailed discussion of programming style. However, in my opinion, the two most important maxims for good programming are:

- When in doubt, favor readability over cleverness or elegance.

- Fill your programs with lots of *meaningful* comments.

Comments

Let us take the second point first. It is not possible to overestimate the importance of adding meaningful comments to your programs—at least any program with more than a few lines.

The problem is this: Good programs are generally used many times during a reasonably long lifetime, which may be measured in months or even years. Inevitably, a programmer will want to return to his or her code to make changes (such as adding additional features) or to fix bugs. However, despite all efforts, programming languages are not as easy to read as spoken languages. It is just inevitable that a programmer will not understand (or perhaps even recognize!) code that was written several months or years earlier, and must rely on carefully written comments to help reacquaint himself or herself with the code. (This has happened to me more times that I would care to recall.)

Let me emphasize that commenting code is almost as much of an art as writing the code itself. I have often seen comments similar to the following:

```
' Set x equal to 5
x = 5
```

This comment is pretty useless, since the actual code is self-explanatory. It simply wastes time and space. (In a teaching tool, such as this book, you may find some comments that would otherwise be left out of a professionally written program.)

A good test of the quality of your comments is to read just the comments (not the code) to see if you get a good sense not only of what the program is designed to do, but also of the steps that are used to accomplish the program's goal. For example, here are the comments from a short BASIC program that appears in Appendix F:

```
' BASIC program to compute the average
' of a set of at most 100 numbers

' Ask for the number of numbers

' If Num is between 1 and 100 then proceed
   ' Loop to collect the numbers to average
      ' Ask for next number
      ' Add the number to the running sum
   ' Compute the average
   ' Display the average
```

Readability

Readability is also a subjective matter. What is readable to one person may not be readable to another. In fact, it is probably fair to say that what is readable to the author of a program is likely to be less readable to *everyone else*, at least to some degree. It is wise to keep this in mind when you start programming (that is, assuming you *want* others to be able to read your programs).

One of the greatest offenders to code readability is the infamous GOTO statement, of which many languages (including VBA) have some variety or other. It is not my intention to dwell upon the GOTO statement, but it will help illustrate the issue of good programming style.

The GOTO statement is very simple—it just redirects program execution to another location. For instance, the following BASIC code asks the user for a positive number. If the user enters a nonpositive number, the GOTO portion of the code redirects execution to the first line of the program (the label TryAgain). This causes the entire program to be executed again. In short, the program will repeat until the user enters a positive number:

```
TryAgain:
INPUT "Enter a positive number: ", x
IF x <= 0 THEN GOTO TryAgain
```

While the previous example may not be good programming style, it is at least readable. However, the following code is much more difficult to read:

```
TryAgain:
INPUT "Enter a number between 1 and 100: ", x
IF x > 100 THEN GOTO TooLarge
IF x <= 0 THEN GOTO TooSmall
```

```
PRINT "Your number is: ", x
GOTO Done
TooLarge:
PRINT "Your number is too large"
GOTO TryAgain
TooSmall:
PRINT "Your number is too small"
GOTO TryAgain
Done:
END
```

Because we need to jump around in the program in order to follow the possible flows of execution, this type of programming is sometimes referred to as *spaghetti code*. Imagine this style of programming in a program that was thousands of lines long! The following version is much more readable, although it is still not the best possible style:

```
TryAgain:
INPUT "Enter a number between 1 and 100: ", x
IF x > 100 THEN
   PRINT "Your number is too large"
   GOTO TryAgain
ELSEIF x <= 0 THEN
   PRINT "Your number is too small"
   GOTO TryAgain
END IF
PRINT "Your number is: ", x
END
```

The following code does the same job, but avoids the use of the GOTO statement altogether, and would no doubt be considered better programming style by most programmers:

```
DO
   INPUT "Enter a number between 1 and 100: ", x
   IF x > 100 THEN
     PRINT "Your number is too large"
   ELSEIF x <= 0 THEN
     PRINT "Your number is too small"
   END IF
LOOP UNTIL x >= 1 AND x <= 100
PRINT "Your number is: ", x
END
```

Readability can also suffer at the hands of programmers who like to think that their code is especially clever or elegant but in reality just turns out to be hard to read and error-prone. This is especially easy to do when programming in the C language. For instance, as a very simple example, consider the following three lines in C:

```
x = x + 1;
x = x + i;
i = i - 1;
```

The first line adds 1 to *x*, the second line adds *i* to *x*, and the third line subtracts 1 from *i*. This code is certainly readable (if not terribly meaningful). However, it can also be written as:

```
x = ++x+i--;
```

This may be some programmer's idea of clever programming, but to me it is just obnoxious. This is why a sagacious programmer always favors readability over cleverness or elegance.

Modularity

Another major issue that relates to readability is that of *modular programming*. In the early days of PC programming (in BASIC), most programs were written as a single code unit, sometimes with many hundreds or even thousands of lines of code. It is not easy to follow such a program, especially six months after it was written. Also, these programs tended to contain the same code segments over and over, which is a waste of time and space.

The following BASIC example will illustrate the point. Line numbers have been added for reference. (Don't worry too much about following each line of code. You can still follow the discussion in any case.)

```
10   ' Program to reverse the letters in your name

20   ' Do first name
30   INPUT "Enter your first name: ", name$
40   reverse$ = ""
50   FOR i = LEN(name$) TO 1 STEP -1
60      reverse$ = reverse$ + MID$(name$, i, 1)
70   NEXT i
80   PRINT "First name reversed: " + reverse$

90   ' Do middle name
100  INPUT "Enter your middle name: ", name$
110  reverse$ = ""
120  FOR i = LEN(name$) TO 1 STEP -1
130     reverse$ = reverse$ + MID$(name$, i, 1)
140  NEXT i
150  PRINT "Middle name reversed: " + reverse$

160  ' Do last name
170  INPUT "Enter your last name: ", name$
180  reverse$ = ""
190  FOR i = LEN(name$) TO 1 STEP -1
200     reverse$ = reverse$ + MID$(name$, i, 1)
210  NEXT i
220  PRINT "Last name reversed: " + reverse$
```

Now, observe that lines 40–70, 110–140, and 180–210 (in bold) are identical. This is a waste of space. A better approach would be to separate the code that does the reversing of a string *name* into a separate *code module* and call upon that module thrice, as in the following example:

```
' Program to reverse your name

DECLARE FUNCTION Reverse$ (name$)

' Do first name
INPUT "Enter your first name: ", name$
PRINT "First name reversed: " + Reverse$(name$)

' Do middle name
INPUT "Enter your middle name: ", name$
PRINT "Middle name reversed: " + Reverse$(name$)

' Do last name
INPUT "Enter your last name: ", name$
PRINT "Last name reversed: " + Reverse$(name$)
```

The separate code module to reverse a string is:

```
' Reverses a string
FUNCTION Reverse$ (aname$)
    Temp$ = ""
    FOR i = LEN(aname$) TO 1 STEP -1
        Temp$ = Temp$ + MID$(aname$, i, 1)
    NEXT i
    Reverse$ = Temp$
END FUNCTION
```

Of course, the saving in space is not great in this example, but you can imagine what would happen if we replace the reversing procedure by one that requires several hundred lines of code and if we want to perform this procedure a few hundred times in the main program. This modularization could save thousands of lines of code.

There is another very important advantage to modular programming. If we decide to write another program that requires reversing some strings, we can simply add our string-reversing code module to the new program, without having to write any new code. Indeed, professional programmers often compile custom *code libraries* containing useful code modules that can be slipped into new applications when necessary.

It is hard to overestimate the importance of modular programming. Fortunately, as we will see, VBA makes it easy to create modular programs.

Generally speaking, there are two main groups of code modules: *functions* and *subroutines*. The difference between them is that functions return a value whereas subroutines do not. (Of course, we may choose not to use the value returned from a function.) For instance, the *Reverse* function described in the previous example returns the reversed string. On the other hand, the following code module performs a service but does not return a value—it simply pauses a certain number of seconds (given by *sec*):

```
SUB delay (sec)
    ' Get the current time
    StartTime = TIMER
    ' Enter a do-nothing loop for sec seconds
    DO
    LOOP UNTIL TIMER - StartTime > sec
END SUB
```

Functions and subroutines are extremely common in modern coding. Together, they are referred to as *procedures*.

I

The VBA
Environment

3

The Visual Basic Editor, Part I

The first step in becoming an Excel VBA programmer is to become familiar with the environment in which Excel VBA programming is done. Each of the main Office applications has a programming environment referred to as its *Integrated Development Environment* or IDE. Microsoft also refers to this programming environment as the *Visual Basic Editor*.

Our plan in this chapter and Chapter 4, *The Visual Basic Editor, Part II*, is to describe the major components of the Excel IDE. We realize that you are probably anxious to get to some actual programming, but it is necessary to gain some familiarity with the IDE before you can use it. Nevertheless, you may want to read quickly through this chapter and the next and then refer back to them as needed.

In Office 97, the Word, Excel, and PowerPoint IDEs have the same appearance, shown in Figure 3-1. (Beginning with Office 2000, Microsoft Access also uses this IDE.) To start the Excel IDE, simply choose Visual Basic Editor from the Macros submenu of the Tools menu, or hit Alt-F11.

Let us take a look at some of the components of this IDE.

The Project Window

The window in the upper-left corner of the client area (below the toolbar) is called the *Project Explorer*. Figure 3-2 shows a close-up of this window.

Note that the Project Explorer has a treelike structure, similar to the Windows Explorer's folders pane (the left-hand pane). Each entry in the Project Explorer is called a *node*. The top nodes, of which there are two in Figure 3-2, represent the currently open Excel VBA *projects* (hence the name Project Explorer). The view of

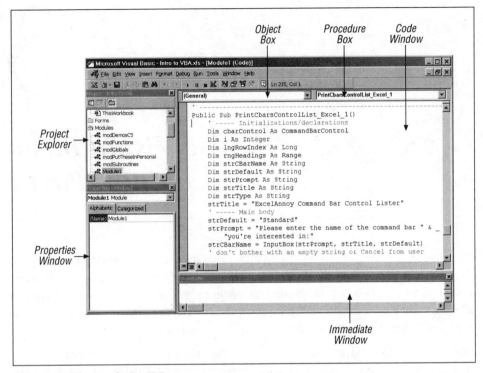

Figure 3-1. The Excel VBA IDE

each project can be expanded or contracted by clicking on the small boxes (just as with Windows Explorer). Note that there is one project for each currently open Excel workbook.

Project Names

Each project has a name, which the programmer can choose. The default name for a project is VBAProject. The top node for each project is labeled:

    ProjectName (*WorkbookName*)

where *ProjectName* is the name of the project and *WorkbookName* is the name of the Excel workbook.

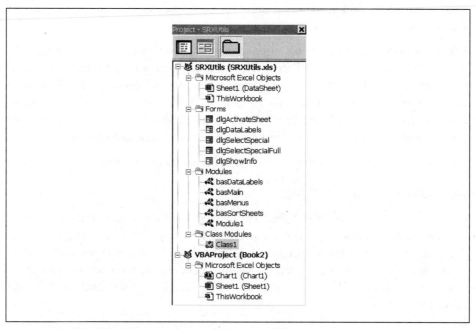

Figure 3-2. The Project Explorer

Project Contents

At the level immediately below the top (project) level, as Figure 3-2 shows, there are nodes named:

    Microsoft Excel Objects
    Forms
    Modules
    Classes

Under the Microsoft Excel Objects node, there is a node for each worksheet and chartsheet in the workbook, as well as a special node called ThisWorkbook, which represents the workbook itself. These nodes provide access to the code windows for each of these objects, where we can write our code.

Under the Forms node, there is a node for each form in the project. Forms are also called UserForms or custom dialog boxes. We will discuss UserForms later in this chapter.

Under the Modules node, there is a node for each code module in the project. Code modules are also called standard modules. We will discuss modules later in this chapter.

Under the Classes node, there is a node for each class module in the project. We will discuss classes later in this chapter.

The main purpose of the Project Explorer is to allow us to navigate around the project. Worksheets and UserForms have two components—a visible component (a worksheet or dialog) and a code component. By right-clicking on a worksheet or UserForm node, we can choose to view the object itself or the code component for that object. Standard modules and class modules have only a code component, which we can view by double-clicking on the corresponding node.

Let us take a closer look at the various components of an Excel project.

The ThisWorkbook object

Under each node in the Project Explorer labeled Microsoft Excel Objects is a node labeled ThisWorkbook. This node represents the project's workbook, along with the code component (also called a code module) that stores event code for the workbook. (We can also place independent procedures in the code component of a workbook module, but these are generally placed in a standard module, discussed later in this chapter.)

Simply put, the purpose of events is to allow the VBA programmer to write code that will execute whenever one of these events fires. Excel recognizes 19 events related to workbooks. We will discuss these events in Chapter 11, *Excel Events*; you can take a quick peek at this chapter now if you are curious. Some examples are:

- The Open event, which occurs when the workbook is opened.

- The BeforeClose event, which occurs just before the workbook is closed.

- The NewSheet event, which occurs when a new worksheet is added to the workbook.

- The BeforePrint event, which occurs just before the workbook or anything in it is printed.

Sheet objects

Under each Microsoft Excel Objects node in the Project Explorer is a node for each sheet. (A *sheet* is a worksheet or a chartsheet.) Each sheet node represents a worksheet or chartsheet's visible component, along with the code component (also called a code module) that stores event code for the sheet. We can also place independent procedures in the code component of a sheet module, but these are generally placed in a standard module, discussed next.

Excel recognizes seven events related to worksheets and 13 events related to chartsheets. We will discuss these events in Chapter 11.

Standard modules

A *module*, also more clearly referred to as a *standard module*, is a code module that contains general procedures (functions and subroutines). These procedures may be macros designed to be run by the user, or they may be support programs used by other programs. (Remember our discussion of modular programming.)

Class modules

Class modules are code modules that contain code related to custom objects. As we will see, the Excel object model has a great many built-in objects (almost 200), such as workbook objects, worksheet objects, chart objects, font objects, and so on. It is also possible to create custom objects and endow them with various properties. To do so, we would place the appropriate code within a class module.

However, since creating custom objects is beyond the scope of this book, we will not be using class modules. (For an introduction to object-oriented programming using VB, allow me to suggest my book, *Concepts of Object-Oriented Programming with Visual Basic*, published by Springer-Verlag, New York.)

UserForm objects

As you no doubt know, Excel contains a great many built-in dialog boxes. It is also possible to create custom dialog boxes, also called *forms* or *UserForms*. This is done by creating UserForm objects. Figure 3-3 shows the design environment for the Select Special UserForm that we mentioned in Chapter 1, *Introduction*.

The large window on the upper-center in Figure 3-3 contains the custom dialog box (named dlgSelectSpecial) in its design mode. There is a floating Toolbox window on the right that contains icons for various Windows controls.

To place a control on the dialog box, simply click on the icon in the Toolbox and then drag and size a rectangle on the dialog box. This rectangle is replaced by the control of the same size as the rectangle. The properties of the UserForm object or of any controls on the form can be changed by selecting the object and making the changes in the Properties window, which we discuss in the next section.

In addition to the form itself and its controls, a UserForm object contains code that the VBA programmer writes in support of these objects. For instance, a command button has a Click event that fires when the user clicks on the button. If we place such a button on the form, then we must write the code that is run when the Click event fires; otherwise, clicking the button does nothing. For instance, the following is the code for the Close button's Click event in Figure 3-3. Note that the Name property of the command button has been set to *cmdClose*:

```
Private Sub cmdClose_Click()
    Unload Me
End Sub
```

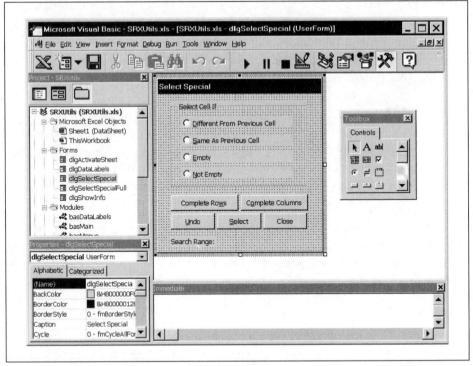

Figure 3-3. A UserForm dialog box

All this code does is unload the form.

Along with event code for a form and its controls, we can also include support procedures within the UserForm object.

Don't worry if all this seems rather vague now. We will devote an entire chapter to creating custom dialog boxes (that is, UserForm objects) later in the book and see several real-life examples throughout the book.

The Properties Window

The Properties window (see Figure 3-1) displays the properties of an object and allows us to change them.

When a standard module is selected in the Project window, the only property that appears in the Properties window is the module's name. However, when a workbook, sheet, or UserForm is selected in the Projects window, many of the object's properties appear in the Properties window, as shown in Figure 3-4.

The Properties window can be used to change some of the properties of the object while no code is running—that is, at *design time*. Note, however, that some properties are read-only and cannot be changed. While most properties can be changed either at design time or *run time*, some properties can only be changed at design time and some can only be changed at run time. Run-time properties generally do not appear in the Properties window.

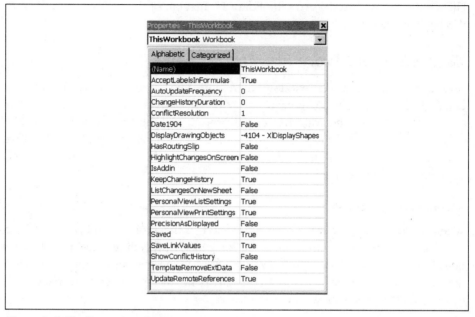

Figure 3-4. The Properties window

The Code Window

The Code window displays the code that is associated with the selected item in the Project window. To view this code, select the object in the Projects window and either choose Code from the View menu or hit the F7 key. For objects with only a code component (no visual component), you can just double-click on the item in the Projects window.

Procedure and Full-Module Views

Generally, a code module (standard, class, or UserForm) contains more than one procedure. The IDE offers the choice between viewing one procedure at a time (called *procedure view*) or all procedures at one time (called *full-module view*), with a horizontal line separating the procedures. Each view has its advantages and disadvantages, and you will probably want to use both views at different times. Unfortunately, Microsoft has not supplied a menu choice for selecting the view. To change views, we need to click on the small buttons in the lower-left corner of the

Code window. (The default view can be set using the Editor tab of the Options dialog box.)

Incidentally, the default font for the module window is Courier, which has a rather thin looking appearance and may be somewhat difficult to read. You may want to change the font to FixedSys (on the Editor Format tab of the Options dialog, under the Tools menu), which is very readable.

The Object and Procedure List Boxes

At the top of the Code window there are two drop-down list boxes (see Figure 3-1). The Object box contains a list of the objects (such as forms and controls) that are associated with the current project, and the Procedure box contains a list of all of the procedures associated with the object selected in the Object box. The precise contents of these boxes varies depending on the type of object selected in the Project Explorer.

A workbook or sheet object

When a workbook or sheet object is selected in the Project window, the Object box contains only two entries: General, for general procedures, and the object in question, either *Workbook*, *Worksheet*, or *Chart*. When the object entry is selected, the Procedure box contains empty code shells for the events that are relevant to that object. Figure 3-5 shows an example.

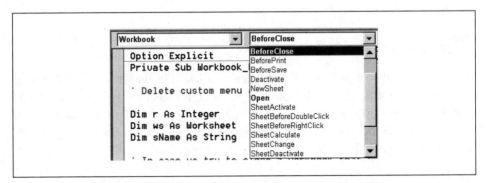

Figure 3-5. The events for a Workbook object

If, for example, we choose the BeforeClose event in the Procedures box, Excel will create the following code shell for this event, and place the cursor within this procedure:

```
Private Sub Workbook_BeforeClose(Cancel As Boolean)

End Sub
```

A standard module

When a standard module is selected in the Project window, the Object box contains only the entry General, and an Procedure box lists all of the procedures we have written for that module (if any). Figure 3-6 shows the open Procedure box, with a list of the current procedures for a particular module. The (Declarations) section is where we place variable declarations for *module-level variables*—that is, for variables that we want to be available in every procedure within the module. We will discuss this in detail in Chapter 5, *Variables, Data Types, and Constants.*

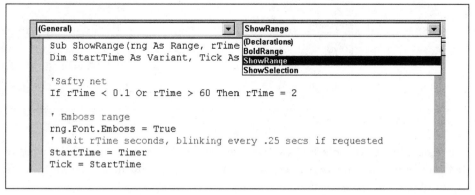

Figure 3-6. The Procedure box

A UserForm object

When a UserForm object is selected in the Project Explorer, the Object box contains a list of all of the objects contained in the UserForm. For instance, Figure 3-7 shows the contents of the Object box for the UserForm object in Figure 3-3. Note that there are entries for the various command buttons (such as *cmdClose*), the various other controls, and even for the UserForm itself.

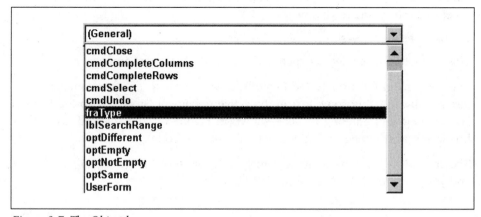

Figure 3-7. The Object box

Figure 3-8 shows the contents of the Procedure box when the *cmdClose* object is selected in the Object box. This list contains the names of the 13 different events that are associated with a command button.

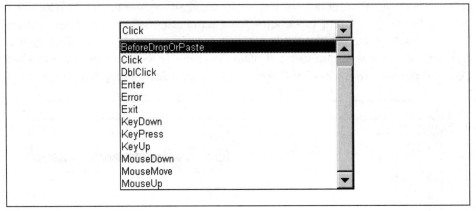

Figure 3-8. The Procedure box

For example, if we select Click, we will be placed within the Code window between the following two lines, where we can write event code for the Click event of the *cmdClose* command button:

```
Private Sub cmdClose_Click()

End Sub
```

The Immediate Window

The Immediate window (see Figure 3-1) has two main functions. First, we can send output to this window using the command `Debug.Print`. For instance, the following code will print whatever text is currently in cell A1 of the active worksheet to the Immediate window:

```
Debug.Print ActiveSheet.Range("A1").Text
```

This provides a nice way to experiment with different code snippets.

The other main function of the Immediate window is to execute commands. For instance, by selecting some text in the active document, switching to the Immediate window, and entering the line shown in Figure 3-9, the selected text will be boldfaced (after hitting the Enter key to execute the code).

The Immediate window is an extremely valuable tool for *debugging* a program, and you will probably use it often (as I do).

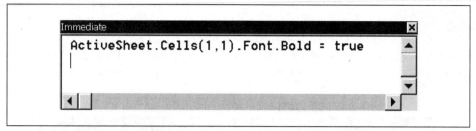

Figure 3-9. The Immediate Window

Arranging Windows

If you need more space for writing code, you can close the Properties window, the Project window, and the Immediate window. On the other hand, if you are fortunate enough to have a large monitor, you can split your screen as shown in Figure 3-10 in order to see the Excel VBA IDE and an Excel workbook at the same time. Then you can trace through each line of your code and watch the results in the workbook! (You can toggle between Excel and the IDE using the Alt-F11 key combination.)

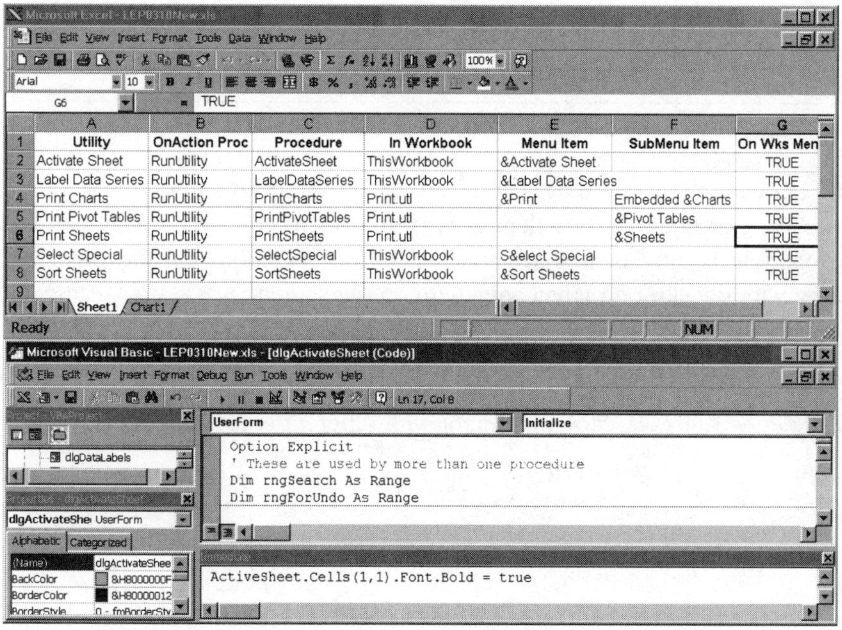

Figure 3-10. A split screen approach

Docking

Many of the windows in the IDE (including the Project, Properties, and Immediate windows) can be in one of two states: docked or floating. This state can be set using the Docking tab on the Options dialog box, which is shown in Figure 3-11.

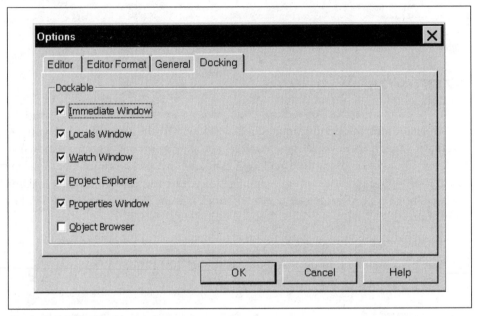

Figure 3-11. The Docking options

A *docked* window is one that is attached, or anchored, to an edge of another window or to one edge of the client area of the main VBA window. When a dockable window is moved, it snaps to an anchored position. On the other hand, a floating window can be placed anywhere on the screen.

4

The Visual Basic Editor, Part II

In this chapter, we conclude our discussion of the Visual Basic Editor. Again, let us remind the reader that he or she may want to read quickly through this chapter and refer to it later as needed.

Navigating the IDE

If you prefer the keyboard to the mouse (as I do), then you may want to use keyboard shortcuts. Here are some tips.

General Navigation

The following keyboard shortcuts are used for navigating the IDE:

F7
> Go to the Code window.

F4
> Go to the Properties window.

Ctrl-R
> Go to the Project window.

Ctrl-G
> Go to the Immediate window.

Alt-F11
> Toggle between Excel and the VB IDE.

Navigating the Code window at design time

Within the code window, the following keystrokes are very useful:

F1

>   Help on the item under the cursor.

Shift-F2

>   Go to the definition of the item under the cursor. (If the cursor is over a call to a function or subroutine, hitting Shift-F2 sends you to the definition of that procedure.)

Ctrl-Shift-F2

>   Return to the last position where editing took place.

Tracing code

The following keystrokes are useful when tracing through code (discussed in the "Debugging" section, later in this chapter):

F8

>   Step into

Shift-F8

>   Step over

Ctrl-Shift-F8

>   Step out

Ctrl-F8

>   Run to cursor

F5

>   Run

Ctrl-Break

>   Break

Shift-F9

>   Quick watch

F9

>   Toggle breakpoint

Ctrl-Shift-F9

>   Clear all breakpoints

Bookmarks

It is also possible to insert *bookmarks* within code. A bookmark marks a location to which we can return easily. To insert a bookmark, or to move to the next or previous bookmark, use the Bookmarks submenu of the Edit menu. The presence of a bookmark is indicated by a small blue square in the left margin of the code.

Getting Help

If you are like me, you will probably make extensive use of Microsoft's Excel VBA help files while programming. The simplest way to get help on an item is to place the cursor on that item and hit the F1 key. This works not only for VBA language keywords but also for portions of the VBA IDE.

Note that Microsoft provides multiple help files for Excel, the VBA language, and the Excel object model. While this is quite reasonable, occasionally the help system gets a bit confused and refuses to display the correct help file when we strike the F1 key. (I have not found a simple resolution to this problem, other than shutting down Excel and the Visual Basic Editor along with it.)

Note also that a standard installation of Microsoft Office does *not* install the VBA help files for the various applications. Thus, you may need to run the Office setup program and install Excel VBA help by selecting that option in the appropriate setup dialog box. (Do not confuse Excel help with Excel VBA help.)

Creating a Procedure

There are two ways to create a new procedure (that is, a subroutine or a function) within a code module. First, after selecting the correct project in the Project Explorer, we can select the Procedure option from the Insert menu. This will produce the dialog box shown in Figure 4-1. Just type in the name of the procedure and select Sub or Function (the Property choice is used with custom objects in a class module). We will discuss the issue of Public versus Private procedures and static variables later in this chapter.

A simpler alternative is to simply begin typing:

```
Sub SubName
```

or:

```
Function FunctionName
```

in any code window (following the current **End Sub** or **End Function** statement, or in the general declarations section). As soon as the Enter key is struck, Excel will move the line of code to a new location and thereby create a new subroutine. (It will even add the appropriate ending—**End Sub** or **End Function**.)

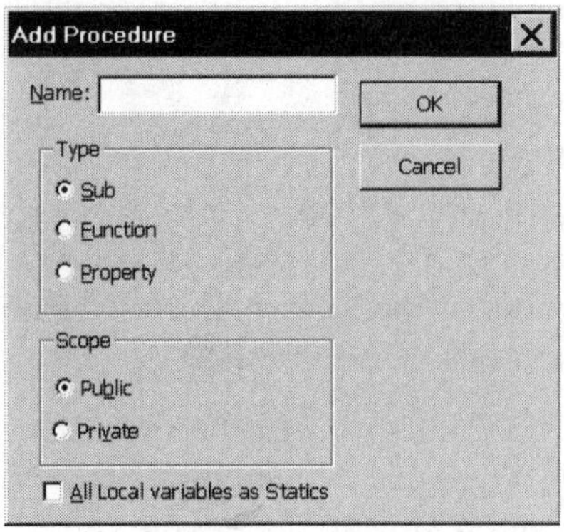

Figure 4-1. The Add Procedure dialog box

Run Time, Design Time, and Break Mode

The VBA IDE can be in any one of three modes: run mode, break mode, or design mode. When the IDE is in design mode, we can write code or design a form.

Run mode occurs when a procedure is running. To run (or execute) a procedure, just place the cursor anywhere within the procedure code and hit the F5 key (or select Run from the Run menu). If a running procedure seems to be hanging, we can *usually* stop the procedure by hitting Ctrl-Break (hold down the Control key and hit the Break key).

Break mode is entered when a running procedure stops because of either an error in the code or a deliberate act on our part (described a bit later). In particular, if an error occurs, Excel will stop execution and display an error dialog box, an example of which is shown in Figure 4-2.

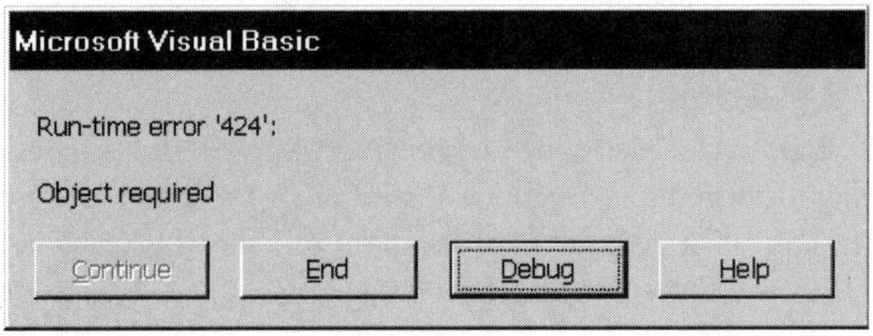

Figure 4-2. An error message

Error dialog boxes offer a few options: end the procedure, get help (such as it may be) with the problem, or enter break mode to debug the code. In the latter case, Excel will stop execution of the procedure at the offending code and highlight that code in yellow. We will discuss the process of debugging code a bit later.

Aside from encountering an error, there are several ways we can deliberately enter break mode for debugging purposes:

- Hit the Ctrl-Break key and choose Debug from the resulting dialog box.

- Include a `Stop` statement in the code, which causes Excel to enter break mode.

- Insert a *breakpoint* on an existing line of executable code. This is done by placing the cursor on that line and hitting the F9 function key (or using the Toggle Breakpoint option on the Debug menu). Excel will place a red dot in the left margin in front of that line and will stop execution when it reaches the line. You may enter more than one breakpoint in a procedure. This is generally preferred over using the `Stop` statement, because breakpoints are automatically removed when we close down the Visual Basic Editor, so we don't need to remember to remove them, as we do with `Stop` statements.

- Set a *watch* statement that causes Excel to enter break mode if a certain condition becomes true. We will discuss watch expressions a bit later.

To exit from Break mode, choose Reset from the Run menu.

Note that the caption in the title bar of the VBA IDE indicates which mode is currently active. The caption contains the word "[running]" when in run mode and "[break]" when in break mode.

Errors

In computer jargon, an error is referred to as a *bug*. In case you are interested in the origin of this word, the story goes that when operating the first large-scale digital computer, called the Mark I, an error was traced to a moth that had found its way into the hardware. Incidentally, the Mark I (circa 1944) had 750,000 parts, was 51 feet long, and weighed over five tons. How about putting that on your desktop? It also executed about one instruction every six seconds, as compared to over 200 million instructions per second for a Pentium!

Errors can be grouped into three types based on when they occur—*design time*, *compile time*, or *run time*.

Design-Time Errors

As the name implies, a *design-time error* occurs during the writing of code. Perhaps the nicest feature of the Visual Basic Editor is that it can be instructed to watch as we type code and stop us when we make a syntax error. This automatic syntax checking can be enabled or disabled in the Options dialog box shown in Figure 4-3, but I strongly suggest that you keep it enabled.

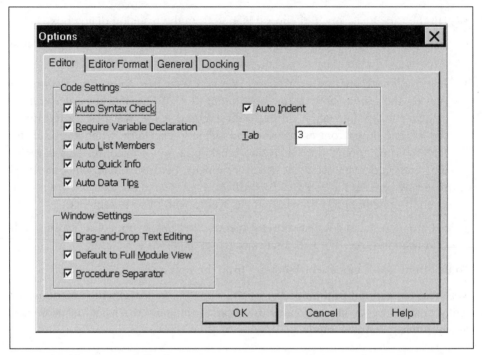

Figure 4-3. The Options dialog box

Notice also that there are other settings related to the design-time environment, such has how far to indent code in response to the Tab key. We will discuss some of these other settings a bit later.

To illustrate automatic syntax checking, Figure 4-4 shows what happens when we deliberately enter the syntactically incorrect statement x == 5 and then attempt to move to another line. Note that Microsoft refers to this type of error as a *compile error* in the dialog box and perhaps we should as well. However, it seems more descriptive to call it a design-time error or just a syntax error.

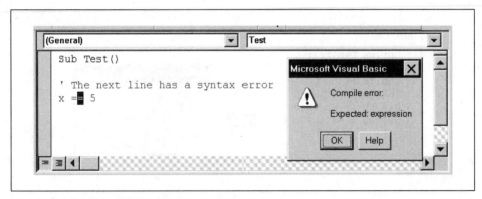

Figure 4-4. A syntax error message

Compile-Time Errors

Before a program can be executed, it must be *compiled*, or translated into a language that the computer can understand. The compilation process occurs automatically when we request that a program be executed. We can also specifically request compilation by choosing the Compile Project item under the Debug menu.

If Excel encounters an error while compiling code, it displays a compile error message. For example, the code in Figure 4-5 contains a compile-time error. In particular, the first line:

```
Dim wb as Workbook
```

defines a variable of type *Workbook* to represent an Excel workbook. (We will go into all of this in Chapter 17, *The Workbook Object*, so don't worry about the details now.) However, the second line:

```
Set wb = ActiveWorkbook.Name
```

attempts to assign the variable *wb* not to the active workbook, which would be legal, but to the *name* of the active workbook. This error is not caught during design time because it is not a syntax error. It is only at compile time, when Excel considers the statement in the context of the first statement, that the error becomes evident.

Run-Time Errors

An error that occurs while a program is running is called a *run-time error.* Figure 4-6 illustrates a run-time error and its corresponding error message. In this example, the code:

```
Workbooks.Open "d:\temp\ExistNot.xls"
```

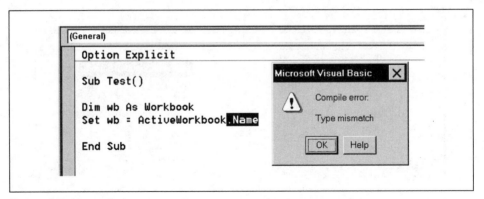

Figure 4-5. A compilation error message

Figure 4-6. A run-time error message

attempts to open an Excel workbook that does not exist. Notice that this error message is actually quite friendly—not only does it describe the error in clear terms (the file could not be found), but it also offers some suggestions for eliminating the problem.

Logical Errors

There is one more type of error that we should discuss, since it is the most insidious type of all. A *logical error* can be defined as the production of an unexpected and incorrect result. As far as Excel is concerned, there is no error, because Excel has no way of knowing what we intend. (Thus, a logical error is *not* a run-time error, in the traditional sense, even though it does occur at run time.)

To illustrate, the following code purports to compute the average of some numbers:

```
Dim x(3) As Integer
Dim Ave As Single
x(0) = 1
x(1) = 3
```

```
x(2) = 8
x(3) = 5
Ave = (x(0) + x(1) + x(2) + x(3)) / 3
MsgBox "Average is: " & Ave
```

The result is the message box shown in Figure 4-7. Unfortunately, it is incorrect. The penultimate line in the preceding program should be:

```
Ave = (x(0) + x(1) + x(2) + x(3)) / 4
```

Note the 4 in the denominator, since there are 4 numbers to average. The correct average is 4.25. Of course, Excel will not complain because it has no way of knowing whether we really want to divide by 3.

Figure 4-7. The result of a logical error

Precisely because Excel cannot warn us about logical errors, they are the most dangerous, because we *think* that everything is correct.

Debugging

Invariably, you will encounter errors in your code. Design-time and compile-time errors are relatively easy to deal with because Excel helps us out with error messages and by indicating the offending code. Logical errors are much more difficult to detect and to fix. This is where debugging plays a major role. The Excel IDE provides some very powerful ways to find bugs.

Debugging can be quite involved, and we could include a whole chapter on the subject. There are even special software applications designed to assist in complex debugging tasks. However, for most purposes, a few simple techniques are sufficient. In particular, Excel makes it easy to *trace* through our programs, executing one line at a time, watching the effect of each line as it is executed.

Let us try a very simple example, which you should follow along on your PC. If possible, you should arrange your screen as in Figure 4-8. This will make it easier to follow the effects of the code, since you won't need to switch back and forth between the Excel window and the Excel VBA window. The code that we will

trace is shown in Example 4-1. Note that lines beginning with an apostrophe are
comments that are ignored by Excel.

Example 4-1. A Simple Program to Trace

```
Sub Test()

Dim ws As Worksheet

Set ws = ActiveSheet

' Insert a value into cell A1
ws.Cells(1, 1).Value = "sample"
' Make it bold
ws.Cells(1, 1).Font.Bold = True
' Copy cell
ws.Cells(1, 1).Copy
' Paste value only
ws.Cells(2, 1).PasteSpecial Paste:=xlValues

End Sub
```

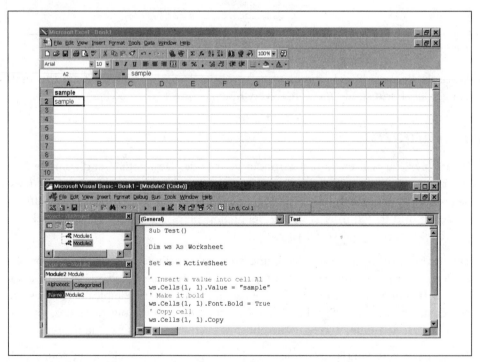

Figure 4-8. Top-and-bottom windows for easy debugging

Make sure that an empty worksheet is active in Excel. Switch to the VBA IDE and place the insertion point somewhere in the code. Then hit the F8 key once, which starts the tracing process. (You can also choose Step Into from the Debug menu.)

Continue striking the F8 key, pausing between keystrokes to view the effect of each instruction in the Excel window. (You can toggle between Excel and the IDE using Alt-F11.) As you trace through this code, you will see the word "sample" entered into cell A1 of the active worksheet, changed to appear in boldface, copied to the Clipboard, and pasted as normal text into the cell A2. Now you can begin to see what Excel VBA programming is all about!

Let us discuss some of the tools that Excel provides for debugging code.

Tracing

The process of executing code one line at a time, as we did in the previous example, is referred to as *tracing* or *code stepping*. Excel provides three options related to tracing: stepping into, stepping over, and stepping out of. The difference between these methods refers to handling calls to other procedures.

To illustrate the difference, consider the code shown in Example 4-2. In *ProcedureA*, the first line of code sets the value of cell A1 of the active worksheet. The second line calls *ProcedureB* and the third line boldfaces the contents of the cell. *ProcedureB* simply changes the size and name of the font used in cell A1. Don't worry about the exact syntax of this code. The important thing to notice is that the second line of *ProcedureA* calls *ProcedureB*.

Example 4-2. Sample Code for Tracing Methods

```
Sub ProcedureA()
    ActiveSheet.Cells(1, 1).Value = "sample"
    Call ProcedureB
    ActiveSheet.Cells(1, 1).Font.Bold = True
End Sub

Sub ProcedureB()
    ActiveSheet.Cells(1, 1).Font.Size = 24
    ActiveSheet.Cells(1, 1).Font.Name = "Arial"
End Sub
```

Stepping into

Step Into executes code one statement (or instruction) at a time. If the statement being executed calls another procedure, stepping into that statement simply transfers control to the first line in the called procedure. For instance, with reference to the previous code, stepping into the line:

```
    Call ProcedureB
```

in *ProcedureA* transfers control to the first line of *ProcedureB*:

```
ActiveSheet.Cells(1, 1).Font.Size = 24
```

Further tracing proceeds in *ProcedureB*. Once all of the lines of *ProcedureB* have been traced, control returns to *ProcedureA* at the line immediately following the call to *ProcedureB*—that is, at the line:

```
ActiveSheet.Cells(1, 1).Font.Bold = True
```

Step Into has another important use. If we choose Step Into while still in design mode, that is, before any code is running, execution begins but break mode is entered *before* the first line of code is actually executed. This is the proper way to begin tracing a program.

Step Over (Shift-F8 or choose Step Over from the Debug menu)

Step Over is similar to Step Into, except that if the current statement is a call to another procedure, the entire called procedure is executed without stopping (rather than tracing through the called procedure). Thus, for instance, stepping over the line:

```
Call ProcedureB
```

in the previous procedure executes *ProcedureB* and stops at the next line:

```
ActiveSheet.Cells(1, 1).Font.Bold = True
```

in *ProcedureA*. This is useful if we are certain that *ProcedureB* is not the cause of our problem and we don't want to trace through that procedure line by line.

Step Out (Ctrl-Shift-F8 or choose Step Out from the Debug menu)

Step Out is intended to be used within a called procedure (such as *ProcedureB*). Step Out executes the remaining lines of the called procedure and returns to the calling procedure (such as *ProcedureA*). This is useful if we are in the middle of a called procedure and decide that we don't need to trace any more of that procedure, but want to return to the calling procedure. (If you trace into a called procedure by mistake, just do a Step Out to return to the calling procedure.)

Run To Cursor (Ctrl-F8 or choose Run To Cursor from the Debug menu)

If the Visual Basic Editor is in break mode, we may want to execute several lines of code at one time. This can be done using the *Run To Cursor* feature. Simply place the cursor on the statement *immediately following* the last line you want to execute and then execute Run To Cursor.

Set Next Statement (Ctrl-F9 or choose Set Next Statement from the Debug menu)

We can also change the flow of execution while in break mode by placing the cursor on the statement that we want to execute next and selecting Set Next Statement. This will set the selected statement as the next statement to execute, but will not execute it until we continue tracing.

Breaking out of Debug mode

When we no longer need to trace our code, we have two choices. To return to design mode, we can choose Reset from the Run menu (there is no hotkey for this). To have Excel finish executing the current program, we can hit F5 or choose Run from the Run menu.

Watching Expressions

It is often useful to watch the values of certain expressions or variables as we trace through a program. Excel provides several ways to do this.

Quick Watch (Shift-F9)

This feature is used to quickly check the value of a variable or expression while in break mode. We just place the insertion point over the variable name and hit Shift-F9 (or choose Quick Watch from the Debug menu). For instance, Figure 4-9 shows the Quick Watch dialog box when the expression $x + 2$ is selected in the code in Figure 4-10. According to Figure 4-9, at the time that Quick Watch was invoked, the expression $x + 2$ had the value 8. Note that if we had just placed the insertion point in front of the letter **x**, then Quick Watch would have reported the value of this variable alone.

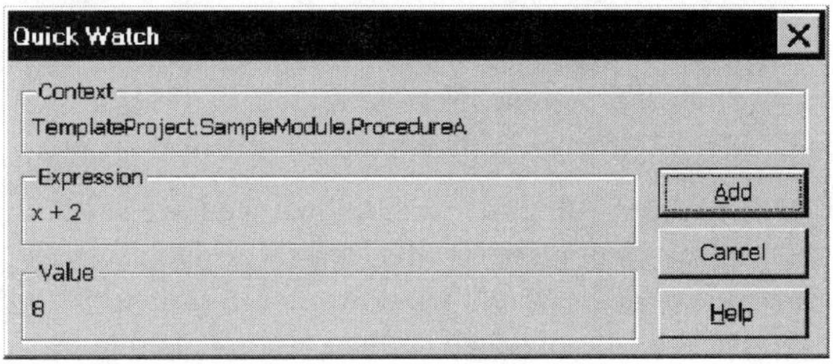

Figure 4-9. The Quick Watch window

Another way to quickly get values for expressions or variables is to enable Auto Data Tips on the Editor tab of Excel VBA's Options dialog box. With this feature enabled, when we place the mouse pointer over a variable or select an expression and place the mouse pointer over it, after a slight delay, a small yellow window will appear containing the value of the variable or expression. This is *very* useful!

The Locals and Watches windows

There are two special windows that aid in watching expressions: the Watches window and the Locals window. These are shown in Figure 4-10.

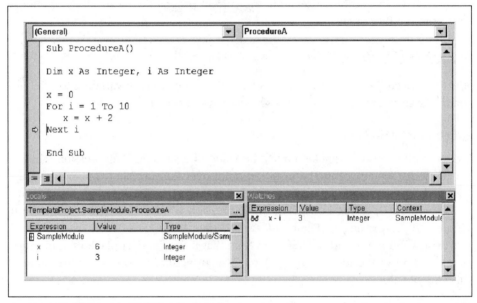

Figure 4-10. The Locals and Watches windows

The *Locals window* shows the values of all local variables. A *local variable* is a variable defined within the current procedure, and is therefore not valid in any other procedure. (We will discuss local variables in the next chapter.)

The *Watches window* shows all of the watches that we have set. A *watch* is a variable or expression that we place in the Watch window. Excel automatically updates the expressions in the Watch window after each line of code is executed and acts according to the type of watch defined, as described in the following list.

To add a watch, choose Add Watch from the Debug menu. This will produce the dialog box shown in Figure 4-11. We can then enter a variable or expression, such as **x > 6**, in the Expression text box. Note that there are three types of watches:

- Watch Expression simply adds the expression to the Watches window, so we can watch its value as code is executed. In this example, the value of the expression will be either **True** or **False**, depending upon whether **x** is greater than 6.

- Break When Value Is True asks Excel to stop execution and enter break mode whenever the expression is **true**. In this example, VBA will break execution when **x** > 6 is **true**, that is, when **x** becomes greater than 6.

- Break When Value Changes asks Excel to enter break mode when the value of the expression changes in any way. (In this case, from **True** to **False** or vice-versa.)

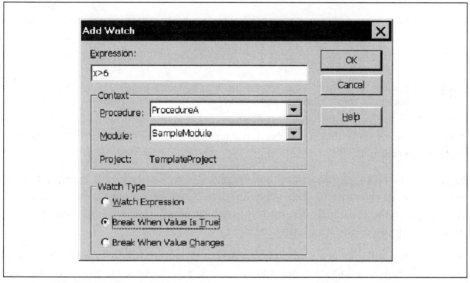

Figure 4-11. The Add Watch dialog box

Altogether, the various tracing modes and watch types provide a very powerful set of tools for debugging code. I use them often!

Macros

In earlier days, a *macro* consisted of a series of keystrokes that was recorded and assigned to a hot key. When a user invoked the hot key, the recording would play and the recorded keystrokes would be executed.

These days, macros (at least for Microsoft Office) are much more sophisticated. In fact, an Excel macro is just a special type of subroutine—one that does not have any parameters. (We will discuss subroutines and parameters in Chapter 6, *Functions and Subroutines.*)

Recording Macros

Excel has the capability of recording very simple macros. When we ask Excel to record a macro by selecting Macro → Record New Macro from Excel's (not Excel VBA's) Tools menu, it takes note of our keystrokes and converts them into a VBA subroutine (with no parameters).

For example, suppose we record a macro that does a find and replace, replacing the word "macro" by the word "subroutine." When we look in the Projects window under the project in which the macro was recorded, we will find a new subroutine in a standard code module:

```
Sub Macro1()
'
' Macro1 Macro
' Macro recorded 9/13/98 by sr
'

    '

    Cells.Replace What:="macro", Replacement:="subroutine", _
        LookAt:=xlPart, SearchOrder:=xlByRows, MatchCase:=False
End Sub
```

This is the same code that we might have written in order to perform this find and replace operation.

In certain situations, the macro recorder can serve as a very useful learning tool. If we can't figure out how to code a certain action, we can record it in a macro and cut and paste the resulting code into our own program. (In fact, you might want to try recording the creation of a pivot table.)

However, before you get too excited about this cut-and-paste approach to programming, we should point out that it is not anywhere near the panacea one might hope. One problem is that the macro recorder has a tendency to use ad hoc code rather than code that will work in a variety of situations. For instance, recorded macro code will often refer to the current selection, which may work at the time the macro was recorded but is not of much use in a general setting, because the programmer cannot be sure what the current selection will be when the user invokes the code.

Another problem is that the macro recorder is only capable of recording very simple procedures. Most useful Excel programs are far too complicated to be recorded automatically by the macro recorder.

Finally, since the macro recorder does such a thorough job of translating our actions into code, it tends to produce very bloated code, which often runs very slowly.

Running Macros

As you may know, to run a macro from the user interface, we just choose Macros from the Macro submenu of the Tools menu (or hit Alt-F8). This displays the Macro dialog box shown in Figure 4-12. This dialog box lists all macros in the current workbook or in all workbooks. From here, we can do several things, including running, editing, creating, or deleting macros. (Choosing Edit or Create places us in the VB Editor.)

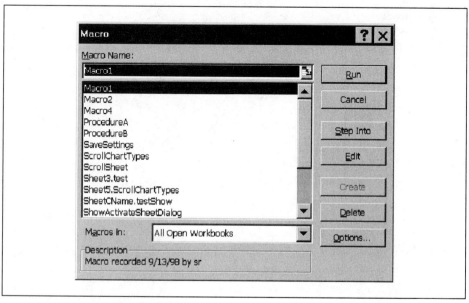

Figure 4-12. Excel's Macro dialog box

We should also comment on what appears and does not appear in the Macro list box. All macros that we write will appear in the Macros dialog box (as will all recorded macros). However, there are a few variations. If we give the macro a unique name (within the context given in the "Macros in" list box), then only the name of the macro will appear in the list box. If the name is not unique, then it must be qualified by the name of the module in which the macro appears, as in:

```
Sheet5.ScrollChartTypes
```

in Figure 4-12. Unfortunately, the first version of a macro with a nonunique name is not qualified. (Note the presence of another ScrollChartTypes macro in Figure 4-12.)

Note that we can prevent a macro procedure from appearing in the Macros list box by making the procedure private, using the **Private** keyword, as in:

```
Private Sub HideThisMacro()
```

We will discuss `Private` and `Public` procedures in Chapter 6.

Finally, if you are like me, you will collect a great many macros over the years. As time goes by, you may forget the names of some of these macros and thus have trouble finding a macro when you need it. I would advise you to give some careful thought to creating a consistent naming convention for macros. I begin the names of all macros with a word that categorizes the macro. For instance, all of my macros that deal with worksheets begin with the letters Wks, as in:

```
Wks_Sort
Wks_Compare
Wks_Print
```

II

The VBA Programming Language

5

Variables, Data Types, and Constants

In the next few chapters, we will discuss the basics of the VBA programming language, which underlies all of the Microsoft Office programming environments. During our discussion, we will consider many short coding examples. I hope that you will take the time to key in some of these examples and experiment with them.

Comments

We have already discussed the fact that comments are important. Any text that follows an apostrophe is considered a comment and is ignored by Excel. For example, the first line in the following code is a comment, as is everything following the apostrophe on the third line:

```
' Declare a string variable
Dim WksName as String
WksName = Activesheet.Name    ' Get name of active sheet
```

When debugging code it is often useful to temporarily comment out lines of code so they will not execute. The lines can subsequently be uncommented to restore them to active duty. The CommentBlock and UncommentBlock buttons, which can be found on the Edit toolbar, will place or remove comment marks from each currently selected line of code and are very useful for commenting out several lines of code in one step. (Unfortunately, there are no keyboard shortcuts for these commands, but they can be added to a menu and given menu accelerator keys.)

Line Continuation

The very nature of Excel VBA syntax often leads to long lines of code, which can be difficult to read, especially if we need to scroll horizontally to see the entire line. For this reason, Microsoft recently introduced a line-continuation character into VBA. This character is the underscore, which *must* be preceded by a space and cannot be followed by any other characters (including comments). For example, the following code is treated as one line by Excel:

```
ActiveSheet.Range("A1").Font.Bold = True
```

It is important to note that a line continuation character cannot be inserted in the middle of a literal string constant, which is enclosed in quotation marks.

Constants

The VBA language has two types of constants. A *literal constant* (also called a *constant* or *literal*) is a specific value, such as a number, date, or text string, that does not change, and that is used exactly as written. Note that string constants are enclosed in double quotation marks, as in **"Donna Smith"** and date constants are enclosed between number signs, as in **#1/1/96#**.

For instance, the following code stores a date in the variable called *dt*:

```
Dim dt As Date
dt = #1/2/97#
```

A *symbolic constant* (also sometimes referred to simply as a *constant*) is a name for a literal constant.

To define or declare a symbolic constant in a program, we use the **Const** keyword, as in:

```
Const InvoicePath = "d:\Invoices\"
```

In this case, Excel will replace every instance of **InvoicePath** in our code with the string **"d:\Invoices\"**. Thus, **InvoicePath** is a constant, since it never changes value, but it is not a literal constant, since it is not used as written.

The virtue of using symbolic constants is that, if we decide later to change **"d:\Invoices\"** to **"d:\OldInvoices\"**, we only need to change the definition of **InvoicePath** to:

```
Const InvoicePath = "d:\OldInvoices\"
```

rather than searching through the entire program for every occurrence of the phrase **"d:\Invoices\"**.

It is generally good programming practice to declare any symbolic constants at the beginning of the procedure in which they are used (or in the Declarations section of a code module). This improves readability and makes housekeeping simpler.

In addition to the symbolic constants that you can define using the Const statement, VBA has a large number of built-in symbolic constants (about 700), whose names begin with the lowercase letters *vb*. Excel VBA adds additional symbolic constants (1266 of them) that begin with the letters *xl*. We will encounter many of these constants throughout the book.

Among the most commonly used VBA constants are **vbCrLf**, which is equivalent to a carriage return followed by a line feed, and **vbTab**, which is equivalent to the tab character.

Enums

Microsoft has recently introduced a structure into VBA to categorize the plethora of symbolic constants. This structure is called an *enum*, which is short for *enumeration*. For instance, among Excel's 152 enums, there is one for the fill type used by the AutoFill method, defined as follows:

```
Enum XlAutoFillType
    xlFillDefault = 0
    xlFillCopy = 1
    xlFillSeries = 2
    xlFillFormats = 3
    xlFillValues = 4
    xlFillDays = 5
    xlFillWeekdays = 6
    xlFillMonths = 7
    xlFillYears = 8
    xlLinearTrend = 9
    xlGrowthTrend = 10
End Enum
```

(The Excel documentation incorrectly refers to this enum as **XlFillType**.) Note that enum names begin with the letters *Xl* (with an uppercase *X*).

Thus, the following line of code will autofill the first seven cells in the first row of the active sheet with the days of the week, assuming that the first cell contains the word Monday:

```
ActiveSheet.Range("A1").AutoFill ActiveSheet.Range("A1:G1"), xlFillDays
```

This is far more readable than:

```
ActiveSheet.Range("A1").AutoFill ActiveSheet.Range("A1:G1"), 5
```

Note that this enum is built in, so we do not need to add it to our programs in order to use these symbolic constants. (We can create our own enums, but this is generally not necessary in Excel VBA programming, since Excel has done such a good job of this for us.)

As another example, the built-in enum for the constant values that can be returned when the user dismisses a message box (by clicking on a button) is:

```
Enum VbMsgBoxResult
     vbOK = 1
     vbCancel = 2
     vbAbort = 3
     vbRetry = 4
     vbIgnore = 5
     vbYes = 6
     vbNo = 7
End Enum
```

For instance, when the user hits the OK button on a dialog box (assuming it has one), VBA returns the value **vbOK**. Certainly, it is a lot easier to remember that VBA will return the symbolic constant **vbOK** than to remember that it will return the constant 1. (We will discuss how to get and use this return value later.)

VBA also defines some symbolic constants that are used to set the types of buttons that will appear on a message box. These are contained in the following enum (which includes some additional constants not shown):

```
Enum VbMsgBoxStyle
     vbOKOnly = 0
     vbOKCancel = 1
     vbAbortRetryIgnore = 2
     vbYesNoCancel = 3
     vbYesNo = 4
     vbRetryCancel = 5
End Enum
```

To illustrate, consider the following code:

```
If MsgBox("Proceed?", vbOKCancel) = vbOK Then

    ' place code to execute when user hits OK button

Else

    ' place code to execute when user hits any other button

End If
```

In the first line, the code **MsgBox("Proceed?", vbOKCancel)** causes Excel to display a message box with an OK button and a Cancel button and the message "Proceed?", as shown in Figure 5-1.

If the user clicks the OK button, Excel will return the constant value **vbOK**; otherwise it will return the value **vbCancel**. Thus, the **If** statement in the first line will distinguish between the two responses. (We will discuss the **If** statement in detail in Chapter 8, *Control Statements*. Here we are interested in the role of symbolic constants.)

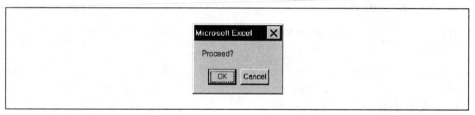

Figure 5-1. Example message box

In case you are not yet convinced of the value of symbolic constants, consider the following enum for color constants:

```
Enum ColorConstants
        vbBlack = 0
        vbBlue = 16711680
        vbMagenta = 16711935
        vbCyan = 16776960
        vbWhite = 16777215
        vbRed = 255
        vbGreen = 65280
        vbYellow = 65535
End Enum
```

Consider which you'd rather type, this:

```
ATextBox.ForeColor = vbBlue
```

or this:

```
ATextBox.ForeColor = 16711680
```

Need I say more?

Variables and Data Types

A *variable* can be thought of as a memory location that can hold values of a specific type. The value in a variable may change during the life of the program—hence the name variable.

In VBA, each variable has a specific *data type*, which indicates which type of data it may hold. For instance, a variable that holds text strings has a String data type and is called a string variable. A variable that holds integers (whole numbers) has an Integer data type and is called an integer variable. For reference, Table 5-1 shows the complete set of VBA data types, along with the amount of memory that they consume and their range of values. We will discuss a few of the more commonly used data types in a moment.

Table 5-1. VBA Data Types

Type	Size in Memory	Range of Values
Byte	1 byte	0 to 255
Boolean	2 bytes	True or False
Integer	2 bytes	-32,768 to 32,767
Long (long integer)	4 bytes	-2,147,483,648 to 2,147,483,647
Single (single-precision real)	4 bytes	Approximately -3.4E38 to 3.4E38
Double (double-precision real)	8 bytes	Approximately -1.8E308 to 4.9E324
Currency (scaled integer)	8 bytes	Approximately -922,337,203,685,477.5808 to 922,337,203,685,477.5807
Date	8 bytes	1/1/100 to 12/31/9999
Object	4 bytes	Any Object reference.
String	Variable length: 10 bytes + string length; Fixed length: string length	Variable length: <= about 2 billion (65,400 for Win 3.1) Fixed length: up to 65,400
Variant	16 bytes for numbers 22 bytes + string length	Number: same as Double String: same as String
User-defined	Varies	

Variable Declaration

To *declare* a variable means to define its data type. Variables are declared with the `Dim` keyword (or with the keywords `Private` and `Public`, which we will discuss later in this chapter). Here are some examples:

```
Dim Name As String
Dim Holiday As Date
Dim Age As Integer
Dim Height As Single
Dim Money As Currency
Dim wbk As Workbook
Dim ch As Chart
```

The general syntax of a variable declaration is:

```
Dim VariableName As DataType
```

If a particular variable is used without first declaring it, or if it is declared without mentioning a data type, as in:

```
Dim Age
```

then VBA will treat the variable as having type Variant. As we can see from Table 5-1, this is generally a waste of memory, since variants require more memory than most other types of variables.

For instance, an integer variable requires 2 bytes, whereas a variant that holds the same integer requires 16 bytes, which is a waste of 14 bytes. It is not uncommon to have hundreds or even thousands of variables in a complex program, and so the memory waste could be significant. For this reason, it is a good idea to declare all variables.

Perhaps more importantly, much more overhead is involved in maintaining a Variant than its corresponding String or Integer, for example. This in turn means that using Variants typically results in worse performance than using an equivalent set of explicit data types.

We can place more than one declaration on a line to save space. For instance, the following line declares three variables:

```
Dim Age As Integer, Name As String, Money As Currency
```

Note, however, that a declaration such as:

```
Dim Age, Height, Weight As Integer
```

is legal, but **Age** and **Height** are declared as Variants, not Integers. In other words, we must specify the type for *each* variable explicitly.

It is also possible to tell VBA the type of the variable by appending a special character to the variable name. In particular, VBA allows the type-declaration suffixes shown in Table 5-2. (I personally dislike these suffixes, but they do save space.)

Table 5-2. Type-Declaration Suffixes

Suffix	Type
%	integer
&	long
!	single
#	double
@	currency
$	string

For instance, the following line declares a variable called **Name$** of type String:

```
Dim Name$
```

We can then write:

```
Name$ = "Donna"
```

Finally, let us note that although Excel allows variable and constant declarations to be placed anywhere within a procedure (before the item is used, that is), it is generally good programming practice to place all such declarations at the *beginning* of the procedure. This improves code readability and makes housekeeping much simpler.

The Importance of Explicit Variable Declaration

We have said that using the Variant data type generally wastes memory and often results in poorer performance. There is an additional, even more important reason to declare all variables explicitly. This has to do with making typing errors, which we all do from time to time. In particular, if we accidentally misspell a variable name, VBA will think we mean to create a *new* variable!

To illustrate how dangerous this can be, consider the *NewBook* procedure in Example 5-1, whose purpose is to take the first open workbook, change its contents, ask the user for a name under which to save the changed workbook, and then save the workbook under the new name.

Example 5-1. A Procedure with a Typo

```
Sub NewBook()

Dim Wbk As Workbook
Dim WbkName As String

' Get first open workbook
Set Wbk = Workbooks(1)

' Get the workbook name
WbkName = Wbk.Name

' Code to change the contents of the workbook
' goes here . . .

' Ask user for new name for document
WkbName = InputBox("Enter name for workbook " & WbkName)

' Save the workbook
Wbk.SaveAs WbkName

End Sub
```

Observe that there is a typographical error (the b and k are transposed) in the following line:

```
    WkbName = InputBox("Enter name for workbook " & WbkName)
```

Since the variable *WkbName* is not declared, Excel will treat it as a new variable and give it the Variant data type. Moreover, VBA will assume that we want the new filename to be assigned to the variable *WkbName*, and will save the changed document under its original name, which is stored in *WbkName*. Thus, we will lose the original workbook when it is inadvertently overwritten without warning!

Option Explicit

To avoid the problem described in the previous example, we need a way to make Excel refuse to run a program if it contains any variables that we have not explicitly declared. This is done simply by placing the line:

```
Option Explicit
```

in the Declarations section of each code module. Since it is easy to forget to do this, VBA provides an option called Require Variable Declaration in its Options dialog box. When this option is selected, VBA automatically inserts the Option Explicit line for us. Therefore, I *strongly* recommend that you enable this option.

Now let us briefly discuss some of the data types in Table 5-1.

Numeric Data Types

The numeric data types include Integer, Long, Single, Double, and Currency. A long is also sometimes referred to as a *long integer.*

Boolean Data Type

A Boolean variable is a variable that takes on one of two values: **True** or **False**. This is a very useful data type that was only recently introduced into VBA. Prior to its introduction, VBA recognized 0 as **False** and any nonzero value as **True**, and you may still see this usage in older code.

String Data Type

A string is a sequence of characters. (An empty string has no characters, however.) A string may contain ordinary text characters (letters, digits, and punctuation) as well as special control characters such as **vbCrLf** (carriage return/line feed characters) or **vbTab** (tab character). As we have seen, a string constant is enclosed within quotation marks. The empty string is denoted by a pair of adjacent quotation marks, as in:

```
EmptyString = ""
```

There are two types of string variables in VBA: fixed-length and variable-length. A fixed-length string variable is declared as follows:

```
Dim FixedStringVarName As String * StringLen
```

For instance, the following statement declares a fixed-length string of length 10 characters:

```
Dim sName As String * 10
```

Observe that the following code, which concatenates two strings:

```
Dim s As String * 10
s = "test"
Debug.Print s & "/"
```

and produces the output:

```
test       /
```

This shows that the content of a fixed-length string is padded with spaces in order to reach the correct length.

A variable-length string variable is a variable that can hold strings of varying lengths (at different times, of course). Variable-length string variables are declared simply as:

```
Dim VariableStringVarName As String
```

As an example, the code:

```
Dim s As String
s = "test"
Debug.Print s & "/"
s = "another test"
Debug.Print s & "/"
```

produces the output:

```
test/
another test/
```

Variable-length string variables are used much more often than fixed-length strings, although the latter have some very specific and important uses (which we will not go into in this book).

Date Data Type

Variables of the Date data type require 8 bytes of storage and are actually stored as decimal (floating-point) numbers that represent dates ranging from January 1, 100 to December 31, 9999 (no year 2000 problem here) and times from 0:00:00 to 23:59:59.

As discussed earlier, literal dates are enclosed within number signs, but when assigning a date to a date variable, we can also use valid dates in string format. For example, the following are all valid date/time assignments:

```
Dim dt As Date
dt = #1/2/98#
dt = "January 12, 2001"
dt = #1/1/95#
dt = #12:50:00 PM#
dt = #1/13/76 12:50:00 PM#
```

VBA has many functions that can manipulate dates and times. If you need to manipulate dates or times in your programs, you should probably spend some time with the Excel VBA help file. (Start by looking under "Date Data Type.")

Variant Data Type

The Variant data type provides a catch-all data type that is capable of holding data of any other type except fixed-length string data and user-defined types. We have already noted the virtues and vices of the Variant data type, and discussed why variants should generally be avoided.

Excel Object Data Types

Excel VBA has a large number of additional data types that fall under the general category of Object data type. We will see a complete list in the chapter on the Excel object model. To get the feel for the types of objects in the Excel object model, here is a partial list of the more prominent objects:

Chart-related objects:

Axis	ChartTitle	Legend	Series
AxisTitle	DataLabel	LegendEntry	SeriesCollection
Chart	DataTable	LegendKey	TickLabels
ChartArea	Floor	PlotArea	Walls
ChartColorFormat	Gridlines	Point	

Pivot table-related objects:

PivotCache	PivotField	PivotFormula	PivotItem	PivotTable

General objects:

Comment	Font	Range	Workbook
FillFormat	Outline	Sheets	Worksheet
Filter	PageSetup	Window	WorksheetFunction

Thus, we can declare variables such as:

```
Dim wb As Workbook
Dim wks As Worksheet
Dim chrt As Chart
Dim ax As axis
Dim pf As PivotField
```

We will devote much of this book to studying the objects in the Excel object model, for it is through these objects that we can manipulate Excel programmatically.

The generic As Object declaration

It is also possible to declare any Excel object using the generic object data type `Object`, as in the following example:

```
Dim chrt As Object
```

While you may see this declaration from time to time, it is much less efficient than a specific object declaration, such as:

```
Dim chrt As Chart
```

This is because Excel cannot tell what type of object the variable *chrt* refers to until the program is running, so it must use some execution time to make this determination. This is referred to as *late binding* and can make programs run significantly more slowly. (For more on late versus early binding, see Appendix E, *Programming Excel from Another Application.*) Thus, generic object declarations should be avoided.

We will discuss object variables in some detail in Chapter 9, *Object Models.* However, we should briefly discuss the `Set` statement now, since it will appear from time to time in upcoming code examples.

The Set statement

Declaring object variables is done in the same way as declaring nonobject variables. For instance, here are two variable declarations:

```
Dim int As Integer    ' nonobject variable declaration
Dim chrt As Chart     ' object variable declaration
```

On the other hand, when it comes to assigning a value to variables, the syntax differs for object and nonobject variables. In particular, we must use the `Set` keyword when assigning a value to an object variable. For example, the following line assigns the currently active Excel chart to the variable *chrt*:

```
Set chrt = ActiveChart
```

(If the currently active object is not a chart, then the variable *chrt* will be set to the special value `Nothing`. We will discuss `Nothing` later.)

Arrays

An *array variable* is a collection of variables that use the same name, but are distinguished by an index value. For instance, to store the first 100 cells in the first row of a worksheet, we could declare an array variable as follows:

```
Dim Cell(1 To 100) As Range
```

(There is no Cell object in the Excel object model: a cell is a special Range object.) The array variable is `Cell`. It has size 100. The lower bound of the array is 1 and the upper bound is 100. Each of the following variables are Range variables (that is, variables of the object type Range):

```
Cell(1), Cell(2),..., Cell(100)
```

Note that if we omit the first index in the declaration, as in:

```
Dim Cell(100) As Range
```

then VBA will automatically set the first index to 0 and so the size of the array will be 101.

The virtue of declaring array variables is clear, since it would be very unpleasant to have to declare 100 separate variables! In addition, as we will see, there are ways to work collectively with all of the elements in an array, using a few simple programming constructs. For instance, the following code boldfaces the values in each of the 100 cells in the array:

```
For i = 1 To 100
    Cell(i).Font.Bold = True
Next i
```

The dimension of an array

The Cell array defined in the previous example has *dimension* one. We can also define arrays of more than one dimension. For instance, the array:

```
Dim Cell(1 To 10, 1 To 100) As Range
```

is a two-dimensional array, whose first index ranges from 1 to 10 and whose second index ranges from 1 to 100. Thus, the array has size 10*100 = 1000.

Dynamic arrays

When an array is declared, as in:

```
Dim FileName(1 To 10) As String
```

the upper and lower bounds are both specified and so the size of the array is fixed. However, there are many situations in which we do not know at declaration time how large an array we may need. For this reason, VBA provides dynamic arrays and the ReDim statement.

A dynamic array is declared with empty parentheses, as in:

```
Dim FileName() as String
```

Dynamic arrays can be sized (or resized) using the ReDim statement, as in:

```
ReDim FileName(1 to 10)
```

This same array can later be resized again, as in:

```
ReDim FileName(1 to 100)
```

Note that resizing an array will destroy its contents *unless* we use the `Preserve` keyword, as in:

```
ReDim Preserve FileName(1 to 200)
```

However, when `Preserve` is used, we can only change the upper bound of the array (and only the last dimension in a multidimensional array).

The UBound function

The *UBound* function is used to return the current upper bound of an array. This is very useful in determining when an array needs redimensioning. To illustrate, suppose we want to collect an unknown number of filenames in an array named *FileName*. If the next file number is *iNextFile*, the following code checks to see if the upper bound is less than *iNextFile*; if so, it increases the upper bound of the array by 10, preserving its current contents, to make room for the next filename:

```
If UBound(FileName) < iNextFile Then
    ReDim Preserve FileName(UBound(FileName) + 10)
End If
```

Note that redimensioning takes time, so it is wise to add some "working room" at the top to cut down on the number of times the array must be redimensioned. This is why we added 10 to the upper bound in this example, rather than just 1. (There is a trade-off here between the extra time it takes to redimension and the extra space that may be wasted if we do not use the entire redimensioned array.)

Variable Naming Conventions

VBA programs can get very complicated, and we can use all the help we can get in trying to make them as readable as possible. In addition, as time goes on, the ideas behind the program begin to fade, and we must rely on the code itself to refresh our memory. This is why adding copious comments to a program is so important.

Another way to make programs more readable is to use a consistent *naming convention* for constants, variables, procedure names, and other items. In general, a name should have two properties. First, it should remind the reader of the purpose or function of the item. For instance, suppose we want to assign Chart variables to several Excel charts. The code:

```
Dim chrt1 As Chart, chrt2 as Chart
Set chrt1 = Charts("Sales")
Set chrt2 = Charts("Transactions")
```

is perfectly legal, but 1000 lines of code and six months later, will we remember which invoice is *chrt1* and which is *chrt2*? Since we went to the trouble of naming the charts in a descriptive manner, we should do the same with the Chart variables, as in:

```
Dim chrtSales As Chart, chrtTrans as Chart
Set chrtSales = Charts("Sales")
Set chrtTrans = Charts("Transactions")
```

Of course, there are exceptions to all rules, but in general, it is better to choose descriptive names for variables (as well as other items that require naming, such as constants, procedures, controls, forms, and code modules).

Second, a variable name should reflect something about the properties of the variable, such as its data type. Many programmers use a convention in which the first few characters of a variable's name indicate the data type of the variable. This is sometimes referred to as a Hungarian naming convention, after the Hungarian programmer Charles Simonyi, who is credited with its invention.

Table 5-3 and Table 5-4 describe the naming convention that we will *generally* use for standard and object variables, respectively. Of course, you are free to make changes for your own personal use, but you should try to be reasonably consistent. These prefixes are intended to remind us of the data type, but it is not easy to do this perfectly using only a couple of characters, and the longer the prefix, the less likely it is that we will use it! (Note the *c* prefix for integers or longs. This is a commonly used prefix when the variable is intended to *count* something.)

Table 5-3. Naming Convention for Standard Variables

Variable	Prefix
Boolean	b or f
Byte	b or bt
Currency	cur
Date	dt
Double	d or dbl
Integer	i, c, or int
Long	l, c, or lng
Single	s or sng
String	s or str
User-defined type	u or ut
Variant	v or var

Table 5-4. Naming Convention for Some Object Variables

Variable	Prefix
Chart	ch or chrt
Workbook	wb or wbk

Table 5-4. Naming Convention for Some Object Variables (continued)

Variable	Prefix
Worksheet	ws or wks
Pivot Table	pt or pvt
Font	fnt
Range	rng

In addition to a data type, every variable has a *scope* and a *lifetime*. Some programmers advocate including a hint as to the scope of a variable in the prefix, using *g* for global, and *m* for module level. For example, the variable `giSize` is a global variable of type Integer. We will discuss the scope and lifetime of a variable next (but we will not generally include scope prefixes in variable names).

Variable Scope

Variables and constants have a *scope*, which indicates where in the program the variable or constant is recognized (or visible to the code). The scope of a variable or constant can be either procedure-level (also called local), module-level private, or module-level public. The rules may seem a bit involved at first, but they do make sense.

Procedure-level (local) variables

A *local* or *procedure-level* variable or constant is a variable or constant that is declared within a procedure, as is the case with the variable `LocalVar` and the constant `LocalConstant` in Figure 5-2. A local variable or constant is not visible outside of the procedure. Thus, for instance, if we try to run *ProcedureB* in Figure 5-2, we will get the error message, "Variable not defined," and the name `LocalVar` will be highlighted.

One of the advantages of local variables is that we can use the same name in different procedures without conflict, since each variable is visible only to its own procedure.

Module-level variables

A *module-level* variable (or constant) is one that is declared in the declarations section of a code module (standard, class, or UserForm). Module-level variables and constants come in two flavors: private and public.

Simply put, a module-level *public* variable (or constant) is available to all procedures in all of the modules in the project, not just the module in which it is declared, whereas a module-level *private* variable (or constant) is available only to the procedures in the module in which it was declared.

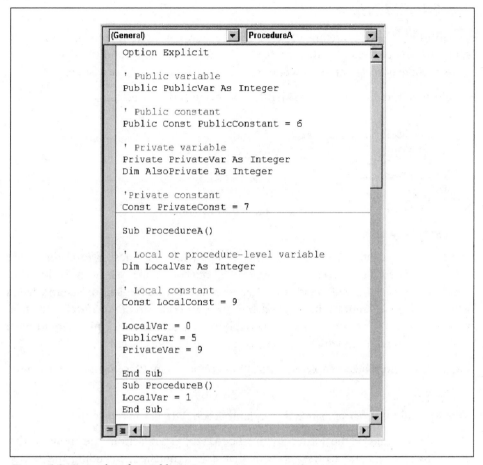

```
(General)                    ▼   ProcedureA                    ▼

  Option Explicit                                                     ▲

  ' Public variable
  Public PublicVar As Integer

  ' Public constant
  Public Const PublicConstant = 6

  ' Private variable
  Private PrivateVar As Integer
  Dim AlsoPrivate As Integer

  'Private constant
  Const PrivateConst = 7

  Sub ProcedureA()

  ' Local or procedure-level variable
  Dim LocalVar As Integer

  ' Local constant
  Const LocalConst = 9

  LocalVar = 0
  PublicVar = 5
  PrivateVar = 9

  End Sub
  Sub ProcedureB()
  LocalVar = 1
  End Sub                                                             ▼
```

Figure 5-2. Examples of variable scope

Public variables and constants are declared using the **Public** keyword, as in:

```
Public APubInt As Integer
Public Const APubConst = 7
```

Private variables and constants are declared using the **Private** keyword, as in:

```
Private APrivateInt As Integer
Private Const APrivateConst = 7
```

The **Dim** keyword, when used at the module level, has the same scope as **Private**, but is not as clear, so it should be avoided.

Public variables are also referred to as *global variables*, but this descriptive term is not *de rigueur*.

Variable Lifetime

Variables also have a lifetime. The difference between lifetime and scope is quite simple: *lifetime* refers to how long (or when) the variable is valid (that is, retains a value) whereas *scope* refers to where the variable is accessible or visible.

To illustrate the difference, consider the following procedure:

```
Sub ProcedureA()
    Dim LocalVar As Integer
    LocalVar = 0
    Call ProcedureB
    LocalVar = 1.
End Sub
```

Note that *LocalVar* is a local variable. When the line:

```
Call ProcedureB
```

is executed, execution switches to *ProcedureB*. While the lines of *ProcedureB* are being executed, the variable `LocalVar` is out of scope, since it is local to *ProcedureA*. But it is still valid. In other words, the variable still exists and has a value, but it is simply not accessible to the code in *ProcedureB*. In fact, *ProcedureB* could also have a local variable named *LocalVar*, which would have nothing to do with the variable of the same name in *ProcedureA*.

Once *ProcedureB* has completed, execution continues in *ProcedureA* with the line:

```
LocalVar = 1
```

This is a valid instruction, since the variable *LocalVar* is back in scope.

Thus, the lifetime of the local variable *LocalVar* extends from the moment that *ProcedureA* is entered to the moment that it is terminated, including the period during which *ProcedureB* is being executed as a result of the call to this procedure, even though during that period, *LocalVar* is out of scope.

Incidentally, you may notice that the Microsoft help files occasionally get the notions of scope and visibility mixed up a bit. The creators of the files seem to understand the difference, but they don't always use the terms correctly.

Static variables

To repeat, a variable may go in and out of scope and yet remain valid during that time—that is, retain a value during that time. However, once the lifetime of a variable expires, the variable is destroyed and its value is lost. It is the lifetime that determines the *existence* of a variable; its scope determines its visibility.

Thus, consider the following procedures:

```
Sub ProcedureA()
    Call ProcedureB
    Call ProcedureB
    Call ProcedureB
    Call ProcedureB
    Call ProcedureB
End Sub
Sub ProcedureB()
    Dim x As Integer
    x = 5
    . . .
End Sub
```

When *ProcedureA* is executed, it simply calls *ProcedureB* five times. Each time *ProcedureB* is called, the local variable *x* is created anew and destroyed at the end of that call. Thus, *x* is created and destroyed five times.

Normally, this is just want we want. However, there are times when we would like the lifetime of a local variable to persist longer than the lifetime of the procedure in which it is declared. As an example, we may want a procedure to do something special the first time it is called, but not subsequent times. For instance, the following one-line macro changes the font of the selected cells to Comic Sans:

```
Sub ToComic()
    Selection.Font.Name = "Comic Sans"
End Sub
```

Suppose, however, that we wish to warn the user that Comic Sans is a bit informal and ask if he or she really wants to make this change. We don't want to make a pest of ourselves by asking every time the user invokes this macro. What we need is a local variable with a "memory" that will allow it to keep track of whether or not a particular call to *ToComic* is the first call or not. This is done with a static variable.

A *static variable* is a local variable whose lifetime is the lifetime of the entire module, not just the procedure in which it was declared. In fact, a static variable retains its value as long as the document or template containing the code module is active (even if no code is running).

Thus, a static variable has the scope of a local variable, but the lifetime of a module-level variable. *C'est tout dire!*

Consider now the modification of the preceding macro, which is shown in Example 5-2. The code first declares a static Boolean variable called `NotFirstTime`. It may seem simpler to use a variable called `FirstTime`, but there is a problem. Namely, Boolean variables are automatically initialized as False, so the first time that the *ToComic* macro is run, `FirstTime` would be False, which is not want we want. (We will discuss variable initialization a bit later.)

Example 5-2. ToComic() Modified to Use a Static Variable

```
Sub ToComic()

' Declare static Boolean variable
Static NotFirstTime As Boolean

' If first time, then ask for permission
If NotFirstTime = False Then

    If MsgBox("Comic Sans is a bit informal. Proceed?", _
                vbYesNo) = vbYes Then

        ' Make the change
        Selection.Font.Name = "Comic Sans MS"

    End If

    ' No longer the first time
    NotFirstTime = True

Else

    ' If not the first time, just make the change
    Selection.Font.Name = "Comic Sans MS"

End If

End Sub
```

The `If` statement checks to see if the value of *NotFirstTime* is False, as it will be the first time the procedure is called. In this case, a message box is displayed, as shown in Figure 5-3. If the user chooses the Yes button, the font is changed. In either case, the static Boolean variable *NotFirstTime* is set to True. Precisely because *NotFirstTime* is static, this value will be retained even after the macro ends (but not if the document is closed).

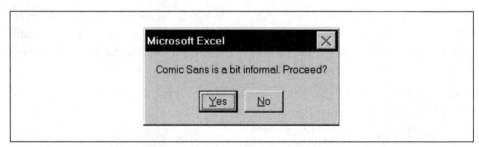

Figure 5-3. Dialog that appears if the static NotFirstTime is false

The next time the macro is executed, the variable *NotFirstTime* will be True, and so the `If` condition:

```
If NotFirstTime = False Then
```

will be `False` and the *MsgBox* function will not be executed. Instead, the `Else` code will execute. This code just changes the font, without bothering the user with a message box.

Static variables are not used very often, but they can be quite useful at times.

It may have occurred to you that we could accomplish the same effect by using a module-level private variable to keep a record of whether or not the macro has been called, instead of a static local variable. However, it is considered better programming style to use the most restrictive scope possible which, in this case, is a local variable with an "extended" lifetime. This helps prevent accidental alteration of the variable in other portions of the code. (Remember that this code may be part of a much larger code module, with a lot of things going on. It is better to hide the *NotFirstTime* variable from this other code.)

Variable Initialization

When a procedure begins execution, all of its local variables are automatically *initialized*, that is, given initial values. In general, however, it is not good programming practice to rely on this initialization, since it makes the program less readable and somewhat more prone to logical errors. Thus, it is a good idea to initialize all local variables explicitly, as in the following example:

```
Sub Example()

Dim x As Integer
Dim s As String

x = 0        ' Initialize x to 0
s = ""       ' Initialize s to empty string

' more code here . . .

End Sub
```

Note, however, that static variables cannot be initialized, since that defeats their purpose! Thus, it is important to know the following rules that VBA uses for variable initialization (note also that they are intuitive):

*   Numeric variables (Integer, Long, Single, Double, Currency) are initialized to zero.

*   A variable-length string is initialized to a zero-length (empty) string.

*   A fixed-length string is filled with the character represented by the ASCII character code 0, or *Chr*(0).

*   Variant variables are initialized to **Empty**.

*   Object variables are initialized to **Nothing**.

The Nothing keyword actually has several related uses in Excel VBA. As we will see in Chapter 8, it is used to release an object variable. Also, it is used as a return value for some functions, generally to indicate that some operation has failed. Finally, it is used to initialize object variables.

VBA Operators

VBA uses a handful of simple operators and relations, the most common of which are shown in Table 5-5.

Table 5-5. VBA Operators and Relations

Type	Name	Symbol
Arithmetic Operators	Addition	+
	Subtraction	−
	Multiplication	*
	Division	/
	Division with Integer result	\
	Exponentiation	∧
	Modulo	Mod
String Operator	Concatenation	&
Logical Operators	AND	AND
	OR	OR
	NOT	NOT
Comparison Relations	Equal	=
	Less than	<
	Greater than	>
	Less than or equal to	<=
	Greater than or equal to	>=
	Not equal to	<>

The Mod operator returns the remainder after division. For example:

```
8 Mod 3
```

returns 2, since the remainder after dividing 8 by 3 is 2.

To illustrate string concatenation, the expression:

```
"To be or " & "not to be"
```

is equivalent to:

```
"To be or not to be"
```

6

Functions and Subroutines

As we have seen, VBA allows two kinds of procedures: functions and subroutines. As a reminder, the only difference between a function and a subroutine is that a function returns a value, whereas a subroutine does not.

Calling Functions

A function declaration has the form:

```
[Public or Private] Function FunctionName(Param1 As DataType1, _
        Param2 As DataType2,...) As ReturnType
```

Note that we must declare the data types not only of each parameter to the function, but also of the return type. Otherwise, VBA declares these items as variants.

We will discuss the optional keywords **Public** and **Private** later in this chapter, but you can probably guess that they are used here to indicate the scope of the function, just as they are used in variable declarations.

For example, the *AddOne* function in Example 6-1 adds 1 to the original value.

Example 6-1. The AddOne Function

```
Public Function AddOne(Value As Integer) As Integer
    AddOne = Value + 1
End Function
```

To use the return value of a function, we just place the call to the function within the expression, in the location where we want the value. For instance, the code:

```
MsgBox "Adding 1 to 5 gives: " & AddOne(5)
```

produces the message box in Figure 6-1, where the expression *AddOne*(5) is replaced by the return value of *AddOne*, which in this case is 6.

Figure 6-1. The message dialog displayed by Example 6-1

Note that, in general, any parameters to a function must be enclosed in parentheses within the function call.

In order to return a value from a function, we must assign the function's name to the return value somewhere within the body of the function. Example 6-2 shows a slightly more complicated example of a function.

Example 6-2. Assigning a Function's Return Value

```
Function ReturnCount() As Variant

' Return count of cells in current selection

If TypeName(Selection) = "Range" Then
   ReturnCount = Selection.Count
Else
   ReturnCount = "Not applicable"
End If

End Function
```

This function returns a count of the number of cells in the current selection, provided that the selection is a range of cells. If the selection is another type of object (such as a chart), the function returns the words "Not applicable." Note that since the return value may be a number or a string, we declare the return type as Variant. Note also that *ReturnCount* is assigned twice within the body of the function. Its value, and hence the value of the function, is set differently depending upon the value returned by the *TypeName(Selection)* function. Since these assignments are mutually exclusive, only one of them will occur each time the function is called.

Because functions return values, you can't call them directly from the Macro dialog that appears when you select Tools → Macro → Macros, nor can you assign them to an Excel toolbar or menu through Excel's user interface. If you want to be able to call a function, you'll have to "wrap" it in—that is, have it called by—a subroutine, the topic that we'll cover next.

Calling Subroutines

A subroutine declaration has the form:

```
[Public or Private] Sub SubroutineName(Param1 As DataType1, _
        Param2 As DataType2,...)
```

This is similar to the function declaration, with the notable absence of the `As ReturnType` portion. (Note also the word `Sub` in place of `Function`.)

Since subroutines do not return a value, they cannot be used within an expression. To call a subroutine named *SubroutineA*, we can write either:

```
Call SubroutineA(parameters, . . .)
```

or simply:

```
SubroutineA parameters, . . .
```

Note that any parameters must be enclosed in parentheses when using the `Call` keyword, but not otherwise.

Parameters and Arguments

Consider the following very simple subroutine, which does nothing more than display a message box declaring a person's name:

```
Sub DisplayName(sName As String)
    MsgBox "My name is " & sName
End Sub
```

To call this subroutine, we would write, for example:

```
DisplayName "Wolfgang"
```

or:

```
Call DisplayName("Wolfgang")
```

The variable *sName* in the procedure declaration:

```
Sub DisplayName(sName As String)
```

is called a *parameter* of the procedure. The call to the procedure should contain a string variable or a literal string that is represented by the variable *sName* in this procedure (but see the discussion of optional parameters in the next section). The value used in place of the parameter when we make the procedure call is called an *argument*. Thus, in the previous example, the argument is the string "Wolfgang."

Note that many programmers fail to make a distinction between parameters and arguments, using the names interchangeably. However, since a parameter is like a variable and an argument is like a *value* of that variable, failing to make this distinction is like failing to distinguish between a variable and its value!

Optional Arguments

In VBA, the arguments to a procedure may be specified as optional, using the `Optional` keyword. (It makes no sense to say that a parameter is optional; it is the value that is optional.) To illustrate, consider the procedure in Example 6-3, which simply changes the font name and font size of the current selection:

Example 6-3. Using an Optional Argument

```
Sub ChangeFormatting(FontName As String, _
                Optional FontSize As Variant)

' Change font name
Selection.Font.Name = FontName

' Change font size if argument is supplied
If Not IsMissing(FontSize) Then
   Selection.Font.Size = CInt(FontSize)
End If

End Sub
```

The second parameter is declared with the `Optional` keyword. Because of this, we may call the procedure with or without an argument for this parameter, as in:

```
ChangeFormatting("Arial Narrow", 24)
```

and:

```
ChangeFormatting("Arial Narrow")
```

Note that the *IsMissing* function is used in the body of the procedure to test whether the argument is present. If the argument is present, then the font size is changed. Note also that we declared the *FontSize* parameter as type Variant because *IsMissing* works only with parameters of type Variant (unfortunately). Thus, we converted the Variant to type Integer using the *CInt* function.

A procedure may have any number of optional arguments, but they must all come at the end of the parameter list. Thus, for instance, the following declaration is *not* legal:

```
Sub ChangeFormatting(Optional FontName As String, FontSize As Single)
```

If we omit an optional argument in the middle of a list, we must include an empty space when calling that procedure. For instance, if a procedure is declared as follows:

```
Sub ChangeFormatting(Optional FontName As String, _
                     Optional FontSize As Single, _
                     Optional FontBold as Boolean)
```

then a call to this procedure to set the font name to Arial and the boldfacing to True would look like:

```
ChangeFormat "Arial", , True
```

To avoid confusion, we should point out that some built-in Excel procedures have optional arguments and others do not. Of course, we cannot leave out an argument unless the documentation or declaration for the procedure specifically states that it is optional.

Named Arguments

Some VBA procedures can contain a large number of parameters. For example, one form of the Excel *SaveAs* function has the declaration:

```
SaveAs (Filename As string, FileFormat As VARIANT, Password As VARIANT, _
        WriteResPassword As VARIANT, ReadOnlyRecommended As VARIANT, _
        CreateBackup As VARIANT, AddToMru As VARIANT, TextCodepage As _
        VARIANT, TextVisualLayout As VARIANT)
```

where all of the parameters are optional. Here is an example of a call to this procedure:

```
SaveAs "c:\temp\test.xls", , , , , True , , , True
```

Not very readable, is it?

The arguments shown in the previous call are said to be *positional arguments* because it is their position that tells VBA which parameters they are intended to replace. This is why we need to include space for missing arguments.

However, VBA can also use *named arguments*, in which case the previous call would be written as:

```
SaveAs FileName:="c:\temp\test.xls", _
       CreateBackup:=True, _
       AddToMru:=True
```

Note the special syntax for named arguments, in particular, the colon before the equal sign.

This function call is a great improvement over the positional argument version. In general, the advantages of named arguments over positional arguments are three-fold:

- Named arguments can improve readability and clarity.

- Blank spaces (separated by commas) are required for missing optional arguments when using a positional declaration, but not when using named arguments.

- The order in which named arguments are listed is immaterial which, of course, is not the case for positional arguments.

Named arguments can improve readability quite a bit, and are highly recommended. However, they can require considerably more space, so for the short examples in this book, we usually will not use them.

ByRef Versus ByVal Parameters

Parameters come in two flavors:`ByRef` and `ByVal`. Many programmers do not have a clear understanding of these concepts, but they are very important and not that difficult to understand.

To explain the difference, consider the two procedures in Example 6-4. *ProcedureA* simply sets the value of the module-level variable *x* to 5, displays that value, calls the procedure *AddOne* with the argument *x*, and then displays the value of *x* again.

Example 6-4. Testing the ByVal and ByRef Keywords

```
Sub ProcedureA()
    x = 5               ' Set x to 5
    MsgBox x            ' Display x
    Call AddOne(x)       ' Call AddOne
    MsgBox x            ' Display x again
End Sub

Sub AddOne(ByRef i As Integer)
    i = i + 1
End Sub
```

Note the presence of the **ByRef** keyword in the *AddOne* procedure declaration. This keyword tells VBA to pass a reference to the variable *x* to the *AddOne* procedure. Therefore, the *AddOne* procedure, in effect, replaces its parameter *i* by the variable *x*. As a result, the line:

```
    i = i + 1
```

effectively becomes:

```
    x = x + 1
```

So, after *AddOne* is called, the variable *x* has the value 6.

On the other hand, suppose we change the *AddOne* procedure, replacing the keyword **ByRef** with the keyword **ByVal**:

```
Sub AddOne(ByVal i As Integer)
    i = i + 1
End Sub
```

In this case, VBA does not pass a reference to the variable **x**, but rather it passes its *value*. Hence, the variable *i* in *AddOne* simply takes on the value 5. Adding 1 to that value gives 6. Thus, *i* equals 6, but the value of the argument **x** is not affected! Hence, both message boxes will display the value 5 for **x**.

ByRef and ByVal both have their uses. When we want to change the value of an argument, we must declare the corresponding parameter as ByRef, so that the called procedure has access to the actual argument itself. This is the case in the previous example. Otherwise, the *AddOne* procedure does absolutely nothing, since the local variable *i* is incremented, and it is destroyed immediately afterwards, when the procedure ends.

On the other hand, when we pass an argument for informational purposes only, and we do not want the argument to be altered, it should be passed by value, using the ByVal keyword. In this way, the called procedure gets only the *value* of the argument.

To illustrate further, *ProcedureA* in Example 6-5 gets the text of the first cell and feeds it to the *CountCharacters* function. The returned value (the number of characters in the active document) is then displayed in a message box.

Example 6-5. Passing an Argument by Value

```
Sub ProcedureA()
    Dim sText As String
    sText = ActiveSheet.Cells(1,1).Text
    MsgBox CountCharacters(sText)
End Sub

Function CountCharacters(ByVal sTxt As String)
    CountCharacters = Len(sTxt)
End Function
```

Now, *CountCharacters* does not need to, and indeed should not, change the text. It only counts the number of characters in the text. This is why we pass the argument by value. In this way, the variable *sTxt* gets the value of the text in *sText*, that is, it gets a *copy* of the text.

To appreciate the importance of this, imagine for a moment that *CountCharacters* is replaced by a procedure that contains hundreds or thousands of lines of code, written by someone else, perhaps not as reliable as we are. Naturally, we do not want this procedure to change our text. Rather than having to check the code for errors, all we need to do is notice that the *sTxt* parameter is called by value, which tells us that the procedure does not even have access to our text. Instead, it gets only a copy of the text.

There is one downside to passing arguments by value: it can take a lot of memory (and time). For instance, in the previous example, VBA needs to make a copy of the text to pass to the parameter *sTxt*.

Thus, we can summarize by saying that if we want the procedure to modify an argument, the argument must be passed by reference. If not, the argument should be passed by value unless this will produce an unacceptable decrease in performance, or unless we are very sure that it will not get changed by accident.

It is important to note that VBA defaults to `ByRef` if we do not specify otherwise. This means that the values of arguments are subject to change by the called procedure, unless we explicitly include the keyword `ByVal`. *Caveat scriptor!*

Exiting a Procedure

VBA provides the `Exit Sub` and `Exit Function` statements, should we wish to exit from a procedure before the procedure would terminate naturally. For instance, if the value of a parameter is not suitable, we may want to issue a warning to the user and exit, as Example 6-6 shows.

Example 6-6. Using the Exit Sub Statement

```
Sub DisplayName(sName As String)
    If sName = "" then
        Msgbox "Please enter a name."
        Exit Sub
    End If
    MsgBox "Name entered is " & sName
End Sub
```

Public and Private Procedures

Just as variables and constants have a scope, so do procedures. We can declare a procedure using the `Public` or `Private` keyword, as in:

```
    Public Function AddOne(i As Integer) As Integer
```

or:

```
    Private Function AddOne(i As Integer) As Integer
```

The difference is simple: a `Private` procedure can only be called from within the module in which it is defined, whereas a `Public` procedure can be called from within any module in the project.

Note that if the `Public` or `Private` keyword is omitted from a procedure declaration, then the procedure is considered to be `Public`.

Project References

In order for code in one project to call a public procedure in another project, the calling project must have a reference to the called project.

Generally, a project that is associated with a workbook is interested only in procedures that lie in that project. In fact, it would in general be bad programming practice to require a procedure in one project to call a procedure in another project. Nonetheless, there may be occasions when this is required. To add a reference to the calling project, we use the References dialog box (under the Tools menu), shown in Figure 6-2.

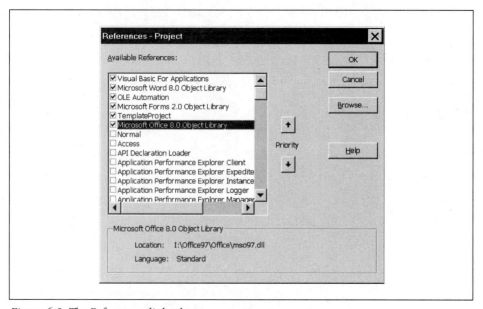

Figure 6-2. The References dialog box

Fully Qualified Procedure Names

When we call a public procedure that lies in another module, there is a potential problem with ambiguity, for there may be more than one public procedure with the same name in another module. VBA will execute the first one it finds, and this may not be the one we had in mind!

The solution is to use a *qualified procedure name*, which has the form:

```
ModuleName.ProcedureName
```

For instance, if a public procedure named *AddOne* lies in a module named Utilities, then we can call this procedure using the syntax:

```
Utilities.AddOne
```

If necessary, we can also specify the project name, using the syntax (don't forget to set the reference first):

```
ProjectName.ModuleName.ProcedureName
```

It is important to note that `ProjectName` is the code name of the project, not the filename. (The default code name is VBAProject.)

7

Built-in Functions and Statements

VBA has a large number of built-in functions and statements. For possible reference, Table 7-1 shows the VBA functions, and Table 7-2 shows the statements. We will take a look at a few of the more commonly used functions and statements for programming Excel VBA in this chapter and Chapter 8, *Control Statements*.

Table 7-1. VBA Functions

Abs	DDB	IsError	RightB
Array	Dir	IsMissing	Rnd
Asc	DoEvents	IsNull	RTrim
AscB	Environ	IsNumeric	Second
AscW	EOF	IsObject	Seek
Atn	Error	Lbound	Sgn
Cbool	Exp	Lcase	Shell
Cbyte	FileAttr	Left	Sin
Ccur	FileDateTime	LeftB	SLN
Cdate	FileLen	Len	Space
CDbl	Fix	LenB	Spc
Cdec	Format	LoadPicture	Sqr
Choose	FreeFile	Loc	Str
Chr	FV	LOF	StrComp
ChrB	GetAllSettings	Log	StrConv
ChrW	GetAttr	Ltrim	String
Cint	GetAutoServerSettings	Mid	Switch
CLng	GetObject	MidB	SYD
Command	GetSetting	Minute	Tab

Table 7-1. VBA Functions (continued)

Cos	Hex	MIRR	Tan
CreateObject	Hour	Month	Time
CSng	Iif	MsgBox	Timer
CStr	IMEStatus	Now	TimeSerial
CurDir	Input	Nper	TimeValue
Cvar	InputB	NPV	Trim
CVDate	InputBox	Oct	TypeName
CVErr	InStr	Partition	UBound
Date	InStrB	Pmt	UCase
DateAdd	Int	PPmt	Val
DateDiff	Ipmt	PV	VarType
DatePart	IRR	QBColor	Weekday
DateSerial	IsArray	Rate	Year
DateValue	IsDate	RGB	
Day	IsEmpty	Right	

Table 7-2. VBA Statements

AppActivate	Do...Loop	Mid	Reset
Beep	End	MidB	Resume
Call	Enum	MkDir	Return
ChDir	Erase	Name	RmDir
ChDrive	Error	On Error	RSet
Close	Event	On...GoSub	SavePicture
Const	Exit	On...GoTo	SaveSetting
Date	FileCopy	Open	Seek
Declare	For Each...Next	Option Base	Select Case
DefBool	For...Next	Option Compare	SendKeys
DefByte	Function	Option Explicit	Set
DefCur	Get	Option Private	SetAttr
DefDate	GoSub...Return	Print #	Static
DefDbl	GoTo	Private	Stop
DefDec	If...Then...Else	Property Get	Sub
DefInt	Implements	Property Let	Time
DefLng	Input #	Property Set	Type
DefObj	Kill	Public	Unload
DefSng	Let	Put	Unlock
DefStr	Line Input #	RaiseEvent	While...Wend

Table 7-2. VBA Statements (continued)

DefVar	Load	Randomize	Width #
DeleteSetting	Lock	ReDim	With
Dim	LSet	Rem	Write #

To help simplify the exposition, we will follow Microsoft's lead and use square brackets to indicate optional parameters. Thus, for instance, the second parameter in the following procedure is optional:

```
Sub ChangeFormat(FontName [, FontSize])
```

Note that we have also omitted the data type declarations, which will be discussed separately.

The MsgBox Function

We have been using the *MsgBox* function unofficially for some time now. Let us introduce it officially. The *MsgBox* function is used to display a message and wait for the user to respond by pushing a button. The most commonly used syntax is:

```
MsgBox(prompt [, buttons] [, title])
```

This is not the function's complete syntax. There are some additional optional parameters related to help contexts that you can look up in the help documentation.

prompt is a String parameter containing the message to be displayed in the dialog box. Note that a multiline message can be created by interspersing the `vbCrLf` constant within the message.

buttons is a Long parameter giving the sum of values that specify various properties of the message box. These properties are the number and type of buttons to display, the icon style to use, the identity of the default button, and the modality of the message box. (A *system modal* dialog box remains on top of all currently open windows and captures the input focus systemwide, whereas an *application modal* dialog box remains on top of the application's windows only and captures the application's focus.) The various values of *Buttons* that we can sum are shown in Table 7-3. (They are officially defined in the `VbMsgBoxStyle` enum.)

Table 7-3. The MsgBox Buttons Argument Values

Purpose	Constant	Value	Description
Button Types	vbOKOnly	0	Display OK button only
	vbOKCancel	1	Display OK and Cancel buttons
	vbAbortRetryIgnore	2	Display Abort, Retry, and Ignore buttons

Table 7-3. The MsgBox Buttons Argument Values (continued)

Purpose	Constant	Value	Description
	vbYesNoCancel	3	Display Yes, No, and Cancel buttons
	vbYesNo	4	Display Yes and No buttons
	vbRetryCancel	5	Display Retry and Cancel buttons
Icon Types	vbCritical	16	Display Critical Message icon
	vbQuestion	32	Display Warning Query icon
	vbExclamation	48	Display Warning Message icon
	vbInformation	64	Display Information Message icon
Default Button	vbDefaultButton1	0	First button is default
	vbDefaultButton2	256	Second button is default
	vbDefaultButton3	512	Third button is default
	vbDefaultButton4	768	Fourth button is default
Modality	vbApplicationModal	0	Application modal message box
	vbSystemModal	4096	System modal message box

For instance, the code:

```
MsgBox "Proceed?", vbQuestion + vbYesNo
```

displays the message box shown in Figure 7-1, which includes a question mark icon and two command buttons, labeled Yes and No.

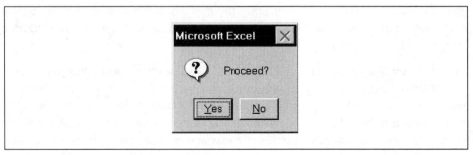

Figure 7-1. A MsgBox dialog box

The *title* parameter is a string expression that is displayed in the title bar of the dialog box. If we omit this argument, then "Microsoft Excel" will be displayed, as in Figure 7-1.

The *MsgBox* function returns a number indicating which button was selected. These return values are given in Table 7-4. (They are officially defined in the VbMsgBoxResult enum.)

Table 7-4. MsgBox Return Values

Constant	Value	Description
vbOK	1	OK button pressed
vbCancel	2	Cancel button pressed
vbAbort	3	Abort button pressed
vbRetry	4	Retry button pressed
vbIgnore	5	Ignore button pressed
vbYes	6	Yes button pressed
vbNo	7	No button pressed

The InputBox Function

The *InputBox* function is designed to get input from the user. The most commonly used (but not the complete) syntax is:

```
InputBox(prompt [, title] [, default])
```

where *prompt* is the message in the input box, *title* is the title for the input box, and *default* is the default value that is displayed in the text box. For instance, the code:

```
sName = InputBox("Enter your name.", "Name", "Albert")
```

produces the dialog box in Figure 7-2.

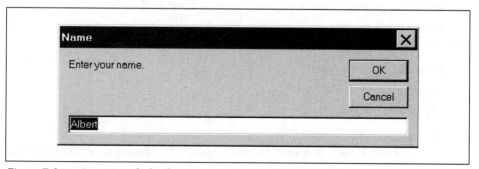

Figure 7-2. An InputBox dialog box

The *InputBox* function returns the string that the user enters into the text box. Thus, in our example, the string variable *sName* will contain this string.

Note that if we want a number from the user, we can still use the *InputBox* function and simply convert the returned string (such as "12.55") to a number (12.55) using the *Val* function, discussed later in the chapter.

VBA String Functions

Here are a handful of useful functions that apply to strings (both constants and variables):

The Len function

The *Len* function returns the length of a string—that is, the number of characters in the string. Thus, the code:

```
Len("January Invoice")
```

returns the number 15.

The UCase and LCase functions

These functions return an all uppercase or all lowercase version of the string argument. The syntax is:

```
UCase(string)
LCase(string)
```

For instance:

```
MsgBox UCase("Donna")
```

will display the string DONNA.

The Left, Right and Mid functions

These functions return a portion of a string. In particular:

```
Left(string, number)
```

returns the leftmost *number* characters in *string*, and:

```
Right(string, number)
```

returns the rightmost *number* characters in *string*. For instance:

```
MsgBox Right("Donna Smith", 5)
```

displays the string Smith.

The syntax for *Mid* is:

```
Mid(string, start, length)
```

This function returns the first *length* number of characters of *string*, starting at character number *start*. For instance:

```
Mid("Library.xls",9,3)
```

returns the string xls. If the *length* parameter is missing, as in:

```
Mid("Library.xls",9)
```

the function will return the rest of the string, starting at *start*.

The Instr function

The syntax for this very useful function is:

```
Instr(Start, StringToSearch, StringToFind)
```

The return value is the position, starting at *Start*, of the first occurrence of *StringToFind* within *StringToSearch*. If *Start* is missing, then the function starts searching at the beginning of *StringToSearch*. For instance:

```
MsgBox Instr(1, "Donna Smith", "Smith")
```

displays the number 7, because "Smith" begins at the seventh position in the string "Donna Smith."

The Str and Val functions

The *Str* function converts a number to a string. For instance:

```
Str(123)
```

returns the string 123. Conversely, the *Val* function converts a string that represents a number into a number (so that we can do arithmetic with it, for instance). For example:

```
Val("4.5")
```

returns the number 4.5 and:

```
Val("1234 Main Street")
```

returns the number 1234. Note, however, that *Val* does not recognize dollar signs or commas. Thus:

```
Val($12.00)
```

returns 0, not 12.00.

The Trim, LTrim, and RTrim functions

The *LTrim* function removes leading spaces from a string. Similarly, *RTrim* removes trailing spaces, and *Trim* removes both leading and trailing spaces. Thus:

```
Trim("  extra    ")
```

returns the string extra.

The String and Space functions

The *String* function provides a way to quickly create a string that consists of a single character repeated a number of times. For instance:

```
sText = String(25, "B")
```

sets *sText* to a string consisting of 25 Bs. The *Space* function returns a string consisting of a given number of spaces. For instance:

```
sText = Space(25)
```

sets *sText* to a string consisting of 25 spaces.

The Like operator and StrCmp function

The Like operator is very useful for comparing two strings. Of course, we can use the equal sign, as in:

```
string1 = string2
```

which is true when the two strings are identical. However, `Like` will also make a case-insensitive comparison or allow the use of pattern matching. The expression:

string `Like` *pattern*

returns `True` if *string* fits *pattern*, and `False` otherwise. (Actually, the expression can also return `Null`.) We will describe *pattern* in a moment.

The type of string comparison that the `Like` operator uses depends upon the setting of the `Option Compare` statement. There are two possibilities, one of which should be placed in the Declarations section of a module (in the same place as `Option Explicit`):

```
Option Compare Binary
Option Compare Text
```

Note that the default is `Option Compare Binary`.

Under `Option Compare Binary`, string comparison is in the order given by the ANSI character code, as shown here:

A < B < . . . < Z < a < b < . . . < z < À < . . . < Ø < à < . . . < ø

Under `Option Compare Text`, string comparison is based on a case-insensitive sort order (determined by your PC's locale setting). This gives a sort order as shown here:

A = a < À = à < B = b < . . . < Z = z < Ø = ø

By the way, the last item in the `Text` sort order is the "[" character, with ANSI value 91. This is useful to know if you want to place an item last in alphabetical order—just surround it by square brackets.

The pattern-matching features of the `Like` operator allow the use of wildcard characters, character lists, or character ranges. For example:

?

   Matches any single character

*

   Matches zero or more characters

#

   matches any single digit (0–9)

[charlist]

   Matches any single character in *charlist*

[!charlist]

   Matches any single character not in *charlist*

For more details, check the VBA help file.

The *StrCmp* function also compares two strings. Its syntax is:

```
StrComp(string1, string2 [, compare])
```

and it returns a value indicating whether **string1** is equal to, greater than, or less than **string2**. For more details, check the VBA help file.

Miscellaneous Functions and Statements

Of the wealth of functions offered by the VBA language, we'll focus on the *Is...* functions to determine an attribute of a variable or object, the conversion functions, and two functions, *IIf* and *Switch*, that return a conditional result.

The Is Functions

VBA has several *Is* functions that return Boolean values indicating whether or not a certain condition holds. We have already discussed the *IsMissing* function in connection with optional arguments. Here are some additional Is functions.

The IsDate function

This function indicates whether an expression can be converted to a date. It also applies to a cell, in which case it evaluates the contents of the cell. If the contents represent a valid date, the function returns **True**. For instance, the code:

```
IsDate(Range("F3"))
```

will return **True** if the contents of cell F3 represent a date.

The IsEmpty function

This function indicates whether a variable has been initialized or whether a worksheet cell is empty. For example, the code:

```
If IsEmpty(Range("A1")) Then . . .
```

tests whether or not cell A1 is empty.

The IsNull function

This function is used to test whether a variable is **Null** (that is, contains no data). Note that code such as:

```
If var = Null Then
```

will always return **False** because most expressions that involve **Null** automatically return **False**. The proper way to determine if the variable **var** is **Null** is to write:

```
If IsNull(var) Then
```

The IsNumeric function

This function indicates whether an expression can be evaluated as a number or whether a cell contains a value that can be evaluated as a number. For instance, if cell A1 contains the data 123 (even if this cell is formatted as text), then the condition in:

```
If IsNumeric(Range("A1")) Then
```

will evaluate to **True**. On the other hand, if the cell contains the data 123 Main Street, then the condition will evaluate to **False**.

The Immediate If Function

The Immediate If function has the syntax:

```
IIf(Expression, TruePart, FalsePart)
```

If **Expression** is True, then the function returns **TruePart**. If **Expression** is False, the function returns **FalsePart**. For instance, the following code displays a dialog indicating whether or not the first row in the active worksheet is empty:

```
Dim rng As Range
Set rng = ActiveSheet.Rows(1)
MsgBox IIf(IsEmpty(ActiveSheet.Cells(1, 1)), _
    "Cell is empty", "Cell is not empty")
```

It is very important to note that the Immediate If function always evaluates *both* **TruePart** and **FalsePart**, even though it returns only one of them. Hence, we must be careful about undesirable side effects. For example, the following code will produce a division by zero error because even though the *IIf* function returns $1/x$ only when x is not equal to 0, the expression $1/x$ is evaluated in all cases, including when x is equal to 0:

```
x = 0
y = IIf(x = 0, x ^ 2, 1 / x)
```

The Switch Function

The syntax of the *Switch* function is:

```
Switch(expr1, value1, expr2, value2, ... , exprn, valuen)
```

where **exprn** and **valuen** are expressions. Note that there need only be one expression-value pair, but the function is more meaningful if there are at least two such pairs.

The *Switch* function evaluates each expression **exprn**. When it encounters the first True expression, it returns the corresponding value. As with the *IIf* function,

Switch always evaluates all of the expressions. If none of the expressions is True, the function returns `Null`. This can be tested with the *IsNull* function.

The procedure in Example 7-1 displays the type of file based on its extension: Template, Workbook, or Add-in.

Example 7-1. The Switch Function

```
Sub ShowFileType(FileExt As String)

Dim FileType As Variant

FileType = Switch(FileExt = "xlt", "Template", _
                  FileExt = "xls", "Workbook", _
                  FileExt = "xla", "Addin")

' Display result
If Not IsNull(FileType) Then
   MsgBox FileType
Else
   MsgBox "Unrecognized type"
End If

End Sub
```

There is one subtlety in this code. Since the *Switch* function can return a `Null` value, we cannot assign the return value to a String variable, as we might first try to do:

```
Dim FileType As String

FileType = Switch(FileExt = "xlt", "Template", _
                  FileExt = "xls", "Workbook", _
                  FileExt = "xla", "Addin")
```

This will not produce an error unless *FileExt* is *not* "xlt," "xls," or "xla," in which case we will get the very annoying error message, "Invalid use of Null." The solution is to declare *FileType* as a Variant, which can hold any data type, including *no* data type, which is indicated by the `Null` keyword. (This issue can also be avoided by using a `Select Case` statement, discussed in Chapter 8.)

Units Conversions

The *InchesToPoints* function converts a measurement given in inches to one given in points. The reason this is important is that many Excel values need to be given (or are returned) in points, but most of us prefer to think in inches (there are 72 points in one inch).

This applies especially to positioning properties, such as Top and Left. For instance, the Top property of a ChartObject specifies the location of the top of the chart object, measured in points, from Row 1 of the worksheet. Thus, to set this value to .25 inches, we would write:

```
ActiveChart.ChartObject.Top = InchesToPoints(.25)
```

There is also a *PointsToInches* function that is useful for displaying the return value of a function in inches when the function returns the value in points.

The Beep Statement

This simple statement, whose syntax is:

```
Beep
```

sounds a single tone through the computer's speakers. It can be useful (when used with restraint) if we want to get the user's attention. However, there is a caveat: The results are dependent upon the computer's hardware, and so the statement may not produce a sound at all! Thus, if you use this statement in your code, be sure to warn the user. (It is possible, and probably better in general, to use the Excel status bar to display messages to the user that do not interfere with execution of a program. This is done using the StatusBar property of the Application object.)

Handling Errors in Code

We discussed the various types of errors in Chapter 3, but we have scrupulously avoided the question of how to handle run-time errors in code. Indeed, VBA provides several tools for handling errors (`On Error`, `Resume`, the Err object, and so on), and we could include an entire chapter on the subject in this book.

Proper error handling is *extremely* important. Indeed, if you are, or intend to become, a professional application developer, you should familiarize yourself with error-handling procedures.

On the other hand, if your intention is to produce Excel VBA code for your own personal use, the reasons for adding error handling routines are somewhat mitigated. For when an error occurs within one of your own programs, VBA will stop execution, display an error message, and highlight the offending code. This should enable you to debug the application and fix the problem. (It would be unreasonable to expect another user of your program to debug your code, however.)

Let us undertake a brief discussion of the highlights of error handling. (For more details, may I suggest my book *Concepts of Object-Oriented Programming in Visual Basic*, published by Springer-Verlag. It has a detailed chapter on error handling.)

The On Error Goto Label Statement

The On Error statement tells VBA what to do when a run-time error occurs. The most common form of the statement is:

```
On Error GoTo label
```

where *label* is a label. For instance, consider the following code:

```
Sub example()

On Error GoTo ERR_EXAMPLE
MsgBox Selection.Cells.Count

Exit Sub

ERR_EXAMPLE:
  MsgBox Err.Description, vbCritical
  Exit Sub

End Sub
```

The purpose of this procedure is simply to display the number of cells in the current selection. When the current selection is a worksheet range, the Cells property returns the collection of cells in the selection and the Count property then returns the number of cells.

However, if the current selection is not a worksheet range (it might be a drawing object or a chart, for instance), then the Cells property fails. To deal with this possibility in a friendly manner, we add some error checking. The line:

```
On Error GoTo ERR_EXAMPLE
```

tells VBA to move execution to the label **ERR_EXAMPLE** if an error occurs. The code following this label is called the *error-handling code*. If an error should occur, the next line executed is the *MsgBox* line, in which case the dialog in Figure 7-3 will be displayed. This message gives a description of the error, obtained from the Error object, which we discuss in the next section.

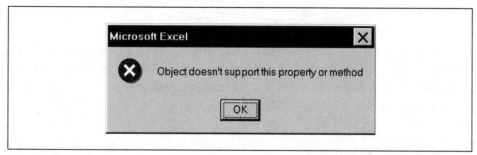

Figure 7-3. An error dialog

It is important to note the line just before the **ERR_EXAMPLE** label:

```
Exit Sub
```

Without this statement, the error-handling code will always be executed, even when there is no error! Omitting this line is a common mistake. Note also that labels always end with a colon.

The Error Object

The error object, Err object, belongs to the VBA object model. The most important properties of this object are:

Number
> The VBA error number

Source
> The name of the current VBA project

Description
> A description of the error

Note that the Clear method of the Err object will clear all of the properties of the Err object, setting its Number property to 0 (which indicates the absence of an error).

The On Error GoTo 0 Statement

The statement:

```
On Error GoTo 0
```

turns off any previous **On Error GoTo** *label* statements. Any error occurring subsequently will be handled by VBA in its own inimitable way.

The On Error Resume Next Statement

The syntax:

```
On Error Resume Next
```

tells VBA to continue executing the code immediately following the line that caused the error. There are two important uses for this form of **On Error**. The first is to cause VBA to ignore an error. For instance, the code:

```
Sub example()

On Error Resume Next
MsgBox Selection.Cells.Count

End Sub
```

will report the cell count when the selection is a worksheet range and do nothing when the selection is not a worksheet range.

Another important use for the `On Error Resume Next` syntax is for *in-line error checking*, where we check for errors immediately following the line that may have caused an error. For instance, another way to handle errors in the previous example is:

```
Sub example()

On Error Resume Next
MsgBox Selection.Cells.Count
If Err.Number <> 0 Then
  MsgBox Err.Description, vbCritical
End If

End Sub
```

The Resume Statement

It is also possible to include the `Resume` statement in the error-handling portion of the code. This will cause VBA to resume execution at the line that follows the one that caused the error. Thus, the previous code is equivalent to the following:

```
Sub example()

On Error GoTo ERR_EXAMPLE
MsgBox Selection.Cells.Count

Exit Sub
ERR_EXAMPLE:
  MsgBox Err.Description, vbCritical
  Resume Next

End Sub
```

There are three variations on the `Resume` statement:

- Resume
- Resume Next
- Resume *ALabel*

The first version will cause VBA to resume with the line that caused the error. This is useful if your error-handling code actually repairs the error condition and you want the line that caused the original error to be executed again.

To illustrate, the procedure in Example 7-2 is designed to open a workbook named *a:\test.xls*. If it does not exist, an error will occur. The error-handling code gives the user a chance to enter a new workbook name, in which case we want to execute the Open method again. Hence the use of the `Resume` statement.

Example 7-2. Error Handling with the Resume Statement

```
Sub test()

Dim sNew As String
sNew = "a:\test.xls"
On Error GoTo ERR_DISK
Workbooks.Open sNew

Exit Sub

ERR_DISK:
  If Err.Number = 1004 Then
    sNew = InputBox("Cannot find file. Enter new location or leave blank to
                    cancel.")
    If sNew <> "" Then
      Resume
    Else
      Exit Sub
    End If
  End If

End Sub
```

The third variation:

```
Resume ALabel
```

causes VBA to resume execution at the line labeled *ALabel*.

8

Control Statements

We conclude our discussion of the VBA language with a discussion of the main VBA *control statements*, which are statements that affect the flow of control (or flow of execution) in a program.

The If...Then Statement

The If...Then statement is used for conditional control. The syntax is:

```
If Condition Then
    ' statements go here . . .
ElseIf AnotherCondition Then
    ' more statements go here . . .
Else
    ' more statements go here . . .
End If
```

Note that we may include more than one ElseIf part, and that both the ElseIf part(s) and the Else part are optional. We can also squeeze all parts of this statement onto a single line, which is generally only a good idea when the ElseIf and Else parts are missing. As an example, the following code deletes the current selection in the active worksheet if it contains more than one cell:

```
If Selection.Count > 1 Then Selection.Delete
```

The following example changes the color of the current selection based upon its location—selected cells in odd-numbered rows are colored red, those in even-numbered rows are colored blue:

```
Dim oCell As Range
For Each oCell In Selection.Cells
  If (oCell.Row Mod 2) = 1 Then
    ' odd
    oCell.Interior.ColorIndex = 3    ' red
```

```
    Else
       ' even
       oCell.Interior.ColorIndex = 5      ' blue
    End If
Next
```

The For Loop

The For..Next statement provides a method for repeatedly looping through a block of code (that is, one or more lines of code). This loop is naturally referred to as a For loop. The basic syntax is:

```
For counter = start To end
    ' block of code goes here . . .

Next counter
```

The first time that the block of code is executed, the variable *counter* (called the loop variable for the For loop) is given the value *start*. Each subsequent time that the block of code is executed, the loop variable *counter* is incremented by 1. When *counter* exceeds the value *end*, the block of code is no longer executed. Thus, the code block is executed a total of *end* – *start* + *1* times, each time with a different value of *counter*.

Note that we can omit the word *counter* in the last line of a For loop (replacing Next counter with just Next). This may cause the For loop to execute a bit more quickly, but it also detracts a bit from readability.

To illustrate, the following code loops through the collection of all cells in the current selection. If a cell has a date in it, then the font color is changed to red:

```
Dim i As Integer
Dim oCell As Range

For i = 1 To Selection.Count

    ' Get the next cell
    Set oCell = Selection.Cells(i)
    ' Color it if a date
    If IsDate(oCell) Then
       oCell.Font.ColorIndex = 3
    End If

Next i
```

For loops are often used to initialize an array. For instance, the following code assigns a value of 0 to each of the 11 variables *iArray*(0) through *iArray*(10):

```
For i = 0 To 10
    iArray(i) = 0
Next i
```

Note that the loop variable *counter* will usually appear within the block of code, as it does in this array initialization example, but this is not a requirement. However, if it does appear, we need to be very careful not to change its value, since that will certainly mess up the **For** loop. (VBA automatically increments the loop variable each time through the loop, so we should leave it alone.)

Exit For

VBA provides the **Exit For** statement to exit a **For** loop prematurely. For instance, the code in Example 8-1 finds the first nonempty cell in the first row of the active worksheet. If none exists, a message is displayed. Note the use of a Boolean variable to keep track of the existence question.

Example 8-1. Finding the First Nonempty Cell

```
Sub FindFirstNonEmpty()

Dim oCell As Range
Dim bNone As Boolean

bNone = True
For Each oCell In ActiveSheet.Rows(1).Cells
  If Not IsEmpty(oCell) Then
    oCell.Select
    bNone = False
    Exit For
  End If
Next

If bNone Then MsgBox "No nonempty cells in row 1", vbInformation

End Sub
```

We can also control the step size and direction for the counter in a **For** loop using the **Step** keyword. For instance, in the following code, the counter *i* is incremented by 2 each time the block of code is executed:

```
For i = 1 to 10 Step 2
  ' code block goes here
Next i
```

The following loop counts down from 10 to 1 in increments of −1. This can be useful when we want to examine a collection (such as the cells in a row or column) from the bottom up:

```
For i = 10 to 1 Step -1
  ' code block goes here
Next i
```

The For Each Loop

The `For Each` loop is a variation on the `For` loop that was designed to iterate through a collection of objects (as well as through elements in an array), and is generally much more efficient than using the traditional `For` loop. The general syntax is:

```
For ObjectVar In CollectionName
    ' block of code goes here . . .

Next ObjectVar
```

where *ObjectVar* is a variable of the same object type as the objects within the collection. The code block will execute once for each object in the collection.

The *FindFirstNonEmpty* procedure shown in Example 8-1 illustrates the `For Each` loop.

Thus, when iterating through a collection of objects, we have two choices:

```
For Each object in Collection
    ' code block here
Next object
```

or:

```
For i = 1 to Collection.Count
    ' code block here
Next i
```

It is important to keep in mind that the `For Each` loop can be *much* faster than the `For` loop when dealing with collections of Excel objects. Thus, except for small collections, it is the preferred method.

The Do Loop

The `Do` loop has several variations. To describe these variations, we use the notation:

```
{While | Until}
```

to represent either the word `While` or the word `Until`, but not both. With this in mind, here are the possible syntaxes for the `Do` loop:

```
Do {While | Until} condition

    ' code block here

Loop
```

or:

```
Do

    ' code block here

Loop {While | Until} condition
```

Actually, there is a fifth possibility, because we can dispense with *condition* completely and write:

```
Do

    ' code block here

Loop
```

Some of these variations are actually quite subtle. For instance, the following code cycles through the cells in the first row of the active worksheet as long as the cells are nonempty:

```
i = 1
Do While IsEmpty(ActiveSheet.Rows(1).Cells(i))
  i = i + 1
Loop
ActiveSheet.Rows(1).Cells(i).Select
```

(This code will cause some problems if the first row has no nonempty cells, but let's not worry about that now.) Consider also the following code, whose purpose is similar:

```
i = 1
Do
  i = i + 1
Loop While Not IsEmpty(ActiveSheet.Rows(1).Cells(i))
ActiveSheet.Rows(1).Cells(i).Select
```

The difference between these two versions is that, in the first case, the `IsEmpty` condition is checked immediately, before any code within the Do loop is executed. Thus, if the first cell is empty, the condition will fail, no code will be executed within the Do loop, and so this cell will be selected (as it should).

On the other hand, in the second case, the condition is checked at the end of each loop, so the loop will execute the first time, even if the first cell is empty.

Just as the `For` loop has an `Exit For` statement for terminating the loop, a Do loop as an `Exit Do` statement for exiting the Do loop.

The Select Case Statement

As we have seen, the `If...Then...` construct is used to perform different tasks based on different possibilities. An alternative construct that is often more readable is the `Select Case` statement, whose syntax is:

```
Select Case testexpression
  Case value1
    ' statements to execute if testexpression = value1
  Case value2
    ' statements to execute if testexpression = value2
    . . .

  Case Else
    ' statements to execute otherwise
End Select
```

Note that the **Case Else** part is optional. To illustrate, the following code is the **Select Case** version of Example 7-1 in Chapter 7, *Built-in Functions and Statements*, (see the discussion of the *Switch* function) that displays the type of a file based on its extension. I think you will agree that this is a bit more readable than the previous version:

```
Sub ShowFileType(FileExt As String)

Dim FileType As Variant

Select Case FileExt
  Case "xlt"
    FileType = "Template"
  Case "xls"
    FileType = "Worksheet"
  Case "xla", "utl"
    FileType = "Addin"
  Case Else
    FileType = "unknown"
End Select

' Display result
MsgBox FileType

End Sub
```

Note the penultimate case statement:

```
Case "xla", "utl"
```

VBA allows us to place more than one condition in a case statement, separated by commas. This is useful when more than one case produces the same result.

A Final Note on VBA

There is a lot more to the VBA language than we have covered here. In fact, the VBA reference manual is about 300 pages long. However, we have covered the main points needed to begin Excel VBA programming.[*]

---

[*] If you'd like a good reference guide to the VBA language, see *VB & VBA in a Nutshell: The Language*, written by Paul Lomax and published by O'Reilly & Associates.

Actually, many Excel VBA programming tasks require only a small portion of VBA's features and you will probably find yourself wrestling much more with Excel's object model than with the VBA language itself.

We conclude our discussion of the VBA language per se with a brief outline of topics for further study, which you can do using the VBA help files.

File-Related Functions

VBA has a large number of functions related to file and directory housekeeping. Table 8-1 contains a selection of them.

Table 8-1. Some VBA File and Directory Functions

Function	Description
Dir	Find a file with a certain name.
FileLen	Get the length of a file.
FileTimeDate	Get the date stamp of a file.
FileCopy	Copy a file.
Kill	Delete a file.
Name	Rename a file or directory.
RmDir	Delete a directory.
MkDir	Make a new directory.

In addition to the file-related functions in Table 8-1, there may be times when it is useful to create new text files to store data. VBA provides a number of functions for this purpose, headed by the **Open** statement, whose (simplified) syntax is:

```
Open pathname For mode As [#] filenumber
```

Once a file has been opened, we can read or write to it.

Date and Time-Related Functions

VBA has a large number of functions related to manipulating dates and times. Table 8-2 contains a selection.

Table 8-2. Some Date- and Time-Related Functions

Function	Description
Date, Now, Time	Get the current date or time.
DateAdd, DateDiff, DatePart	Perform date calculations.
DateSerial, DateValue	Return a date.
TimeSerial, TimeValue	Return a time.

Table 8-2. Some Date- and Time-Related Functions (continued)

Function	Description
Date, Time	Set the date or time.
Timer	Time a process.

The Format Function

The *Format* function is used to format strings, numbers, and dates. Table 8-3 gives a few examples.

Table 8-3. Format Function Examples

Expression	Return Value
Format(Date, "Long Date")	Thursday, April 30, 1998
Format(Time, "Long Time")	5:03:47 PM
Format(Date, "mm/dd/yy hh:mm:ss AMPM")	04/30/98 12:00:00 AM
Format(1234.5, "$##,##0.00")	$1,234.50
Format("HELLO", "<")	"hello"

III

Excel Applications and the Excel Object Model

9

Object Models

In this chapter, we present a general overview of object models and the syntax used to manipulate them in code.

As we have discussed, VBA is the programming language that underlies several important Windows applications, including Microsoft Excel, Word, Access, Power-Point, Visual Basic, and, in Office 2000, Outlook. Any application that uses VBA in this way is called a *host application*. We also discussed the fact that each host application enhances VBA by providing an *object model* (perhaps more than one) to deal with the objects that are particular to that application.

Microsoft provides over a dozen different object models for its Office application suite and related products. These include object models for Excel, Word, Access, DAO (Data Access Objects), Outlook, PowerPoint, Binder, Graph, Forms, VBA, VB, ASP (Active Server Pages), and more. Of course, our interest in this book is with the Excel object model, and we will devote most of the rest of the book to describing the major portions of this model. (We will also discuss a portion of the Office object model in the chapter on customizing Excel menus and toolbars.)

Objects, Properties, and Methods

In the parlance of VBA programming, an *object* is something that is identified by its properties and its methods. For example, workbooks, worksheets, charts, and fonts are all examples of objects in the Excel object model. Actually, the Excel object model contains 192 different objects, including several hidden and obsolete ones.

Properties

The term *property* is used in the present context in pretty much the same way that it is used in everyday English; it is a trait or attribute or characteristic of an object. For instance, a Worksheet object has 55 properties, among which are Cells, Name, ProtectionMode, and UsedRange. A property's value can be any valid data type, such as Integer, Single, String, or even another object type.

When the value of a property has type Integer, for instance, we will refer to the property as an *integer property*. Integer properties are quite common, and so Microsoft has defined a large number of built-in enums (152, to be exact, with 1266 individual constants) to give symbolic names to these property values. For instance, the Calculation property of the Application object can take on any of the values in the enum defined by:

```
Enum XlCalculation
    xlCalculationManual = -4135
    xlCalculationAutomatic = -4105
    xlCalculationSemiautomatic = 2
End Enum
```

If a property's value is an object, it is referred to as an *object property*. For instance, a Workbook object has an ActiveChart property that returns a Chart object. Of course, the Chart object has its own set of properties and methods.

Because a Chart object can be obtained from a Workbook object, we refer to Chart as a *child object* of Workbook, and Workbook as a *parent* of Chart. We will have more to say about this parent-child relationship a bit later.

Methods

A *method* of an object is an action that can be performed on (or on behalf of) the object. For instance, a Worksheet object has a Protect method that causes the worksheet to be protected.

In programming terms, the properties and methods of an object are just built-in functions or subroutines. It is important to emphasize that the distinction between property and method is one of intent and is often made somewhat arbitrarily. (In fact, the Item member is sometimes classified as a property and sometimes as a method, depending upon the object in question; it appears that even Microsoft has trouble making up its collective mind from time to time.)

The properties and methods of an object are collectively referred to as the object's *members*. This should not be confused with an object's children.

Collection Objects

In programming with the Excel object model (or indeed any object model), it is common to have a great many objects "alive" at the same time. For instance, each cell within the current selection is an object (a Range object), as is each row and column in each open worksheet. Hence, at any given time, there are thousands of objects in existence. To manage these objects, the designers of an object model generally include a special type of object called a *collection object.*

As the name implies, collection objects represent collections of objects—generally objects of a single type. For instance, the Excel object model has a collection object called Rows that represents the set of all rows in the worksheet in question (as Range objects). It is customary to say that the Rows collection object *contains* the rows in the sheet, so we will use this terminology as well. There is one Rows collection for each open worksheet.

Collection objects are generally just called *collections*, but it is very important to remember that a collection is just a special type of object. As we will see, the properties and methods of a Collection object are specifically designed to manage the collection.

We can generally spot a collection object by the fact that its name is the plural of the name of the objects contained within the collection. For instance, the Worksheets collection contains Worksheet objects. However, in some cases, this naming convention is not followed. For instance, the Rows collection contains Range objects. In the Excel object model, there are no Cell, Row, or Column objects. These are all represented by Range objects. We will devote an entire chapter (Chapter 19) to the important Range object.

Collections are extremely common in the Office object models. In fact, almost one-half of all of the objects in the Excel object model are collections! Table 9-1 shows some of the more commonly used collections in the Excel object model.

Table 9-1. Some Excel Collection Objects

Areas	FormatConditions	SeriesCollection
Axes	LegendEntries	Sheets
Borders	Names	Windows
ChartObjects	PivotFields	Workbooks
Charts	PivotTables	Worksheets
DataLabels	Points	
Filters	Range	

We emphasize the fact that a collection is just a special type of object. Indeed, the properties and methods of a Collection object are specifically designed to manage the collection. Accordingly, the *basic* requirements for a collection object are:

- A property called Count that returns the number of objects in the collection. This is a read-only property; that is, it cannot be set by the programmer. It is automatically updated by VBA itself.

- A method called Add (or something similar, such as AddNew) that allows the programmer to add a new object to the collection.

- A method called Remove, Close, or Delete, or something similar, that allows the programmer to remove an object from the collection.

- A method called Item that permits the programmer to access any particular object in the collection. The item is usually identified either by name or by an index number.

Note that these basic requirements are not hard and fast. Some collection objects may not implement all of these members, and many implement additional members. For instance, the Areas and Borders collections do not have an Add method, since we are not allowed to add objects to these collections. We can only manipulate the properties of these collections.

Some Excel collections are considerably more complicated than others, since they have several properties and methods that relate specifically to the type of object they contain. For instance, the Sheets collection has 10 properties and eight methods. Several of these members, such as the PrintOut method, are included specifically so that they can operate on all of the sheets in the collection at the same time. (A *sheet* is either a worksheet or a chartsheet.)

The Base of a Collection

Note that collections can be either 0-based or 1-based. In a *0-based collection*, the first member has index 0, and in a *1-based collection*, the first member has index 1. Most, but not all, collections in the Excel object model and in VBA itself are 1-based. However, some older collections tend to be 0-based. (I guess that Microsoft got a lot of complaints about 0-based collections so they decided to switch.)

It is important to determine the base of any collection before trying to access members by index. This can be done by checking the help system (sometimes) or trying some sample code. For instance, the code:

```
For i = 1 To Selection.Cells.Count
    Debug.Print Selection.Cells(i).Value
Next i
```

is correct, since the Cells collection is 1-based. However, the UserForms collection, which represents all currently loaded user forms in Excel, is 0-based, so the code:

```
For i = 1 To UserForms.Count
    Debug.Print UserForms(i).Name
Next i
```

will produce an error. The correct code is:

```
For i = 0 To UserForms.Count - 1
    Debug.Print UserForms(i).Name
Next i
```

(Note that this reports the number of *loaded* forms in the project.)

Object Model Hierarchies

The fact that one object's properties and methods can return another object, thus creating the concept of *child objects*, is of paramount importance, for it adds a very useful structure to the object model.

It seems by looking at the literature that there is not total agreement on when one object is considered a child of another object. For our purposes, if object A has a property or method that returns object B, then we will consider object B to be a child of object A and object A to be a parent of object B. For example, the Range object has a Font property, which returns a Font object. Hence Font is a child of Range and Range is a parent of Font. The Font object is also a child of the Chart-Area object, which represents the chart area within an Excel chart. (We will discuss this object in Chapter 21, *The Chart Object*.) In fact, an object may have many parents and many children.

It is important not to take the parent-child analogy too literally. For instance, the object hierarchy is full of circular parent-child relationships. As an example, Range is a child of Worksheet and Worksheet is a child of Range. Indeed, in most object models, most objects have a property that returns the top object of the model. In the Excel object model, almost every object has an Application property that returns the Application object, which is the top object in the Excel object model. This provides a quick way to return to the top of the object hierarchy. Hence, almost every object in the object model is a parent of the top object!

The object hierarchy of an object model is often pictured in a tree-like structure. A small portion of the Excel object model is shown in Figure 9-1. This figure was taken from the object browser that I wrote as an aid to programming the object model. A coupon for this object browser is included in the back of the book.

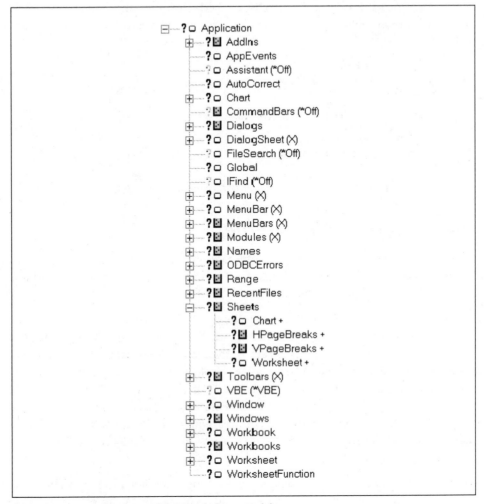

Figure 9-1. A small portion of the Excel object model

Object Model Syntax

It is time that we formally discuss the basic syntax that is used when programming with an object model.

The general syntax for referring to an object's properties and methods is very simple. If *objVar* is an object variable that refers to a particular object and **AProperty** is a property of this object, then we can access this property (for reading or for changing) using the syntax:

```
objVar.AProperty(any required parameters)
```

For instance, the following code sets the font name property of the first row in the active worksheet:

```
' Declare object variable
Dim rng As Range

' Set rng to refer to first row
Set rng = ActiveSheet.Rows(1)

' Set font name
rng.Font.Name = "Arial"
```

Note that the last line of code actually invokes two properties; the Font property of *rng* returns a Font object, whose Name property is set to Arial.

If *AMethod* is a method for this object, then we can invoke that method with the syntax:

```
objVar.AMethod(any required parameters)
```

Note that this syntax is quite similar to the syntax used to call an ordinary VBA subroutine or function, except that here we require qualification with the name of the variable that points to the object whose property or method is being called.

For instance, continuing the previous code, we can apply the CheckSpelling method to the row referred to by *rng* as follows:

```
rng.CheckSpelling
```

We could include the name of a custom dictionary as a parameter to this method.

Object Variables

To access a property of an object, or to invoke a method, we can generally take two approaches: *direct* or *indirect.* The indirect approach uses an object variable—that is, a variable that has an object data type—whereas the direct approach does not.

For instance, to set the Bold property of the Font object for the first row in the active worksheet, we can take a direct approach, as in:

```
ActiveSheet.Rows(1).Font.Bold = True
```

Alternatively, we can assign an object variable. Here are two possibilities:

```
Dim rng As Range
Set rng = ActiveSheet.Rows(1)
rng.Font.Bold = True

Dim fnt As Font
Set fnt = ActiveSheet.Rows(1).Font
fnt.Bold = True
```

Object variables are more important than they might seem at first. The most obvious reason for their use is that they can improve code readability when we need to refer to the same object more than once. For instance, instead of writing:

```
ActiveSheet.Rows(1).Font.Bold = True
ActiveSheet.Rows(1).Font.Italic = True
ActiveSheet.Rows(1).Font.Underline = False
ActiveSheet.Rows(1).Font.Size = 12
ActiveSheet.Rows(1).Font.Name = "Arial"
```

we can use a Font variable to improve readability as follows:

```
Dim fnt As Font
Set fnt = ActiveSheet.Rows(1).Font
fnt.Bold = True
fnt.Italic = True
fnt.Underline = False
fnt.Size = 12
fnt.Name = "Arial"
```

The With Statement

In fact, VBA provides a `With` statement to handle just the situation in the previous example, which could be written as follows:

```
Dim fnt As Font
Set fnt = ActiveSheet.Rows(1).Font
With fnt
    .Bold = True
    .Italic = True
    .Underline = False
    .Size = 12
    .Name = "Arial"
End With
```

The general syntax of the `With` statement is:

```
With object
    ' statements go here

End With
```

where the statements generally refer to the object, but do not require qualification using the object's name, as in the previous example.

Object Variables Save Execution Time

The main reason that object variables are important is not to improve readability, but to save execution time. In particular, to execute each of the five lines in the first version of the previous code, VBA needs to resolve the references to the various Excel objects ActiveSheet, Rows(1), and Font. That is, VBA needs to "climb down" the Excel object model. This takes time.

However, in the code that uses an object variable of type Font, VBA only needs to resolve these references once. Therefore, the second version runs much more quickly. This difference can be very noticeable when there are hundreds or thousands of references to resolve.

An Object Variable Is a Pointer

There are some very important differences between object variables and nonobject variables, such as those of type Integer, Single, or String. As we have mentioned, a nonobject variable can be thought of as a name for a location in the computer's memory that holds some data. For instance, in the code:

```
Dim iVar As Integer
iVar = 123
```

the variable *iVar* is a 4-byte memory location that holds the integer value 123. This can be pictured as in Figure 9-2. (Actually, the 4-byte memory location holds the value 123 in binary format, but that is not relevant to our discussion.)

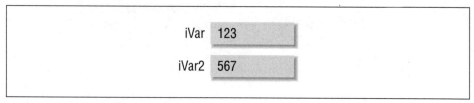

Figure 9-2. Integer variables in memory

Now, if we were to further write:

```
Dim iVar2 As Integer
iVar2 = iVar
iVar2 = 567
```

we would not expect the last line of code to have any effect upon the value of the variable *iVar*, which should still be 123. This is because *iVar* and *iVar2* represent different areas of memory, as pictured in Figure 9-2.

However, an object variable is *not* the name of a memory location that holds the object. Rather, an object variable is the name of a memory location that holds the *address* of the memory location that holds the object, as shown in Figure 9-3. Put another way, the object variable holds a *reference to*, or *points to* the object. For this reason, it is an example of a *pointer variable*, or simply a *pointer*. In Figure 9-3, the object variable *rng* points to an object of type Range, namely, the first column in the active sheet.

The code that goes with Figure 9-3 is:

```
Dim rng as Range
Set rng = ActiveSheet.Columns(1)
```

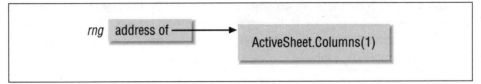

Figure 9-3. An object variable in memory

One of the consequences of the fact that object variables are pointers is that more than one object variable can point to (or refer to) the same object, as in:

```
Dim rng as Range
Dim rng2 as Range
Set rng = ActiveSheet.Columns(1)
Set rng2 = rng
```

This code creates the situation pictured in Figure 9-4.

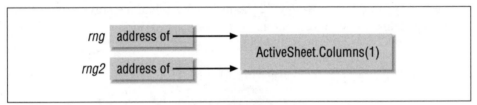

Figure 9-4. Two object variables referencing the same object

We emphasize that while *rng* and *rng2* are different object variables, they hold the same value and so point to the same object. Thus, we can change the first column using either of these object variables.

It is important when programming with objects to keep very careful track of all object variables and what they are referencing. Furthermore, it is generally not a good idea to have more than one object variable pointing to the same object (as in Figure 9-4) unless there is a compelling reason to do so. It is very easy to change the object using one object variable (say *rng*) and then later use the other variable (*rng2*), thinking it refers to the unchanged object.

Freeing an Object Variable: the Nothing Keyword

To free an object variable so that it no longer points to anything, we use the `Nothing` keyword, as in:

```
Set rng2 = Nothing
```

It is good programming practice to free object variables when they are no longer needed, since this can save resources. An object variable is also set to `Nothing` automatically when its lifetime expires.

Note that once an object no longer has any references to it, the object will automatically be destroyed by VBA, thus freeing up its resources (memory). However, *all* references to the object must be freed before the object is destroyed. This is another reason not to point more than one object variable at the same object if possible.

The Is Operator

To compare the values of two ordinary variables, *Var1* and *Var2*, we would just write:

```
If Var1 = Var2 Then . . .
```

However, the syntax for comparing two object variables to see if they refer to the same object is special (as is the syntax for setting the value of an object variable—using the Set statement). It is done using the Is operator:

```
If rng Is rng2 then . . .
```

Similarly, to test whether or not an object variable has been set to Nothing, we write:

```
If rng Is Nothing Then . . .
```

Be advised that there is a problem with the Is operator in the current version of VBA. This problem exists in the version of VBA used by Office 97 *and* Office 2000. (Microsoft has acknowledged the problem.) For example, the code:

```
Dim Wks As Worksheet
Dim Wks2 As Worksheet

Set Wks = ActiveSheet
Set Wks2 = ActiveSheet

MsgBox Wks Is Wks2
```

will correctly display the value True. However, the analogous code:

```
Dim rng As Range
Dim rng2 As Range

Set rng = ActiveSheet.Rows(1)
Set rng2 = ActiveSheet.Rows(1)

MsgBox rng Is rng2
```

incorrectly displays the value False. If we change the penultimate line to:

```
Set rng2 = rng
```

then the message box correctly displays True.

Default Members

In most object models, many objects have a *default member* (property or method) that is invoked when a property or method is expected but we do not specify one. For instance, in the Microsoft Word object model, the default member for the Range object is the Text property. Hence, the VBA Word code:

```
Dim rng As Range
Set rng = ActiveDocument.Words(1)
rng = "Donna"
```

sets the first word in the active document to Donna, since Word applies the default property in the last line, effectively replacing it with:

```
rng.Text = "Donna"
```

Unfortunately, neither the Excel VBA documentation nor the Excel object model itself make an effort to identify the default members of Excel objects. Accordingly, my suggestion is to avoid the issue when programming Excel.

In any case, default members tend to make code less readable, and for this reason, I generally avoid them. One notable exception is for a collection object. It is generally the case that the default member of a collection object is the Item method. Hence, for instance, we can refer to the fourth cell in the current selection by:

```
Selection.Cells(4)
```

rather than by the more clumsy:

```
Selection.Cells.Item(4)
```

Since this use of the default member is not likely to cause any confusion, we will use it.

Global Objects

Many of the properties and methods of the Application object can be used without qualifying them with the word **Application**. These are called *global members*. For instance, the Selection property is global, and so we can write:

```
Selection.Cells.Count
```

instead of:

```
Application.Selection.Cells.Count
```

To identify the global members, the Excel object model has a special object called the Global object. This object is not used directly—its purpose is simply to identify the global members of the object model. Note that the members of the Global object form a proper subset of the members of the Application object (which means that not all of the members of the *Application* object are global).

Table 9-2 lists the (nonhidden) global members of the Excel object model.

Table 9-2. Excel Global Members

ActiveCell	DDEAppReturnCode	Range
ActiveChart	DDEExecute	Run
ActivePrinter	DDEInitiate	Selection
ActiveSheet	DDEPoke	SendKeys
ActiveWindow	DDERequest	Sheets
ActiveWorkbook	DDETerminate	ThisWorkbook
Application	Evaluate	Union
Assistant	Excel4IntlMacroSheets	Windows
Calculate	Excel4MacroSheets	Workbooks
Cells	ExecuteExcel4Macro	WorksheetFunction
Charts	Intersect	Worksheets
CommandBars	Names	
Creator	Parent	

10

Excel Applications

Simply put, we can define an *Office application* to be an Office "document" (for instance, an Access database, Excel workbook, Word document, Word template, or PowerPoint presentation) that contains some special customization. This customization usually takes the form of a combination of VBA procedures and menu and/or toolbar customizations and is generally designed to simplify or automate certain tasks. It may provide *utilities*, which are programs for performing a specific task, such as printing or sorting.

This may seem like a fairly liberal definition. For instance, if we add a single custom menu item to a Word template that simply adds a closing (Sincerely yours, etc.) to the end of a Word document, we could consider this template to be a Word application. However, it is doubtful that we could get anyone to buy this Word application!

The point we want to emphasize is that an Office application is quite different from a traditional Windows application, such as Excel itself. Traditional Windows applications are built around a main executable file. In the case of Excel, this file is called *excel.exe*. Of course, a complex application like Excel involves many additional supporting files, such as additional executables, help files, object library files, resource files, information files, ActiveX control files, and the ubiquitous DLL files.

On the other hand, Office applications do not revolve around standalone executable files. Rather, they are created within an Office document. In particular, an Access application is created within an Access database, an Excel application is created within an Excel workbook, a Word application is created within a Word document, and a PowerPoint application is created within a PowerPoint presentation. Office applications can be created within Office templates or add-ins as well.

This raises a whole new set of issues related to the distribution of Office applications. In developing an Office application for distribution, we must immediately deal with two issues. Where do we put the code for this application, and what means do we provide the user to invoke the features of the application? The first issue is complicated by whether we will allow the user to have access to the application's code and data or not.

The answers to these questions depend, not surprisingly, on the nature of the application.

Providing Access to an Application's Features

I recently created an Excel application for a well-known fast food company. The company wanted to send out data on sales and other things to its field offices, in the form of a rather complicated Excel pivot table. They wanted the field personnel to be able to filter the pivot table by various means (thus creating smaller pivot tables) as well as generate a variety of charts showing different views of the data. (The complete application involved other features, but this will illustrate the point.)

In particular, the main pivot table contains several types of data (sales, transaction counts, and so on) for several Designated Marketing Areas (DMAs) and store types (company, franchise, or both). One feature of the application is a chart-creating utility for this data. But where should the code for this feature go and how should the field personnel be given access to this charting utility?

Since the charting utility directly involves the pivot table, it seems reasonable in this case to simply place a command button labeled Make Chart(s) directly on the pivot table worksheet. When the user clicks the button, a dialog box such as the one shown in Figure 10-1 appears, allowing the user to make various selections and then create the chart or charts.

In general, there are several possible options for providing access to the charting utility, that is, for displaying the dialog box in Figure 10-1 (or, for that matter, for providing access to any macro):

- Select it from the Macro dialog by choosing Tools → Macro → Macros. The Macro dialog was discussed in Chapter 4, *The Visual Basic Editor, Part II*. This is the most efficient method for a user who writes macros and wants to run one quickly (and it provides an easy method to run many of the very short examples presented in this book). But since the dialog displays only the names of macros to be run, it's not suitable for a user who is unfamiliar with the macros, nor is it a very efficient method of running frequently used macros.

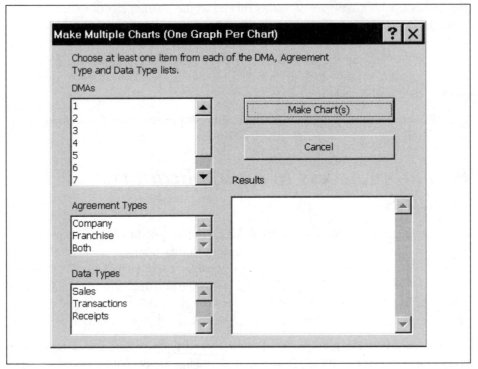

Figure 10-1. Dialog for a charting utility

- Run or display it automatically when a workbook opens by attaching code to one of Excel's events, in this case the Open event. Events are discussed in detail in Chapter 11, *Excel Events*.

- Place a button directly on the worksheet.

- Place a button on an existing Excel toolbar. This can be done programmatically (a topic discussed in Chapter 12, *Custom Menus and Toolbars*) or through the user interface (see "Assigning Macros to Menus and Toolbars" later in this section).

- Create a new toolbar and add the button to it, either programmatically or through the user interface. For information on the latter, see "Working with Toolbars and Menus Interactively" later in this section.

- Add a menu item to an existing Excel menu, either programmatically or through the user interface.

- Create a new menu bar and add a menu item, either programmatically or through the user interface.

In this case, since we did not want the user to be able to invoke the chart-printing utility unless the worksheet containing the pivot table was active, we opted for the button on the worksheet approach. This is not to say, however, that the other approaches would not work.

On the other hand, if the utility in question has wider applicability, then it would probably make more sense to use a toolbar or add a menu item. (I much prefer menu items over toolbar buttons, because they are easily invoked using the keyboard and don't get in the way of other windows.) Indeed, an application that has many features might benefit from a dedicated toolbar or menu bar or a dedicated popup menu on, say, the main Excel worksheet and chart menu bars.

In short, the decision as to how to provide access to the features of an Office application depends on several things, including the complexity of the application, the scope of its features, and personal preferences.

Working with Toolbars and Menus Interactively

Whether we choose to place a command button for a macro on an existing Excel toolbar or on a custom toolbar of our own making, we may need to specify, using the Excel user interface, when the toolbar in question will be displayed. We can create a new toolbar and display or hide existing toolbars by selecting the Customize option from the Tools menu. The Toolbars tab for the Customize dialog box is shown in Figure 10-2.

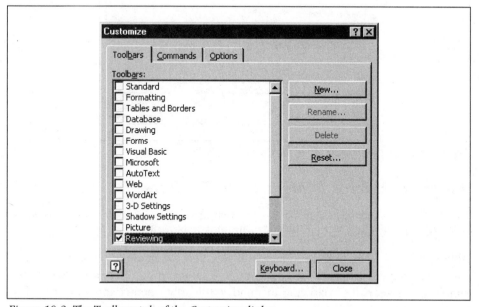

Figure 10-2. The Toolbars tab of the Customize dialog

To create a new toolbar, simply click the New button. Excel opens the New Tool-bar dialog, which prompts us for a name for the toolbar. After we assign it a unique name, Excel will create the toolbar, list it in the Toolbars list box, and display the toolbar. We can then populate the toolbar with buttons.

To display or hide existing toolbars, we simply check or uncheck their boxes in the Toolbars list box.

We can also create a new submenu, which can then be added to an existing menu or toolbar. To do this, we select the Commands tab of the Customize dialog (see Figure 10-3), then select the New Menu option in the Categories list box. Click on the New Menu item in the Commands list box and drag it to the appropriate menu or toolbar. Finally, we right-click on the new menu and enter its caption in the context menu's Name field.

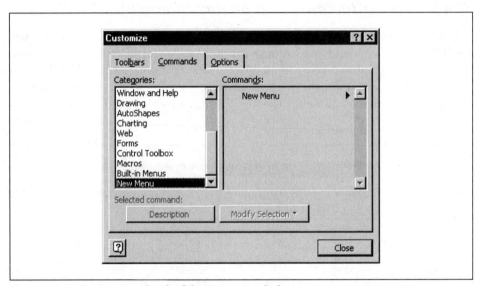

Figure 10-3. The Commands tab of the Customize dialog

Assigning Macros to Menus and Toolbars

Excel also allows us to assign macros to existing menus and toolbars, which is also done from the Commands tab of the Customize dialog shown in Figure 10-3.

Although many users find the Commands tab, and the menu and toolbar customization features in Office, to be confusing and intimidating, they are actually quite simple if we keep the following in mind: Ordinarily, menus and toolbars are in *run mode*. In this mode, selecting a menu item or a toolbar button causes the corresponding action to be performed. On the other hand, whenever the Customize dialog is visible, menus and toolbars are in *edit mode*. While in edit mode, clicking on a menu item or button has an entirely different effect. In particular, right-clicking on a menu item displays a menu with the item's properties. Also, we can move, delete, or add items to a menu simply by dragging and dropping these items!

 Since edit mode is active whenever the Customize dialog is visible, you should be very careful not to inadvertently drag a menu item (or toolbar button) off of a menu (or toolbar), because this will delete that item from the menu (or toolbar).

So, to assign a macro to a toolbar or menu item, make sure the Customize dialog is visible, select Macros in the Categories list (see Figure 10-3), and drag the macro from the Commands list to the appropriate location on the menu or toolbar. That's it.

It is worth pointing out that customizing menus and toolbars through the Customize dialog, as we have just described, may be the right way to proceed for developers, but it also may be too much to ask a client to perform this customization himself or herself. The alternative is to create the custom object programmatically, as discussed in Chapter 12. This is something you will need to judge for yourself.

Where to Store an Application

In the case of the Excel application for the aforementioned fast food company, all of the data for the application is contained in a single workbook. Since none of this data needs to be hidden from the user, it is reasonable to distribute the code and any concomitant data for the application directly in the workbook that contains the data (the pivot table). This makes the workbook totally self-contained and eliminates the need for an installation procedure. All the main office needs to do is email the workbook to its field offices. There are several possibilities here, however:

- Store the application and its data in the document in which it will be used. This is suitable for a standalone application like the one shown in Figure 10-1. It is also suitable for small macros, such as those contained in code fragments throughout this book, that we want to run just to see how some Excel VBA feature is implemented.

- Store the application and its data in an Excel template. This is suitable, of course, when the template will serve as the basis of multiple spreadsheets.

- Store the application and its data in a hidden Excel workbook in Excel's startup directory.

- Store the application and its data in an Excel add-in.

Each of these choices has its advantages and disadvantages, which, incidentally, vary among the Office applications. For instance, templates are much more useful in Word than in Excel, and add-ins are more useful in Excel than in Access. In any case, our interest here is in Excel.

The Excel Startup Folder

When Excel loads, it automatically loads any spreadsheets stored in its startup and alternate startup folders. The default location of the startup folder is usually a sub-folder of the main Excel folder named *XlStart*. By default, there is no alternate startup folder, although one can be defined using the General tab of the Options dialog; to open it, select Options from the Tools menu.

Because the contents of these folders are opened at startup as ordinary work-books, their macros are easily accessible to all other Excel workbooks. This makes them ideal as a storage location for macros. The only drawback is that Excel actually opens the spreadsheets stored in these directories; to prevent this, they should be hidden by selecting the Hide option from Excel's Window menu (*not* the For-mat menu) when the spreadsheet to be hidden is active.

Macros that are stored in the startup and alternate startup folders are available from the Macro dialog, and we can assign them to toolbars and menus through the Excel user interface, as well as programmatically. (On the other hand, an add-in, which is discussed later in this chapter, does not make its subroutines directly accessible to other Excel workbooks, but instead requires that they be assigned to toolbar or menu items programmatically.)

A workbook stored in either of these folders is an excellent choice for a library of macros that you want to be globally available to your spreadsheets. It is also suit-able for developing Excel macros for others to use, although Excel add-ins (which are discussed in the section "Excel Add-Ins" later in this chapter) provide greater flexibility and control, and are much more suitable for macros intended for distri-bution.

We will assume in this book that you want to store macros in an add-in. As we will see, there are clear advantages to using add-ins. Moreover, this will give us a chance to discuss how add-ins are created in Excel. However, you can feel free to place the example macros in a spreadsheet that is kept in the startup or alternate startup folder.

Excel Templates

The purpose of an Excel template is to provide a starting place for a new work-book, worksheet, chart, or code module. Creating a template is easy. We simply create a new workbook and save it as a template using the Save As command.

For instance, suppose we start a new workbook and enter the number 123 in the first cell of the first sheet. Then we save the workbook in the templates directory (more on this later) as a template called *test.xlt*. When we next invoke the New command from the File menu, Excel will display a New dialog with an icon for our template, as shown in Figure 10-4. When we select the *test.xlt* icon, Excel will create a new workbook and *copy* the data from the template into the workbook.

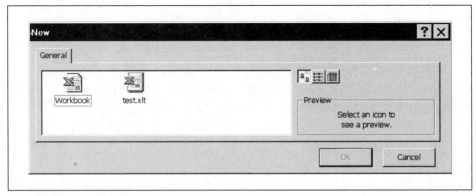

Figure 10-4. The New dialog showing template icons

It is very important to note that the data (and other things such as formatting) as well as macros are actually copied to the workbook, after which all connection between the template and the new workbook is severed. This is quite different from the way that Microsoft Word uses templates. A Word template remains attached to the document. Certain changes, such as the addition of styles or mac-ros, can be saved either in the template or in the document itself, but Word never copies macros from a template into a document. Also, several templates can be opened at one time (the so-called global templates), each of which may affect the document. Word templates are dynamic; Excel templates are static.

This reduces the usefulness of Excel templates considerably, for if we create a template that contains lots of code, for instance, then each workbook that is based on that template will contain its own copy of that code. This can be a major waste of space and can also make it very difficult to maintain and upgrade the code. For these reasons, I generally avoid using Excel templates whenever possible.

For the record, however, we should note that the following items are transferred to a new workbook or worksheet that is based on a template:

- The number and type of sheets in a workbook
- Cell and sheet formats set using the Format menu
- Cell styles
- Page formats and print-area settings for each sheet
- Cell contents
- Worksheet graphics
- Custom toolbars, macros, hyperlinks, and ActiveX controls on forms; custom toolbars must be attached to the template
- Protected and hidden areas of the workbook
- Workbook calculation options and window display options set using the Options command on the Tools menu

We should also note that Excel supports several types of special templates called *autotemplates*. They are templates with the following names:

- *Book.xlt*
- *Sheet.xlt*
- *Chart.xlt*
- *Dialog.xlt*
- *Module.xlt*
- *Macro.xlt* (for Excel version 4 macros)

When the *Book.xlt* template is stored in the *XlStart* subdirectory, Excel bases all new workbooks on this template when you select the *Workbook* icon in the New dialog (see Figure 10-2).

If you want new worksheets to have a special format, then you can create a template named *Sheet.xlt* and place it in the *XlStart* folder. Then every time the Insert Worksheet menu item is invoked, Excel will make copies of all of the worksheets in the *Sheet.xlt* template and place them in the current workbook. Note that this can be more than one sheet if there is more than one sheet in *Sheet.xlt*.

By now you get the idea. The other autotemplates work similarly.

It is also important to know that all of the Office applications use the same default directory for templates. Hence, this directory may contain Word, Excel, Power-Point, and Access templates. But Word is the only Office application (as of Office 97) that provides a way for the user to change this directory (from the File Locations tab of the Options dialog under the Word Tools menu). It follows that, changing this directory using Word will change it for all Office applications!

Excel Add-Ins

An Excel add-in is a special type of workbook that is usually saved with an *.xla* file extension. (We will discuss how to create add-ins later in this section.) An add-in can be connected to Excel by checking its check box in the Add-Ins dialog (see Figure 10-5), which is displayed by selecting Add-Ins from the Tools menu.

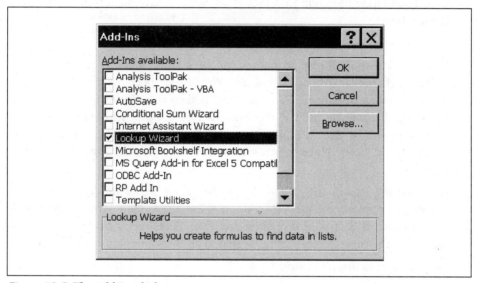

Figure 10-5. The Add-Ins dialog

Once an add-in is connected, it remains so (even if Excel is closed and reopened) until the check box in the Add-Ins dialog is unchecked. When connected, an add-in's functionality (VBA procedures) is accessible from any Excel workbook. Thus, it is truly an extension of Excel.

Typically, an add-in contains code that creates new menu items or toolbar items that provide the user with access to the procedures in the add-in. This code is placed in the Workbook_Open event of the add-in so that the menus (or toolbars) are created/customized as soon as the add-in is connected. (We will see examples of this soon.)

Creating an add-in

Creating an add-in is a simple process. It begins with an Excel workbook, say *SRXUtils.xls*. (This stands for Steven Roman's Excel Utilities.) The workbook, of course, contains a number of macros. To create an add-in from the workbook, follow these steps:

1. Compile the project using Excel's VBA Editor.

   When the code in any VBA procedure is edited and then executed, Excel must first *compile* the code; that is, translate the code into a language that the computer can understand. This is why there may be a slight delay the first time code is executed. Subsequent execution of the same code does not require compilation unless the code has been changed since the previous compilation. To compile the code in *SRXUtils.xls*, select the Compile option from the Debug menu.

2. Set a few worksheet properties and a few project properties.

   We should also set a few properties for the add-in. When *SRXUtils.xls* is the active workbook in Excel, choose the Properties option from the Excel File menu, and then display the Summary tab, as shown in Figure 10-6. The Title is the string that will be used in the Add-Ins dialog, shown in Figure 10-7. The Comments will be shown at the bottom of the Add-Ins dialog. Therefore, you should fill in both of these sections in the Properties dialog, as shown in Figure 10-6.

   Next, we use Excel's VBA Editor to set the properties of the VBA project. In the Project Explorer of the VBA Editor, select the project whose filename is *SRXUtils.xls*. Then choose Properties from the Tools menu to display the dialog. Fill in the project name and description as shown in Figure 10-8.

3. Protect the code from viewing.

   To protect the code in an Excel workbook from unauthorized viewing, we can use the VBA Project Properties dialog. Selecting the dialog's Protection tab, we get the dialog shown in Figure 10-9. Checking "Lock project for viewing" and entering a password protects the code from viewing (and from alteration). The project will still appear in the VBIDE Project window, but Excel will not allow the user to expand the tree for this project without the password.

4. Save the workbook as an add-in in a directory of your choice.

   Select the Save As option from the File menu, select "Microsoft Excel Add-In (*.xla)" from the "Save as type" drop-down list, navigate to the directory in which you'd like to save the file, enter the filename in the "File name" drop-down list box (in the case of our example, it's *SRXUtils.xla*) and press the Save button.

   Every Excel workbook has a property called IsAddIn. When this property is True, Excel considers the workbook to be an add-in. One of the consequences of this is that the workbook becomes invisible, so we cannot simply

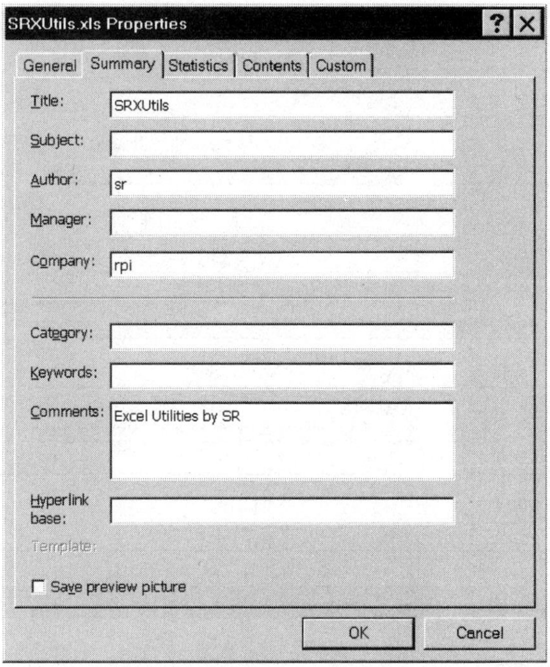

Figure 10-6. Add-in Properties

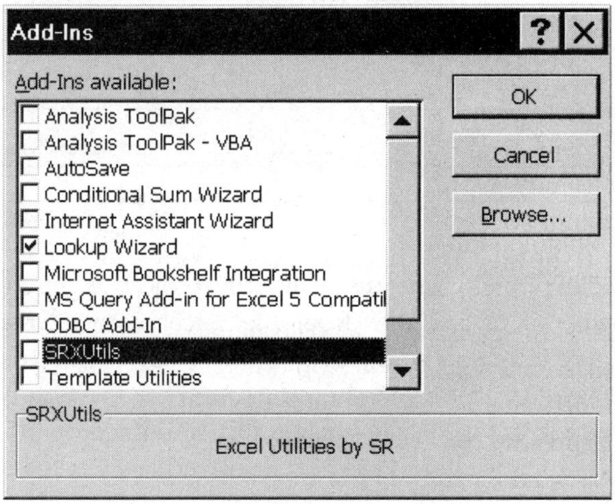

Figure 10-7. The Add-Ins dialog

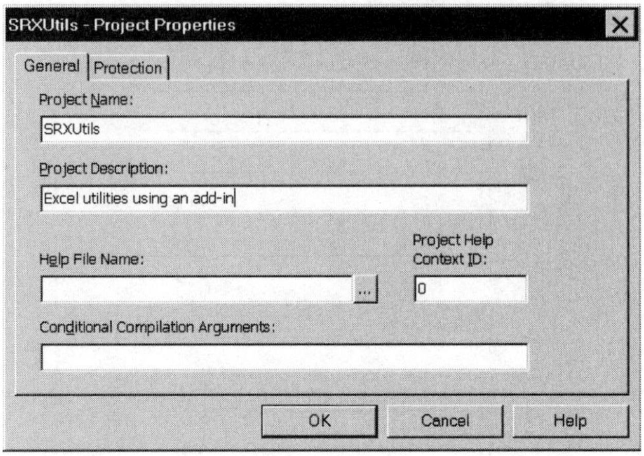

Figure 10-8. VBA project properties

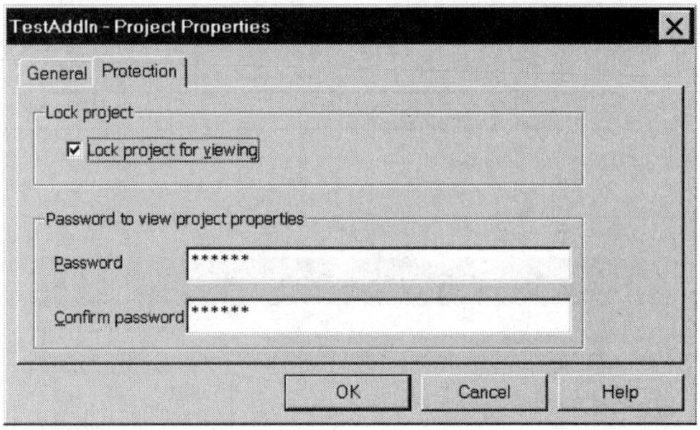

Figure 10-9. Protection tab

set the IsAddIn property and then save the project as an XLA file, since its workbook will be inaccessible from the Excel user interface. Fortunately, Microsoft realized this and arranged it so that when we save the file as an add-in using the Save As dialog and choosing *xla* in the "Save as type" drop-down listbox, Excel will automatically change the IsAddIn property value to `True`. (We can change the value to `False` as discussed later, in the section, "Debugging add-ins.")

Characteristics of an add-in

An add-in has the following characteristics that set it apart from ordinary Excel workbooks:

- The workbook window and any worksheets in an add-in are hidden from view. The intention is that the creator of the add-in can use worksheets to store supporting data for the add-in. However, this data should not be visible to the user of the add-in. In fact, an add-in is designed to be transparent to the user; both the code and any supporting data are hidden from the user. Thus, if you want your add-in to expose worksheets to the user, they must be placed in separate Excel workbook files, which can be opened by code in the add-in at the desired time.

- As you probably know, when an Excel workbook is changed and the user tries to close the workbook, Excel displays a warning message asking if the user wants to save the changes before closing the workbook. No such message is displayed for an add-in. Thus, the creator of an add-in can change the data in an add-in worksheet through code without worrying that the user of the add-in will be bothered by a message to which he or she could not possibly respond intelligently. (Of course, it is up to the add-in's creator to save any changes if desired, using the Save As method of the Worksheet object.)

- When an Excel workbook is opened, the Workbook_Open even is fired. For an ordinary Workbook, the user can suppress this event by holding down the Shift key. The Open event for an add-in cannot be suppressed. This is in keeping with the tamper-proof nature of add-ins.

- Add-in macros are not displayed in the Macros dialog box, thus hiding them from the user.

Add-ins and COM Add-ins

Excel 2000 supports the same add-in model that is supported by Excel 97. This is the add-in model that we use to create the SRXUtils add-in.

In addition, the Office 2000 suite supports a new add-in model called the COM add-in model. A COM add-in is an ActiveX DLL or executable file that can be connected to multiple Office 2000 applications. Since this type of add-in is an ActiveX DLL or executable, it must be created using a programming environment, such as Visual Basic or Visual C++, that is capable of creating these types of files. However, Visual Basic for Applications cannot create ActiveX DLLs or executables, so it cannot be used to create COM add-ins.

Debugging add-ins

An add-in can be debugged just like any other Excel workbook. You do not need to refer again to the original XLS file.

In particular, an add-in can be opened like any other Excel workbook. However, unless you know the password (assuming that the add-in has one), you will not be able to see either the add-in's code or its workbook window. Using the password, you can expand the project node in the Project window to view the code and, if you select the ThisWorkbook node and open the Properties window, change the IsAddIn property to `False` to display the workbook window. Now you can treat the workbook just like any other Excel workbook. Once the necessary changes have been made, you can recompile the code and return the IsAddIn property to `True`.

Deleting an add-in

You may have noticed that the Add-Ins dialog shown in Figure 10-5 does not have a Delete button. To remove an add-in from the list, uncheck the add-in, rename the XLA file, and then check the add-in again. You will get a message asking if Excel should remove the add-in from the list. And while we are on the subject of idiosyncratic behavior, note that changes to an add-in's Title property may not be reflected in the Add-Ins dialog until Excel is shut down and reopened.

An Example Add-In

Let's begin the creation of an Excel add-in by creating an add-in shell. This will demonstrate the process of add-in creation and provide a starting point from which we can create a full-fledged add-in–based Excel application, adding new features as we proceed through the book. I strongly suggest that you follow along in the creation process.

In this chapter, we will create the add-in shell whose features just display message boxes (for now). At this time, we do not want to cloud the issue of add-in creation by implementing any real features. In Chapter 12, we will increase the number of mock features so that we can demonstrate how to handle multiple features in an add-in, as well as how to create a custom menu system for an add-in. In later chapters, we will implement these features and add additional ones.

Creating the Source Workbook

The first step is to create a new workbook that will act as the source for the add-in. Please do this now. This workbook will eventually be saved as an add-in. I will refer to the workbook as *SRXUtils.xls*, but you can feel free to name your version anything you like.

Incidentally, as we make changes to our add-in, we will do so in the *SRXUtils.xls* worksheet and then save that worksheet over the current add-in. Before doing so, of course, we must unload the current version of the add-in.

Setting Up the Custom Menus

To activate the mock features of our add-in shell, we will create a custom menu. We will discuss the creation of menus and toolbars at length in Chapter 12. For now, we will keep the details to a minimum so we can get the overall picture of add-in creation.

Our custom menu should be created automatically when the add-in loads and destroyed when the add-in unloads. Accordingly, we begin by placing some code in the Open and BeforeClose events of ThisWorkbook, as shown in Example 10-1.

Example 10-1. The Workbook's Open and BeforeClose Event Handlers

```
Private Sub Workbook_BeforeClose(Cancel As Boolean)
    DeleteCustomMenuItem
End Sub

Private Sub Workbook_Open()
    CreateCustomMenuItem
End Sub
```

This event code just calls procedures to create or delete the custom menu. These procedures should be placed in a new code module, so add a module to the *SRXUtils* project and name it **basMenus**. Next, place the *CreateCustomMenuItem* procedure shown in Example 10-2 in **basMenus**. It is not necessary to completely understand this procedure now, since we will go over the details in Chapter 12. For the moment, note that Example 10-2 creates an ActivateSheet menu item on the Custom menu, and that when we click the item, the routine defined by its OnAction property—in this case, the *ActivateSheet* subroutine—is run.

Example 10-2. The CreateCustomMenuItem Procedure

```
Sub CreateCustomMenuItem()
Dim cbpop As CommandBarControl
Dim cbpop As CommandBarControl
' Check for custom menu. If it exists then exit.
Set cbcpop = Application.CommandBars( _
    "Worksheet menu bar"). _
    FindControl(Type:=msoControlPopup, _
    Tag:="SRXUtilsCustomMenu")
If Not cbcpop Is Nothing Then Exit Sub
' Create a popup control on a menu bar
Set cbpop = Application.CommandBars( _
    "Worksheet menu bar"). _
    Controls.Add(Type:=msoControlPopup, _
```

Example 10-2. The CreateCustomMenuItem Procedure (continued)

```
    Temporary:=True)
cbpop.Caption = "Cu&stom"
' Set tag property to find it later for deletion
cbpop.Tag = "SRXUtilsCustomMenu"
' Add menu item to popup menu
With cbpop.Controls.Add(Type:=msoControlButton, _
    Temporary:=True)
        .Caption = "&ActivateSheet"
        .OnAction = "ActivateSheet"
End With
End Sub
```

Also place the *DeleteCustomMenuItem* procedure shown in Example 10-3 into **basMenus**:

Example 10-3. The DeleteCustomMenuItem Procedure

```
Sub DeleteCustomMenuItem()
Dim cbc As CommandBarControl
Set cbc = Application.CommandBars( _
    "Worksheet menu bar"). _
    FindControl(Type:=msoControlPopup, _
    Tag:="SRXUtilsCustomMenu")
If Not cbc Is Nothing Then cbc.Delete
End Sub
```

Implementing the Features of the Add-In

Since the *ActivateSheet* utility (which is invoked when the user selects the ActivateSheet custom menu item created by the code in Example 10-2) is very simple, it does not require its own code module. We simply add the following procedure to the **basMain** code module, which we also must create:

```
Public Sub ActivateSheet()
    MsgBox "This is the ActivateSheet utility"
End Sub
```

Final Steps

Finally, you should follow these steps:

1. *Compile the project.* Use the Debug menu to compile the *SRXUtils.xls* project.

2. *Set the properties.* Set the workbook and project properties as shown in Figures 10-4 and 10-6, making any necessary changes based on the name you have chosen for your add-in.

3. *Protect the add-in.* Under the Protection tab of the project's Properties dialog, check the "Lock project for viewing" checkbox and enter a password.

4. *Save the add-in*. Save the project as an add-in named *SRXUtils.xla* in a directory of your choice.

Now we are ready to try the add-in. Close the *SRXUtils.xls* workbook and open a new workbook. Select the Add-Ins menu item under the Tools menu and hit the Browse button on the Add-Ins dialog. Locate your *SRXUtils.xla* file. Then check the entry in the Add-Ins dialog. You should see the new Custom menu in the worksheet menu bar. Select the ActivateSheet item. You should get the expected message box. *Finis.*

As mentioned earlier, as we progress through the book, we will make this example add-in much more meaningful.

11

Excel Events

During the course of using Excel, certain *events* happen. For instance, when a worksheet is created, that is an event. When a chart is resized, that is an event. Microsoft Excel defines a total of 63 different events. When an event occurs, programmers like to say that the event *fires*.

The purpose of an event is simply to allow the VBA programmer to write code that will execute whenever an event fires. As we will see, this code is placed in an *event procedure*. The code itself is referred to as *event code*. We wrote some simple event code for the Open and BeforeClose workbook events when we created the *SRXUtils* add-in in the previous chapter.

Most Excel events break naturally into five groups, as indicated in Tables 11-1 through 11-5. These groups partially reflect the level at which the event takes place—the application level (highest), the workbook level (middle), or the worksheet/chartsheet level (lowest).

To illustrate, when a worksheet is activated by the user or through code (by calling the Activate method) several events will fire. They are, in firing order:

- The Activate event of the worksheet. This event fires whenever the worksheet is activated.

- The SheetActivate event of the workbook. This event fires whenever any worksheet in the workbook is activated.

- The SheetActivate event of the application. This event fires whenever any worksheet in any workbook in the currently running instance of Excel is activated. (However, as we will discuss later, to enable this event, we must write some special code.)

The EnableEvents Property

It is important to note that no Excel event will fire unless the EnableEvents property is set to **True** (although it is set to **True** by default). Thus, the programmer has control over whether Excel events are enabled. The EnableEvents property is a property of the Application object, so, for instance, to prevent the Save event from firing when the active workbook is saved, we can write:

```
Application.EnableEvents = False
ActiveWorkbook.Save
Application.EnableEvents = True
```

Events and the Excel Object Model

The Excel object model contains several objects that exist simply as a convenience, in order to include the Excel events in the object model. (We do not actually program with these objects.) These objects are AppEvents, DocEvents, ChartEvents, WorkBookEvents, OLEObjectEvents, and RefreshEvents. The events associated with a worksheet, for instance, are methods of the DocEvents object, which is a child of the Worksheet object and the Chart object.

Accessing an Event Procedure

By now you are probably wondering how to write an event procedure. The short answer is that for each event, Excel provides us with an *event code shell* where we can place the event code for that event.

To illustrate, consider the SelectionChange event of the Worksheet object. Figure 11-1 shows the code window for a worksheet (Sheet1). Note that the Worksheet object is selected in the objects list box. This causes the procedures list box to be filled with the names of the worksheet events. We can simply choose the event for which we want to write event code.

For instance, if we choose the SelectionChange event, Excel will automatically produce the following code shell:

```
Private Sub Worksheet_SelectionChange(ByVal Target As Excel.Range)

End Sub
```

Excel will even place the cursor between the two code lines so we can begin entering event code.

As the name implies, this event fires when the current selection is changed in the worksheet. Note that Excel will fill in the *Target* parameter with the Range object that represents the *new* selection. Thus, our event code has access to the new

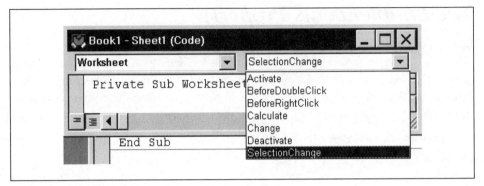

Figure 11-1. Events for the Worksheet object

selection, but not to the previous selection. Many events have parameters associated with them. This provides a way for Excel to pass us information related to the event.

The same approach will work for the workbook and chart events, but Application events require a different approach, which we will discuss later in the chapter.

The Excel events are listed in Tables 11-1 through 11-5.

Worksheet Events

The worksheet-related events are shown in Table 11-1. These events are also referred to as document events.

Table 11-1. Worksheet Events (DocEvents)

Event Name	Description
Activate	Occurs when a worksheet is activated.
BeforeDoubleClick	Occurs when a worksheet is double-clicked, before the default double-click action.
BeforeRightClick	Occurs when a worksheet is right-clicked, before the default right-click action.
Calculate	Occurs after the worksheet is recalculated.
Change	Occurs when cells on the worksheet are changed by the user or by an external link.
Deactivate	Occurs when the worksheet is deactivated.
SelectionChange	Occurs when the selection changes on a worksheet.

WorkBook Events

Table 11-2 shows the workbook-related events.

Table 11-2. Workbook Events

Event Name	Description
Activate	Occurs when a workbook is activated.
AddinInstall	Occurs when the workbook is installed as an add-in.
AddinUninstall	Occurs when the workbook is uninstalled as an add-in.
BeforeClose	Occurs before the workbook closes.
BeforePrint	Occurs before the workbook (or anything in it) is printed.
BeforeSave	Occurs before the workbook is saved.
Deactivate	Occurs when the workbook is deactivated.
NewSheet	Occurs when a new sheet is created in the workbook.
Open	Occurs when the workbook is opened.
SheetActivate	Occurs when any sheet is activated.
SheetBeforeDoubleClick	Occurs when any worksheet is double-clicked, before the default double-click action.
SheetBeforeRightClick	Occurs when any worksheet is right-clicked, before the default right-click action.
SheetCalculate	Occurs after any worksheet is recalculated or after any changed data is plotted on a chart.
SheetChange	Occurs when cells in any worksheet are changed by the user or by an external link.
SheetDeactivate	Occurs when any sheet is deactivated.
SheetSelectionChange	Occurs when the selection changes on any worksheet (does not occur if the selection is on a chart sheet).
WindowActivate	Occurs when any workbook window is activated.
WindowDeactivate	Occurs when any workbook window is deactivated.
WindowResize	Occurs when any workbook window is resized.

Incidentally, a user can suppress the Open event for a workbook by holding down the Shift key when opening the workbook.

Chart Events

Table 11-3 shows the chart-related events.

Table 11-3. Chart Events

Event Name	Description
Activate	Occurs when a chart sheet or embedded chart is activated.
BeforeDoubleClick	Occurs when an embedded chart is double-clicked, before the default double-click action.

Table 11-3. Chart Events (continued)

Event Name	Description
BeforeRightClick	Occurs when an embedded chart is right-clicked, before the default right-click action.
Calculate	Occurs after the chart plots new or changed data.
Deactivate	Occurs when the chart is deactivated.
DragOver	Occurs when a range of cells is dragged over a chart.
DragPlot	Occurs when a range of cells is dragged and dropped on a chart.
MouseDown	Occurs when a mouse button is pressed while the pointer is over a chart.
MouseMove	Occurs when the position of the mouse pointer changes over a chart.
MouseUp	Occurs when a mouse button is released while the pointer is over a chart.
Resize	Occurs when the chart is resized.
Select	Occurs when a chart element is selected.
SeriesChange	Occurs when the user changes the value of a chart data point.

Application Events

Table 11-4 shows the Application-level events. These events apply to all objects in the currently running instance of Excel.

Table 11-4. Application Events

Event Name	Description
NewWorkbook	Occurs when a new workbook is created.
SheetActivate	Occurs when any sheet is activated.
SheetBeforeDoubleClick	Occurs when any worksheet is double-clicked, before the default double-click action.
SheetBeforeRightClick	Occurs when any worksheet is right-clicked, before the default right-click action.
SheetCalculate	Occurs after any worksheet is recalculated or after any changed data is plotted on a chart.
SheetChange	Occurs when cells in any worksheet are changed by the user or by an external link.
SheetDeactivate	Occurs when any sheet is deactivated.
SheetSelectionChange	Occurs when the selection changes on any worksheet (does not occur if the selection is on a chart sheet).
WindowActivate	Occurs when any workbook window is activated.
WindowDeactivate	Occurs when any workbook window is deactivated.
WindowResize	Occurs when any workbook window is resized.

Table 11-4. Application Events (continued)

Event Name	Description
WorkbookActivate	Occurs when any workbook is activated.
WorkbookAddinInstall	Occurs when a workbook is installed as an add-in.
WorkbookAddinUninstall	Occurs when any add-in workbook is uninstalled.
WorkbookBeforeClose	Occurs immediately before any open workbook closes.
WorkbookBeforePrint	Occurs before any open workbook is printed.
WorkbookBeforeSave	Occurs before any open workbook is saved.
WorkbookDeactivate	Occurs when any open workbook is deactivated.
WorkbookNewSheet	Occurs when a new sheet is created in any open workbook.
WorkbookOpen	Occurs when a workbook is opened.

Unfortunately, Excel makes it a bit more difficult to reach the Application events than events in the other categories. Here is a step-by-step procedure for reaching the event code shells for the Application events:

1. Use the VBA Insert menu to insert a class module into your project. Let us call this class module **CApp** (short for **Class Application**). In the declaration section of the class module, add the line:

   ```
   Public WithEvents App As Application
   ```

   Choosing the App object in the objects drop-down should now give you access to the Application event code shells, as shown in Figure 11-2.

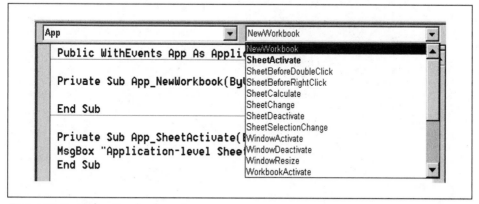

Figure 11-2. Application-level events

2. In the code module in which you want to activate Application-level events (say the code module associated with a workbook, worksheet, or chart), place the following declaration in the declarations section of the module:

   ```
   Dim AppObj As New CApp
   ```

   (You can use any variable name you wish in place of *AppObj*).

3. Finally, assign the App property of *AppObj* to the Application object. This is done by executing the code:

```
Set AppObj.App = Excel.Application
```

It is up to you where to place this line of code, but it must be executed in order to activate Application-level events. (There is a certain circularity here, since a natural place to put this code is in the WorkbookOpen event. However, this event will not fire until this code has been executed.)

In addition to using the EnableEvents property, you can turn off Application-level events by executing the code:

```
Set AppObj.App = Nothing
```

QueryTable Refresh Events

Table 11-5 shows the events related to QueryTables. We will not discuss Query-Tables in this book, but at least now you are aware of the existence of these events should you decide to pursue this matter on your own.

Table 11-5. Refresh Events

Event Name	Description
AfterRefresh	Occurs after a query is completed or canceled.
BeforeRefresh	Occurs before any refreshes of the query table.

12

Custom Menus and Toolbars

In this chapter, we discuss methods for programmatically controlling menus and toolbars. Even though the subject of menus and toolbars is fairly straightforward, it can seem very confusing, especially since the documentation is less helpful than it might be.

Menus and Toolbars: An Overview

Actually, Excel's menu and toolbar objects do not belong to the Excel object model. The menus and toolbars throughout the Microsoft Office application suite belong to the Office object model. The portion of the Office object model that relates to menus and toolbars is shown in Figure 12-1.

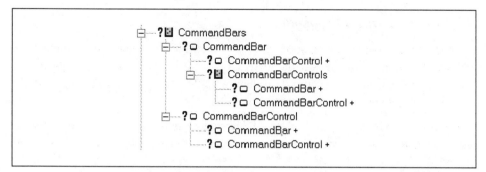

Figure 12-1. The menu and toolbar portion of the Office object model

Note that this model is actually quite small, containing only two objects and their corresponding collections:

- CommandBar objects and the CommandBars collection
- CommandBarControl objects and the CommandBarControls collection

Menu Terminology

To help set the notation, Figure 12-2 shows the components of the Office menu structure (this happens to be a Word menu, but no matter).

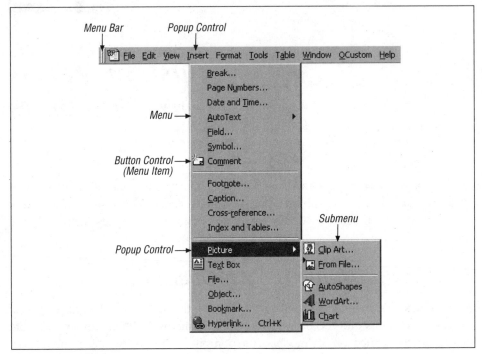

Figure 12-2. An Office menu

The CommandBar Object

Toolbars, menu bars, menus, submenus, and shortcut menus are all CommandBar objects. (A shortcut menu is a menu that pops up in response to a right mouse click.) Thus, every item pictured in Figure 12-2 is a command bar except the popup controls and the button control.

Of course, toolbars, menu bars, and shortcut menus are "top level" objects, whereas menus and submenus emanate from toolbars, menu bars, or shortcut menus.

It is important to note that Office VBA does not treat each of these CommandBar objects in the same way. For instance, the Count property of the CommandBars collection counts only the top-level items: menu bars, toolbars, and shortcut menus. It does not count menus or submenus. Also, the Add method of the CommandBars collection can be used to create toolbars or menu bars, but not menus or submenus.

The CommandBar object has a Type property that can assume one of the constants in the following enum:

```
Enum MsoBarType
    msoBarTypeNormal = 0    ' toolbar
    msoBarTypeMenuBar = 1   ' menu bar
    msoBarTypePopup = 2     ' menu, submenu, or shortcut menu
End Enum
```

Command-Bar Controls

The items on a toolbar, menu bar, menu, or submenu are actually controls, called *command-bar controls*; that is, they are CommandBarControl objects. As we will see, there are various types of command-bar controls, falling into two broad categories: custom command-bar controls (including custom text boxes, drop-down list boxes, and combo boxes) and built-in command-bar controls. Note that command-bar controls are not the same as the controls that we can place on a *UserForm;* they are designed specifically for toolbars and menus.

There are two special types of custom command-bar controls that are not typical of other types of controls. These are Popup controls and Button controls.

Popup controls

A command-bar control of type `msoControlPopup` is a control whose sole purpose is to pop up a menu (when the control is on a menu bar) or a submenu (when the control is on a menu). These controls are naturally referred to as *popup controls* (see Figure 12-2). Popup controls that are located on a menu bar take on the appearance of a recessed button when the mouse pointer is over the control. Popup controls on a menu or submenu have a small arrow on the far right to identify them.

Thus, the term *popup* is used in two different ways. A popup *control* is a command-bar control of type `msoControlPopup` and is used to pop up a menu or submenu. A popup *command bar* is a command bar of type `msoBarTypePopup` and is either a menu, submenu, or shortcut menu. Note that to display a popup command bar, the user needs to activate a popup control.

Button controls

A command-bar control of type `msoControlButton` is called a *button control.* When a button control is activated (using an accelerator key or mouse click), a macro is executed. Button controls have a string property called OnAction, which we can set to the name of the macro that is executed when the control is activated.

Adding a Menu Item

It is worth mentioning now that there are a few counterintuitive wrinkles in the process of menu creation. In particular, we might think at first that adding a new menu should be done using the Add method of the CommandBars collection, specifying the name of the parent menu and the location of the new menu on the parent. After all, a menu is a CommandBar object, and this procedure would be consistent with other cases of adding objects to a collection.

However, this is not how it is done. Instead, as we will see, a new menu (or sub-menu) is created by adding a command-bar control of type `msoControlPopup` to the CommandBarControls collection of the parent menu (and specifying the new control's position on the parent). Actually, this represents a savings of effort on our behalf. For, as we have remarked, a menu or submenu requires a popup control for activation. Thus, Microsoft makes the task of creating menus and submenus easier by automatically creating the corresponding (empty) menu or submenu in response to our creation of a popup control. (We will see an example of this later, so don't worry too much if this is not perfectly clear yet.)

One word of advice before proceeding: As we will see, when creating a new tool-bar or menu, you can set one of the parameters to make the object temporary, meaning that it will be destroyed when Excel is closed. In this way, if anything unexpected happens, it is easy to recover—just close Excel and reopen it. Alterna-tively, by opening the Customize dialog box (from the Tools menu), you can delete menu items by dragging them off of the menu, and you can delete toolbars by using the Delete button.

The CommandBars Collection

The topmost object that relates to menus and toolbars is the CommandBars collec-tion, which contains all of the application's CommandBar objects. The Command-Bars collection is accessible through the CommandBars property of the Application object, that is:

```
Application.CommandBars
```

The code in Example 12-1 will print a list of all of the CommandBar objects to the immediate window. You may be surprised at the large number of objects, most of which are not currently visible.

Example 12-1. Listing Excel's CommandBar Objects

```
Public Sub ShowCmdBars()

Dim sType as string, cbar as CommandBar
For Each cbar In Application.CommandBars
```

Example 12-1. Listing Excel's CommandBar Objects (continued)

```
Select Case cbar.Type
Case msoBarTypeNormal      ' A toolbar
    sType = "Normal"
Case msoBarTypeMenuBar      ' A menu bar
    sType = "Menu bar"
Case msoBarTypePopup        ' Menu, submenu
    sType = "Popup"
End Select
Debug.Print cbar.Name & "," & sType & "," & cbar.Visible
Next

End Sub
```

If you execute this code, you should get the following entries, among many others:

```
Worksheet Menu Bar,Menu bar,True
Chart Menu Bar,Menu bar,False
```

This indicates that Excel's main menu bars are different for worksheets than for chartsheets, as is evident if you look at the menus themselves. The worksheet menu bar has different controls than the Chart menu bar. Thus, if you want to add a custom menu item to Excel's "main" menu bar, regardless of what type of sheet is currently active, you will need to do so for both the Worksheet Menu Bar and the Chart Menu Bar.

There is a slight complication concerning the CommandBars property that we should discuss. When qualified with the Application object, as in `Application.CommandBars`, this property returns the collection of all available built-in and custom command bars for the application which, in this case, is Excel. This is why we used the fully qualified expression `Application.Workbook` in Example 12-1. Note that from a *standard* code module, we can skip the qualification and just write CommandBars.

However, from a Workbook, the CommandBars property returns a different collection. In particular, there are two possibilities. When the workbook is embedded within another application and Excel is activated by double-clicking on that embedded workbook, the CommandBars collection returns the collection of command bars that are available in that setting. This may be different from the full collection of Excel command bars. If the workbook is not embedded in another application, then the CommandBars property returns `Nothing`.

Note also that the Workbook object has a CommandBars property. However, this property is meaningful only when the workbook is embedded within another application, in which case the property returns the CommandBars collection for that application. When applied to a nonembedded workbook, the property returns `Nothing`. Moreover, there is no programmatic way to return the set of command bars attached to a workbook.

Creating a New Menu Bar or Toolbar

As we have said, one way in which menu bars and toolbars differ from menus and submenus is in their creation. To create a new menu bar or shortcut menu, we use the Add method of the CommandBars collection. The syntax for the Add method is:

```
CommandBarsObject.Add(Name, Position, MenuBar, Temporary)
```

The optional *Name* parameter is the name of the new command bar. If this argument is omitted, Excel VBA assigns a default name (such as "Custom 1") to the command bar. The optional *Position* parameter gives the position of the new command bar. This can be set to **msoBarLeft**, **msoBarTop**, **msoBarRight**, **msoBarBottom**, **msoBarFloating** (for a floating command bar), or **msoBarPopup** (for a shortcut menu).

The optional Boolean *MenuBar* parameter is set to **True** for a menu bar and **False** for a toolbar. The default value is **False**, so if the argument is omitted, a toolbar is created. Note that if you create a new menu bar and make it visible, it will replace the existing Excel menu bar! If this happens, you can still exit Excel by typing Alt-F4, and the normal Excel menu will reappear the next time that you launch Excel.

Setting the optional *Temporary* parameter to **True** makes the new command bar temporary. Temporary command bars are deleted when Excel is closed. The default value is **False**.

To illustrate, the following code creates a new floating toolbar called "Custom Toolbar" and makes it visible:

```
Dim cbar As Office.CommandBar
Set cbar = Application.CommandBars.Add("Custom Toolbar", _
    msoBarFloating, False, True)
cbar.Visible = True
```

It is important to note that, if a CommandBar object by the name Custom Toolbar already exists, the previous code will produce a runtime "Invalid procedure call" error. Thus, we really should test for the existence of the CommandBar object before using the Add method, as shown in Example 12-2.

Example 12-2. Creating a New Toolbar

```
Public Sub CreateToolbar()

Dim cbar As Office.CommandBar
Dim bExists As Boolean
bExists = False
For Each cbar In Application.CommandBars
    If cbar.Name = "Custom Toolbar" Then bExists = True
Next
If Not bExists Then
```

Example 12-2. Creating a New Toolbar (continued)

```
  Set cbar = Application.CommandBars.Add("Custom Toolbar", _
    msoBarFloating, False, True)
  cbar.Visible = True
End If

End Sub
```

Command-Bar Controls

Initially, one of the most confusing aspects of the Office menu system is that the items that appear on a menu bar are *not* menus, or even names of menus. Rather, they are *controls* of type CommandBarControl. Command-bar controls can be added to a menu bar, toolbar, menu, submenu, or shortcut menu. (Think of toolbars, menu bars, and so on as "forms" upon which you place controls.)

Every command-bar control is an object of type CommandBarControl and so it belongs to the CommandBarControls collection. (We are *not* saying that the Type property of a command-bar control is CommandBarControl.) In addition, every command-bar control is an object of one of the following three object types:

- CommandBarButton
- CommandBarComboBox
- CommandBarPopup

This dual identity of CommandBarControl objects allows the various types of command-bar controls to possess on the one hand a common set of properties and methods (those of the CommandBarControl object) and on the other hand an additional set of properties and methods that reflects the diversity of these controls. This makes sense, since, for instance, text boxes are quite different from popup controls. Moreover, as we will see, CommandBarPopup objects need a special property (called Controls) that provides access to the *associated menu's* controls. (The other types of CommandBarControl objects do not need, and do not have, this property.)

The Type property of a CommandBarControl helps to identify the data type of the control. It can assume any of the values in the following enum:

```
Enum MsoControlType
    msoControlCustom = 0
    msoControlButton = 1              ' CommandBarButton
    msoControlEdit = 2               ' CommandBarComboBox
    msoControlDropdown = 3           ' CommandBarComboBox
    msoControlComboBox = 4           ' CommandBarComboBox
    msoControlButtonDropdown = 5     ' CommandBarComboBox
    msoControlSplitDropdown = 6      ' CommandBarComboBox
    msoControlOCXDropdown = 7        ' CommandBarComboBox
```

```
        msoControlGenericDropdown = 8
        msoControlGraphicDropdown = 9          ' CommandBarComboBox
        msoControlPopup = 10                   ' CommandBarPopup
        msoControlGraphicPopup = 11            ' CommandBarPopup
        msoControlButtonPopup = 12             ' CommandBarPopup
        msoControlSplitButtonPopup = 13        ' CommandBarPopup
        msoControlSplitButtonMRUPopup = 14     ' CommandBarPopup
        msoControlLabel = 15
        msoControlExpandingGrid = 16
        msoControlSplitExpandingGrid = 17
        msoControlGrid = 18
        msoControlGauge = 19
        msoControlGraphicCombo = 20            ' CommandBarComboBox
    End Enum
```

The comments that follow some of the constants in this enum indicate the data
type of the control. This information comes from the Microsoft help files. The
missing comments mean either that some command-bar controls do not belong to
one of the three data types in question or else that the help file has not kept up
with later additions to the enum.

Creating a New Command-Bar Control

To create and add a command-bar control to a command bar, use the Add method
of the CommandBarControls collection. This method returns a CommandBar-
Button, CommandBarComboBox, or CommandBarPopup object, depending on the
value of the Type parameter. The syntax is:

```
CommandBarControlsObject.Add(Type, Id, Parameter, Before, Temporary)
```

Type is the type of control to be added to the specified command bar. Table 12-1
shows the possible values for this parameter, along with the corresponding control and the return type of the Add method.

Table 12-1. msoControlType Values for the Type Parameter

Type Parameter (Value)	Control	Returned Object
msoControlButton (1)	Button	CommandBarButton
msoControlEdit (2)	Text box	CommandBarComboBox
msoControlDropdown (3)	List box	CommandBarComboBox
soControlComboBox (4)	Combo box	CommandBarComboBox
msoControlPopup (10)	Popup	CommandBarPopup

The optional *Before* parameter is a number that indicates the position of the new
control on the command bar. The new control will be inserted before the control
that is at this position. If this argument is omitted, the control is added at the end
of the command bar.

To add a so-called custom control of one of the types listed in Table 12-1, set the *Id* parameter to 1 or leave it out. To add a built-in control, set the *Id* parameter to the ID number of the control (and leave out the *Type* argument). We will discuss built-in control IDs, and consider some examples, in the following section.

As with command bars, we can set the optional *Temporary* parameter to **True** to make the new command-bar control temporary. It will then be deleted when Excel is closed.

It is very important to note that a CommandBar object does not have a Command-BarControls property, as might be expected. In order to return a CommandBar-Controls object, we must use the Controls property, as in:

```
CommandBars("Worksheet Menu bar").Controls
```

It is equally important to note that, among all of the types of CommandBar-Controls, one and only one type has a Controls property. In particular, a Com-mandBarControl of type CommandBarPopup has a Controls property, which provides access to the CommandBarControls collection associated with the corresponding menu for the popup control. As we will see in an upcoming example, the Controls property thus provides the means by which we can add controls to the menu!

Built-in Command-Bar-Control IDs

As we will see in Example 12-3, it is possible to place built-in command-bar controls on toolbars (or menus). This is done by setting the *Id* parameter of the Add method of the CommandBarControls collection to the ID of the built-in command-bar control.

We must now address the issue of how to determine the IDs for the built-in controls. One approach to finding the ID of a particular control is to use the FindControl method to get a reference to the control. Once this is done, we can examine the control's ID property. The syntax for FindControl is:

```
expression.FindControl(Type, Id, Tag, Visible, Recursive)
```

where *expression* is either a CommandBar or CommandBars object. The other parameters are optional. The method returns the *first* CommandBarControl object that fits the criteria specified by the parameters, or **Nothing** if the search is unsuccessful. Briefly, the parameters are:

Type
   One of the **MsoControlType** constants in the enum given earlier in this chapter

Id
   The ID of the control

Tag

The tag value of the control

Visible

Set to **True** to include only visible command-bar controls in the search

Recursive

True to include the command bar and all of its popup subtoolbars in the search

While the FindControl method can be quite useful, the problem in this situation is that the method requires another way to identify the control, such as through its Tag property. Thus, the FindControl method is most useful in finding a custom control that we have created and assigned a Tag value.

An alternative approach to getting built-in control IDs is to create a one-time list for future reference. The code in Example 12-3 will create a text file and fill it with a list of all built-in control names and IDs. (Note that it requires that a directory named *temp* exist on your D: drive; feel free to change the drive and path to one suitable for your system.) The code creates a temporary toolbar, adds a built-in control for each possible control ID using a simple **For** loop, and then examines each of these controls. This is a rather ad hoc approach, but seems to be the only approach available.

Example 12-3. Code to Generate a List of Control IDs

```
Public Sub ListControlIDs()

Dim fr As Integer
Dim cbar As Office.CommandBar
Dim ctl As CommandBarControl
Dim i As Integer
Const maxid = 4000
fr = FreeFile
Open "d:\temp\ids.txt" For Output As #fr
' Create temporary toolbar
Set cbar = Application.CommandBars.Add("temporary", msoBarTop, _
    False, True)
For i = 1 To maxid
    On Error Resume Next ' skip if cannot add
    cbar.Controls.Add Id:=i
Next i
On Error GoTo 0
For Each ctl In cbar.Controls
    Print #fr, ctl.Caption & " (" & ctl.Id & ")"
Next
cbar.Delete
Close #fr
```

Example 12-4 shows a small portion of the resulting file when the code is run on my system. Appendix C, *Command Bar Controls*, contains a complete list.

Example 12-4. Outputting the IDs of Command-Bar Controls

```
<Custom>    1
&Spelling...    2
&Save    3
&Print...    4
&New...    18
&Copy    19
Cu&t    21
&Paste    22
Open    23
Can't Repeat    37
&Microsoft Word    42
Clear Contents    47
Custom    51
&Piggy Bank    52
Custom    59
&Double Underline    60
Custom    67
Custom    68
&Close    106
AutoFormat    107
&Format Painter    108
Print Pre&view    109
Custom    112
&Bold    113
&Italic    114
&Underline115
```

We will consider an example that uses built-in controls later in the chapter (at which time it should become clearer just what a built-in control is.)

Example: Creating a Menu

The program shown in Example 12-5 creates the menu system shown in Figure 12-3 on Excel's worksheet menu bar. Note that the macros that are invoked by the selection of the menu items are named *ExampleMacro1* and *ExampleMacro2*.

Example 12-5. An Example Menu

```
Sub CreatePopup()
Dim cbpop As CommandBarControl
Dim cbctl As CommandBarControl
Dim cbsub As CommandBarControl
' Create a popup control on the main menu bar
Set cbpop = Application.CommandBars("Worksheet Menu Bar"). _
    Controls.Add(Type:=msoControlPopup)
cbpop.Caption = "&Custom"
```

Example 12-5. An Example Menu (continued)

```
cbpop.Visible = True
' Add a menu item
Set cbctl = cbpop.Controls.Add(Type:=msoControlButton)
cbctl.Visible = True
' Next is required for caption
cbctl.Style = msoButtonCaption
cbctl.Caption = "MenuItem&1"
' Action to perform
cbctl.OnAction = "ExampleMacro1"
' Add a popup for a submenu
Set cbsub = cbpop.Controls.Add(Type:=msoControlPopup)
cbsub.Visible = True
cbsub.Caption = "&SubMenuItem1"
' Add a menu item to the submenu
Set cbctl = cbsub.Controls.Add(Type:=msoControlButton)
cbctl.Visible = True
' Next is required for caption
cbctl.Style = msoButtonCaption
cbctl.Caption = "SubMenuItem&2"
' Action to perform
cbctl.OnAction = "ExampleMacro2"
End Sub
```

	A	B	C	D	E	F	G	H
1	Utility	OnAction Proc	Procedure	In Workbook	Menu Item	SubMenu Item	On Wks Menu	On Chart Menu
2	Activate Sheet	RunUtility	ActivateSheet	ThisWorkbook	&Activate Sheet		TRUE	TRUE
3	Print Charts	RunUtility	PrintCharts	Print.utl	&Print	Embedded &Charts	TRUE	TRUE
4	Print Pivot Tables	RunUtility	PrintPivotTables	Print.utl		&Pivot Tables	TRUE	TRUE
5	Print Sheets	RunUtility	PrintSheets	Print.utl		&Sheets	TRUE	TRUE

Figure 12-3. An example custom menu

Note also the use of the ampersand character (&) in the Caption properties. This character signals a hot key (or accelerator key). Thus, "&Custom" appears as <u>C</u>ustom in the menu bar and can be invoked using the keystroke combination Alt-C.

Example: Creating a Toolbar

Let us construct a custom toolbar with four different types of controls, as shown in Figure 12-4. This will illustrate the use of the built-in controls. The code in Example 12-6 does the job. We will discuss various portions of the code after you have glanced at it.

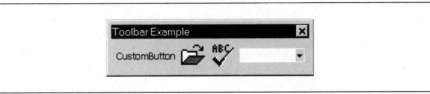

Figure 12-4. A custom toolbar

Example 12-6. An Example Toolbar

```
Sub CreateToolbar()
Dim cbar As CommandBar, cbctl As CommandBarControl

' Delete if it exists
For Each cbar In Application.CommandBars
    If cbar.Name = "Toolbar Example" Then cbar.Delete
Next

' Create a floating toolbar
Set cbar = Application.CommandBars.Add(Name:="Toolbar Example", _
  Position:=msoBarFloating)
cbar.Visible = True

' Add a custom button control to execute a macro
Set cbctl = cbar.Controls.Add(Type:=msoControlButton)
cbctl.Visible = True
cbctl.Style = msoButtonCaption
cbctl.Caption = "CustomButton"

' Run the following macro
cbctl.OnAction = "ExampleMacro"

' Add built-in Open... control
Set cbctl = cbar.Controls.Add(Id:=23)

' Icon for button
cbctl.FaceId = 23
cbctl.Visible = True

' Add built-in spell checking button
Set cbctl = cbar.Controls.Add(Id:=2)
cbctl.FaceId = 2
cbctl.Visible = True

' Add a list box
Set cbctl = cbar.Controls.Add(Type:=msoControlDropdown)

' Add a tag so macro can find it
cbctl.Tag = "ComposerList"
cbctl.Visible = True
cbctl.Caption = "ListCaption"

' Set list properties of the list box
```

Example 12-6. An Example Toolbar (continued)

```
With cbctl
    .AddItem "Chopin", 1
    .AddItem "Mozart", 2
    .AddItem "Bach", 3
    .DropDownLines = 0
    .DropDownWidth = 75
    ' select nothing to start
    .ListIndex = 0
End With


' Set macro to execute when an item
' is selected
cbctl.OnAction = "ExampleListMacro"
End Sub
```

The first step is to check for an existing toolbar named Toolbar Example. If it exists, we delete it. Then we create a floating toolbar named Toolbar Example. The name is important, since we will use it later for identification.

Next, we add a custom button control (*Id* argument missing) and assign it the macro *ExampleMacro*, whose code, which is shown in Example 12-7, simply tells us that we pushed the button.

Example 12-7. The ExampleMacro Macro

```
Sub ExampleMacro()
    MsgBox "Custom button pressed"
End Sub
```

Next, we add a built-in File Open… custom control, whose *Id* happens to be 23. (We have already discussed how to get built-in control IDs.) This custom control automatically displays the Open dialog box. Note that we set the *FaceId* to 23 as well. This displays the default icon for the Open command, but we could choose another icon if desired.

Then we add the built-in Spelling custom control, which checks the spelling of the active document.

Finally, we add a custom list box and populate it with the names of three composers. Note that we set the Tag property of this list box. The reason is that we want to be able to use the FindControl method to find the list box from within the macro that is assigned to the OnAction property, which is shown in Example 12-8.

Example 12-8. Macro Invoked by Selecting a Composer from the List Box

```
Sub ExampleListMacro()
    Dim cbctl As CommandBarControl
    Find the list box control
    Set cbctl = CommandBars("Toolbar Example"). _
        FindControl(Tag:="ComposerList")
```

Example 12-8. Macro Invoked by Selecting a Composer from the List Box (continued)

```
    If Not cbctl Is Nothing Then
        MsgBox "You selected " & cbctl.List(cbctl.ListIndex)
    End If
End Sub
```

In this macro, we use the FindControl method to locate the list box control, via its tag, on the toolbar. Once we have located the list box, we can get the currently selected item (which we simply display for this example). Note that if two or more controls fit the search criteria, FindControl returns the first control that it finds. Also, if no control fits the criteria, FindControl returns **Nothing**, so we can check this as we have done in our program.

Example: Adding an Item to an Existing Menu

Of course, rather than creating a custom toolbar or adding a custom menu to Excel's menu system, you may prefer to add a button to an existing toolbar or a menu item to an existing menu. In that case, you simply need to retrieve a reference to the CommandBar object to which you wish to add the item and call the Controls collection's Add method to add an item to it. In addition, you can retrieve the Index property of the item before which you'd like to position your new menu item or toolbar button. Example 12-9, which contains the source code for a Workbook_Open event that adds an "About SRXUtils" menu item immediately before the "About Microsoft Excel" item, shows how this can be done. Note that the procedure is able to determine the precise location of the About Microsoft Excel menu item by retrieving a reference to its CommandBarControl object and its Index property.

Example 12-9. Adding a Menu Item to an Existing Menu

```
Private Sub Workbook_Open()

Dim lngPos As Long
Dim objHelpMenu As CommandBar
Dim objHelpMenuItem As CommandBarControl
Dim objExcelAbout As CommandBarControl

'Get reference to Help menu
Set objHelpMenu = Application.CommandBars("Help")

' Determine position of "About Microsoft Excel"
Set objExcelAbout = objHelpMenu.Controls("About Microsoft Excel")
If Not objExcelAbout Is Nothing Then
    lngPos = objExcelAbout.Index
Else
    lngPos = objHelpMenu.Controls.Count
```

Example 12-9. Adding a Menu Item to an Existing Menu (continued)

```
End If


' Add "About SRXUtils" menu item
Set objHelpMenuItem = objHelpMenu.Controls.Add(msoControlButton, 1, , _
                      lngPos, True)
objHelpMenuItem.Caption = "About &SRXUtils"
objHelpMenuItem.BeginGroup = True
objHelpMenuItem.OnAction = "ShowAboutMacros"

End Sub
```

Augmenting the SRXUtils Application

Armed with our knowledge of Office CommandBars, we can augment our add-in shell, first discussed in Chapter 10, *Excel Applications*.

Creating the Data Worksheet

As an Excel application gets more complex, the associated menu gets more complex. Rather than store all data directly in code, it makes sense to use a worksheet. Recall that add-in worksheets are hidden from the user, and so they are the perfect place to keep data for the add-in.

Open the *SRXUtils.xls* source workbook, delete all sheets but one, and name that sheet DataSheet. Fill in the sheet as shown in Figure 12-5. This sheet contains one row for each procedure (or utility) of the add-in (we will add more rows later in the book). The first row is for the *ActivateSheet* utility whose code shell we included earlier. We will add code shells for the other utilities a bit later. In later chapters, we will implement these utilities properly.

	A	B	C	D	E	F	G	H
1	Utility	OnAction Proc	Procedure	In Workbook	Menu Item	SubMenu Item	On Wks Menu	On Chart Menu
2	Activate Sheet	RunUtility	ActivateSheet	ThisWorkbook	&Activate Sheet		TRUE	TRUE
3	Print Charts	RunUtility	PrintCharts	Print.utl	&Print	Embedded &Charts	TRUE	TRUE
4	Print Pivot Tables	RunUtility	PrintPivotTables	Print.utl		&Pivot Tables	TRUE	TRUE
5	Print Sheets	RunUtility	PrintSheets	Print.utl		&Sheets	TRUE	TRUE

Figure 12-5. DataSheet of SRXUtils.xls

Let us take a closer look at the contents of DataSheet. The first column is the name of the utility. This is not used outside of the sheet.

The second column is the name of the procedure that is activated when the utility is invoked by the user through a menu item created by the add-in. In this case, all menu items fire the same utility: *RunUtility*. This utility will determine the menu item that was clicked and call the appropriate procedure.

The third column gives the location of this procedure. As you can see, we have placed the printing procedures in a separate workbook called *Print.utl.* As an application gets more complex, you may want to split it up into several workbooks. In this way, your add-in can be written to load a file only when it is needed, thus saving resources. (In this example, we are splitting up the application for demonstration purposes only. The printing utilities are not really complex enough to warrant a separate workbook.)

The fourth column contains the caption for the menu item that will invoke the utility. Note the ampersand character (&), which determines the menu hot key. For example, the ActivateSheet menu item can be invoked using the A key. The fifth column gives the menu item name in case there is a submenu. Thus, the print utilities are accessed through the Print submenu.

The final two columns determine whether the menu (or submenu) item will be enabled or disabled when a worksheet or chartsheet is active. As we have seen, Excel uses a different main menu bar when a worksheet is active (Worksheet Menu Bar) than when a chartsheet is active (Chart Menu Bar). For a utility that pertains only to charts, for instance, we may not want the corresponding menu item to be available from the Worksheet menu bar and vice-versa.

Next, you should create a new standard code module called **basMain** and place the following constant declarations in the Declarations section:

```
Public Const Utility_Col = 1
Public Const OnAction_Col = 2
Public Const Procedure_Col = 3
Public Const InWorkbook_Col = 4
Public Const MenuItem_Col = 5
Public Const SubMenuItem_Col = 6
Public Const OnWksMenu_Col = 7
Public Const OnChartMenu_Col = 8
```

By using these constants throughout the add-in, if we need to move any columns in the DataSheet sheet, all we need to do is change the values of these constants. (This is precisely what symbolic constants are for!)

Setting Up the Custom Menus

The first step in creating the custom menus for our features is to make a slight alteration in the code for the Open event for **ThisWorkbook**. Change the code as shown in Example 12-10.

Example 12-10. The Revised Versions of ThisWorkbook's Open and Close Events

```
Private Sub Workbook_Open()
  CreateCustomMenus
End Sub
```

The code for creating the custom menu is more complicated than the one from Chapter 10 because we must now extract the necessary information from the DataSheet worksheet. There are many ways to do this, but we have elected to split the process into two procedures. The first procedure, *CreateCustomMenus*, checks for the existence of the custom menus using the Tag property. If the menu exists, it is deleted. Then the procedure calls the second procedure, *CreateCustomMenu*, which actually does the menu creation. This is done once for the worksheet menu bar and once for the chart menu bar. The first procedure is shown in Example 12-11.

Example 12-11. The CreateCustomMenus Procedure

```
Sub CreateCustomMenus()

' Create custom menu on both worksheets and chartsheets
' menu bars if they do not already exist.
' Use the control's tag property to identify it.

Dim cbc As CommandBarControl

Set cbc = Application.CommandBars( _
  "Worksheet menu bar").FindControl( _
  Type:=msoControlPopup, Tag:="SRXUtilsCustomMenu")

If Not cbc Is Nothing Then cbc.Delete
CreateCustomMenu "Worksheet Menu Bar"

Set cbc = Application.CommandBars( _
  "Chart menu bar").FindControl( _
  Type:=msoControlPopup, Tag:="SRXUtilsCustomMenu")
If Not cbc Is Nothing Then cbc.Delete
CreateCustomMenu "Chart Menu Bar"

End Sub
```

The *CreateCustomMenu* procedure is shown in Example 12-12. Note that the OnAction property of every menu item is set to a procedure called *RunUtility*, as the "onActivation Proc" column in Figure 12-3 shows. This procedure will sort out which menu item was selected and call the appropriate procedure. To pass the information to *RunUtility*, we set each control's Tag property to the name of the procedure and its Parameter property to the name of the workbook that contains the procedure. (The Tag and Parameter properties are "spare" properties designed to allow the programmer to store important information, which is precisely what we are doing.) In the *RunUtility* procedure, we can use the ActionControl property to return the control that caused the *RunUtility* procedure to execute. Then it is a simple matter to read the Tag and Parameter properties of that control.

Example 12-12. The CreateCustomMenu Procedure

```
Sub CreateCustomMenu(sBarName As String)

Dim cbpop As CommandBarControl
Dim cbctl As CommandBarControl
Dim cbctlCurrentPopup As CommandBarControl
Dim iEnabledColumn As Integer
Dim iLastRow As Integer
Dim iCurrentRow As Integer
Dim sCurrentMenuItem As String
Dim sCurrentSubMenuItem As String
Dim sCurrentProcedure As String
Dim sCurrentWorkbook As String
Dim sCurrentOnAction As String
Dim ws As Worksheet

iEnabledColumn = OnWksMenu_Col   ' Column for worksheet menu bar
If LCase(sBarName) = "chart menu bar" Then _
    iEnabledColumn = OnChartMenu_Col


Set ws = ThisWorkbook.Worksheets("DataSheet")

' Create a popup control on main menu bar sBarName
Set cbpop = Application.CommandBars(sBarName). _
   Controls.Add(Type:=msoControlPopup, Temporary:=True)
With cbpop
  .Caption = "Cu&stom"
  .Tag = "SRXUtilsCustomMenu"
End With

' Get last used row of DataSheet
iLastRow = Application.WorksheetFunction.CountA(ws.Range("A:A"))

' Go through DataSheet to get menu items
For iCurrentRow = 2 To iLastRow

  ' Set the values
  sCurrentProcedure = ws.Cells(iCurrentRow, Procedure_Col).Value
  sCurrentWorkbook = ws.Cells(iCurrentRow, InWorkbook_Col).Value
  sCurrentMenuItem = ws.Cells(iCurrentRow, MenuItem_Col).Value
  sCurrentSubMenuItem = ws.Cells(iCurrentRow, SubMenuItem_Col).Value
  sCurrentOnAction = ThisWorkbook.Name & "!" & _
    ws.Cells(iCurrentRow, OnAction_Col).Value

  ' If no Submenu item then this is a button control
  ' else it is a popup control
  If sCurrentSubMenuItem = "" Then
    ' Add button control
    With cbpop.Controls.Add(Type:=msoControlButton, Temporary:=True)
      .Caption = sCurrentMenuItem
      .OnAction = sCurrentOnAction
      .Tag = sCurrentProcedure        ' to pass this on
```

Example 12-12. The CreateCustomMenu Procedure (continued)

```
            .Parameter = sCurrentWorkbook   ' to pass this on
            .Enabled = ws.Cells(iCurrentRow, iEnabledColumn).Value
        End With
    Else
        ' Add popup control if it is not already added
        If sCurrentMenuItem <> "" Then
            Set cbctlCurrentPopup = cbpop.Controls.Add( _
                Type:=msoControlPopup, Temporary:=True)
            cbctlCurrentPopup.Caption = sCurrentMenuItem
        End If
        ' Now add the submenu item, which is a button control
        With cbctlCurrentPopup.Controls.Add( _
            Type:=msoControlButton, Temporary:=True)
            .Caption = sCurrentSubMenuItem
            .OnAction = sCurrentOnAction
            .Tag = sCurrentProcedure       ' to pass this on
            .Parameter = sCurrentWorkbook   ' to pass this on
            .Enabled = ws.Cells(iCurrentRow, iEnabledColumn).Value
        End With
    End If

Next     ' row

End Sub
```

Implementing the Features of the Add-in

We are now ready to "implement" the features of the add-in. As discussed earlier, for now we will just supply a message box for each feature.

The *ActivateSheet* utility has already been taken care of, since there should be a code module named **basMain** in the *SRXUtils.xls* project. For now, this module should contain only the following procedure:

```
Public Sub ActivateSheet()
    MsgBox "This is the ActivateSheet utility"
End Sub
```

For the printing utilities, we need a new Excel workbook. Create a new workbook and name it *Print.xls*. Add a code module (with any name) containing the code shown in Example 12-13.

Example 12-13. Code for the Printing Procedures

```
Public Sub PrintCharts()
  MsgBox "This is the print charts utility"
End Sub

Public Sub PrintPivotTables()
  MsgBox "This is the print pivot tables utility"
End Sub
```

Example 12-13. Code for the Printing Procedures (continued)

```
Public Sub PrintSheets()
  MsgBox "This is the print sheets utility"
End Sub
```

Now, the *Print.xls* workbook is an ordinary Excel workbook, so if our add-in opens this workbook in order to call one of its procedures, the workbook will be visible to the user. This is not good. Hence, we need to create an add-in from this worksheet as well. Let us call it *Print.utl*. (You can save the worksheet under this name by placing the name in quotation marks in the File name box in Excel's Save As dialog. If you omit the quotation marks, Excel will save the file as *Print.utl.xla*.) Don't forget to perform the usual add-in creation rituals for this workbook (compile the code, set the workbook and project properties, and lock the workbook from viewing) before saving it as an add-in.

We now need to implement the *RunUtility* procedure. This procedure, which should be placed in the **basMain** code module, is shown in Example 12-14.

Example 12-14. The RunUtility Procedure

```
Sub RunUtility()

' Use Tag and Parameter properties to find the procedure for
' the requested utility. Procedure name is in Tag property
' and workbook name is in the Parameter property.
' Use ActionControl to return the control.

Dim WkbName As String
Dim ProcName As String

WkbName = Application.CommandBars.ActionControl.Parameter
If WkbName = "" Or WkbName = "ThisWorkbook" Then _
    WkbName = ThisWorkbook.Name

ProcName = Application.CommandBars.ActionControl.Tag

' Open workbook if necessary
On Error GoTo WkbNotFound
If Not IsBookOpen(WkbName) Then
 Workbooks.Open ThisWorkbook.Path & Application.PathSeparator & WkbName
End If

' Run procedure
On Error GoTo ProcNotFound
Application.Run WkbName & "!" & ProcName

Exit Sub

WkbNotFound:
  MsgBox "Cannot find workbook " & WkbName & " in " & _
    ThisWorkbook.Path, vbCritical, "Test Add-In"
```

Example 12-14. The RunUtility Procedure (continued)

```
   Exit Sub

ProcNotFound:
   MsgBox "Cannot find procedure " & ProcName & " in " & _
      WkbName, vbCritical, "Test Add-In"
   Exit Sub

End Sub
```

Example 12-14 makes a call to the *IsBookOpen* function (which is shown in Example 12-15) to see if the workbook containing the procedure is open. Perhaps the obvious choice for determining whether or not a workbook is open is to look through the *Workbooks* collection, which is the collection of all "open" workbooks (more on this in Chapter 17, *The Workbook Object*). However, an add-in is hidden, even from this collection. Fortunately, we can still refer to an add-in workbook by name, so we just try to get this name using the line:

```
   sName = Workbooks(sWkbName).Name
```

If this generates an error, we know that the workbook is not open. Otherwise, it will return the name of the workbook. (Of course, we already knew the name in this case, but that doesn't matter.)

Example 12-15. The IsBookOpen Function

```
Private Function IsBookOpen(sWkbName) As Boolean

' Check to see if workbook is open
' Note that an add-in workbook does not appear in
' the Workbooks collection, so we need another method.
' However, an add-in can be referenced by name, so we simply
' access its Name property. If an error occurs, then
' the workbook is not open.

Dim sName As String
On Error GoTo WkbNotOpen
IsBookOpen = True
sName = Workbooks(sWkbName).Name

Exit Function

WkbNotOpen:
IsBookOpen = False

End Function
```

Closing Any Open Add-Ins

When the user unchecks the SRXUtils item in the Add-Ins dialog, Excel will close the *SRXUtils.xla* workbook. But it will not close any add-ins, such as *Print.utl*, that were opened in code. The place to close all open add-ins is in the workbook's BeforeClose event, which currently only deletes the custom menu.

A simple (but perhaps not elegant) approach is to close every add-in listed in the DataSheet except the main *SRXUtils.xla* (which is closed when the user deselects the add-in). For this, we need an **On Error Resume Next** line so that an attempt to close a workbook that is not open will be ignored. Thus, you should change the code for the existing BeforeClose event to that shown in Example 12-16.

Example 12-16. The Workbook_BeforeClose Event Handler

```
Private Sub Workbook_BeforeClose(Cancel As Boolean)

' Delete custom menu and close all add-ins

Dim r As Integer
Dim ws As Worksheet
Dim sName As String

' In case we try to close a workbook that is not open
On Error Resume Next

DeleteCustomMenus

Set ws = ThisWorkbook.Worksheets("DataSheet")
For r = 2 To Application.WorksheetFunction.CountA(ws.Range("A:A"))
    sName = ws.Cells(r, InWorkbook_Col).Value
    If sName <> "" And sName <> "ThisWorkbook" Then
      Workbooks(sName).Close
    End If
Next r

End Sub
```

The *DeleteCustomMenus* procedure is shown in Example 12-17.

Example 12-17. The DeleteCustomMenus Procedure

```
Sub DeleteCustomMenus()

Dim cbc As CommandBarControl

Set cbc = Application.CommandBars("Worksheet menu bar"). _
    FindControl(Type:=msoControlPopup, Tag:="TestAddInCustomMenu")
If Not cbc Is Nothing Then cbc.Delete

Set cbc = Application.CommandBars("Chart menu bar"). _
    FindControl(Type:=msoControlPopup, Tag:="TestAddInCustomMenu")
If Not cbc Is Nothing Then cbc.Delete

End Sub
```

The pieces are now complete, so you can save the *SRXUtils.xls* file as an add-in, just as we did in Chapter 10. (If you have a problem, you can download the source code for this add-in from the O'Reilly web site and compare it with your code.)

13

Built-In Dialog Boxes

The Excel object model contains a Dialog object for each of Excel's built-in dialog boxes. These Dialog objects are kept in the Dialogs collection and are indexed by the `XlBuiltInDialog` constants shown in Table 13-1 and Table 13-2. The Dialogs collection is returned by the Dialogs property of the Application object.

Table 13-1. The XlBuiltInDialog Constants and Their Values

xlDialogActivate (103)	xlDialogFormatMove (128)	xlDialogPivotTableWizard (312)
xlDialogActiveCellFont (476)	xlDialogFormatNumber (42)	xlDialogPlacement (300)
xlDialogAddChartAutoformat (390)	xlDialogFormatOverlay (226)	xlDialogPrint (8)
xlDialogAddinManager (321)	xlDialogFormatSize (129)	xlDialogPrinterSetup (9)
xlDialogAlignment (43)	xlDialogFormatText (89)	xlDialogPrintPreview (222)
xlDialogApplyNames (133)	xlDialogFormulaFind (64)	xlDialogPromote (202)
xlDialogApplyStyle (212)	xlDialogFormulaGoto (63)	xlDialogProperties (474)
xlDialogAppMove (170)	xlDialogFormulaReplace (130)	xlDialogProtectDocument (28)
xlDialogAppSize (171)	xlDialogFunctionWizard (450)	xlDialogProtectSharing (620)
xlDialogArrangeAll (12)	xlDialogGallery3dArea (193)	xlDialogPushbuttonProperties (445)
xlDialogAssignToObject (213)	xlDialogGallery3dBar (272)	xlDialogReplaceFont (134)
xlDialogAssignToTool (293)	xlDialogGallery3dColumn (194)	xlDialogRoutingSlip (336)

Table 13-1. The XlBuiltInDialog Constants and Their Values (continued)

xlDialogAttachText (80)	xlDialogGallery3dLine (195)	xlDialogRowHeight (127)
xlDialogAttachToolbars (323)	xlDialogGallery3dPie (196)	xlDialogRun (17)
xlDialogAutoCorrect (485)	xlDialogGallery3dSurface (273)	xlDialogSaveAs (5)
xlDialogAxes (78)	xlDialogGalleryArea (67)	xlDialogSaveCopyAs (456)
xlDialogBorder (45)	xlDialogGalleryBar (68)	xlDialogSaveNewObject (208)
xlDialogCalculation (32)	xlDialogGalleryColumn (69)	xlDialogSaveWorkbook (145)
xlDialogCellProtection (46)	xlDialogGalleryCustom (388)	xlDialogSaveWorkspace (285)
xlDialogChangeLink (166)	xlDialogGalleryDoughnut (344)	xlDialogScale (87)
xlDialogChartAddData (392)	xlDialogGalleryLine (70)	xlDialogScenarioAdd (307)
xlDialogChartLocation (527)	xlDialogGalleryPie (71)	xlDialogScenarioCells (305)
xlDialogChartOptionsData-Labels (505)	xlDialogGalleryRadar (249)	xlDialogScenarioEdit (308)
xlDialogChartOptions-DataTable (506)	xlDialogGalleryScatter (72)	xlDialogScenarioMerge (473)
xlDialogChartSourceData (541)	xlDialogGoalSeek (198)	xlDialogScenarioSummary (311)
xlDialogChartTrend (350)	xlDialogGridlines (76)	xlDialogScrollbarProperties (420)
xlDialogChartType (526)	xlDialogInsert (55)	xlDialogSelectSpecial (132)
xlDialogChartWizard (288)	xlDialogInsertHyperlink (596)	xlDialogSendMail (189)
xlDialogCheckbox-Properties (435)	xlDialogInsertNameLabel (496)	xlDialogSeriesAxes (460)
xlDialogClear (52)	xlDialogInsertObject (259)	xlDialogSeriesOptions (557)
xlDialogColorPalette (161)	xlDialogInsertPicture (342)	xlDialogSeriesOrder (466)
xlDialogColumnWidth (47)	xlDialogInsertTitle (380)	xlDialogSeriesShape (504)
xlDialogCombination (73)	xlDialogLabelProperties (436)	xlDialogSeriesX (461)
xlDialogConditional-Formatting (583)	xlDialogListboxProperties (437)	xlDialogSeriesY (462)
xlDialogConsolidate (191)	xlDialogMacroOptions (382)	xlDialogSetBackground-Picture (509)

Table 13-1. The XlBuiltInDialog Constants and Their Values (continued)

xlDialogCopyChart (147)	xlDialogMailEditMailer (470)	xlDialogSetPrintTitles (23)
xlDialogCopyPicture (108)	xlDialogMailLogon (339)	xlDialogSetUpdateStatus (159)
xlDialogCreateNames (62)	xlDialogMailNextLetter (378)	xlDialogShowDetail (204)
xlDialogCreatePublisher (217)	xlDialogMainChart (85)	xlDialogShowToolbar (220)
xlDialogCustomizeToolbar (276)	xlDialogMainChartType (185)	xlDialogSize (261)
xlDialogCustomViews (493)	xlDialogMenuEditor (322)	xlDialogSort (39)
xlDialogDataDelete (36)	xlDialogMove (262)	xlDialogSortSpecial (192)
xlDialogDataLabel (379)	xlDialogNew (119)	xlDialogSplit (137)
xlDialogDataSeries (40)	xlDialogNote (154)	xlDialogStandardFont (190)
xlDialogDataValidation (525)	xlDialogObjectProperties (207)	xlDialogStandardWidth (472)
xlDialogDefineName (61)	xlDialogObjectProtection (214)	xlDialogStyle (44)
xlDialogDefineStyle (229)	xlDialogOpen (1)	xlDialogSubscribeTo (218)
xlDialogDeleteFormat (111)	xlDialogOpenLinks (2)	xlDialogSubtotalCreate (398)
xlDialogDeleteName (110)	xlDialogOpenMail (188)	xlDialogSummaryInfo (474)
xlDialogDemote (203)	xlDialogOpenText (441)	xlDialogTable (41)
xlDialogDisplay (27)	xlDialogOptionsCalculation (318)	xlDialogTabOrder (394)
xlDialogEditboxProperties (438)	xlDialogOptionsChart (325)	xlDialogTextToColumns (422)
xlDialogEditColor (223)	xlDialogOptionsEdit (319)	xlDialogUnhide (94)
xlDialogEditDelete (54)	xlDialogOptionsGeneral (356)	xlDialogUpdateLink (201)
xlDialogEditionOptions (251)	xlDialogOptionsListsAdd (458)	xlDialogVbaInsertFile (328)
xlDialogEditSeries (228)	xlDialogOptionsTransition (355)	xlDialogVbaMakeAddin (478)
xlDialogErrorbarX (463)	xlDialogOptionsView (320)	xlDialogVbaProcedureDefinition (330)
xlDialogErrorbarY (464)	xlDialogOutline (142)	xlDialogView3d (197)
xlDialogExtract (35)	xlDialogOverlay (86)	xlDialogWindowMove (14)
xlDialogFileDelete (6)	xlDialogOverlayChartType (186)	xlDialogWindowSize (13)
xlDialogFileSharing (481)	xlDialogPageSetup (7)	xlDialogWorkbookAdd (281)

Table 13-1. The XlBuiltInDialog Constants and Their Values (continued)

xlDialogFillGroup (200)	xlDialogParse (91)	xlDialogWorkbookCopy (283)
xlDialogFillWorkgroup (301)	xlDialogPasteNames (58)	xlDialogWorkbookInsert (354)
xlDialogFilter (447)	xlDialogPasteSpecial (53)	xlDialogWorkbookMove (282)
xlDialogFilterAdvanced (370)	xlDialogPatterns (84)	xlDialogWorkbookName (386)
xlDialogFindFile (475)	xlDialogPhonetic (538)	xlDialogWorkbookNew (302)
xlDialogFont (26)	xlDialogPivotCalculated-Field (570)	xlDialogWorkbookOptions (284)
xlDialogFontProperties (381)	xlDialogPivotCalculated-Item (572)	xlDialogWorkbookProtect (417)
xlDialogFormatAuto (269)	xlDialogPivotFieldGroup (433)	xlDialogWorkbookTabSplit (415)
xlDialogFormatChart (465)	xlDialogPivotField-Properties (313)	xlDialogWorkbookUnhide (384)
xlDialogFormatCharttype (423)	xlDialogPivotFieldUngroup (434)	xlDialogWorkgroup (199)
xlDialogFormatFont (150)	xlDialogPivotShowPages (421)	xlDialogWorkspace (95)
xlDialogFormatLegend (88)	xlDialogPivotSolveOrder (568)	xlDialogZoom (256)
xlDialogFormatMain (225)	xlDialogPivotTableOptions (567)	

Table 13-2. Additional XlBuiltInDialog Constants and Their Values for Excel 9.0

_xlDialogChartSourceData (541)	xlDialogOptionsME (647)	xlDialogWebOptionsFonts (687)
_xlDialogPhonetic (538)	xlDialogPivotClientServer-Set (689)	xlDialogWebOptions-General (683)
xlDialogExternalData-Properties (530)	xlDialogPublishAs-WebPage (653)	xlDialogWebOptions-Pictures (685)
xlDialogImportTextFile (666)	xlDialogWebOptions-Encoding (686)	
xlDialogNewWebQuery (667)	xlDialogWebOptionsFiles (684)	

Note that each of the constants in Table 13-1 and Table 13-2 are formed from the prefix `xlDialog` followed by the name of the dialog box. For example, the Open dialog box constant is `xlDialogOpen` and so the corresponding Dialog object is:

```
Application.Dialogs(xlDialogOpen)
```

The Open dialog box is shown in Figure 13-1.

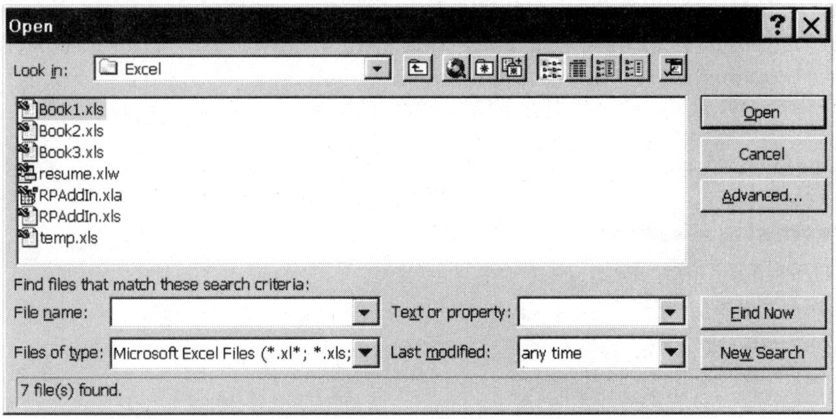

Figure 13-1. The Open File dialog box

Unfortunately, the Dialog object has only one useful property or method: the Show method.

The Show Method

The Show method displays a dialog box. This provides a convenient way to "lead" the user to a built-in dialog box. Unfortunately, we cannot access the values that the user enters into that dialog. Until the dialog is dismissed by the user and the actions specified in the dialog are completed, we have no control over the chain of events. (In Word 97, for instance, we can use built-in dialog boxes to get values from the user, without letting Word act automatically on those values.)

To illustrate, the code:

```
Application.Dialogs(xlDialogOpen).Show
```

displays the Open dialog box in Figure 13-1. The Show method returns **True** if the user clicks the OK button and **False** if the user clicks the Cancel button.

When the dialog box is dismissed by the user using the OK button, any appropriate actions indicated by the fields in the dialog box are carried out. In the case of the Open dialog, this means, of course, that the file selected by the user is actually opened in Excel. However, no actions are taken if the user dismisses the dialog box using the Cancel button.

The Show method has syntax:

```
DialogObject.Show(arg1, arg2, ..., arg30)
```

where the arguments are used to set some dialog options.

In particular, it is possible to set some of the values on a built-in Excel dialog box using arguments to the *Show* method. These arguments are listed in the Excel VBA Help file under "Built-In Dialog Box Argument Lists." For instance, the xlDialogOpen dialog box has the following arguments:

> *file_text*
> *update_links*
> *read_only*
> *format*
> *prot_pwd*
> *write_res_pwd*
> *ignore_rorec*
> *file_origin*
> *custom_delimit*
> *add_logical*
> *editable*
> *file_access*
> *notify_logical*
> *converter*

Hence, the code:

```
Application.Dialogs(xlDialogOpen).Show "*.*", False, True
```

displays the Open dialog, sets the "Files of type" drop-down box to All Files "*.*" so that the dialog will display the names of all files, sets *update_links* to False (so that Excel links are not automatically updated) and *read_only* to True (thus any file that is opened will be read-only).

Unfortunately, Microsoft does not seem to have documented the *meaning* of the various arguments. Also, the arguments are not named arguments, so we must include space for all arguments that precede the arguments that we want to set. Thus, a trial-and-error approach seems to be the only solution if you must set some dialog options. (Have fun.)

14

Custom Dialog Boxes

As we have seen, Excel's built-in dialogs offer very restricted communication with the user. Fortunately, Excel makes it possible to create custom dialog boxes that allow much more flexible communication. Custom dialog boxes are also called *forms* or *UserForms*. Our intention here is to present an introduction to the subject, which will provide a good jumping-off point for further study.

Generally speaking, most Excel applications will require only very simple forms. For example, we may want to display a form with a text box for text input, a list box to allow user selection, or some option buttons to select from several choices. Of course, we will want some command buttons to allow the user to execute procedures.

In fact, Microsoft's Visual Basic is a more appropriate programming environment than Microsoft Office for creating applications that involve complex forms, since it was designed specifically for that purpose. And Visual Basic allows you to access any of the object models in the Microsoft Office suite, just as Excel does.

What Is a UserForm Object?

A *UserForm object* can be thought of as a standard code module with a visual interface (a form) that is used to interact with the user (hence the term *UserForm*). However, we must be careful taking this description too literally. For instance, procedures (even public ones) that are declared in the General section of a UserForm module are generally intended to support objects (or code) on the form itself, whereas public procedures declared in a standard module are generally intended to support code anywhere in the project (not just in its own module).

To illustrate the point, suppose we declare a public procedure called *ProcedureA* in the General section of a UserForm module called UserForm1. Even though this procedure is public, we cannot access it from another module (even within the same project) by simply writing:

```
ProcedureA
```

as we could if the procedure was defined within a standard module. Instead, we must use the qualified name:

```
UserForm1.ProcedureA
```

Creating a UserForm Object

To create a user form at design time, we just select the project in which the form will reside and choose UserForm from the Insert menu. (Forms can be created at run time using the Add method of the UserForms collection, but we will confine our attention to creating forms at design time.) Figure 14-1 shows the design environment when a UserForm object is selected in the Project window.

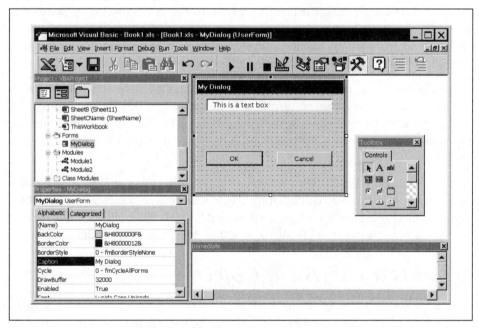

Figure 14-1. A UserForm dialog box (design time)

Note that the window on the right in Figure 14-1 contains the dialog box, in which we have placed a text box control and two command button controls. There is also a Toolbox window that contains icons used to add various Windows controls to the form.

To place a control on a form, we simply click on the icon in the Toolbox and then drag a rectangle on the form. This rectangle is replaced by the control. We can change the properties of the form itself (or any controls on the form) by selecting the object and making the changes in the Properties window. (Note the change to the form's caption in Figure 14-1.)

Additional controls may also be available on your system. These can be accessed by choosing "Additional controls" under the Tools menu. (This menu option is enabled, though, only, only if a user form has the focus in the VB IDE.)

ActiveX Controls

If you have been using Microsoft Windows for some time (as we presume you have, since you are reading this book), then you are quite familiar with controls at the user level. The following are examples of controls:

- Command buttons
- Text boxes
- List boxes
- Combo boxes
- Option buttons
- Check boxes
- Labels
- Tabs
- Scroll bars

All of these controls have a *visual interface* for interaction with the user. However, some controls do not have a visual interface. One example is the Timer control, which can be set to fire an event at regular intervals. Thus, the programmer can write code that will execute at regular intervals.

Generally speaking, a *control* (or *ActiveX control*) can be thought of as a special type of code component that can be placed within a larger container object (such as a form) and has the following properties:

- Controls generally (but not always) provide a visual interface for communication with the user.
- Controls can have *methods* that can be invoked by the user.
- Controls can have *properties* that can be read and set by the user.
- Controls can have *events* for which the user can write event code.

We discussed events that are associated with Excel objects (worksheets, work-books, charts, and so on) in Chapter 11, *Excel Events*. Control events work in pre-cisely the same way, as we will see in the upcoming examples.

Adding UserForm Code

In general, VBA programmers add two types of code to a UserForm module: event code that underlies the various controls on the form (and perhaps the form itself), and additional procedures that perform utility functions needed by the applica-tion. The latter code is added to the general section of the UserForm code module.

To illustrate the point with a very simple example, suppose we want to create an application that sorts selected columns (treating each column as a single object) using the first row as the sort key. Our form might look something like the one shown in Figure 14-2.

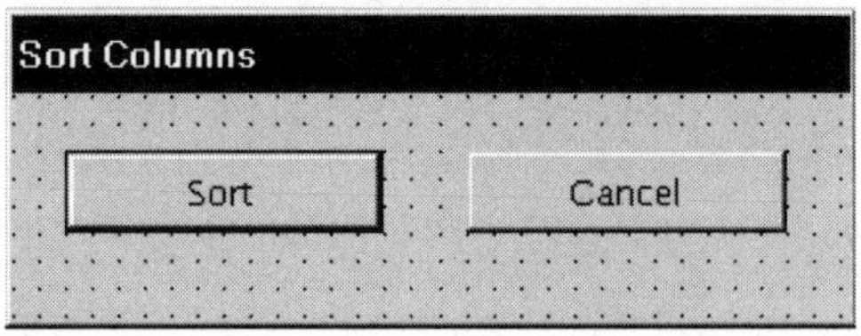

Figure 14-2. A Sort dialog box

When the user clicks the Sort button, VBA will ask him or her to confirm the sort operation and then act accordingly. Now, when the Sort button is selected by the user, VBA fires the Click event for this button. If the button is named cmdSort, then VBA provides the event code shell:

```
Private Sub cmdSort_Click()

End Sub
```

Clearly, we want to perform the sorting operation when this event is fired. How-ever, it would not be a good idea to place the actual code to perform the sort in this event code shell. Instead, we write a separate sorting procedure to do the sort-ing and place it in the General section of the UserForm module, or perhaps make it a public procedure in a separate standard code module within the project:

```
Public Sub SortColumns()
    ' code here to sort text
End Sub
```

There are several reasons why it is better to place the sorting code in a separate procedure. This *code modularity* makes it easier to:

- Use the code in other locations in the application
- Move the code to other applications
- Find and repair bugs in the code
- Make improvements or additions to the code
- Just plain read the code

Once the sorting procedure is complete, we can add the following code to the *Click* event:

```
Private Sub cmdSort_Click()
If MsgBox("Sort currently selected columns?", _
    vbQuestion + vbYesNo) = vbYes Then SortColumns
End Sub
```

Incidentally, the Click event for the Cancel button is often just the following:

```
Private Sub cmdCancel_Click()
    Unload Me
End Sub
```

All this does is unload the form.

While on the subject of unloading a form, it is important to understand the distinction between unloading a form and hiding a form. We can hide a form by setting the form's Visible property to **False**. This makes the form invisible, but it still consumes resources, such as memory. When we unload a form, it no longer consumes resources. (Well, this is not quite true. We need to not only unload the form, but also to set any variables that reference the form to **Nothing**.)

Excel's Standard Controls

Excel 97 has two types of controls. Figure 14-3 shows two toolboxes, each of which provides access to one type of control. (Below each toolbox is a control created using that toolbox.)

The controls on the Control Toolbox (on the left in Figure 14-3) are ActiveX controls. These controls can be placed either on a UserForm or directly on a worksheet (but not a chartsheet). They are the same as the controls that are accessible from the VB editor's Toolbox when designing a UserForm. ActiveX controls are very flexible and generally support a wide range of events. The Control Toolbox can be opened from within Excel (not the Excel VBA IDE) by selecting the Customize option from the Tools menu and checking the Control Toolbox toolbar in the Toolbars tab.

Note that the Control Toolbox in Figure 14-3 is not the same as the Toolbox in Figure 14-1, even though both are used to access ActiveX controls. The Toolbox in

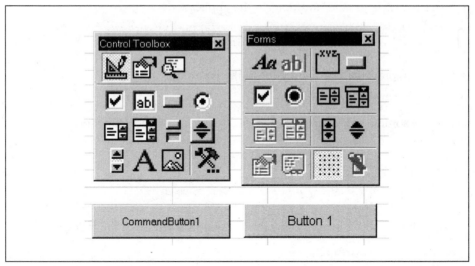

Figure 14-3. Control toolbars

Figure 14-1 is used to place ActiveX controls on user forms; the Control Toolbox in Figure 14-3 is used to place ActiveX controls on worksheets. The first button on the Control Toolbox, called the Design Mode button, is particularly important. Pressing it puts the worksheet in *design mode* at least with respect to its controls. When in design mode, we can move and resize the controls on the worksheet using the mouse. We can also right-click the control to bring up a dialog box with control options. When the Design Mode button is not depressed, clicking on a control with the mouse simply fires the Click event!

By selecting the Customize option from the Tools menu and checking the Forms toolbar in the Toolbars tab, you open the Forms toolbox. The controls on the Forms toolbox (on the right in Figure 14-3) are referred to as "standard Excel worksheet controls" and are a remnant from Excel 5.0. They can be placed on worksheets or chartsheets (but not UserForms) and have only a single event: the Click event.

For instance, if you place a standard button on a worksheet, Excel immediately opens the Assign Macro dialog box, as shown in Figure 14-4. This allows you to assign a macro to the button's Click event.

Since standard Excel controls are the only controls that can be placed on a chartsheet, they remain useful. But ActiveX controls are far more flexible and should be used whenever possible. We will speak no further about the standard Excel controls.

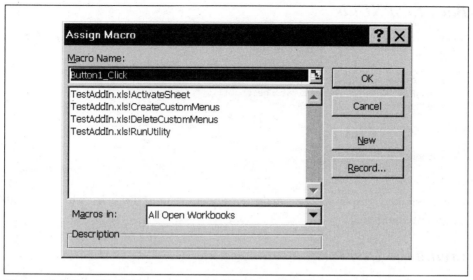

Figure 14-4. Response to placing a standard Excel command button

Example: The ActivateSheet Utility

It is time now to implement the *ActivateSheet* utility in our *SRXUtils* application. This will demonstrate the use of UserForms.

In particular, when the user selects *ActivateSheet*, we would like to present him or her with a custom dialog that lists all of the sheets in the active workbook, as shown in Figure 14-5. The user can select one of these sheets, which will then be activated.

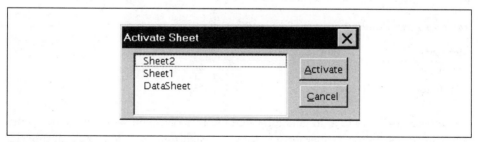

Figure 14-5. The activate sheet dialog

To implement this utility, we need to do the following things:

- Change the *ActivateSheet* procedure in **basMain** to open the Activate Sheet dialog (instead of displaying the current message).

- Design the Activate Sheet dialog itself.

- Write the code behind the Activate Sheet dialog.

Back to SRXUtils

So crank up the *SRXUtils.xls* worksheet and replace the *ActivateSheet* procedure in
basMain:

```
Public Sub ActivateSheet()
  MsgBox "This is the ActivateSheet utility"
End Sub
```

with the procedure:

```
Public Sub ActivateSheet()
  dlgActivateSheet.Show
End Sub
```

which simply displays the Activate Sheet dialog (which we will call
dlgActivateSheet).

Create the UserForm

After you insert a UserForm into your project, you should use the Properties window to change its Name property to *dlgActivateSheet* and its Caption property
to "Activate Sheet." Then you can add the controls to the form. The UserForm in
Figure 14-5 has two command buttons and one list box.

List box

Place a List box on the form as in Figure 14-5. Using the Properties window, set
the properties shown in Table 14-1. Note that the TabIndex property determines
not only the order that the controls are visited as the user hits the Tab key, but
also determines which control has the initial focus. Since we want the initial focus
to be on the list box, we set its tab index to 0.

Table 14-1. Nondefault Properties of the ListBox Control

Property	Value
Name	lstSheets
TabIndex	0

We should also note that, in general, there are two places in which a control property can be set: in the Properties window at design time, or using code during run
time. Some properties should be (or must be) set at design time, whereas others
can only be set at run time. However, most properties can be set at either time.

As a simple example, a control's Visible or Enabled property is often set during
run time, in response to actions by the user. For instance, we may want to disable
a command button labeled Print until the user has selected an object to print from

a list of objects. Setting the Enabled property of a command button whose name is *PrintButton* is easily done:

```
PrintButton.Enabled = False
```

In general, the choice of where to set a given property of a control is partly a matter of taste. I favor setting properties in code because it tends to make the code more complete and therefore more readable. It can also make changing properties simpler. However, some fundamental properties, such as Name and Caption, are best set at design time.

Activate button

Place a command button on the form, as in Figure 14-5. Using the Properties window, set the properties shown in Table 14-2.

Table 14-2. Nondefault Properties of the Activate Button

Property	Value
Name	cmdActivate
Accelerator	A
Caption	Activate
TabIndex	1

Cancel button

Place another command button on the form, as in Figure 14-5. Using the Properties window, set the properties shown in Table 14-3.

Table 14-3. Nondefault Properties of the Cancel Button

Property	Value
Name	cmdCancel
Accelerator	C
Caption	Cancel
TabIndex	2
Cancel	True

Create the Code Behind the UserForm

Now it is time to create the code behind these controls.

Cancel button code

Double click on the Cancel button to display the Click event code shell. Adding the line:

```
Unload Me
```

will fill out the code shell as follows and cause the form to be unloaded when the user hits the Cancel button:

```
Private Sub cmdCancel_Click()
    Unload Me
End Sub
```

ActivateSelectedSheet procedure

Next, we create a procedure that will activate the selected sheet. We want this procedure to be called in three situations; namely, when the user:

- Selects a sheet name from the list box and clicks the Activate button (or uses the Alt-A hot key)
- Double-clicks on a sheet name in the list box
- Selects a sheet name from the list box and hits the Enter key

Since this code will be used in three different situations, we can avoid repeating the code by placing it in its own procedure in the General section of a UserForm, as shown in Example 14-1.

Example 14-1. The ActivateSelectedSheet Procedure

```
Sub ActivateSelectedSheet()
If lstSheets.ListIndex > -1 Then
  Sheets(lstSheets.List(lstSheets.ListIndex)).Activate
End If
Unload Me
End Sub
```

This code demonstrates some list box properties. First, the ListIndex property returns the index number (starting at 0) of the currently selected item in the list box. Thus, the following code checks to see if an item is selected (otherwise ListIndex = -1):

```
If lstSheets.ListIndex > -1 Then
```

The code:

```
lstSheets.List(i)
```

returns the *i*th item in the list box (as a string). Thus:

```
lstSheets.List(lstSheets.ListIndex))
```

is the currently selected item—that is, the currently selected sheet name. Finally, the code:

```
Sheets(lstSheets.List(lstSheets.ListIndex)).Activate
```

activates that worksheet by invoking its Activate method. We will discuss the Activate method in Chapter 18, *The Worksheet Object*. For now, we simply note that if a worksheet has the name MySheet, then the code:

```
Sheets("MySheet").Activate
```

activates that sheet.

Finally, the last thing done in the cmdActivate_Click event is to unload the form, since it is no longer needed.

Activate button code

To set the code behind the Activate button, select cmdActivate in the Objects drop-down box (above the upper-left corner of the code window) and select Click in the Procedures drop-down box (above the upper-right corner of the code window). You can now fill in the code for the Click event of the **cmdActivate** button:

```
Private Sub cmdActivate_Click()
    ActivateSelectedSheet
End Sub
```

Double-click lstSheets code

We also want *ActivateSelectedSheet* to be called when the user double-clicks on a sheet name. The DblClick event for the list box fires when the user double-clicks on an item in the list box. Select lstSheets in the Objects drop-down and DblClk in the Procedures drop-down. Then fill in the DblClk event code shell:

```
Private Sub lstSheets_DblClick(ByVal Cancel As _
    MSForms.ReturnBoolean)
        ActivateSelectedSheet
End Sub
```

Enter key event

We also want to invoke *ActivateSelectedSheet* when the user selects a sheet name and hits the Enter key. When the list box has the focus, any keystroke fires the KeyDown event. Choose this event in the Procedures drop-down and add the code shown in Example 14-2 to the event shell.

Example 14-2. The lstSheets_KeyDown Event Procedure

```
Private Sub lstSheets_KeyDown(ByVal KeyCode As _
    MSForms.ReturnInteger, ByVal Shift As Integer)
If KeyCode = vbKeyReturn Then ActivateSelectedSheet
End Sub
```

In this case, we must add code to determine whether the Enter key was struck. Fortunately, Excel will fill in the *KeyCode* parameter of the KeyDown event with the key code for the key that caused the event to be fired. (For a list of key codes, check "KeyCode" in the Excel VBA help file.)

Fill the lstSheets list box

Next, we need to fill the *lstSheets* list box with a list of all of the sheets in the current workbook. We want this to be done automatically, so we will place the required code in the Initialize event of the UserForm. This event is fired by Excel when the form is loaded, but before it becomes visible. As the name implies, it is designed to initialize various properties of the form and its controls.

Select UserForm in the Object drop-down and Initialize in the Procedures drop-down. You should get the UserForm_Initialize event code shell. Fill it with the code shown in Example 14-3.

Example 14-3. The UserForm_Initialize Event Procedure

```
Private Sub UserForm_Initialize()
' Fill lstSheets with the list of sheets
Dim cSheets As Integer
Dim i As Integer
cSheets = Sheets.Count
lstSheets.Clear
For i = 1 To cSheets
   lstSheets.AddItem Sheets(i).Name
Next
End Sub
```

This code first gets the total number of sheets (worksheets and charts) in the current workbook. (We will discuss this in detail in later chapters, so don't worry about it now.) The list box is then cleared of any previous content. Then we have a `For` loop that adds the sheet names to the list box. This is done using the List-Box control's AddItem method. The name of a sheet is given by its Name property.

Trying the Activate Utility

If all has gone well, you can now save SRXUtils as an add-in, load it through the Tools menu (if it is currently loaded, you will need to unload it before saving the add-in or Excel will complain) and try out the new ActivateSheet feature.

ActiveX Controls on Worksheets

As you may know, ActiveX controls (and standard Excel controls) can be placed directly on a worksheet. Care must be taken, however, not to clutter up a worksheet with controls that would be better placed on a UserForm. When only a small number of controls are required, then placing these controls directly on a worksheet may be appropriate.

There are some special considerations when controls are placed directly on a worksheet. In particular, each ActiveX control on a *worksheet* (not on a User-Form) is represented by an OLEObject in the Excel object model. However, it is important to note that OLEObject objects can also represent embedded OLE objects. Thus, for instance, if we insert a bitmap on a worksheet (select Object from Excel's Insert menu), this bitmap object will be represented by an OLEObject.

The Worksheet object has a property called OLEObjects that returns the OLEObjects collection consisting of all OLEObject objects on the worksheet. Thus, the OLEObjects collection for the active worksheet is:

```
ActiveSheet.OLEObjects
```

Because OLEObjects also represent embedded OLE objects (such as bitmaps), we cannot be certain that, say:

```
ActiveSheet.OLEObjects(1)
```

is a control. Thus, it is wise when adding a control or embedded OLE object to a worksheet to immediately assign the control or object a name and then refer to it by this name rather than by index, as in:

```
ActiveSheet.OLEObjects("MyButton")
```

Referring to a Control on a Worksheet

Fortunately, Excel lets us refer to an ActiveX control on a worksheet by using its name, without reference to the OLEObjects collection. For instance, if we place a command button on a worksheet, Excel will give it the default name CommandButton1. Both of the following lines set the height of this command button to 20 points:

```
ActiveSheet.OLEObjects("CommandButton1").Height = 20
ActiveSheet.CommandButton1.Height = 20
```

Unfortunately, however, the properties and methods that we access in this manner are the properties and methods of the OLEObject, not the control itself. These properties are shown in Table 14-4.

Table 14-4. Members of the OLEObject Object

Activate	Height	ProgId
Application	Index	Select
AutoLoad	Interior	SendToBack
AutoUpdate	Left	Shadow
Border	LinkedCell	ShapeRange
BottomRightCell	ListFillRange	SourceName
BringToFront	Locked	Top

Table 14-4. Members of the OLEObject Object (continued)

Copy	Name	TopLeftCell
CopyPicture	Object	Update
Creator	OLEType	Verb
Cut	OnAction	Visible
Delete	Parent	Width
Duplicate	Placement	ZOrder
Enabled	PrintObject	

Thus, for instance, while we can set the Height property of the command button, we cannot set its Caption property in this way. That is, the code:

```
ActiveSheet.OLEObjects("CommandButton1").Caption = "ClickMe"
```

will generate an error.

The way to reach the members of the control itself is to use the Object property of an OLEObject object, which returns the underlying control, and makes its properties and methods accessible. Thus, the following two lines each set the button's caption:

```
ActiveSheet.OLEObjects("CommandButton1").Object.Caption = "ClickMe"
ActiveSheet.CommandButton1.Object.Caption = "ClickMe"
```

In addition to the standard properties available for ActiveX controls, the following properties can be used with ActiveX controls embedded in sheets in Microsoft Excel:

BottomRightCell
> Returns a Range object that represents the cell that lies under the lower-right corner of the object.

LinkedCell
> Returns or sets the worksheet range that is linked to the value of the control. Thus, if we place a value in the linked cell, the control will assume this value, and vice-versa.

ListFillRange
> Returns or sets the worksheet range that is used to fill a list box control.

Placement
> Returns or sets the way that the control is attached to the cells below it. The possible values are the XlPlacement constants: xlMoveAndSize, xlMove, and xlFreeFloating.

PrintObject
> If this property is set to True, the control will be printed when the worksheet is printed.

TopLeftCell

> Returns a Range object that represents the cell that lies under the top-left corner of the object.

ZOrder

> Returns the ZOrder position of the control.

Note also that Table 14-4 has some properties that are not properties of controls themselves. They relate to the OLEObject, which is the container for the control, and thus to the control's relationship with the worksheet. For instance, the code:

```
ActiveSheet.CommandButton1.TopLeftCell.Address
```

returns the address of the top-left cell of the worksheet that lies under the control (or rather, the control's container: the OLEObject).

As another example, the following code will locate the top-left cell under the command button and then scroll the active window so that this cell (and therefore the command button) is at the upper-left corner of the window:

```
Dim rng As Range
Set rng = ActiveSheet.CommandButton1.TopLeftCell
With ActiveWindow
   .ScrollRow = rng.Row
   .ScrollColumn = rng.Column
End With
```

It is important to note that some properties and methods of some Excel objects are disabled when an ActiveX control has the focus. For example, the Sort method of the Range object cannot be used when a control is active. Since a control on a worksheet remains active after it is clicked, the following code will fail:

```
Private Sub CommandButton1_Click
    Range("A:A").Sort Key1:=Range("A:A")
End Sub
```

(We will discuss the sort method in Chapter 19, *The Range Object.* Don't worry about that now.) This is one disadvantage of placing controls directly on worksheets.

Of course, one way to avoid this problem is to activate another object before calling the sort method. For instance, we can amend the previous code as follows:

```
Private Sub CommandButton1_Click
    Range("A:A").Activate
    Range("A:A").Sort Key1:=Range("A:A")
    CommandButton1.Activate        ' Optional
End Sub
```

It is also worth mentioning that if you save an Excel 97 or Excel 2000 workbook in Excel 5.0/95 Workbook file format, all ActiveX control information will be lost.

Adding a Control to a Worksheet Programmatically

To programmatically add an ActiveX control to a worksheet, we use the Add method of the OLEObjects collection. The syntax is:

```
OLEObjectCollection.Add(ClassType, FileName, Link, DisplayAsIcon, _
    IconFileName, IconIndex, IconLabel, Left, Top, Width, Height)
```

The *ClassType* parameter is the so-called *programmatic identifier* (or ProgID) for the control. Table 14-5 shows the ProgIDs for various controls.

Table 14-5. ProgIDs for ActiveX Controls

Control	ProgID
CheckBox	Forms.CheckBox.1
ComboBox	Forms.ComboBox.1
CommandButton	Forms.CommandButton.1
Frame	Forms.Frame.1
Image	Forms.Image.1
Label	Forms.Label.1
ListBox	Forms.ListBox.1
MultiPage	Forms.MultiPage.1
OptionButton	Forms.OptionButton.1
ScrollBar	Forms.ScrollBar.1
SpinButton	Forms.SpinButton.1
TabStrip	Forms.TabStrip.1
TextBox	Forms.TextBox.1
ToggleButton	Forms.ToggleButton.1

The only other parameters that are relevant to adding ActiveX controls (this method is used for other types of OLE objects as well) are the Left, Top, Width, and Height parameters, which specify in points the location (with respect to the upper-left corner of cell A1) and size of the control. All other parameters should be omitted. (This is a good place for named arguments!)

For instance, the code:

```
ActiveSheet.OLEObjects.Add ClassType:="Forms.Textbox.1", _
    Left:=72, Top:=72, Height:=20, Width:=100
```

places a new text box approximately one inch from the top and left edges of the active worksheet. (The dimensions do not seem to be terribly accurate.)

15

The Excel Object Model

The Excel object model is one of the most extensive object models in Microsoft's arsenal, with almost 200 objects and over 5000 properties and methods. As we have mentioned, however, many of these objects and members are included solely for backward compatibility with earlier versions of Excel. When we ignore these objects and members, the object count drops to 140 and the member count is about 3000. This makes the Excel object model second in size only to the Word object model.

We will not discuss the objects and members that are included for backward compatibility only. However, since you should at least be aware of the existence of these objects, we will include them in our pictures of the model (appropriately marked) but not in the tables.

It is certainly not our intention in this book to cover all, or even most, of the objects and members of the Excel object model. Our goal is to acquaint you with the major portions of this model, so that you can easily learn more as needed.

It seems appropriate to begin by trying to present an overall view of the Excel object model.

A Perspective on the Excel Object Model

To put the Excel object model in some perspective, Table 15-1 gives some statistics on various Microsoft object models. (The Excel 8 Small Model is the Excel object model without the objects and members that are included solely for backward compatibility with versions of Excel prior to Excel 8.)

Table 15-1. Some Object Model Statistics

Application	Objects	Properties	Methods	Enums	Constants
Access 8	51	1596	532	31	485
Binder 8	4	37	15	4	11
DAO 3.5	37	235	174	26	185
Excel 8	192	3245	1716	152	1266
Excel 8 Small Model	140	1974	985	152	1266
Forms 2	64	588	352	42	191
Graph 8	44	1120	234	58	447
Office 97	40	615	209	78	801
Outlook 8	42	1568	534	34	154
PowerPoint 8	110	1197	322	53	370
Word 8	188	2300	837	192	1969

For reference, Table 15-2 shows all objects in the Excel (small) object model, along with the number of children for each object.

Table 15-2. Excel Objects and Their Child Counts

AddIn (0)	Filters (1)	PivotTable (7)
AddIns (1)	Floor (3)	PivotTables (1)
Adjustments (0)	Font (0)	PlotArea (3)
AppEvents (0)	FormatCondition (3)	Point (4)
Application (21)	FormatConditions (1)	Points (1)
Areas (1)	FreeformBuilder (1)	QueryTable (2)
AutoCorrect (0)	Global (0)	QueryTables (1)
AutoFilter (2)	Gridlines (1)	Range (17)
Axes (1)	GroupShapes (1)	RecentFile (1)
Axis (4)	HiLoLines (1)	RecentFiles (1)
AxisTitle (5)	HPageBreak (2)	RefreshEvents (0)
Border (0)	HPageBreaks (1)	RoutingSlip (0)
Borders (1)	Hyperlink (2)	Scenario (1)
CalculatedFields (1)	Hyperlinks (1)	Scenarios (1)
CalculatedItems (1)	Interior (0)	Series (11)
CalloutFormat (0)	LeaderLines (1)	SeriesCollection (1)
Characters (1)	Legend (6)	SeriesLines (1)
Chart (22)	LegendEntries (1)	ShadowFormat (1)
ChartArea (4)	LegendEntry (2)	Shape (19)
ChartColorFormat (0)	LegendKey (3)	ShapeNode (0)
ChartEvents (0)	LineFormat (1)	ShapeNodes (1)

Table 15-2. Excel Objects and Their Child Counts (continued)

ChartFillFormat (1)	LinkFormat (0)	ShapeRange (14)
ChartGroup (8)	Mailer (0)	Shapes (3)
ChartGroups (1)	Name (1)	Sheets (4)
ChartObject (5)	Names (1)	SoundNote (0)
ChartObjects (4)	ODBCError (0)	Style (3)
Charts (3)	ODBCErrors (1)	Styles (1)
ChartTitle (5)	OLEFormat (1)	TextEffectFormat (0)
ColorFormat (0)	OLEObject (5)	TextFrame (1)
Comment (2)	OLEObjectEvents (0)	ThreeDFormat (1)
Comments (1)	OLEObjects (4)	TickLabels (1)
ConnectorFormat (1)	Outline (0)	Trendline (2)
ControlFormat (0)	PageSetup (0)	Trendlines (1)
Corners (0)	Pane (1)	UpBars (3)
CustomView (0)	Panes (1)	Validation (0)
CustomViews (1)	Parameter (1)	VpageBreak (2)
DataLabel (5)	Parameters (1)	VpageBreaks (1)
DataLabels (5)	Phonetic (1)	Walls (3)
DataTable (2)	PictureFormat (0)	Window (7)
Dialog (0)	PivotCache (0)	Windows (1)
Dialogs (1)	PivotCaches (1)	Workbook (14)
DocEvents (0)	PivotField (4)	WorkbookEvents (0)
DownBars (3)	PivotFields (2)	Workbooks (1)
DropLines (1)	PivotFormula (0)	Worksheet (19)
ErrorBars (1)	PivotFormulas (1)	WorksheetFunction (0)
FillFormat (1)	PivotItem (3)	Worksheets (3)
Filter (0)	PivotItems (2)	

Table 15-3 shows the Excel objects that have at least four children. As we can see by comparing the sizes of Tables 15-2 and 15-3, most objects by far have fewer than 4 children. In fact, 35 of the 140 objects (almost one-fourth) have no children at all.

Table 15-3. Objects with Four or More Children

Application (21)	DataLabel (5)	Series (11)
Axis (4)	DataLabels (5)	Shape (19)
AxisTitle (5)	Legend (6)	ShapeRange (14)
Chart (22)	OLEObject (5)	Sheets (4)
ChartArea (4)	OLEObjects (4)	Window (7)

Table 15-3. Objects with Four or More Children (continued)

ChartGroup (8)	PivotField (4)	Workbook (14)
ChartObject (5)	PivotTable (7)	Worksheet (19)
ChartObjects (4)	Point (4)	
ChartTitle (5)	Range (17)	

Table 15-4 lists the the top 20 objects with regard to member count (that is, the number of properties and methods that an object supports).

Table 15-4. The Top 20 Objects by Member Count

Application (304)	Window (96)	OLEObjects (66)
Range (198)	Series (90)	OLEObject (65)
WorksheetFunction (185)	Shape (81)	ChartGroup (58)
Chart (158)	Axis (78)	ChartObjects (58)
Workbook (154)	PageSetup (73)	Global (57)
Worksheet (130)	ShapeRange (72)	Style (57)
PivotTable (96)	PivotField (72)	

As we can see, the member count drops off fairly rapidly. Moreover, the member count is concentrated in a few areas:

Application
Range
WorksheetFunction
Workbook
Worksheet
PivotTable and related objects
Chart and related objects

Of course, the WorksheetFunction object has lots of members because it has one member for each Excel worksheet function.

By looking at Tables 15-3 and 15-4, we get the feeling that much of the power of the Excel object hierarchy is concentrated in the six objects:

Application
Chart
PivotTable
Range
Workbook
Worksheet

Indeed, we will devote much of our time in the remainder of the book to these objects.

Excel Enums

It is also interesting to glance over the list of Excel enums, whose names begin with Xl (with the sole exception of the **Constants** enum). Table 15-5 shows these enums for Excel 8, along with a count of the number of constants per enum. Table 15-6 shows the new enums added for Excel 9. Note that there are some rather large enums in the object model. The enums with at least 20 constants are:

- `XlBuiltInDialog` (221)
- `Constants` (163)
- `XlChartType` (73)
- `XlApplicationInternational` (45)
- `XlPaperSize` (42)
- `XlFileFormat` (39)
- `XlClipboardFormat` (33)
- `XlChartItem` (29)
- `XlPivotFormatType` (22), for Excel 9
- `XlRangeAutoFormat` (21)
- `XlParameterDataType` (20)
- `XlPattern` (20)

Table 15-5. The Excel Enums and Their Number of Constants (Excel 8)

Constants (163)	XlEnableSelection (3)	XlPivotFieldOrientation (5)
XlApplicationInternational (45)	XlEndStyleCap (2)	XlPivotTableSourceType (4)
XlApplyNamesOrder (2)	XlErrorBarDirection (2)	XlPlacement (3)
XlArrangeStyle (4)	XlErrorBarInclude (4)	XlPlatform (3)
XlArrowHeadLength (3)	XlErrorBarType (5)	XlPrintLocation (3)
XlArrowHeadStyle (5)	XlFileAccess (2)	XlPriority (3)
XlArrowHeadWidth (3)	XlFileFormat (39)	XlPTSelectionMode (6)
XlAutoFillType (11)	XlFillWith (3)	XlRangeAutoFormat (21)
XlAutoFilterOperator (6)	XlFilterAction (2)	XlReferenceStyle (2)
XlAxisCrosses (4)	XlFindLookIn (3)	XlReferenceType (4)
XlAxisGroup (2)	XlFormatCondition-Operator (8)	XlRoutingSlipDelivery (2)

Table 15-5. The Excel Enums and Their Number of Constants (Excel 8) (continued)

XlAxisType (3)

XlBackground (3)

XlBarShape (6)

XlBordersIndex (8)

XlBorderWeight (4)

XlBuiltInDialog (221)

XlCalculation (3)

XlCategoryType (3)

XlCellInsertionMode (3)

XlCellType (10)

XlChartGallery (3)

XlChartItem (29)

XlChartLocation (3)

XlChartPicturePlacement (7)

XlChartPictureType (3)

XlChartSplitType (4)

XlChartType (73)

XlClipboardFormat (33)

XlColorIndex (2)

XlCommandUnderlines (3)

XlCommentDisplayMode (3)

XlConsolidationFunction (11)

XlCopyPictureFormat (2)

XlCreator (1)

XlCutCopyMode (2)

XlCVError (7)

XlDataLabelPosition (11)

XlDataLabelsType (6)

XlDataSeriesDate (4)

XlDataSeriesType (4)

XlDeleteShiftDirection (2)

XlDirection (4)

XlDisplayBlanksAs (3)

XlDisplayShapes (3)

XlFormatConditionType (2)

XlFormControl (10)

XlFormulaLabel (4)

XlHAlign (8)

XlHighlightChangesTime (3)

XlIMEMode (11)

XlInsertShiftDirection (2)

XlLegendPosition (5)

XlLineStyle (8)

XlLink (4)

XlLinkInfo (2)

XlLinkInfoType (3)

XlLinkType (2)

XlLocationInTable (9)

XlLookAt (2)

XlMailSystem (3)

XlMarkerStyle (12)

XlMouseButton (3)

XlMousePointer (4)

XlMSApplication (7)

XlObjectSize (3)

XlOLEType (3)

XlOLEVerb (2)

XlOrder (2)

XlOrientation (4)

XlPageBreak (2)

XlPageBreakExtent (2)

XlPageOrientation (2)

XlPaperSize (42)

XlParameterDataType (20)

XlParameterType (3)

XlPasteSpecialOperation (5)

XlPasteType (6)

XlPattern (20)

XlRoutingSlipStatus (3)

XlRowCol (2)

XlRunAutoMacro (4)

XlSaveAction (2)

XlSaveAsAccessMode (3)

XlSaveConflictResolution (3)

XlScaleType (2)

XlSearchDirection (2)

XlSearchOrder (2)

XlSheetType (5)

XlSheetVisibility (3)

XlSizeRepresents (2)

XlSortMethod (2)

XlSortMethodOld (2)

XlSortOrder (2)

XlSortOrientation (2)

XlSortType (2)

XlSpecialCellsValue (4)

XlSubscribeToFormat (2)

XlSummaryColumn (2)

XlSummaryReportType (2)

XlSummaryRow (2)

XlTabPosition (2)

XlTextParsingType (2)

XlTextQualifier (3)

XlTickLabelOrientation (5)

XlTickLabelPosition (4)

XlTickMark (4)

XlTimeUnit (3)

XlToolbarProtection (5)

XlTrendlineType (6)

XlUnderlineStyle (5)

XlVAlign (5)

XlWBATemplate (4)

Table 15-5. The Excel Enums and Their Number of Constants (Excel 8) (continued)

XlDVAlertStyle (3)	XlPhoneticAlignment (4)	XlWindowState (3)
XlDVType (8)	XlPhoneticCharacterType (4)	XlWindowType (5)
XlEditionFormat (4)	XlPictureAppearance (2)	XlWindowView (2)
XlEditionOptionsOption (8)	XlPictureConvertorType (13)	XlXLMMacroType (3)
XlEditionType (2)	XlPivotFieldCalculation (9)	XlYesNoGuess (3)
XlEnableCancelKey (3)	XlPivotFieldDataType (3)	

Table 15-6. Additional Enums for Excel 9.0

XlCmdType (4)	XlHtmlType (4)	XlSourceType (7)
XlColumnDataType (10)	XlLayoutFormType (2)	XlSubtototalLocationType (2)
XlCubeFieldType (2)	XlPivotFormatType (22)	XlWebFormatting (3)
XlDisplayUnit (9)	XlQueryType (6)	XlWebSelectionType (3)

The VBA Object Browser

Microsoft does supply a tool for viewing the objects, properties, methods, events, and enums in an object model. It is called the Microsoft Object Browser, and it is accessible from the View menu in the VBA IDE (or hit the F2 key). Figure 15-1 shows the Microsoft Object Browser.

The topmost drop-down list box lets us select an object model for viewing; in the case of Figure 15-1, we are viewing the Excel object model. The second list box is for searching the object model. On the left, we find a list of the classes in the object model. There is one class per object and one class per enum. The right-hand list box shows the properties, methods, and events of the object that is selected in the Classes list box. The text box at the bottom gives some information about the selected item.

The Object Browser is certainly a useful tool, and you will probably want to spend some time experimenting with it. (Perhaps its best feature is that it is easily accessible from the IDE.) However, it gives only a flat, one-dimensional view of the object model. For this reason, I have written an object browser that provides a two-dimensional view of an object model. In fact, many of the figures in this book are screen shots taken from my object browser. For more information on this browser, please see the coupon in the back of this book.

Figure 15-1. The Microsoft Object Browser

16

The Application Object

As we discussed in Chapter 15, *The Excel Object Model*, the majority of the action in the Excel object model rests in the six objects Application, Chart, PivotTable, Range, Workbook, and Worksheet. In this book, we will concentrate on the following objects, along with some of their children:

Application
Chart
CommandBars
Dialogs
Global
Names
Range
Sheets
Window/Windows
Workbook/Workbooks
Worksheet
WorkSheetFunctions

This constitutes the vast majority of the Excel object model. With this knowledge, you should be able to program most Excel tasks and be in a position to easily pick up any additional information from the Excel help files that you might need for less common programming tasks.

As you might imagine, several of these objects are complicated enough to deserve a complete chapter, so we will devote this chapter to discussing some of the properties and methods of the Application object itself, along with some of its simpler children.

Figure 16-1 shows the Application object, which sits atop the Excel object model and represents Excel itself, and its children. Each object is preceded by an icon that indicates whether it is a collection object (the little basket) or a noncollection object (the little oval).

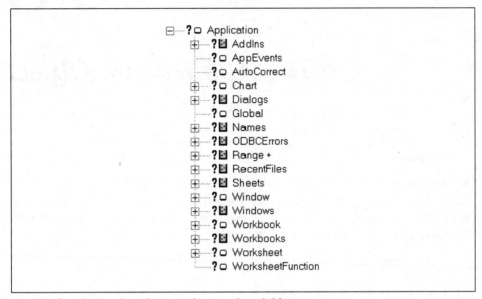

Figure 16-1. The Excel Application object and its children

Figure 16-2 shows all children of the Application object, including those that are included in the Excel object model strictly for backward compatibility. These latter objects are marked with an (X). The objects in Figure 16-2 that are marked (*Off) actually belong to the Microsoft Office object model, but are included here because they are accessible from the Excel object model and are sometimes used when programming the Excel model. There is also one object that belongs to the Visual Basic Extensibility model. It is marked (*VBE).

Properties and Methods of the Application Object

The Application object has a whopping 218 properties and methods, of which 188 are neither hidden nor obsolete (by obsolete we mean included for backward compatibility only). These 188 members are shown in Table 16-1.

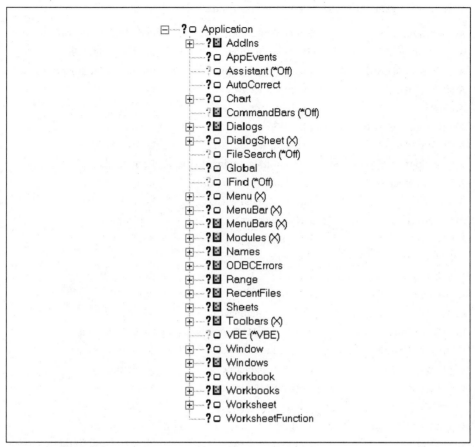

Figure 16-2. The Excel Application object along with its obsolete children

Recall that a member is global if it can be used without qualification. Global members are indicated by (g) in Table 16-1. Thus, for instance, since the ActiveCell property is global, we may write:

```
MsgBox ActiveCell.Formula
```

in place of:

```
MsgBox Application.ActiveCell.Formula
```

Table 16-1. Application Object Members[a]

ActivateMicrosoftApp	DisplayNoteIndicator	OperatingSystem
ActiveCell (g)	DisplayRecentFiles	OrganizationName
ActiveChart (g)	DisplayScrollBars	Parent (g)
ActivePrinter (g)	DisplayStatusBar	Path
ActiveSheet (g)	DoubleClick	PathSeparator

Table 16-1. Application Object Members^a (continued)

ActiveWindow (g)	EditDirectlyInCell	PivotTableSelection
ActiveWorkbook (g)	EnableAnimations	PreviousSelections
AddChartAutoFormat	EnableAutoComplete	PromptForSummaryInfo
AddCustomList	EnableCancelKey	Quit
AddIns (g)	EnableEvents	Range (g)
AlertBeforeOverwriting	EnableSound	RecentFiles
AltStartupPath	Evaluate (g)	RecordMacro
Application	Excel4IntlMacroSheets (g)	RecordRelative
AskToUpdateLinks	Excel4MacroSheets (g)	ReferenceStyle
Assistant (g)	ExecuteExcel4Macro (g)	RegisteredFunctions
AutoCorrect	FileConverters	RegisterXLL
Build	FileFind	Repeat
Calculate (g)	FileSearch	RollZoom
CalculateBeforeSave	FindFile	Rows (g)
Calculation	FixedDecimal	Run (g)
Caller	FixedDecimalPlaces	Run2 (g)
CanPlaySounds	GetCustomListContents	SaveWorkspace
CanRecordSounds	GetCustomListNum	ScreenUpdating
Caption	GetOpenFilename	Selection (g)
CellDragAndDrop	GetSaveAsFilename	SendKeys (g)
Cells (g)	Goto	SetDefaultChart
CentimetersToPoints	Height	Sheets (g)
Charts (g)	Help	SheetsInNewWorkbook
CheckSpelling	IgnoreRemoteRequests	ShowChartTipNames
ClipboardFormats	InchesToPoints	ShowChartTipValues
Columns (g)	InputBox	ShowToolTips
CommandBars (g)	Interactive	StandardFont
CommandUnderlines	International	StandardFontSize
ConstrainNumeric	Intersect (g)	StartupPath
ControlCharacters	Iteration	StatusBar
ConvertFormula	Left	TemplatesPath
CopyObjectsWithCells	LibraryPath	ThisWorkbook (g)
Creator (g)	MacroOptions	Top
Cursor	MailLogoff	TransitionMenuKey
CursorMovement	MailLogon	TransitionMenuKeyAction
CustomListCount	MailSession	TransitionNavigKeys
CutCopyMode	MailSystem	UILanguage

Table 16-1. Application Object Members[a] (continued)

DataEntryMode	MathCoprocessorAvailable	Undo
DDEAppReturnCode (g)	MaxChange	Union (g)
DDEExecute (g)	MaxIterations	UsableHeight
DDEInitiate (g)	MemoryFree	UsableWidth
DDEPoke (g)	MemoryTotal	UserControl
DDERequest (g)	MemoryUsed	UserName
DDETerminate (g)	MouseAvailable	Value
Default	MoveAfterReturn	VBE
DefaultFilePath	MoveAfterReturnDirection	Version
DefaultSaveFormat	Name	Visible
DefaultSheetDirection	Names (g)	Volatile
DeleteChartAutoFormat	NetworkTemplatesPath	Wait
DeleteCustomList	NextLetter	Width
Dialogs	ODBCErrors	Windows (g)
DisplayAlerts	ODBCTimeout	WindowsForPens
DisplayClipboardWindow	OnKey	WindowState
DisplayCommentIndicator	OnRepeat	Workbooks (g)
DisplayExcel4Menus	OnTime	WorksheetFunction (g)
DisplayFormulaBar	OnUndo	Worksheets (g)
DisplayFullScreen	OnWindow	WSFunction

[a] (g) indicates a global member.

Of course, this is far too many members to discuss even the majority in a nonreference book, so we will pick out a few of the more interesting and useful members. The important point is that you can use Table 16-1 to find a member that suits a particular purpose and then check the Excel help files for more information if it is not covered in this book.

We will also discuss additional properties and methods of the Application object throughout the remainder of the book, hopefully at times when the discussion will be more relevant.

In the hope of making our discussion a bit more structured, we will try to break the members in Table 16-1 into separate groups. Note, however, that this is in many cases a bit arbitrary.

Members that Return Children

Many of the members of the Application object are designed simply to gain access to a child object of the Application object. For instance, the Workbooks property simply returns the Workbooks collection object, which represents all of the currently open Workbook objects (i.e., workbooks). We will discuss many of these objects at the proper time, but it is worth taking a look at the members that return these objects now.

Table 16-2 shows the 35 members of the Application object that return child objects.

Table 16-2. Members that Return Child Objects

Member	Return Type
ActiveCell	Range
ActiveChart	Chart
ActiveSheet	Worksheet
ActiveSheet	Chart
ActiveWindow	Window
ActiveWorkbook	Workbook
AddIns	AddIns
Application	Application
Assistant	Assistant
AutoCorrect	AutoCorrect
Cells	Range
Charts	Sheets
Columns	Range
CommandBars	CommandBars
Dialogs	Dialogs
Excel4IntlMacroSheets	Sheets
Excel4MacroSheets	Sheets
FileFind	IFind
FileSearch	FileSearch
Intersect	Range
Names	Names
NextLetter	Workbook
ODBCErrors	ODBCErrors
Parent	Application
Range	Range
RecentFiles	RecentFiles
Rows	Range
Sheets	Sheets
ThisWorkbook	Workbook
Union	Range

Table 16-2. Members that Return Child Objects (continued)

Member	Return Type
VBE	VBE
Windows	Windows
Workbooks	Workbooks
WorksheetFunction	WorksheetFunction
Worksheets	Sheets

There are some points worth noting in Table 16-2. First, there are several members that begin with the word "Active." It should come as no surprise that these members return the corresponding currently active object. For instance, the ActiveSheet member returns the currently active worksheet or chart, depending upon which is active at the time. (Note that there is no Sheet object. Sheets are either worksheets or stand-alone charts. We will discuss this issue in detail in Chapter 18, *The Worksheet Object*.)

Observe also that often the name of a member is the same as the name of the object that the member returns. For instance, the AddIns property returns the AddIns collection, the Application property returns the Application object, and the Windows property returns the Windows collection.

The notable exceptions to this rule are:

- The ThisWorkBook property returns the Workbook object containing the currently running code. One use of this property is in determining the location (complete path and filename) of the workbook on the user's computer, which is done by writing:

    ```
    ThisWorkbook.FullName
    ```

- Several object properties, such as Cells, Columns, and Rows, return a Range object. This is because there are no Cell, Column, or Row objects in the Excel object model. Instead, each of these "objects" is actually a Range object. (Incidentally, a similar thing happens in the Word object model. In particular, there are no Character, Word, or Sentence objects. Rather, these are Range objects in the Word object model as well.)

Members that Affect the Display

There are several members that affect the display of certain items:

DisplayAlerts property (R/W Boolean)

When **True**, Excel displays various warning messages (such as a confirmation message that precedes the deletion of a worksheet) while a macro is running. If you do not want a macro to be disturbed, then set this to **False**:

```
Application.DisplayAlerts = False
```

The default value of this property is `True`.

DisplayCommentIndicator property (R/W Long)

This property affects the way that Excel indicates the presence of a comment in an unselected cell. It can be any one of the constants in the following enum:

```
Enum XlCommentDisplayMode
    xlCommentIndicatorOnly = -1        ' Display indicator only
    xlNoIndicator = 0                  ' Display
    xlCommentAndIndicator = 1          ' Display indicator and comment
                                       '  itself
End Enum
```

Setting DisplayCommentIndicator to either `xlCommentIndicatorOnly` or `xlCommentAndIndicator` sets the value of the DisplayNoteIndicator property (described later in this section) to `True`, while setting DisplayCommentIndicator to `xlNoIndicator` changes DisplayNoteIndicator to `False`.

DisplayFormulaBar property (R/W Boolean)

This property determines whether the formula bar is displayed. Its default value is `True`.

DisplayFullScreen property (R/W Boolean)

This property determines whether Excel is in full-screen mode. (Note that displaying Excel in full-screen mode is not the same as maximizing Excel's application window.)

DisplayNoteIndicator property (R/W Boolean)

If this property is `True`, its default value, then cells containing notes display cell tips and contain note indicators (which are small dots in the upper-right corner of a cell). Setting DisplayNoteIndicator to `False` also sets DisplayCommentIndicator to `xlNoIndicator`, while setting DisplayNoteIndicator to `True` sets DisplayCommentIndicator to `xlCommentIndicatorOnly`.

Members that Enable Excel Features

Several Application members enable or disable certain Excel features:

EnableAnimations property (R/W Boolean)

This property determines whether animated insertion and deletion is enabled. When animation is enabled inserted worksheet rows and columns appear slowly and deleted worksheet rows and columns disappear slowly. The default value is `False`.

EnableAutoComplete property (R/W Boolean)

This property determines whether Excel's AutoComplete feature is enabled; its default value is `True`.

EnableCancelKey property (R/W Long)

This property controls how Excel handles the Ctrl-Break or Esc key combinations during a running procedure. It can be one of the following `XlEnableCancelKey` constants:

```
Enum XlEnableCancelKey
      xlDisabled = 0
      xlInterrupt = 1
      xlErrorHandler = 2
End Enum
```

The meanings of these constants follow:

`xlDisabled`

Trapping is disabled (the keystrokes are ignored).

`xlInterrupt`

The running procedure is interrupted by the display of a dialog box that enables the user to either debug or end the procedure. This is the default value.

`xlErrorHandler`

The keystroke interrupt is sent to the running procedure as an error that is trappable by an error handler using the **On Error GoTo** statement. The error code is 18.

Note that this property can be dangerous and should be used with great circumspection. In particular, if you set the property to **xlDisabled**, then there is no way to interrupt an infinite loop. Similarly, if you set the property to **xlErrorHandler** but your error handler returns using the **Resume** statement, there is no way to stop nonself-terminating code.

For these reasons, Excel always resets the EnableCancelKey property to **xlInterrupt** whenever Excel returns to the idle state and there is no code running.

EnableEvents property (R/W Boolean)

This property is **True** (its default value) if events are enabled for the Application object. (For more on this, see Chapter 11, *Excel Events.*)

EnableSound property (R/W Boolean)

This property enables and (mercifully) disables sounds for Microsoft Office. The default value is **False**.

Event-Related Members

It is possible to assign macros to certain events. (These are special events—not the events that we discussed in Chapter 11.) For instance, we can assign a macro to play whenever a particular key is pressed. This is done by invoking the OnKey method for the Application object. Let us describe two of the more useful events that can be assigned a macro.

OnKey method

The syntax for the OnKey method is:

```
Application.OnKey(Key, Procedure)
```

where *Key* is the key or key combination (written as a string) that will execute the macro and *Procedure* is the name of that macro.

Note that we can alter the normal behavior of Excel by assigning a key combination to the *Key* parameter that has a normal Excel response (such as Ctrl-S for save). If we assign an empty string to the *Procedure* parameter, then Excel will omit its normal response (so nothing will happen). If we omit the *Procedure* parameter, then Excel will return the key combination to its normal function.

To illustrate, the following code will disable the Ctrl-o key combination, which normally displays the Open dialog box:

```
Application.OnKey "^o",""
```

The following code returns the Ctrl-o key combination to its normal Excel function:

```
Application.OnKey "^o"
```

The *Key* argument can specify a single key or any key combined with one or more of Alt, Ctrl, or Shift. Normal alphanumeric keys are denoted by themselves, as in "a," "A," "1." Table 16-3 shows how to enter special keys. For instance, the F2 key is denoted by "{F2}", and the Enter key is denoted either by "{ENTER}" or "~".

Table 16-3. Special Keys for the Key Parameter

Key	Code
Backspace	{BACKSPACE} or {BS}
Break	{BREAK}
Caps Lock	{CAPSLOCK}
Clear	{CLEAR}
Delete or Del	{DELETE} or {DEL}
Down Arrow	{DOWN}
End	{END}
Enter (numeric keypad)	{ENTER}
Enter	~ (tilde)
Esc	{ESCAPE} or {ESC}
Help	{HELP}

Table 16-3. Special Keys for the Key Parameter (continued)

Key	Code
Home	{HOME}
Ins	{INSERT}
Left Arrow	{LEFT}
Num Lock	{NUMLOCK}
Page Down	{PGDN}
Page Up	{PGUP}
Return	{RETURN}
Right Arrow	{RIGHT}
Scroll Lock	{SCROLLLOCK}
Tab	{TAB}
Up Arrow	{UP}
F1 through F15	{F1} through {F15}

To combine keys with Shift, Ctrl, or Alt, use the following prefixes:

Shift	+ (plus sign)
Ctrl	∧ (caret)
Alt	% (percent sign)

For instance, to denote the Alt-F2 key combination, write "%{F2}". To denote Ctrl-Shift-Enter, write "∧+{ENTER}".

In order to use one of the characters +, ∧, %, {, }, or ~ without having it interpreted as a special key, simply enclose the character in braces. For instance, to reassign the { key, we would assign the Key parameter to "{{}".

OnTime method

This method is used to run a procedure at a specific time or after a specific amount of time has passed. The syntax is:

```
Application.OnTime(EarliestTime, Procedure, LatestTime, Schedule)
```

Of course, the *Procedure* parameter is the name of the macro to run. The *EarliestTime* parameter is the time you want the macro to be run. To specify a time, we use the *TimeValue* function. For instance, the following code executes the macro *test* in the **ThisWorkbook** code module of the *book1* workbook at 3:58 P.M.:

```
Application.OnTime TimeValue("3:58 PM"), _
    "d:\excel\book1.xls!ThisWorkbook.test"
```

LatestTime is an optional parameter that specifies the latest time at which the procedure can *begin* running. We can use the *TimeValue* function to specify a time for this parameter, or we can set *LatestTime* to *EarliestTime* plus some additional time. For instance, the following code requires that Excel run the macro no later than 30 seconds following 3:58 P.M.:

```
Application.OnTime TimeValue("3:58 PM"), _
    "d:\excel\book1.xls!ThisWorkbook.test", _
    TimeValue("3:58 PM") + 30
```

The *LatestTime* parameter may be useful, since if Excel is busy (running another procedure, for instance), then execution of the macro denoted by *Procedure* will be delayed. If you do not want the macro to be run after a certain time, then set the *LatestTime* parameter.

If you want to clear a previously set OnTime macro, you can call the procedure with the *Schedule* parameter set to **False**. Otherwise, the parameter can be omitted, since its default value is **True**.

Note that the *Now* function returns the current time. Thus, to schedule a macro for a certain amount of time from the present, we can set *EarliestTime* to:

```
Now + TimeValue(time)
```

Calculation-Related Members

The Application object has several members related to calculation.

Calculate method

This method calculates all open workbooks, a specific worksheet in a workbook, or a specified range of cells on a worksheet, depending upon how it is applied.

When applied to the Application object, as in:

```
Application.Calculate
```

Excel will calculate all open workbooks. When applied to a specific worksheet, as in:

```
Worksheets(1).Calculate
```

Excel will calculate that worksheet. When applied to a specific range, as in:

```
Worksheets(1).Rows(2).Calculate
```

Excel will calculate the cells in that range. Note that since Calculate is a global method, we can simply write:

```
Calculate
```

in place of:

```
Application.Calculate
```

Calculation property (Read/Write Long)

This property sets Excel's calculation mode and can be set of any of the following constants:

```
Enum XlCalculation
    xlCalculationManual = -4135
    xlCalculationAutomatic = -4105
    xlCalculationSemiautomatic = 2
End Enum
```

The default value is `xlCalculationAutomatic`. As is typical, the documentation does not explain the term semiautomatic (at least I could not find an explanation). However, there is an option in Excel's Calculation tab under the Options dialog that allows us to specify automatic calculation except for data tables; this is what is meant by semiautomatic.

CalculateBeforeSave property (R/W Boolean)

This property is `True` if workbooks are calculated before they are saved to disk. This is relevant only when the Calculation property is set to `xlManual`.

File-Related Members

Let us take a brief look at the members that are related to file operations.

DefaultFilePath property (R/W String)

This property returns or sets the default path that Microsoft Excel uses when it opens or saves files. This setting can also be changed by the user in the General tab of the Options dialog.

DefaultSaveFormat property (R/W Long)

This property returns or sets the default format for saving files. The default for this property is `xlWorkbookNormal`, indicating the normal workbook format for the current version of Excel. The possible values for this property are the `XLFileFormat` constants shown in Table 16-4.

Table 16-4. XLFileFormat Constants

xlAddIn	xlExcel4Workbook	xlWJ3FJ3
xlCSV	xlExcel5	xlWK1
xlCSVMac	xlExcel7	xlWK1ALL
xlCSVMSDOS	xlExcel9795	xlWK1FMT
xlCSVWindows	xlIntlAddIn	xlWK3
xlCurrentPlatformText	xlIntlMacro	xlWK3FM3

Table 16-4. XLFileFormat Constants (continued)

xlDBF2	xlSYLK	xlWK4
xlDBF3	xlTemplate	xlWKS
xlDBF4	xlTextMac	xlWorkbookNormal
xlDIF	xlTextMSDOS	xlWorks2FarEast
xlExcel2	xlTextPrinter	xlWQ1
xlExcel2FarEast	xlTextWindows	xlHTML (Excel 9 only)
xlExcel3	xlWJ2WD1	xlUnicodeText (Excel 9 only)
xlExcel4	xlWJ3	

FindFile method

This method, whose syntax is:

```
Application.FindFile
```

displays the Open dialog box. If a file is opened successfully by the user, the method returns **True**. If the user cancels the dialog box, the method returns **False**.

GetOpenFilename method

This method displays the Open dialog box and gets a filename or filenames from the user but does not open the files. Its syntax is:

```
Application.GetOpenFilename(FileFilter, _
    FilterIndex, Title, ButtonText, MultiSelect)
```

The optional *FileFilter* parameter is a string that specifies what to put in the "Files of type" drop-down list box in the Open dialog. In other words, it specifies file filtering criteria. This string is in two parts, of the form:

```
description, filefilter
```

The first part is the description of the file type, and the second part is the MS-DOS wildcard file-filter specification. The two parts are separated by a comma. Note that the first part is the string that appears in the "Files of type" drop-down box in the Open dialog box. Thus, the first part also includes the wildcard file-filter specification. Perhaps a few examples will help clarify:

Text files
```
Text Files (*.txt),*.txt
```
Lotus files
```
Lotus 1-2-3 (*.wk?), *.wk?
```
Add-In files
```
Add-In Files (*.xla),*.xla
```

It is also possible to use multiple wildcard file filters, as in:

```
Backup Files (*.xlk; *.bak), *.xlk; *.bak
```

(Note the semicolons.) If the *FileFilter* argument is omitted, the default is:

```
All Files (*.*),*.*
```

Note that *FileFilter* can consist of more than one filter specification, separated by commas, as in:

```
Debug.Print Application.GetOpenFilename( _
    "Text Files (*.txt),*.txt, _
    Backup Files (*.xlk; *.bak), *.xlk; *.bak")
```

In this case, the optional *FilterIndex* parameter specifies which of the filters appears in the "Files of type" drop-down list box. For instance, the following will cause the second filter (backup files) to appear in the "Files of type" drop-down list box:

```
Debug.Print Application.GetOpenFilename( _
    "Text Files (*.txt),*.txt, _
    Backup Files (*.xlk; *.bak), *.xlk; *.bak", 2)
```

The optional *Title* parameter specifies the title of the dialog box. If this argument is omitted, the title is Open. The *ButtonText* parameter is ignored by Windows, but used on the Macintosh.

The optional *MultiSelect* property is set to **True** to allow multiple filenames to be selected and **False** to allow only one filename to be selected. The default value is **False**. To select multiple files from the Open dialog, the user must hold down the Ctrl or Shift key.

The method returns the selected filename or the name entered by the user. The returned name may also include a path specification. If the *MultiSelect* parameter is **True**, the return value is an array of the selected filenames (even if only one filename is selected). The method returns **False** if the user cancels the dialog box.

When *Multiselect* is **True**, we can determine the number of files selected by the user by using the *UBound* function to get the upper bound for the returned array, as in:

```
NumFiles = UBound(Application.GetOpenFilename(MultiSelect:=True))
```

Note finally that this method may change the current drive or folder.

GetSaveAsFilename method

This method is similar to the GetOpenFilename method, but instead displays the Save As dialog box and gets a filename from the user without saving any files. The syntax is:

```
Application.GetSaveAsFilename(InitialFilename, _
    FileFilter, FilterIndex, Title, ButtonText)
```

The optional *InitialFilename* parameter specifies the filename that is placed in the "File name" text box on the Save As dialog. If this argument is omitted, Excel uses the name of the active workbook. The other parameters (and return values) are the same as for the GetOpenFilename method. As with GetOpenFilename, this method may change the current drive or folder.

RecentFiles property (Read-Only)

This property returns a RecentFiles collection that represents the list of recently used files. There are two interesting aspects to the RecentFiles collection. First, it has a Maximum property that returns or can be set to the maximum number of files allowed in the recently used files list that appears on Excel's File menu. This number must be an integer between 0 and 9, inclusive. Thus, the code:

```
MsgBox Application.RecentFiles.Maximum
```

displays the current value.

Second, we can print a list of the filenames of the most recently used files as follows (of course, you may want to do more than print this list):

```
Dim rf As RecentFile
For Each rf In Application.RecentFiles
    Debug.Print rf.Name
Next
```

Note that the RecentFiles collection contains RecentFile objects, and not simply the names of the recently used files, as one might expect.

SaveWorkspace method

This method saves the current workspace. Its syntax is:

```
Application.SaveWorkspace(Filename)
```

where *Filename* is an optional filename for the *xlw* file.

Members that Affect the Current State of Excel

The following members have an effect on the current settings of Excel:

CopyObjectsWithCells property (R/W Boolean)
When this property is **True**, objects (such as embedded controls or shapes) are cut, copied, extracted, and sorted along with cells.

Cursor property (R/W Long)
This property returns or sets the appearance of the mouse pointer. It can be one of the following **XlMousePointer** constants:

```
Enum XlMousePointer
    xlDefault = -4143
```

```
        xlNorthwestArrow = 1
        xlWait = 2
        xlIBeam = 3
End Enum
```

It is considered good programming practice to set the mouse pointer to **xlWait** if your code will take more than a second or so to complete. Of course, you will need to return the mouse pointer to its previous state when the procedure terminates. The proper way to do this is to save the original Cursor property value before changing it, so it can be reset to its original value.

CutCopyMode property (R/W Long)

This property returns or sets the status of Cut or Copy mode.

The CutCopyMode property can be set to either **True** or **False**. On the PC, these have the same effect (but differ on the Macintosh); namely, to cancel Cut or Copy mode and remove the moving border that surrounds the region to be cut or copied.

The CutCopyMode property can return **False**, indicating that Excel is in neither Cut nor Copy mode, or else one of the two values from the following enum:

```
Enum XlCutCopyMode
        xlCopy = 1              ' Copy mode
        xlCut = 2               ' Cut mode
End Enum
```

DataEntryMode property (R/W Long)

This property returns or sets Data Entry mode. When in Data Entry mode, data can be entered only in the cells in the currently selected range.

The property can assume any of the following constant values:

xlOn

> Data Entry mode is on.

xlOff

> Data Entry mode is off.

xlStrict

> Data Entry mode is on, and pressing Esc will not turn it off.

EditDirectlyInCell property (R/W Boolean)

When this property is **True** (which is its default value), Excel allows editing in cells. Otherwise, it does not allow editing in the cells (but you can still edit in the formula bar).

FixedDecimal property (R/W Boolean)

When this property is **True**, all numeric data entered will be formatted with the number of fixed decimal places set by the FixedDecimalPlaces property.

The default value of this property is **False**; the value of the FixedDecimal-Places property is ignored.

FixedDecimalPlaces property (R/W Long)

This property returns or sets the number of fixed decimal places used when the FixedDecimal property is set to **True**. For example, if the FixedDecimal-Property is **True** and FixedDecimalPlaces is set to 3, an entry of 100 in a cell will be displayed as 0.1.

Interactive property (R/W Boolean)

When this property is set to **False**, Excel will block all input from the keyboard and mouse *except* for input to dialog boxes that are displayed by code. This will prevent the user from interfering with the currently running macro. The default value of the Interactive property is **True**.

Of course, considerable care must be taken with this property. For instance, if you forget to reset the property to **True**, or if your code terminates unexpectedly, the user may need to restart Excel. Note that the Alt-F4 key combination will work to shut down Excel, but the user will not be able to save any work. Be careful with this one!

MoveAfterReturn property (R/W Boolean)

When this property is **True**, its default value, the active cell will be moved as soon as the Enter key is pressed. The MoveAfterReturnDirection property is used to specify the direction in which the active cell will be moved. If set to **False**, the active cell remains unchanged after the Enter key is pressed.

MoveAfterReturnDirection property (R/W Long)

This property returns or sets the direction in which the active cell is moved when the user presses Enter if the MoveAfterReturn property is set to **True**. It can assume any one of the following values:

```
Enum XlDirection
    xlUp = -4162
    xlToRight = -4161
    xlToLeft = -4159
    xlDown = -4121
End Enum
```

ReferenceStyle property (R/W Long)

This property returns or sets the style (A1 style or R1C1 style) in which Excel displays cell references and row and column headings. It can be one of the following **XlReferenceStyle** constants:

```
Enum XlReferenceStyle
    xlR1C1 = -4150
    xlA1 = 1
End Enum
```

ScreenUpdating property (R/W Boolean)

When this property is `True`, its default value, screen updating is turned on. Since this may slow down some display-intensive procedures considerably, you may want to temporarily turn off screen updating.

SheetsInNewWorkbook property (R/W Long)

This property returns or sets the number of sheets that Excel automatically inserts into new workbooks.

ShowChartTipNames property (R/W Boolean)

When this property is `True`, its default value, Excel charts show chart tip names.

ShowChartTipValues property (R/W Boolean)

When this property is `True`, its default value, Excel charts show chart tip values.

ShowToolTips property (R/W Boolean)

When this property is `True`, its default value, ToolTips are turned on.

StandardFont property (R/W String)

This property returns or sets the name of the standard font. Note that the change does not take effect until Excel is restarted.

StandardFontSize property (R/W Long)

This property returns or sets the standard font size, in points. The change does not take effect until Excel is restarted.

StartupPath property (Read-Only String)

This property returns the complete path of the startup folder, excluding the final separator.

TemplatesPath property (Read-Only String)

This property returns the path where templates are stored.

Members that Produce Actions

Several members of the Application object perform some sort of action.

ConvertFormula method

This method converts cell references in a formula between the A1 and R1C1 reference styles. It can also convert between relative and absolute references. Its syntax is:

```
Application.ConvertFormula(Formula, FromReferenceStyle, ToReferenceStyle, _
    ToAbsolute, RelativeTo)
```

The `Formula` parameter is a string containing the formula to convert. It must be a valid formula, beginning with an equal sign.

The *FromReferenceStyle* parameter must be one of the following constants:

```
Enum XlReferenceStyle
    xlR1C1 = -4150
    xlA1 = 1
End Enum
```

The optional *ToReferenceStyle* parameter is the reference style into which to convert the formula. It is also one of the **XlReferenceStyle** constants. If we omit this argument, the reference style is not changed.

The optional *ToAbsolute* parameter specifies the converted reference type and can be one of the following **XlReferenceType** constants:

```
Enum XlReferenceType
    xlAbsolute = 1
    xlAbsRowRelColumn = 2
    xlRelRowAbsColumn = 3
    xlRelative = 4
End Enum
```

If this argument is omitted, the reference type is not changed.

Finally, the optional *RelativeTo* parameter is a Range object containing a single cell. This cell is used to determine relative references.; that is, we can think of the formula as being placed in this cell and so all relative references are with respect to this cell.

To illustrate, consider the following code:

```
sFormula = "=D2"
Debug.Print Application.ConvertFormula(sFormula, _
    xlA1, xlR1C1, xlRelative, Range("C3"))
Debug.Print Application.ConvertFormula(sFormula, _
    xlA1, xlR1C1, xlRelRowAbsColumn, Range("C3"))
```

The second line converts from A1 notation to R1C1 notation, assuming that the formula is in cell C3. Hence, the output is:

```
= R[-1]C[1]
```

since D2 is one column to the right and one row up from cell C3. The third line of code converts A1 notation to R1C1 notation, but uses an absolute column reference and so produces:

```
= R[-1]C4
```

since column 4 is one column to the right of column 3.

Evaluate method

This method converts an Excel name to an object or a value. Its syntax is:

```
Application.Evaluate(Name)
```

(This method also applies to Chart, DialogSheet, and Worksheet objects).

The *Name* parameter is the name of the object. It can be any of the following types of name:

An A1-style reference

Name can be any A1-style reference to a *single* cell. The reference is considered to be absolute. To illustrate, consider the following code, each line of which purports to place the word Mary in cell A1:

```
Range("A1").Value = "Mary"
A1.Value = "Mary"
Evaluate("A1").Value = "Mary"
[A1].Value = "Mary"
```

The first line uses the Range method. The second line will produce an error because Excel considers A1 a variable rather than a cell reference. The third line uses the Evaluate method to convert the name of a cell to a Range object. The fourth line is shorthand for the third line.

A range

Name can be any range formed by using the range operator (colon), intersect operator (space), and union operator (comma) with references. The Evaluate method will return the corresponding Range object. To illustrate, consider the following code:

```
Evaluate("B2:C4").Select
Evaluate("B2:C4, D5:F6").Select
Evaluate("B2:C4 B1:F2").Select
[B2:C4 B1:F2].Select
```

The first line selects the range B2:C4. The second line selects the union of the two rectangular ranges B2:C4 and D5:F6. The third line selects the intersection of the two rectangular ranges B2:C4 B1:F2. The fourth line is shorthand for the third line.

A Defined Name

Name can be any defined name. For instance, if we name a range **test**, then the following code selects that range:

```
Evaluate("test").Select
```

(Incidentally, I have had some inconsistent results using the syntax [test]. Select. It seems to work some but not all of the time.) We can also use formula names. For instance, the following code displays the sum of the values in cells B2 through B5:

```
MsgBox Evaluate("SUM(B2:B5)")
```

Note that external references (references to other workbooks) can be used as well, as in:

```
Workbooks("BOOK2.XLS").Sheets("MySheet").Evaluate("A1").Select
```

As we have seen, using square brackets is equivalent to calling the Evaluate method with a string argument. Square brackets have the advantage of producing more concise code, but they cannot be used with string variables. For instance, we can write:

```
Dim sFormula As String
sFormula = "SUM(B2:B5)"
MsgBox Evaluate(sFormula)
```

But the code:

```
MsgBox [sFormula]
```

will simply display the string SUM(B2:B5), as it would without the square brackets.

Goto method

This method selects a given range in any workbook. (It can also select a Visual Basic procedure.) The syntax is:

```
Application.Goto(Reference, Scroll)
```

The optional **Reference** parameter specifies the destination. It can be a Range object, a string that contains a cell reference in R1C1-style notation, or a string that contains a Visual Basic procedure name. If the argument is omitted, the destination is the destination used in the previous call to GoTo.

The optional **Scroll** parameter should be set to **True** to scroll through the window so that the upper-left corner of the destination appears in the upper-left corner of the window. The default is **False**, which means the destination will not move if it was visible within the window, or else it will appear at the bottom of the window if it was not visible.

For example, to select the range B5:C6 in the active worksheet, we can write:

```
Application.Goto Reference:=Range("B5:C6")
```

or:

```
Application.Goto Reference:="R5C2:R6C3"
```

The GoTo method also works in conjunction with the PreviousSelections array. In particular, the Application object has a PreviousSelections property that returns an array of Range objects referencing the previous four ranges selected. The syntax is:

```
Application.PreviousSelections(Index)
```

where **Index** is a number between 1 and 4.

Each time the user selects a range or cell either by using the Name box or the Go To command (on the Edit menu), or the Goto method is called in code, the current range (before the action takes place) is added to the top (index 1) of the PreviousSelections array and the other items in the array are moved down one index value. (The item in position 4, of course, drops out of the array.)

As a simple illustration, consider the code:

```
Application.Goto Sheet1.Range("A1")
ActiveCell.Value = 1
Application.Goto Sheet2.Range("A1")
ActiveCell.Value = 2
```

which fills the first cell on each of two sheets, using the GoTo method to add the cell ranges to the PreviousSelections array.

Now the following line will alternate between the two cells when executed repeatedly:

```
Application.Goto Application.PreviousSelections(1)
```

Note that the GoTo method differs from the Select method in several ways:

- Both methods select the given range, but the Select method does not activate the sheet upon which the new selection is made (if it is not already active).

- The Select method does not have a *Scroll* argument.

- The Select method does not add the current selection to the PreviousSelections array.

- The Select method has a *Replace* argument.

Quit method

This method closes Excel. Note that the BeforeClose event will fire when the *Quit* method is executed. (This event has a *Cancel* parameter that can be set to cancel the quit operation.) We discussed workbook events (including BeforeClose) in Chapter 11, *Excel Events*.

Note that if there are any unsaved open workbooks when the Quit method is invoked, Excel will display the usual dialog box asking the user whether he or she wants to save the changes. We can prevent this either by explicitly saving all workbooks (using the Save method) before invoking the Quit method, or by setting the DisplayAlerts property to **False**. However, in the latter case, any unsaved data will be lost without warning!

It is also important to note that Excel checks the Saved property of a workbook in order to determine whether to prompt for saving. Thus, if we set the Saved property to **True** but do not save the workbook, Excel will quit without prompting to save the workbook (and without saving the workbook).

Miscellaneous Members

Here are some additional members of the Application object.

InputBox method

We have already discussed the VBA *InputBox* function, which is used to return input from the user. The InputBox method of the Application object also returns user information, but has the advantage of being able to validate the return type and to return Excel formulas, objects, and error values.

The syntax for the *InputBox method* is:

```
Application.InputBox(Prompt, Title, Default, _
    Left, Top, HelpFile, HelpContextId, Type)
```

The parameters are as follows (note that all of the parameters are optional except the *Prompt* parameter):

Prompt
> The message to be displayed in the dialog box; it can be a string, number, date, or Boolean value.

Title
> The caption for the dialog box. The default caption is Input.

Default
> The value that will appear in the text box when the dialog box is displayed. If this argument is omitted, the text box will be empty.

Left and Top
> The upper-left corner of the dialog box in points, measured from the upper-left corner of the screen.

HelpFile and HelpContextID
> The name of the Help file and the context ID for a help topic to invoke when the user hits the Help button on the input box. If these arguments are omitted, then no Help button is included on the input box dialog.

Type
> The data type that can be entered into the text box by the user (and thus the return type of the method). It can be one or *a sum of* the values in Table 16-5. When the value is a sum of several numbers, then any of the corresponding data types is acceptable. It follows that formulas are *always* acceptable. The default value is 2 for Text.

Table 16-5. Values for the InputBox Method's Type Parameter

Value	Meaning
0	A formula
1	A number
2	Text (a string)
4	A logical value (True or False)
8	A reference to a single cell
16	An error value, such as #N/A
64	An array of values

Unfortunately, the type checking done by the InputBox method does not seem to be very accurate. To illustrate, the InputBox statement:

```
Range("A1").Value = Application.InputBox( _
    Prompt:="Enter data", Type:=0)
```

should accept only formulas and not text. However, entering the text "test" simply puts this text in cell A1. (The help documentation does say that when *Type* is 0, InputBox returns the formula as text and any references in the formula are returned as A1-style references.)

Note that when *Type* is equal to 8, the InputBox method returns a Range object that refers to the cell in the reference. Therefore, we must use the **Set** statement to assign this object to a variable of type Range, as in:

```
Dim rng as Variant
Set rng = Application.InputBox( _
    Prompt:="Enter Cell Reference", Type:=8)
```

If we omit the **Set** statement, the variable is set to the value in the range, rather than the Range object itself. (If we had declared the *rng* variable to be of type Range, then the preceding code, without the **Set** statement, would result in the error message, "Object variable or With block variable not set.")

When *Type* is equal to 64, the user is expected to enter a rectangular cell range that will be treated as a two-dimensional array. For instance, consider a worksheet as shown in Figure 16-3.

The code:

```
Dim a As Variant
a = Application.InputBox( _
    Prompt:="Enter Array", Type:=64)
Debug.Print a(3,2)
```

will accept the input:

```
A1:B6
```

	A	B
1	4	34
2	5	45
3	23	56
4	14	57
5	55	78
6	67	687

Figure 16-3. Illustration of Type = 64

after which a(3,2) will equal 56.

As a final example, if we respond to the code:

```
Dim a As Variant
a = Application.InputBox( Prompt:="Enter Formula", Type:=1)
Range("D1").Formula = a
```

with a formula, Excel does not put the formula in the cell D1 (it puts only the number), even though 1 is a sum of 1 and 0. In other words, we shouldn't take the sum statement too literally.

Selection property

This property simply returns the currently selected object in the active window. For instance, if a cell is selected, the property returns a Range object denoting this cell. The Selection property returns **Nothing** if nothing is selected. Note that the property also applies to a Window object and returns the current selection in that window.

StatusBar property (R/W String)

This useful property returns or sets the text in Excel's status bar. To return control of the status bar to Excel, simply set this property to **False**. (Similarly, this property will return **False** if Excel currently has control over the status bar.)

Intersect method

This method returns a Range object that represents the rectangular intersection of two or more ranges. The syntax is:

```
Application.Intersect(Arg1, Arg2, ...)
```

where *Arg1*, *Arg2*, . . . are the Range objects whose ranges we wish to intersect. At least two *Range* objects must be specified. For instance, the following line selects the intersection, which is the range B2:D5:

```
Application.Intersect(Range("A1:D5"), Range("B2:F9")).Select
```

Union method

This method is the analog of the Intersect method, but returns the union of two or more ranges. The syntax is:

```
Application.Union(Arg1, Arg2, ...)
```

where *Arg1*, *Arg2*, . . . are the Range objects whose ranges we wish to join together. At least two Range objects must be specified. For instance, the following code selects both rectangular regions A1:D5 and B2:F9:

```
Application.Union(Range("A1:D5"), Range("B2:F9")).Select
```

Children of the Application Object

Figure 16-4 shows the children of the Application object. (This repeats Figure 16-1.)

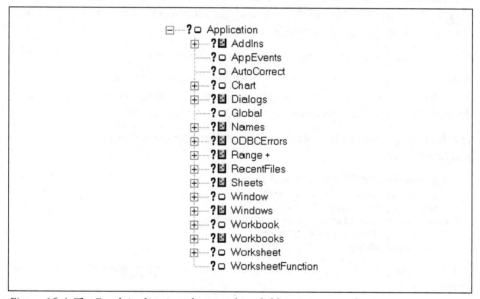

Figure 16-4. The Excel Application object and its children

We will discuss many of the children of the Application object, including App-Events, Chart, Range, Sheets, Workbook, and Worksheet, in later chapters. (We have already discussed the Dialogs object.) For now, let us discuss some of the "smaller" children.

Name Objects and the Names Collections

A Name object represents a defined name for a range of cells. There are two types of names in Excel: built-in names such as `Print_Area` and custom names created by the user or by code.

Name objects are kept in several Names collections. There is a Names collection for the Application object, as well as Names collections for each Workbook and Worksheet object.

There are a variety of ways to create a new Name object. We can add a Name object to a Names collection by calling the collection's Add method, or we can use the CreateNames method of the Range object (discussed in Chapter 19, *The Range Object*).

For instance, the following code creates a Name object that refers to a range on Sheet1 of Book1. The Name object is added to the workbook's Names collection, but not to Sheet1's Names collection:

```
Workbooks("Book1.xls").Names.Add Name:="WkBkName" RefersTo:="=Sheet1!$A$1:$B$1"
```

Note the use of a sheet qualifier in the *RefersTo* parameter and the specification of an absolute address. If the absolute operator ($) is not used, the range will be defined relative to the active cell.

The following code adds a Name object to the Names collection of both Sheet1 and Sheet2:

```
Workbooks("Book1.xls").Worksheets("Sheet1") _
  .Names.Add Name:="WkSheet1Name", _
  RefersTo:="=Sheet1!$A$1:$B$1"
Workbooks("Book1.xls").Worksheets("Sheet2"). _
  Names.Add Name:="WkSheet2Name", _
  RefersTo:="=Sheet2!$A$1:$B$1"
```

Note that this code will also add the Name objects to the workbook's Names collection.

The following code sets the font for the range `WkSheet1Name` to boldface:

```
Sheet1.Names("WkSheet1Name").RefersToRange.Font.Bold = True
```

Note that there is no Names collection for a given Range object, even though a Range object can have more than one name. The best we can do is retrieve the first name for a range object by using the Name property (see the discussion in Chapter 19).

Let us review some of the properties and methods of the Name object:

Delete method

The Delete method, whose syntax is:

```
NameObject.Delete
```

deletes the Name object from the Names collections in which it resides. It does *not* delete the actual range.

Name property

This property returns or sets the name of the Name object.

RefersTo property

This property returns or sets the formula that defines a named range, in A1-style notation, beginning with an equal sign.

RefersToR1C1 property

This property returns or sets the formula that defines a named range, in R1C1-style notation, beginning with an equal sign.

RefersToRange property

This property returns the Range object referred to by the named range. It is read-only. (See the previous example code.)

Value property

This property also returns or sets the formula that defines a named range, in A1-style notation, beginning with an equal sign. Thus, it is equivalent to the RefersTo property.

Visible property

This property returns or sets the visibility of the named range.

The Windows Collection and Window Objects

Of course, a Window object represents an Excel window. The Windows collection of the Application object is the collection of Window objects for all currently open windows in the currently running version of Excel. (Similarly, the Windows collection for a Workbook object contains only the windows in the workbook.)

The Arrange method of the Windows collection is used to arrange the current windows. The syntax is:

```
WindowsObject.Arrange(ArrangeStyle, _
    ActiveWorkbook, SyncHorizontal, SyncVertical)
```

The optional **ArrangeStyle** parameter can be one of the following **XlArrangeStyle** constants:

```
Enum XlArrangeStyle
    xlArrangeStyleVertical = -4166
    xlArrangeStyleHorizontal = -4128
    xlArrangeStyleTiled = 1                ' Default
```

```
        xlArrangeStyleCascade = 7
End Enum
```

We can set the *ActiveWorkbook* parameter to **True** to arrange only the visible windows of the active workbook. The default value is **False**, in which case all windows are arranged.

When *ActiveWorkbook* is True, the remaining parameters are evaluated (otherwise they are ignored). *SyncHorizontal* can be set to **True** to synchronize the horizontal scrolling windows of the active workbook. In other words, all windows scroll at the same time when one window is scrolled horizontally. The default value is False. Similarly, the *SyncVertical* parameter specifies vertical scrolling synchronization. Thus, the following code tiles the visible windows and enables horizontal scrolling synchronization:

```
ActiveWorkbook.Windows.Arrange _
    ArrangeStyle:=xlArrangeStyleTiled, _
    SyncHorizontal:=True
```

To create a new window, we use the NewWindow method of the Workbook object, as in:

```
ThisWorkbook.NewWindow
```

in which case a copy of the active window is created. This method also applies to an existing Window object and creates a copy of the window to which it is applied.

The *Windows* collection has a special property with respect to indexing, namely, the active window is always:

```
Windows(1)
```

The 58 members of the Window object are shown in Table 16-6.

Table 16-6. Members of the Window Object

Activate	EnableResize	SmallScroll
ActivateNext	FreezePanes	Split
ActivatePrevious	GridlineColor	SplitColumn
ActiveCell	GridlineColorIndex	SplitHorizontal
ActiveChart	Height	SplitRow
ActivePane	Index	SplitVertical
ActiveSheet	LargeScroll	TabRatio
Application	Left	Top
Caption	NewWindow	Type
Close	OnWindow	UsableHeight
Creator	Panes	UsableWidth

Table 16-6. Members of the Window Object (continued)

DisplayFormulas	Parent	View
DisplayGridlines	PrintOut	Visible
DisplayHeadings	PrintPreview	VisibleRange
DisplayHorizontalScrollBar	RangeSelection	Width
DisplayOutline	ScrollColumn	WindowNumber
DisplayRightToLeft	ScrollRow	WindowState
DisplayVerticalScrollBar	ScrollWorkbookTabs	Zoom
DisplayWorkbookTabs	SelectedSheets	
DisplayZeros	Selection	

The WorksheetFunction Object

The WorksheetFunction object is returned by the WorksheetFunction property of the Application object. The sole purpose of the WorksheetFunction object is to provide access to Excel's worksheet functions. For instance, the following code illustrates the use of the WorksheetFunction object to access Excel's *Min* function:

```
Dim rng As Range
Dim rMin As Single
Set rng = Worksheets("Sheet1").Range("A1:D10")
rMin = Application.WorksheetFunction.Min(rng)
```

17

The Workbook Object

In this chapter we discuss the Workbook object and the Workbooks collection. Figure 17-1 shows that portion of the Excel object model that relates directly to workbooks.

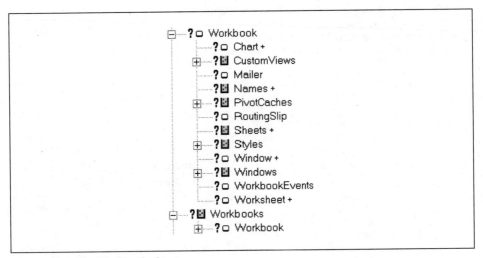

Figure 17-1. The Workbook object

The Workbooks Collection

The Application object has a Workbooks property that returns a Workbooks collection, which contains all of the Workbook objects for the currently open instance of Excel. For instance, the following code displays the number of open workbooks:

```
Dim wbs As Workbooks
```

```
Set wbs = Application.Workbooks
MsgBox wbs.Count
```

Let us look at a few of the properties and methods of the Workbooks collection.

Add Method

The Add method is used to create a new workbook, which is then added to the Workbooks collection. The new workbook becomes the active workbook. The syntax is:

```
WorkbooksObject.Add(Template)
```

where the optional *Template* parameter determines how the new workbook is created. If this argument is a string specifying the name of an existing Excel template file, the new workbook is created with that file as a template.

As you may know, a template is an Excel workbook that may contain content (such as row and column labels), formatting, and macros and other customizations (menus and toolbars for instance). When you base a new workbook on a template, the new workbook receives the content, formatting, and customization from the template.

The *Template* argument can also be one of the following constants:

```
Enum XlWBATemplate
    xlWBATWorksheet = -4167
    xlWBATChart = -4109
    xlWBATExcel4MacroSheet = 3
    xlWBATExcel4IntlMacroSheet = 4
End Enum
```

In this case, the new workbook will contain a single sheet of the specified type. If the *Template* argument is omitted, Excel will create a new workbook with the number of blank sheets set by the Application object's SheetsInNewWorkbook property.

Close Method

The Close method closes all open workbooks. The syntax is simply:

```
WorksbooksObject.Close
```

Count Property

Most collection objects have a Count property, and the Workbooks collection is no exception. This property simply returns the number of currently open workbooks.

Item Property

The Item property returns a particular workbook in the Workbooks collection. For instance:

```
Workbooks.Item(1)
```

returns the Workbook object associated with the first workbook in the Workbooks collection. Since the Item property is the default property, we can also write this as:

```
Workbooks(1)
```

Note that we cannot rely on the fact that a certain workbook will have a certain index. (This applies to all collections.) Thus, to refer to a particular workbook, you should always use its name, as in:

```
Workbooks("Book1.xls")
```

It is important to note that if a user creates a new workbook named, say Book2, using the New menu item on the File menu, then we may refer to this workbook in code by writing:

```
Workbooks("Book2")
```

but the code:

```
Workbooks("Book2.xls")
```

will generate an error (subscript out of range) until the workbook is actually saved to disk.

Open Method

This method opens an existing workbook. The rather complex syntax is:

```
WorkbooksObject.Open(FileName, UpdateLinks, ReadOnly, _
    Format, Password, WriteResPassword, IgnoreReadOnlyRecommended, _
    Origin, Delimiter, Editable, Notify, Converter, AddToMRU)
```

Most of these parameters are rarely used (several of them relate to opening text files, for instance). We discuss the most commonly used parameters and refer the reader to the help files for more information. Note that all of the parameters are optional except *FileName*.

FileName is the file name of the workbook to be opened. To open the workbook in read-only mode, set the *ReadOnly* parameter to **True**.

If a password is required to open the workbook, the *Password* parameter should be set to this password. If a password is required but you do not specify the password, Excel will ask for it.

The *AddToMru* parameter should be set to **True** to add this workbook to the list of recently used files. The default value is **False**.

OpenText Method

This method will load a text file as a new workbook. The method will parse the text data and place it in a single worksheet. The rather complex syntax is:

```
WorkbooksObject.OpenText(Filename, Origin, StartRow, _
    DataType, TextQualifier, ConsecutiveDelimiter, Tab, _
    Semicolon, Comma, Space, Other, OtherChar, FieldInfo)
```

We note first that all of the parameters to this method are optional except the *FileName* parameter.

The *Filename* parameter specifies the filename of the text file to be opened.

The *Origin* parameter specifies the origin of the text file and can be one of the following XlPlatform constants:

```
Enum XlPlatform
    xlMacintosh = 1
    xlWindows = 2
    xlMSDOS = 3
End Enum
```

Note that the **xlWindows** value specifies an ANSI text file, whereas the **xlMSDOS** constant specifies an ASCII file. If this argument is omitted, the current setting of the File Origin option in the Text Import Wizard will be used.

The *StartRow* parameter specifies the row number at which to start parsing text from the text file. The default value is 1.

The optional *DataType* parameter specifies the format of the text in the file and can be one of the following XlTextParsingType constants:

```
Enum XlTextParsingType
    xlDelimited = 1          ' Default
    xlFixedWidth = 2
End Enum
```

The *TextQualifier* parameter is the text qualifier. It can be one of the following XlTextQualifier constants:

```
Enum XlTextQualifier
    xlTextQualifierNone = -4142
    xlTextQualifierDoubleQuote = 1    ' Default
    xlTextQualifierSingleQuote = 2
End Enum
```

The *ConsecutiveDelimiter* parameter should be set to **True** to have Excel consider consecutive delimiters as one delimiter. The default value is **False**.

There are several parameters that require that *DataType* be xlDelimited. When any one of these parameters is set to True, it indicates that Excel should use the corresponding character as the text delimiter. They are described here (all default values are False):

Tab

Set to True to use the tab character as the delimiter.

Semicolon

Set to True to use a semicolon as the delimiter.

Comma

Set to True to use a comma as the delimiter.

Space

Set to True to use a space as the delimiter.

Other

Set to True to use a character that is specified by the *OtherChar* argument as the delimiter.

When *Other* is True, *OtherChar* specifies the delimiter character. If *OtherChar* contains more than one character, only the first character is used.

The *FieldInfo* parameter is an array containing parse information for the individual source columns. The interpretation of *FieldInfo* depends on the value of *DataType*.

When *DataType* is xlDelimited, the *FieldInfo* argument should be an array whose size is the same as or smaller than the number of columns of converted data. The first element of a two-element array is the column number (starting with the number 1), and the second element is one of the following numbers that specifies how the column is parsed:

Value	Description
1	General
2	Text
3	MDY date
4	DMY date
5	YMD date
6	MYD date
7	DYM date
8	YDM date
9	Skip the column

If a two-element array for a given column is missing, then the column is parsed with the General setting. For instance, the following value for *FieldInfo* causes the first column to be parsed as text and the third column to be skipped:

```
Array(Array(1, 2), Array(3, 9))
```

All other columns will be parsed as general data.

To illustrate, consider a text file with the following contents:

```
"John","Smith","Serial Record",1/2/98
"Fred","Gwynn","Serials Order Dept",2/2/98
"Mary","Davis","English Dept",3/5/98
"David","Johns","Chemistry Dept",4/4/98
```

The code:

```
Workbooks.OpenText _
  FileName:="d:\excel\temp.txt", _
  Origin:=xlMSDOS, _
  StartRow:=1, _
  DataType:=xlDelimited, _
  TextQualifier:=xlTextQualifierDoubleQuote, _
  ConsecutiveDelimiter:=True, _
  Comma:=True, _
  FieldInfo:=Array(Array(1, 2), _
    Array(2, 2), Array(3, 2), Array(4, 6))
```

produces the worksheet shown in Figure 17-2. Note that the cells in column D are formatted as dates.

	A	B	C	D
1	John	Smith	Serial Record	1/2/98
2	Fred	Gwynn	Serials Order Dept	2/2/98
3	Mary	Davis	English Dept	3/5/98
4	David	Johns	Chemistry Dept	4/4/98

Figure 17-2. A comma-delimited text file opened in Excel

On the other hand, if *DataType* is xlFixedWidth, the first element of each two-element array specifies the starting character position in the column (0 being the first character) and the second element specifies the parse option (1–9) for the resulting column, as described earlier.

To illustrate, consider the text file whose contents are as follows:

```
0-125-689
2-523-489
3-424-664
4-125-160
```

The code:

```
Workbooks.OpenText _
   FileName:="d:\excel\temp.txt", _
   Origin:=xlMSDOS, _
   StartRow:=1, _
   DataType:=xlFixedWidth, _
   FieldInfo:=Array(Array(0, 2), _
      Array(1, 9), Array(2, 2), Array(5, 9), _
      Array(6, 2))
```

produces the worksheet in Figure 17-3. (Note how we included arrays to skip the hyphens.)

	A	B	C
1	0	125	689
2	2	523	489
3	3	424	664
4	4	125	160

Figure 17-3. A fixed-width text file opened in Excel

Finally, it is important to observe that the text file is opened in Excel, but not converted to an Excel workbook file. To do so, we can invoke the SaveAs method, as in:

```
Application.ActiveSheet.SaveAs _
   FileName:="d:\excel\temp.xls", _
   FileFormat:=xlWorkbookNormal
```

The Workbook Object

A Workbook object represents an open Excel workbook. As we have discussed, Workbook objects are stored in a Workbooks collection.

The Workbook object has a total of 103 properties and methods, as shown in Table 17-1.

Table 17-1. Members of the Workbook Object

AcceptAllChanges	FullName	RefreshAll
AcceptLabelsInFormulas	HasPassword	RejectAllChanges
Activate	HasRoutingSlip	RemoveUser
ActiveChart	HighlightChangesOnScreen	Reply
ActiveSheet	HighlightChangesOptions	ReplyAll
ActiveSheet	IsAddin	ResetColors

Table 17-1. Members of the Workbook Object (continued)

AddToFavorites	IsInplace	RevisionNumber
Application	KeepChangeHistory	Route
AutoUpdateFrequency	LinkInfo	Routed
AutoUpdateSaveChanges	LinkSources	RoutingSlip
BuiltinDocumentProperties	ListChangesOnNewSheet	RunAutoMacros
ChangeFileAccess	Mailer	Save
ChangeHistoryDuration	MergeWorkbook	SaveAs
ChangeLink	MultiUserEditing	SaveCopyAs
Charts	Name	Saved
Close	Names	SaveLinkValues
CodeName	NewWindow	SendMail
Colors	OpenLinks	SendMailer
CommandBars	Parent	SetLinkOnData
ConflictResolution	Path	Sheets
Container	PersonalViewListSettings	ShowConflictHistory
CreateBackup	PersonalViewPrintSettings	Styles
Creator	PivotCaches	TemplateRemoveExtData
CustomDocumentProperties	Post	Unprotect
CustomViews	PrecisionAsDisplayed	UnprotectSharing
Date1904	PrintOut	UpdateFromFile
DeleteNumberFormat	PrintPreview	UpdateLink
DisplayDrawingObjects	Protect	UpdateRemoteReferences
Excel4IntlMacroSheets	ProtectSharing	UserStatus
Excel4MacroSheets	ProtectStructure	VBProject
ExclusiveAccess	ProtectWindows	Windows
FileFormat	PurgeChangeHistoryNow	Worksheets
FollowHyperlink	ReadOnly	WriteReserved
ForwardMailer	ReadOnlyRecommended	WriteReservedBy

Several of the members listed in Table 17-1 exist solely to return the children of the Workbook object. The children are shown in Figure 17-4.

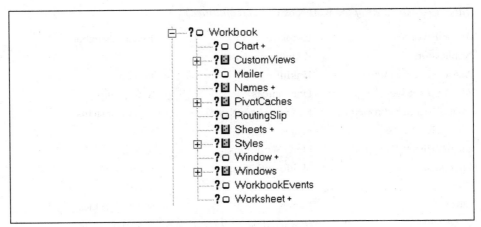

Figure 17-4. Children of the Workbook object

Table 17-2 gives the members of the Workbook object that return children.

Table 17-2. Members of Workbook that Return Objects

Name	ReturnType
ActiveChart	Chart
ActiveSheet	Chart
ActiveSheet	Worksheet
Application	Application
BuiltinDocumentProperties	DocumentProperties
Charts	Sheets
CommandBars	CommandBars
CustomDocumentProperties	DocumentProperties
CustomViews	CustomViews
DialogSheets	Sheets
Excel4IntlMacroSheets	Sheets
Excel4MacroSheets	Sheets
Mailer	Mailer
Names	Names
NewWindow	Window
PivotCaches	PivotCaches
RoutingSlip	RoutingSlip
Sheets	Sheets
Styles	Styles
VBProject	VBProject
Windows	Windows
Worksheets	Sheets

There are a few items worth noting about Table 17-2. First, the ActiveSheet property may return either a Chart object or a Worksheet object, depending upon what type of object is currently active.

Second, the Charts, Sheets, and Worksheets properties all return a (different) Sheets collection. In particular, the Charts object returns the Sheets collection that contains all of the chart sheets in the workbook. (This does not include charts that are embedded in worksheets.) The Worksheets property returns the Sheets collection of all worksheets in the workbook. Finally, the Sheets property returns the Sheets collection of all worksheets and chart sheets. This is a relatively rare example of a collection that contains objects of more than one type. Note that there is no Sheet object in the Excel object model.

Let us look at a few of the more commonly used members from Table 17-1.

Activate Method

This method activates the workbook. The syntax is straightforward, as in:

```
Workbooks("MyWorkBook").Activate
```

Note that Workbooks is global, so we do not need to qualify it with the `Application` keyword.

Close Method

The Close method closes the workbook. Its syntax is:

```
WorkbookObject.Close(SaveChanges, FileName, RouteWorkbook)
```

Note that the Close method of the Workbook object has three parameters, unlike the Close method of the Workbooks object, which has none.

The optional *SaveChanges* parameter is used to save changes to the workbook before closing. In particular, if there are no changes to the workbook, the argument is ignored. It is also ignored if the workbook appears in other open windows. On the other hand, if there are changes to the workbook and it does not appear in any other open windows, the argument takes effect.

In this case, if *SaveChanges* is `True`, the changes are saved. If there is not yet a filename associated with the workbook (that is, if it has not been previously saved), then the name given in *FileName* is used. If *FileName* is also omitted, Excel will prompt the user for a filename. If *SaveChanges* is `False`, changes are not saved. Finally, if the *SaveChanges* argument is omitted, Excel will display a dialog box asking whether the changes should be saved. In short, this method behaves as you would hope.

The optional *RouteWorkbook* refers to routing issues; we refer the interested reader to the Excel VBA help file for more information.

It is important to note that the Close method checks the Saved property of the workbook in order to determine whether or not to prompt the user to save changes. If we set the Saved property to **True**, then the Close method will simply close the workbook with no warning and without saving any unsaved changes.

DisplayDrawingObjects Property

This property returns or sets a value indicating how shapes are displayed. It can be one of the following **XlDisplayShapes** constants:

```
Enum XlDisplayShapes
    XlDisplayShapes = -4104
    xlPlaceholders = 2
    xlHide = 3
End Enum
```

FileFormat Property (Read-Only Long)

This property returns the file format or type of the workbook. It can be one of the following **XlFileFormat** constants:

```
Enum XlFileFormat
    xlCurrentPlatformText = -4158
    xlWorkbookNormal = -4143            ' the default
    xlSYLK = 2
    xlWKS = 4
    xlWK1 = 5
    xlCSV = 6
    xlDBF2 = 7
    xlDBF3 = 8
    xlDIF = 9
    xlDBF4 = 11
    xlWJ2WD1 = 14
    xlWK3 = 15
    xlExcel2 = 16
    xlTemplate = 17
    xlAddIn = 18
    xlTextMac = 19
    xlTextWindows = 20
    xlTextMSDOS = 21
    xlCSVMac = 22
    xlCSVWindows = 23
    xlCSVMSDOS = 24
    xlIntlMacro = 25
    xlIntlAddIn = 26
    xlExcel2FarEast = 27
    xlWorks2FarEast = 28
    xlExcel3 = 29
```

```
              xlWK1FMT = 30
              xlWK1ALL = 31
              xlWK3FM3 = 32
              xlExcel4 = 33
              xlWQ1 = 34
              xlExcel4Workbook = 35
              xlTextPrinter = 36
              xlWK4 = 38
              xlExcel7 = 39
              xlExcel5 = 39
              xlWJ3 = 40
              xlWJ3FJ3 = 41
              xlUnicodeText = 42        ' new for Excel 9
              xlExcel9795 = 43
              xlHTML = 44               ' new for Excel 9
       End Enum
```

Name, FullName, and Path Properties

The Name property returns the name of the workbook, the Path property returns the path to the workbook file, and FullName returns the fully qualified (path and filename) of the workbook file. All of these properties are read-only.

Note that using the Path property without a qualifier is equivalent to:

```
    Application.Path
```

and thus returns the path to Excel itself (rather than to a workbook).

HasPassword Property (Read-Only Boolean)

This read-only property is **True** if the workbook has password protection. Note that a password can be assigned as one of the parameters to the SaveAs method.

PrecisionAsDisplayed Property (R/W Boolean)

When this property is **True**, calculations in the workbook will be done using only the precision of the numbers as they are displayed, rather than as they are stored. Its default value is **False**; calculations are based on the values of numbers as they are stored.

PrintOut Method

The PrintOut method prints an entire workbook. (This method applies to a host of other objects as well, such as Range, Worksheet, and Chart.) The syntax is:

```
    WorkbookObject.PrintOut(From, To, Copies, _
        Preview, ActivePrinter, PrintToFile, Collate)
```

Note that all of the parameters to this method are optional.

The *From* parameter specifies the page number of the first page to print, and the *To* parameter specifies the last page to print. If omitted, the entire object (range, worksheet, etc.) is printed.

The *Copies* parameter specifies the number of copies to print. The default is 1.

Set *Preview* to **True** to invoke print preview rather than printing immediately. The default is **False**.

ActivePrinter sets the name of the active printer. On the other hand, setting *PrintToFile* to True causes Excel to print to a file. Excel will prompt the user for the name of the output file. (Unfortunately, there is no way to specify the name of the output file in code.)

The *Collate* parameter should be set to **True** to collate multiple multipage copies.

PrintPreview Method

This method invokes Excel's print preview feature. Its syntax is:

```
WorkbookObject.PrintPreview
```

Note that the PrintPreview method applies to the same set of objects as the Print-Out method.

Protect Method

This method protects a workbook so that it cannot be modified. Its syntax is:

```
WorkbookObject.Protect(Password, Structure, Windows)
```

The method also applies to charts and worksheets, with a different syntax.

The optional *Password* parameter specifies a password (as a case-sensitive string). If this argument is omitted, the workbook will not require a password in order to unprotect it.

Set the optional *Structure* parameter to **True** to protect the structure of the workbook—that is, the relative position of the sheets in the workbook. The default value is **False**.

Set the optional *Windows* parameter to **True** to protect the workbook windows. The default is **False**.

ReadOnly Property (Read-Only Boolean)

This property is **True** if the workbook has been opened as read-only.

RefreshAll Method

This method refreshes all external data ranges and pivot tables in the workbook. The syntax is:

```
WorkbookObject.RefreshAll
```

Save Method

This method simply saves any changes to the workbook. Its syntax is:

```
WorkbookObject.Save
```

SaveAs Method

This method saves changes to a workbook in the specified file. The syntax is:

```
expression.SaveAs(Filename, FileFormat, Password, WriteResPassword, _
    ReadOnlyRecommended, CreateBackup, AccessMode, ConflictResolution, _
    AddToMru, TextCodePage, TextVisualLayout)
```

The *Filename* parameter specifies the filename to use for the newly saved disk file. If a path is not included, Excel will use the current folder.

The *FileFormat* parameter specifies the file format to use when saving the file. Its value is one of the **XlFileFormat** constants described in our discussion of the FileFormat property.

The *Password* parameter specifies the password to use when saving the file and can be set to any case-sensitive string of up to 15 characters.

The *WriteResPassword* is a string that specifies the write-reservation password for this file. If a file is saved with a write-reservation password and this password is not supplied when the file is next opened, the file will be opened as read-only.

We can set the *ReadOnlyRecommended* parameter to **True** to display a message when the file is opened, recommending that the file be opened as read-only.

Set the *CreateBackup* parameter to **True** to create a backup file.

The *AccessMode* and *ConflictResolution* parameters refer to sharing issues. We refer the interested reader to the Excel VBA help file for details.

Set the *AddToMru* parameter to **True** to add the workbook to the list of recently used files. The default value is **False**.

The remaining parameters are not used in the U.S. English version of Excel.

SaveCopyAs Method

This method saves a copy of the workbook to a file but does not modify the open workbook itself. The syntax is:

```
WorkbookObject.SaveCopyAs(Filename)
```

where *Filename* specifies the filename for the copy of the original file.

Saved Property (R/W Boolean)

This property is **True** if no changes have been made to the specified workbook since it was last saved. Note that this property is read/write, which means we can set the property to **True** even if the workbook has been changed since it was last saved. As discussed earlier, we can set this property to **True**, then close a modified workbook without being prompted to save the current changes.

Children of the Workbook Object

Figure 17-5 shows the children of the *Workbook* object. (This is a repeat of Figure 17-4.)

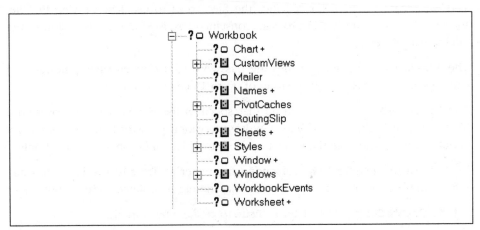

Figure 17-5. Children of the Workbook object

Let us take a quick look at some of these children. (We will discuss the Window, Worksheet, and WorkbookEvents objects later in the book.)

The CustomView Object

The CustomViews property returns the CustomViews collection. Each CustomView object in this collection represents a custom view of the workbook. CustomView objects are pretty straightforward, so we will just consider an example. Look at the sheet shown in Figure 17-6.

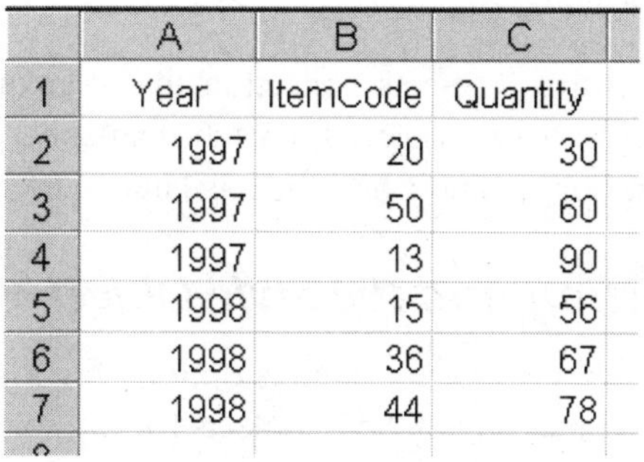

	A	B	C
1	Year	ItemCode	Quantity
2	1997	20	30
3	1997	50	60
4	1997	13	90
5	1998	15	56
6	1998	36	67
7	1998	44	78

Figure 17-6. Example of the CustomView object

Now suppose we use the Autofilter command to filter on the year, as shown in Figure 17-7.

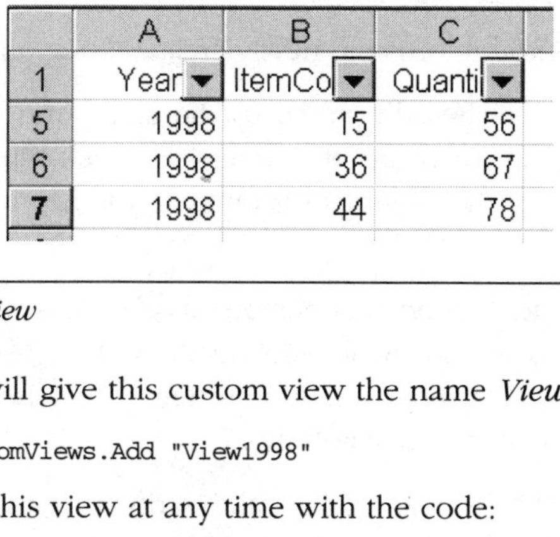

	A	B	C
1	Year ▼	ItemCo ▼	Quanti ▼
5	1998	15	56
6	1998	36	67
7	1998	44	78

Figure 17-7. A filtered view

The following code will give this custom view the name *View1998*:

```
ThisWorkbook.CustomViews.Add "View1998"
```

Now we can display this view at any time with the code:

```
ThisWorkbook.CustomViews!View1998.Show
```

or:

```
strView = "View1998"
ActiveWorkbook.CustomViews(strView).Show
```

The Names Collection

As with the Application object, the Workbook object has a Names property that returns a Names collection. This collection represents the Name objects associated with the workbook. For details on Name objects, see Chapter 16, *The Application Object.*

The Sheets Collection

The Sheets property returns a Sheets collection that contains a Worksheet object for each worksheet and a Chart object for each chartsheet in the workbook. We will discuss Worksheet objects and Chart objects later in the book.

The Styles Collection and the Style Object

A Style object represents a set of formatting options for a range. Each workbook has a Styles collection containing all Style objects for the workbook.

To apply a style to a range, we simply write:

```
RangeObject.Style = StyleName
```

where *StyleName* is the name of a style.

To create a Style object, use the Add method, whose syntax is:

```
WorkbookObject.Add(Name, BasedOn)
```

Note that the Add method returns the newly created Style object.

The *Name* parameter specifies the name of the style, and the optional *BasedOn* parameter specifies a Range object that refers to a cell whose style is used as a basis for the new style. If this argument is omitted, the newly created style is based on the Normal style.

Note that, according to the documentation, if a style with the specified name already exists, the Add method will redefine the existing style based on the cell specified in *BasedOn*. (However, on my system, Excel issues an error message instead, so you should check this carefully.)

The properties of the Style object reflect the various formatting features, such as font name, font size, number format, alignment, and so on. There are also several built-in styles, such as Normal, Currency, and Percent. These built-in styles can be found in the Style name box of the Style dialog box (under the Format menu).

To illustrate, the following code creates a style and then applies it to an arbitrary range of the current worksheet:

```
Dim st As Style
' Delete style if it exists
For Each st In ActiveWorkbook.Styles
   If st.Name = "Bordered" Then st.Delete
Next
' Create style
```

```
With ActiveWorkbook.Styles.Add(Name:="Bordered")
   .Borders(xlTop).LineStyle = xlDouble
   .Borders(xlBottom).LineStyle = xlDouble
   .Borders(xlLeft).LineStyle = xlDouble
   .Borders(xlRight).LineStyle = xlDouble
   .Font.Bold = True
   .Font.Name = "arial"
   .Font.Size = 36
End With
' Apply style
Application.ActiveSheet.Range("A1:B3").Style = "Bordered"
```

Example: Sorting Sheets in a Workbook

Let us add a new utility to our SRXUtils application. If you work with workbooks that contain many sheets (worksheets and chartsheets), then you may want to sort the sheets in alphabetical order.

The basis for the code to order the sheets is the Move method of the Worksheet and Chart objects. Its syntax is:

```
SheetsObject.Move(Before, After)
```

Of course, to use this method effectively, we need a sorted list of sheet names.

The first step is to augment the DataSheet worksheet for SRXUtils by adding a new row for the new utility, as shown in Figure 17-8. (The order of the rows in this DataSheet is based on the order in which we want the items to appear in the custom menu.)

	A	B	C	D	E	F	G	H
1	Utility	OnAction Proc	Procedure	In Workbook	Menu Item	SubMenu Item	On Wks Menu	On Chart Menu
2	Activate Sheet	RunUtility	ActivateSheet	ThisWorkbook	&Activate Sheet		TRUE	TRUE
3	Print Charts	RunUtility	PrintCharts	Print.utl	&Print	Embedded &Charts	TRUE	TRUE
4	Print Pivot Tables	RunUtility	PrintPivotTables	Print.utl		&Pivot Tables	TRUE	TRUE
5	Print Sheets	RunUtility	PrintSheets	Print.utl		&Sheets	TRUE	TRUE
6	Sort Sheets	RunUtility	SortSheets	ThisWorkbook	&Sort Sheets	·	TRUE	TRUE

Figure 17-8. Augmenting the DataSheet worksheet

Next, we insert a new code module called **basSortSheets**, which will contain the code to implement this utility.

We shall include two procedures in **basSortSheets**. The first procedure verifies that the user really wants to sort the sheets. If so, it calls the second procedure, which does the work. The first procedure is shown in Example 17-1. It displays the dialog box shown in Figure 17-8.

Example 17-1. The SortSheets Procedure

```
Sub SortSheets()
  If MsgBox("Sort the sheets in this workbook?", _
  vbOKCancel + vbQuestion, "Sort Sheets") = vbOK Then
    SortAllSheets
  End If
End Sub
```

The action takes place in the procedure shown in Example 17-2. The procedure first collects the sheet names in an array, then places the array in a new worksheet. It then uses the Sort method (applied to a Range object, discussed in Chapter 19) to sort the names. Then it refills the array and finally reorders the sheets using the Move method.

Example 17-2. The SortAllSheets Procedure

```
Sub SortAllSheets()

' Sort worksheets
Dim wb As Workbook
Dim ws As Worksheet
Dim rng As Range
Dim cSheets As Integer
Dim sSheets() As String
Dim i As Integer

Set wb = ActiveWorkbook

' Get true dimension for array
cSheets = wb.Sheets.Count
ReDim sSheets(1 To cSheets)

' Fill array with worksheet names
For i = 1 To cSheets
  sSheets(i) = wb.Sheets(i).Name
Next

' Create new sheet and put names in first column
Set ws = wb.Worksheets.Add
For i = 1 To cSheets
  ws.Cells(i, 1).Value = sSheets(i)
Next

' Sort column
ws.Columns(1).Sort Key1:=ws.Columns(1), _
  Order1:=xlAscending

' Refill array
For i = 1 To cSheets
  sSheets(i) = ws.Cells(i, 1).Value
Next

' Delete extraneous sheet
```

Example 17-2. The SortAllSheets Procedure (continued)

```
Application.DisplayAlerts = False
ws.Delete
Application.DisplayAlerts = True

' Reorder sheets by moving each one to the end
For i = 1 To cSheets
  wb.Sheets(sSheets(i)).Move After:=wb.Sheets(cSheets)
Next

End Sub
```

Once the code is inserted, you can save the *SRXUtils.xls* workbook as an add-in. Don't forget to unload the add-in first, or Excel will complain.

18

The Worksheet Object

A Worksheet object represents an Excel worksheet. Figure 18-1 shows that portion of the Excel object model that relates directly to worksheets.

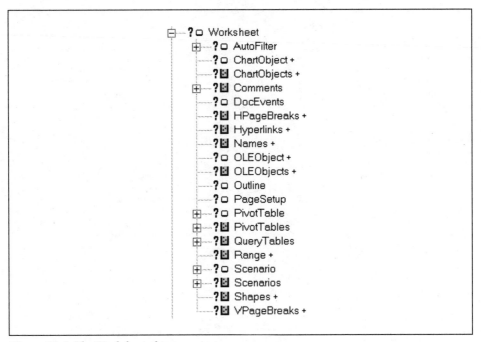

Figure 18-1. The Worksheet object

Properties and Methods of the Worksheet Object

Table 18-1 shows the members of the Worksheet object.

Table 18-1. Members of the Worksheet Object

Activate	EnableOutlining	Protect
Application	EnablePivotTable	ProtectContents
AutoFilter	EnableSelection	ProtectDrawingObjects
AutoFilterMode	Evaluate	ProtectionMode
Calculate	FilterMode	ProtectScenarios
Cells	HPageBreaks	QueryTables
ChartObjects	Hyperlinks	Range
CheckSpelling	Index	ResetAllPageBreaks
CircleInvalid	Move	SaveAs
CircularReference	Name	Scenarios
ClearArrows	Names	ScrollArea
ClearCircles	Next	Select
CodeName	OLEObjects	SetBackgroundPicture
Comments	Outline	Shapes
ConsolidationFunction	PageSetup	ShowAllData
ConsolidationOptions	Parent	ShowDataForm
ConsolidationSources	Paste	StandardHeight
Copy	PasteSpecial	StandardWidth
Creator	PivotTables	Type
Delete	PivotTableWizard	Unprotect
DisplayPageBreaks	Previous	UsedRange
EnableAutoFilter	PrintOut	Visible
EnableCalculation	PrintPreview	VPageBreaks

Many of the members in Table 18-1 exist solely to return the children of the *Worksheet* object. These members and their return types are shown in Table 18-2.

Table 18-2. Members that Return Objects

Name	ReturnType
Application	Application
AutoFilter	AutoFilter
Cells	Range
ChartObjects	ChartObject(s)

Table 18-2. Members that Return Objects (continued)

Name	ReturnType
CircularReference	Range
Columns	Range
Comments	Comments
HPageBreaks	HPageBreaks
Hyperlinks	Hyperlinks
Names	Names
OLEObjects	OLEObject(s)
Outline	Outline
PageSetup	PageSetup
PivotTables	PivotTable(s)
PivotTableWizard	PivotTable
QueryTables	QueryTables
Range	Range
Rows	Range
Scenarios	Scenario(s)
Shapes	Shapes
UsedRange	Range
VPageBreaks	VPageBreaks

Let us discuss some of the members in Table 18-1.

Activate method

This method activates the worksheet, as in:

```
ThisWorkbook.Worksheets("Sheet1").Activate
```

AutoFilterMode property

This property is **True** if the AutoFilter drop-down arrows are currently displayed on the worksheet. (Also see the FilterMode property, discussed later in this section). Note that we can set this property to **False** to remove the arrows, but we cannot set it to **True**. To display the AutoFilter arrows, we use the AutoFilter method, which is discussed in Chapter 19, *The Range Object*.

Calculate method

This method calculates all cells in the worksheet. (Note that the method applies to workbooks and specific ranges as well.) The syntax is simply:

```
WorksheetObject.Calculate
```

CodeName property

This property returns the code name for the worksheet (it also applies to workbook and chart objects). The code name can be used in place of any expression that returns the worksheet. The code name can also be set in the

Properties window. It is referred to as (name) to distinguish it from the Name property.

To illustrate, suppose that we have a worksheet whose code name is Sheet-CodeName and whose name is SheetName. Then the following are equivalent:

```
Worksheets("SheetName").Activate
SheetCodeName.Activate
```

Note that when we first create a worksheet, the name and code name are the same. The two names can then be changed independently. However, the code name can be changed only at design time; it cannot be changed with code at run time.

Copy method

The Copy method has multiple syntaxes. To copy a worksheet, we use the syntax:

```
WorksheetObject.Copy(Before, After)
```

where the optional *Before* parameter is the sheet before which the copied sheet will be placed and the *After* parameter is the sheet after which the copied sheet will be placed. (Only one of *Before* or *After* is allowed at one time.)

Note that if neither *Before* nor *After* is specified, Excel will copy the worksheet to a new workbook.

To illustrate, the following code copies the active worksheet and places the copy at the end of the list of current worksheets:

```
ActiveSheet.Copy After:=Worksheets(Worksheets.Count)
```

Delete method

This method simply deletes the worksheet. The syntax is:

```
WorksheetObject.Delete
```

EnableCalculation property (R/W Boolean)

When this property is **True**, Excel automatically recalculates the worksheet when necessary. Otherwise, the user must request a recalculation. Note that when this property is first set to **True**, Excel will do a recalculation.

Evaluate method

The Evaluate method converts an Excel name to an object or a value. We discussed the details of this method in Chapter 16, *The Application Object*.

FilterMode property (Read-Only Boolean)

This property is **True** if the worksheet is in filter mode. Thus, for instance, if the AutoFilter arrows are displayed but no filtering has taken place, then Auto-FilterMode is **True** whereas FilterMode is **False**. Once filtering is actually performed, then FilterMode is **True**. Put another way, the FilterMode property indicates whether there are hidden rows due to filtering.

Move method

The Move method moves the worksheet to another location in the workbook. The syntax is:

```
WorksheetObject.Move(Before, After)
```

where the parameters have the same meaning as in the Copy method, discussed earlier in this section.

Name property (R/W String)

This property returns or sets the name of the worksheet, as a string.

Names property

This property returns the Names collection representing all the worksheet-specific names. For more on Name objects, see Chapter 16.

PasteSpecial method

This method pastes the contents of the Clipboard onto the worksheet, using a specified format. The most commonly used syntax is simply:

```
WorksheetObject.PasteSpecial(Format)
```

where *Format* specifies the format of the data to paste, as a string. For instance, the following code pastes data in Word document format (assuming that it exists on the Clipboard):

```
ActiveSheet.PasteSpecial "Microsoft Word Document"
```

To learn the syntax of other *Format* strings, you can copy the desired object and then check Excel's Paste Special dialog box.

Note that we must select the destination range before using the PasteSpecial method.

PrintOut method

The PrintOut method prints a worksheet. (The method also applies to Workbook and Range objects.) The syntax is:

```
WorksheetObject.PrintOut(From, To, Copies, _
    Preview, ActivePrinter, PrintToFile, Collate)
```

Note that all of the parameters to this method are optional.

The *From* parameter specifies the page number of the first page to print, and the To parameter specifies the last page to print. If omitted, the entire object (range, worksheet, etc.) is printed.

The *Copies* parameter specifies the number of copies to print. The default is 1.

Set *Preview* to **True** to invoke print preview rather than printing immediately. The default is **False**.

ActivePrinter sets the name of the active printer.

Setting *PrintToFile* to **True** causes Excel to print to a file. Excel will prompt the user for the name of the output file. (Unfortunately, there is no way to specify the name of the output file in code.)

The *Collate* parameter should be set to **True** to collate multiple multipage copies.

PrintPreview method

This method invokes Excel's print preview feature for the worksheet. Its syntax is:

```
WorksheetObject.PrintPreview
```

Protect method

This method protects a worksheet from modification. Its syntax is:

```
WorksheetObject.Protect(Password, DrawingObjects, _
    Contents, Scenarios, UserInterfaceOnly)
```

(Note that the syntax varies from the same method of the Workbook object.)

The optional *Password* parameter is a string that specifies a case-sensitive password for the worksheet.

The optional *DrawingObjects* parameter should be set to **True** to protect shapes. The default value is **False**.

The optional *Contents* parameter should be set to **True**, the default, to protect the cells in the worksheet.

The optional *Scenarios* parameter should be set to **True**, the default, to protect scenarios.

The *Protect* method allows independent protection of cells from changes by the user and by code. In particular, if *UserInterfaceOnly* is set to **True**, then the user cannot make changes to the worksheet, but changes can be made through code. On the other hand, if *UserInterfaceOnly* is **False** (the default), then neither the user nor the programmer can alter the worksheet. Note that it is not the macros themselves that are protected, as the help documentation seems to indicate. Rather, the worksheet is protected from the *effect* of the macros.

Note also that if the *UserInterfaceOnly* argument is set to **True** when protecting a worksheet and then the workbook is saved, the entire worksheet (not just the interface) will be protected when the workbook is reopened. To unprotect the worksheet but reenable user interface protection, we must reapply the Protect method with *UserInterfaceOnly* set to **True**.

ProtectionMode property (Read-Only)

This property is **True** if user-interface-only protection is turned on (via the Protect method). Its default value is **False**.

SaveAs method

This method saves changes to the worksheet in a different file. Its syntax is:

```
WorksheetObject.SaveAs(Filename, FileFormat, Password, _
    WriteResPassword, ReadOnlyRecommended, CreateBackup, _
    AddToMru, TextCodePage, TextVisualLayout)
```

The *Filename* parameter specifies the filename to use for the newly saved disk file. If a path is not included, Excel will use the current folder.

The *FileFormat* parameter specifies the file format to use when saving the file. Its value is one of the **XlFileFormat** constants described in our discussion of the FileFormat property in Chapter 17, *The Workbook Object.*

The *Password* parameter specifies the password to use when saving the file and can be set to any case-sensitive string of up to 15 characters.

The *WriteResPassword* parameter is a string that specifies the write-reservation password for this file. If a file is saved with a write-reservation password and this password is not supplied when the file is next opened, the file will be opened as read-only.

We can set the *ReadOnlyRecommended* parameter to **True** to display a message when the file is opened, recommending that the file be opened as read-only.

Set the *CreateBackup* parameter to **True** to create a backup file.

Set the *AddToMru* parameter to **True** to add the workbook to the list of recently used files. The default value is **False**.

The remaining parameters are not used in the U.S. English version of Excel.

ScrollArea property

This property returns or sets the range where scrolling and cell selection is allowed. The value should be an A1-style range reference. For instance, the code:

```
ActiveSheet.ScrollArea = "A1:B200"
```

allows cell selection and scrolling only within the range A1:B200. To remove any restrictions on cell selection and scrolling, set this property to an empty string, as in:

```
ActiveSheet.ScrollArea = ""
```

Note that setting the scroll area has nothing to do with freezing panes.

Select method

This method selects the worksheet. This is not the same as making it active through the Activate method. In fact, several sheets can be selected at one time (to delete them, for instance). The syntax is:

```
WorksheetObject.Select(Replace)
```

where *Replace* is set to *True* to replace the current selection with the specified worksheet, rather than including the worksheet in the current selection.

SetBackgroundPicture method

This method sets the background graphic for a worksheet (or chart). The syntax is:

```
WorksheetObject.SetBackgroundPicture(FileName)
```

where *FileName* is the name of the graphic file to use for the background.

ShowDataForm method

This method displays the data form associated with the worksheet. Note that in order for the ShowDataForm method to work without generating an error, Excel must be able to determine that the current selection is part of a list. For information on the use of data forms, see the Excel 8 help topic "Guidelines for creating a list on a worksheet" or the Excel 9 help topic "About data forms."

The syntax of this method is simply:

```
WorksheetObject.ShowDataForm
```

Note that the procedure in which the ShowDataForm method is called will pause while the data form is displayed. When the data form is closed, the procedure will resume at the line following the call to ShowDataForm. (In other words, the data form is *modal*.)

Figure 18-2 illustrates the data form for a worksheet.

Unprotect method

This method removes protection from a worksheet. It has no effect if the worksheet is not protected. The syntax is:

```
WorksheetObject.Unprotect(Password)
```

where *Password* is the password used to protect the worksheet (if any). If we omit this argument for a sheet that is password-protected, Excel will prompt the user for the password.

UsedRange property

This ostensibly very useful property returns a Range object that represents the smallest rectangular region that encompasses any currently used cells.

Unfortunately, the UsedRange property has had a rather rocky history in past versions of Excel, and my experience is that the problems have not been completely resolved in Excel 97. (Unfortunately, I know of no single test to check the reliability of this property, and I have not yet used Excel 9 long enough to make a definitive statement about this version.) Thus, I strongly suggest that you use this method with caution, for it sometimes seems to include cells that once had contents but have since been completely cleared.

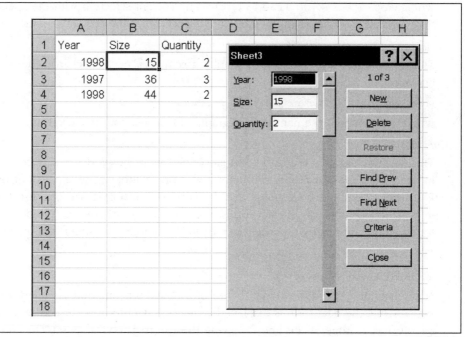

Figure 18-2. A data form

At the end of Chapter 19 we will give an example function that can be used to compute the correct used range.

Visible property

This property returns **True** if the worksheet is visible and **False** otherwise. However, in addition to setting this property to **True** or **False**, we can also set this property to **xlVeryHidden**, in which case the only way to make the worksheet visible is by setting this property to **True** in code. Hence, the user cannot make the worksheet visible.

Children of the Worksheet Object

Let us discuss a few of the children of the Worksheet object. Others will be discussed in later chapters.

Comments

The Comments property returns the Comments collection, which consists of all Comment objects (comments) in the worksheet. We will discuss the Comment object in Chapter 19.

The Names collection

We discussed the Names collection and Name objects in Chapter 16, and so we refer the reader to that earlier discussion.

The Outline object

To illustrate Excel outlining using code, consider the worksheet shown in Figure 18-3. Our goal is to produce the outline in Figure 18-4.

	A	B	C	D
1		Col1	Col2	Col3
2	Row1	78	33	23
3	Row2	123	22	222
4	Row3	231	34	345
5	SubTotal1	432	89	590
6				
7	Row4	223	23	454
8	Row5	345	10	53
9	Row6	11	13	4
10	SubTotal2	579	46	511
11				
12	Total	1011	135	1101

Figure 18-3. Illustrating Excel outlines

1 2 3		A	B	C	D
	1		Col1	Col2	Col3
	2	Row1	78	33	23
	3	Row2	123	22	222
	4	Row3	231	34	345
	5	SubTotal1	432	89	590
	6				
	7	Row4	223	23	454
	8	Row5	345	10	53
	9	Row6	11	13	4
	10	SubTotal2	579	46	511
	11				
	12	Total	1011	135	1101

Figure 18-4. The end result

The first step in obtaining the outline in Figure 18-4 is to set the properties of the Outline object for this worksheet. The Outline property of the Worksheet object returns an Outline object, so we begin with:

```
With ActiveSheet.Outline
   .SummaryRow = xlBelow
   .AutomaticStyles = False
End With
```

Setting the SummaryRow property to `xlBelow` tells Excel that our summary rows (the subtotal and total rows) lie below the detailed data. Thus, Excel will place the expansion/contraction buttons (the small buttons displaying minus signs in Figure 18-4) at the appropriate rows.

Setting AutomaticStyles to `False` prevents Excel from tampering with our formatting. Otherwise, Excel would remove the boldfacing on the summary rows.

As you can see in Figure 18-4, we want to make the following groupings:

```
Rows 2-4
Rows 7-9
Rows 2-11
```

For this, we use the Group method of the Range object. In particular, the following code accomplishes the desired grouping, resulting in Figure 18-4:

```
With ActiveSheet
  .Rows("2:4").Group
  .Rows("7:9").Group
  .Rows("2:11").Group
End With
```

Note that the SummaryColumn property of the Outline object governs the location of the expansion/contraction buttons when columns grouped.

To expand or collapse levels, the user can click the small numbered buttons at the top of the leftmost column in Figure 18-4. Clicking on button number *X* results in all levels above *X* being completely expanded and all levels below and including *X* completely contracted. Thus, all rows at level *X* and above are made visible, but no levels below *X* are visible.

The same thing can be accomplished using the *ShowLevels* method of the *Outline* object, whose syntax is:

```
OutlineObject.ShowLevels(RowLevels, ColumnLevels)
```

For instance, the code:

```
ActiveSheet.Outline.ShowLevels 2
```

is equivalent to clicking on the button labeled 2 and has the effect of showing all levels above and including level 2, as pictured in Figure 18-5.

The PageSetup object

The PageSetup object represents the page formatting (such as margins and paper size) of an Excel worksheet. Each of the page-formatting options is set by setting a corresponding property of the *PageSetup* object.

The PageSetup property of the *Worksheet* object returns the worksheet's PageSetup object.

The properties and methods of the PageSetup object are shown in Table 18-3. (All of the items in Table 18-3 are properties except the PrintQuality method.)

1 2 3		A	B	C	D
	1		Col1	Col2	Col3
+	5	**SubTotal1**	**432**	**89**	**590**
·	6				
+	10	**SubTotal2**	**579**	**46**	**511**
·	11				
−	12	**Total**	**1011**	**135**	**1101**

Figure 18-5. Outline collapsed to level 2

Most of the members in Table 18-3 are self-explanatory (and hold no real surprises), so we will not discuss them.

Table 18-3. Members of the PageSetup Object

Application	FitToPagesWide	PrintGridlines
BlackAndWhite	FooterMargin	PrintHeadings
BottomMargin	HeaderMargin	PrintNotes
CenterFooter	LeftFooter	PrintQuality
CenterHeader	LeftHeader	PrintTitleColumns
CenterHorizontally	LeftMargin	PrintTitleRows
CenterVertically	Order	RightFooter
ChartSize	Orientation	RightHeader
Creator	PaperSize	RightMargin
Draft	Parent	TopMargin
FirstPageNumber	PrintArea	Zoom
FitToPagesTall	PrintComments	

To illustrate, the following code sets some of the properties of the active worksheet:

```
With ActiveSheet.PageSetup
  .LeftMargin = Application.InchesToPoints(1)
  .RightMargin = Application.InchesToPoints(1)
  .PrintTitleRows = "A1"
  .PaperSize = xlPaperLetter
End With
```

Note the use of the *InchesToPoints* function, which is required if we want to express units in inches, since most of the formatting properties require measurement in points. Referring to Figure 18-6, the PrintTitleRows property will cause the word Report, which lies in cell A1, to appear on each page of the printout.

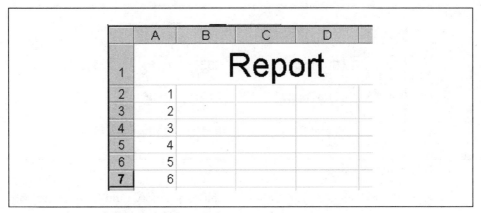

Figure 18-6. A worksheet and the PrintTitleRows property

Example: Printing Sheets

We can now implement the PrintSheets feature of our *SRXUtils* application. Recall that at the present time, this Print utility, located in the *Print.utl* add-in, simply displays a message box. To implement this feature, we want the utility to first display a dialog box, as shown in Figure 18-7. The list box contains a list of all sheets in the active workbook. The user can select one or more sheets and hit the Print button to print these sheets.

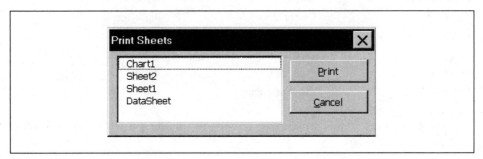

Figure 18-7. Print sheets dialog

The steps to create the print utility are as follows: All the action takes place in the *Print.xls* workbook, so open this workbook. When the changes are finished, you will need to save *Print.xls* as *Print.utl* as well. If *Print.utl* is loaded, the only way to unload it is to unload the add-in *SRXUtils.xla* (if it is loaded) and close the workbook *SRXUtils.xls* (if it is open).

Create the UserForm

Create the dialog shown in Figure 18-7 in the *Print.xls* workbook. Name the dialog *dlgPrintSheets* and set its Caption property to "Print Sheets." Then change the *PrintSheets* procedure to:

```
Public Sub PrintSheets()
   dlgPrintSheets.Show
End Sub
```

The *dlgPrintSheets* dialog has two command buttons and one list box:

```
dlgPrintSheets.Show
```

List box

Place a list box on the form as in Figure 18-7. Using the Properties window, set the properties shown in Table 18-4.

Table 18-4. Nondefault Properties of the List Box

Property	Value
Name	lstSheets
TabIndex	0
MultiSelect	frmMultiSelectExtended

When the Cancel property of the *cmdCancel* button is set to **True**, the button is "clicked" when the user hits the Escape key. Thus, the Escape key will dismiss the print dialog.

The MultiSelect property is set to **frmMultiSelectExtended** so that the user can use the Control key to select multiple (possibly nonconsecutive) entries and the shift key to select multiple consecutive entries.

The TabIndex property determines not only the order in which the controls are visited as the user hits the Tab key, but also determines which control has the initial focus. Since we want the initial focus to be on the list box, we set its tab index to 0.

Print button

Place a command button on the form as in Figure 18-7. Using the Properties window, set the properties shown in Table 18-5.

Table 18-5. Nondefault Properties of the Print Button

Property	Value
Name	cmdPrint
Accelerator	P

Table 18-5. Nondefault Properties of the Print Button (continued)

Property	Value
Caption	Print
TabIndex	1

Cancel button

Place another command button on the form as in Figure 18-7. Using the Properties window, set the properties shown in Table 18-6.

Table 18-6. Nondefault Properties of the Cancel Button

Property	Value
Name	cmdCancel
Accelerator	C
Caption	Cancel
TabIndex	2
Cancel	True

Create the Code Behind the UserForm

Now it is time to create the code behind these controls.

The Declarations section

The Declarations section of the *dlgPrintSheets* UserForm should contain declarations of the module-level variables, as shown in Example 18-1.

Example 18-1. Module-Level Variable Declarations

```
Option Explicit
Dim cSheets As Integer
Dim sSheetNames() As String
```

Cancel button code

The Cancel button code is shown in Example 18-2.

Example 18-2. The cmdCancel_Click Event Handler

```
Private Sub cmdCancel_Click()
    Unload Me
End Sub
```

Print button code

The Print button calls the main print procedure and then unloads the form; its source code is shown in Example 18-3.

Example 18-3. The cmdPrint_Click Event Handler

```
Private Sub cmdPrint_Click()
PrintSelectedSheets
Unload Me
End Sub
```

The Form's Initialize event

The Initialize event of the UserForm is the place to fill the list box with a list of sheets. Our application uses a module-level array, *sSheetNames*, to hold the sheet names and a module-level integer variable, *cSheets*, to hold the sheet count; both were defined in Example 18-1. We fill these variables in the Initialize event and then use the array to fill the list, as Example 18-4 shows. The variables are used again in the main print procedure, which is why we have declared them at the module level.

Note the use of the `ReDim` statement to redimension the arrays. This is necessary since we do not know at the outset how many sheets there are in the workbook.

Example 18-4. The UserForm's Initialize Event Procedure

```
Private Sub UserForm_Initialize()

Dim ws As Object        'Worksheet
ReDim sSheetNames(1 To 10)

lstSheets.Clear
cSheets = 0
For Each ws In ActiveWorkbook.Sheets

  cSheets = cSheets + 1

  ' Redimension arrays if necessary
  If UBound(sSheetNames) < cSheets Then
    ReDim Preserve sSheetNames(1 To cSheets + 5)
  End If

  ' Save name of sheet
  sSheetNames(cSheets) = ws.Name

  ' Add sheet name to list box
  lstSheets.AddItem sSheetNames(cSheets)

Next
End Sub
```

The PrintSheets procedure

The main printing procedure is shown in Example 18-5. Note that we have been careful to deal with two special cases. First, there may not be any sheets in the workbook. Second, the user may hit the Print button without selecting any sheets in the list box.

It is important to note also that list boxes are 0-based, meaning that the first item is item 0. However, our arrays are 1-based (the first item is item 1), so we must take this into account when we move from a selection to an array member; to wit: selection i corresponds to array index $i+1$.

Example 18-5. The PrintSelectedSheets Procedure

```
Sub PrintSelectedSheets()

Dim i As Integer
Dim bNoneSelected As Boolean

bNoneSelected = True

If cSheets = 0 Then
  MsgBox "No sheets in this workbook.", vbExclamation
  Exit Sub
Else
  For i = 0 To lstSheets.ListCount - 1
    If lstSheets.Selected(i) Then
      bNoneSelected = False
      ' List box is 0-based, arrays are 1-based
      ActiveWorkbook.Sheets(sSheetNames(i + 1)).PrintOut
    End If
  Next
End If

If bNoneSelected Then
  MsgBox "No sheets have been selected from the list box.", vbExclamation
End If

End Sub
```

The Range Object

The Range object is one of the workhorse objects in the Excel object model. Simply put, in order to work with a portion of an Excel worksheet, we generally need to first identify that portion as a Range object.

As Microsoft puts it, a Range object "Represents a cell, a row, a column, a selection of cells containing one or more contiguous blocks of cells, or a 3-D range."

Table 19-1 shows the 158 members of the Range object.

Table 19-1. Members of the Range Object[a]

Activate*	EntireColumn*	Parse*
AddComment*	EntireRow*	PasteSpecial*
AddIndent	FillDown*	Phonetic
Address*	FillLeft*	PivotField
AddressLocal	FillRight*	PivotItem
AdvancedFilter	FillUp*	PivotTable
Application	Find*	Precedents*
ApplyNames	FindNext*	PrefixCharacter
ApplyOutlineStyles	FindPrevious*	Previous*
Areas	Font	PrintOut*
AutoComplete	FormatConditions	PrintPreview*
AutoFill*	Formula*	QueryTable
AutoFilter	FormulaArray*	Range*
AutoFit*	FormulaHidden*	ReadingOrder
AutoFormat*	FormulaLabel	RemoveSubtotal
AutoOutline	FormulaLocal	Replace*
BorderAround*	FormulaR1C1*	Resize

Table 19-1. Members of the Range Object[a] (continued)

Borders	FormulaR1C1Local	Row*
Calculate*	FunctionWizard	RowDifferences*
Cells*	GoalSeek	RowHeight*
Characters	Group	Rows*
CheckSpelling	HasArray	Run
Clear*	HasFormula*	Select*
ClearComments	Height*	Show
ClearContents*	Hidden	ShowDependents
ClearFormats*	HorizontalAlignment*	ShowDetail
ClearNotes	Hyperlinks	ShowErrors
ClearOutline	IndentLevel*	ShowPrecedents
Column*	Insert*	ShrinkToFit*
ColumnDifferences*	InsertIndent*	Sort*
Columns*	Interior	SortSpecial
ColumnWidth*	Item	SoundNote
Comment	Justify	SpecialCells*
Consolidate*	Left*	Style
Copy*	ListHeaderRows	SubscribeTo
CopyFromRecordset*	ListNames	Subtotal
CopyPicture	LocationInTable	Summary
Count	Locked*	Table
CreateNames*	Merge*	Text
CreatePublisher	MergeArea*	TextToColumns*
Creator	MergeCells*	Top*
CurrentArray	Name	Ungroup
CurrentRegion*	NavigateArrow	UnMerge*
Cut*	NewEnum	UseStandardHeight
DataSeries	Next*	UseStandardWidth
Default	NoteText	Validation
Delete*	NumberFormat*	Value*
Dependents*	NumberFormatLocal	Value2
DialogBox	Offset*	VerticalAlignment
DirectDependents*	Orientation	Width*
DirectPrecedents*	OutlineLevel	Worksheet
EditionOptions	PageBreak	WrapText*
End*	Parent	

[a] Items marked with an asterisk (*) are discussed in the text.

Our plan in this chapter is to first explore ways of defining Range objects. Then we will discuss many of the properties and methods of this object, as indicated in Table 19-1. As we have mentioned, our goal is not to cover all aspects of the Excel object model, but to cover the main portions of the model and to provide you with a sufficient foundation so that you can pick up whatever else you may need by using the help system.

The Range Object as a Collection

The Range object is rather unusual in that it often acts like a collection object as well as a noncollection object. For instance, it has an Item method and a Count property. On the other hand, the Range object has many more noncollection-type members than is typical of collection objects. In particular, the average member count among all other collection objects is 19, whereas the Range object has 158 members.

Indeed, the Range object should be thought of as a collection object that can hold other Range objects. To illustrate, consider the following code:

```
Dim rng as Range
Set rng = Range("A1", "C5").Cells
MsgBox rng.Count                     ' displays 15
Set rng = Range("A1", "C5").Rows
MsgBox rng.Count                     ' displays 5
Set rng = Range("A1", "C5").Columns
MsgBox rng.Count                     ' displays 3
```

In this code, we alternately set *rng* to the collection of all cells, rows, and columns of the range A1:C5. In each case, *MsgBox* reports the correct number of items in the collection. Note that the Excel model does not have a cell, row, or column object. Rather, these objects are Range objects; that is, the members of *rng* are Range objects.

When we do not specify the member type, a Range object acts like a collection of cells. To illustrate, observe that the code:

```
Dim rng As Range
Set rng = Range("A1", "C5")
MsgBox rng.Count
MsgBox rng(6).Value       ' row-major order
```

displays the number of cells in the range and then the value of cell 6 in that range (counted in row-major order; that is, starting with the first row and counting from left to right). Also, the code:

```
Dim rng As Range
Dim oCell As Range
Set rng = Range("A1", "C5")
For Each oCell In rng
```

```
    Debug.Print oCell.Value
Next
```

will cycle through each cell in the range *rng*, printing cell values in the Immediate window.

Defining a Range Object

As witness to the importance of the Range object, there are a total of 113 members (properties and methods) throughout the Excel object model that return a Range object. This number drops to 51 if we count only *distinct* member names, as shown in Table 19-2. (For instance, BottomRightCell is a property of 21 different objects, as is TopLeftCell.)

Table 19-2. Excel members that return a Range object

ActiveCell	DirectPrecedents	Previous
BottomRightCell	End	Range
Cells	EntireColumn	RangeSelection
ChangingCells	EntireRow	RefersToRange
CircularReference	Find	Resize
ColumnDifferences	FindNext	ResultRange
ColumnRange	FindPrevious	RowDifferences
Columns	Intersect	RowRange
CurrentArray	Item	Rows
CurrentRegion	LabelRange	SourceRange
DataBodyRange	Location	SpecialCells
DataLabelRange	MergeArea	TableRange1
DataRange	Next	TableRange2
Default	Offset	TopLeftCell
Dependents	PageRange	Union
Destination	PageRangeCells	UsedRange
DirectDependents	Precedents	VisibleRange

Let us take a look at some of the more prominent ways to define a Range object.

Range Property

The Range property applies to the Application, Range, and Worksheet objects. Note that:

```
Application.Range
```

is equivalent to:

```
ActiveSheet.Range
```

When Range is used without qualification within the code module of a worksheet, then it is applied to that sheet. When Range is used without qualification in a code module for a workbook, then it applies to the active worksheet in that workbook.

Thus, for example, if the following code appears in the code module for Sheet2:

```
Worksheets(1).Activate
Range("D1").Value = "test"
```

then its execution first activates Sheet1, but still places the word "test" in cell D1 of Sheet2. Because this makes code difficult to read, I suggest that you always qualify your use of the Range property.

The Range property has two distinct syntaxes. The first syntax is:

```
object.Range(Name)
```

where *Name* is the name of the range. It must be an A1-style reference and can include the range operator (a colon), the intersection operator (a space), or the union operator (a comma). Any dollar signs in *Name* are ignored. We can also use the name of a named range.

To illustrate, here are some examples:

```
Range("A2")
Range("A2:B3")
Range("A2:F3 A1:D5")     ' An intersection
Range("A2:F3, A1:D5")    ' A union
```

Of course, we can use the ConvertFormula method to convert a formula from R1C1 style to A1 style before applying the Range property, as in:

```
Range(Application.ConvertFormula("R2C5:R6C9", xlR1C1, xlA1))
```

Finally, if **TestRange** is the name of a range, then we may write:

```
Range(Application.Names("TestRange"))
```

or:

```
Range(Application.Names!TestRange)
```

to return this range.

The second syntax for the Range property is:

```
object.Range(Cell1, Cell2)
```

Here *Cell1* is the cell in the upper-left corner of the range and *Cell2* is the cell in the lower-right corner, as in:

```
Range("D4", "F8")
```

Alternatively, `Cell1` and `Cell2` can be Range objects that represent a row or column. For instance, the following returns the Range object that represents the second and third rows of the active sheet:

```
Range(Rows(2), Rows(3))
```

It is important to note that when the Range property is applied to a Range object, all references are relative to the upper-left corner cell in that range. For instance, if *rng* represents the second column in the active sheet, then:

```
rng.Range("A2")
```

is the second cell in that column, and not cell A2 of the worksheet. Also, the expression:

```
rng.Range("B2")
```

represents the (absolute) cell C2, because this cell is in the second column and second row from cell B1 (which is the upper-left cell in the range *rng*).

Cells Property

The Excel object model does not have an official Cells collection nor a Cell object. Nevertheless, the cells property acts as though it returns such a collection as a Range object. For instance, the following code returns 8:

```
Range("A1:B4").Cells.Count
```

Incidentally, `Cells.Count` returns $16,777,216 = 256 * 65536$.

The Cells property applies to the Application, Range, and Worksheet objects (and is global). When applied to the Worksheet object, it returns the Range object that represents all of the cells on the worksheet. Moreover, the following are equivalent:

```
Cells
Application.Cells
ActiveSheet.Cells
```

When applied to a Range object, the Cells property simply returns the same object, and hence does nothing.

The syntax:

```
Cells(i,j)
```

returns the Range object representing the cell at row *i* and column *j*. Thus, for instance:

```
Cells(1,1)
```

is equivalent to:

```
Range("A1")
```

One advantage of the Cells property over the Range method is that the Cells property can accept integer variables. For instance, the following code searches the first 100 rows of column 4 for the first cell containing the word "test." If such a cell is found, it is selected. If not, a message is displayed:

```
Dim r As Long
For r = 1 To 100
    If Cells(r, 4).Value = "test" Then
        Cells(r, 4).Select
        Exit For
    End If
Next
If r = 101 then MsgBox "No such cell."
```

It is also possible to combine the Range and Cells properties in a useful way. For example, consider the following code:

```
Dim r As Long
Dim rng As Range
With ActiveSheet
  For r = 1 To 100
      If Cells(r, r).Value <> "" Then
        Set rng = .Range(.Cells(1, 1), .Cells(r, r))
        Exit For
      End If
  Next
End With
rng.Select
```

This code searches the diagonal cells (cells with the same row and column number) until it finds a nonempty cell. It then sets **rng** to refer to the range consisting of the rectangle whose upper-left corner is cell A1 and whose lower-right corner is the cell found in this search.

Column, Columns, Row, and Rows Properties

The Excel object model does not have an official Columns or Rows collection. However, the Columns property does return a collection of Range objects, each of which represents a column. Thus:

```
ActiveSheet.Columns(i)
```

is the Range object that refers to the *i*th column of the active worksheet (and is a collection of the cells in that column). Similarly:

```
ActiveSheet.Rows(i)
```

refers to the *i*th row of the active worksheet.

The Columns and Rows properties can also be used with a Range object. Perhaps the simplest way to think of **rng.Columns** is as the collection of all columns in the worksheet *reindexed* so that column 1 is the leftmost column that intersects the range *rng*. To support this statement, consider the following code, whose results are shown in Figure 19-1:

```
Dim i As Integer
Dim rng As Range
Set rng = Range("D1:E1, G1:I1")
rng.Select
MsgBox "First column in range is " & rng.Column      ' Displays 4
MsgBox "Column count is " & rng.Columns.Count        ' Displays 2
For i = -(rng.Column - 2) To rng.Columns.Count + 1
   rng.Columns(i).Cells(1, 1).Value = i
Next
```

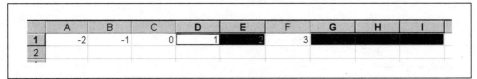

Figure 19-1. A noncontiguous range

Note that the range *rng* is selected in Figure 19-1 (and includes cell D1). The Column property of a Range object returns the leftmost column that intersects the range. (Similarly, the Row property returns the topmost row that intersects the range.) Hence, the first message box will display the number 4.

Now, from the point of view of *rng*, Columns(1) is column number 4 of the worksheet (column D). Hence, Columns(0) is column number 3 of the worksheet (column C) which, incidentally, is not part of *rng*. Indeed, the first column of the worksheet is column number

```
-(rng.Column - 2)
```

which is precisely why we started the For loop at this value.

Next, observe that:

```
rng.Columns.Count
```

is equal to 2 (which is the number displayed by the second message box). This is a bit unexpected. However, for some reason Microsoft designed the Count property of *rng*.Columns to return the number of columns that intersect only the *leftmost area* in the range, which is area D1:E1. (We will discuss areas a bit later.) Finally, note that:

```
rng.Columns(3)
```

is column F, which does not intersect the range at all.

As another illustration, consider the range selected in Figure 19-2. This range is the union B4:C5, E2:E7.

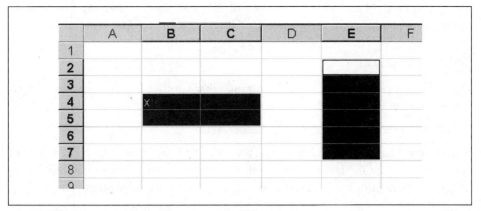

Figure 19-2. The range as a union

The code:

```
Dim rng As Range
Set rng = Range("B4:C5, E2:E7")
MsgBox rng.Columns(1).Cells(1, 1).Value
```

displays a message box containing the **x** shown in cell B4 in Figure 19-2 because the indexes in the Cells property are taken relative to the upper cell in the left-most area in the range.

Note that we can use either integers or characters (in quotes) to denote a column, as in:

```
Columns(5)
```

and:

```
Columns("E")
```

We can also write, for instance:

```
Columns("A:D")
```

to denote columns A through D. Similarly, we can denote multiple rows as in:

```
Rows("1:3")
```

Since a syntax such as:

```
Columns("C:D", "G:H")
```

does not work, the Union method is often useful in connection with the Columns and Rows methods. For instance, the code:

```
Dim rng As Range
Set rng = Union(Rows(3), Rows(5), Rows(7))
rng.Select
```

selects the third, fifth, and seventh rows of the worksheet containing this code or of the active worksheet if this code is in a workbook or standard code module.

Offset Property

The Offset property is used to return a range that is offset from a given range by a certain number of rows and/or columns. The syntax is:

```
RangeObject.Offset(RowOffset, ColumnOffset)
```

where *RowOffset* is the number of rows and *ColumnOffset* is the number of columns by which the range is to be offset. Note that both of these parameters are optional with default value 0, and both can be either positive, negative, or 0.

For instance, the following code searches the first 100 cells to the immediate right of cell D2 for an empty cell (if you tire of the message boxes, simply press Ctrl-Break to halt macro execution):

```
Dim rng As Range
Dim i As Integer
Set rng = Range("D2")
For i = 1 To 100
   If rng.Offset(0, i).Value = "" Then
     MsgBox "Found empty cell at offset " & i & " from cell D2"
   End If
Next
```

Additional Members of the Range Object

Let us now take a quick look at some additional members of the Range object. (Please refer to Table 19-1 for an indication of which members are discussed in this section.)

Activate Method

The Activate method will activate (or select) the range to which it is applied. The Activate method applies to a variety of other objects besides the Range object, such as the Window object, the Worksheet object, and the Workbook object.

AddComment Method

This method adds a Comment object (i.e., a comment) to the *single-cell* range. Its syntax is:

```
RangeObject.AddComment(Text)
```

where *Text* is the text of the comment. For instance, the code:

```
Dim rng As Range
Dim c As Comment
```

```
Set rng = Range("B2")
Set c = rng.AddComment("This is a comment")
```

adds a comment to cell B2 with the text "This is a comment." Note that if *RangeObject* consists of more than a single cell, a runtime error results.

Address Property (Read-Only String)

The Address property returns the range reference of the Range object as a string. The syntax is:

```
RangeObject.Address(RowAbsolute, ColumnAbsolute, _
    ReferenceStyle, External, RelativeTo)
```

RowAbsolute is set to **True** (the default) to return the row part of the reference as an absolute reference. *ColumnAbsolute* is set to **True** (the default) to return the column part of the reference as an absolute reference.

ReferenceStyle can be one of the **XlReferenceStyle** constants **xlA1** or **xlR1C1**. The default value is **xlA1**.

Set the *External* parameter to **True** to return an external reference—that is, a reference that is qualified by the workbook and worksheet names and is thus valid outside the current worksheet. The default value of **False** returns a reference that is not qualified and is therefore valid only within the current worksheet.

Finally, the *RelativeTo* parameter is used when *RowAbsolute* and *ColumnAbsolute* are **False** and *ReferenceStyle* is **xlR1C1**. In this case, we must include a reference point (a cell) to use for the relative addresses.

Let us consider some examples to help clarify this property:

```
Set rng = Range("B2")
rng.Address(ReferenceStyle:=xlA1)                   ' Returns $B$2
rng.Address(ReferenceStyle:=xlA1, _
    External:=True)                                 ' Returns [Book1]Sheet1!$B$2
rng.Address(ReferenceStyle:=xlR1C1)                 ' Returns R2C2
rng.Address(RowAbsolute:=False, _
    ColumnAbsolute:=False, ReferenceStyle:=xlA1)    ' Returns B2
rng.Address(RowAbsolute:=False, _
    ColumnAbsolute:=False, ReferenceStyle:=xlR1C1, _
    RelativeTo:=Range("D1"))                        ' Returns R[1]C[-2]

Set rng = Range("B2:D5")
rng.Address(ReferenceStyle:=xlA1)                   ' Returns $B$2:$D$5
rng.Address(ReferenceStyle:=xlR1C1)                 ' Returns R2C2:R5C4
rng.Address(RowAbsolute:=False, _
    ColumnAbsolute:=False, ReferenceStyle:=xlA1)    ' Returns B2:D5
rng.Address(RowAbsolute:=False, _
    ColumnAbsolute:=False, ReferenceStyle:=xlR1C1, _
    RelativeTo:=Range("D1"))                        ' Returns R[1]C[-2]:R[4]C
```

AutoFill Method

This important method performs an autofill on the cells in the range. Its syntax is:

```
RangeObject.AutoFill(Destination, Type)
```

Here *Destination* is the Range object whose cells are to be filled. The destination must include the source range—that is, the range that contains the data to use for the autofill.

The optional *Type* parameter specifies the fill type. It can be one of the following `XlAutoFillType` constants (note that the Excel documentation refers to a nonexistent `XlFillType` enum):

```
Enum XlAutoFillType
     xlFillDefault = 0
     xlFillCopy = 1
     xlFillSeries = 2
     xlFillFormats = 3
     xlFillValues = 4
     xlFillDays = 5
     xlFillWeekdays = 6
     xlFillMonths = 7
     xlFillYears = 8
     xlLinearTrend = 9
     xlGrowthTrend = 10
End Enum
```

If this argument is `xlFillDefault` or is omitted, Excel will attempt to select the most appropriate fill type, based on the source data.

To illustrate, consider the code:

```
Range("A1:B1").AutoFill Range("A1:K1")
```

which autofills cells C1 through K1 using the source data in cells A1 and B1. If A1 contains 1 and B1 contains 2, then this code will fill the destination cells with consecutive integers starting at 3 (in cell C1). Note that cells A1 and B1 are included in the destination range.

As another illustration, consider the worksheet in Figure 19-3, where cell B1 contains the formula:

```
=A1*A1
```

The code:

```
Range("B1").AutoFill Range("B1:B5")
```

will produce the output shown in Figure 19-4.

We should mention one source of potential problems with the AutoFill method. Apparently, when AutoFill is executed, the formula in the source cell is copied,

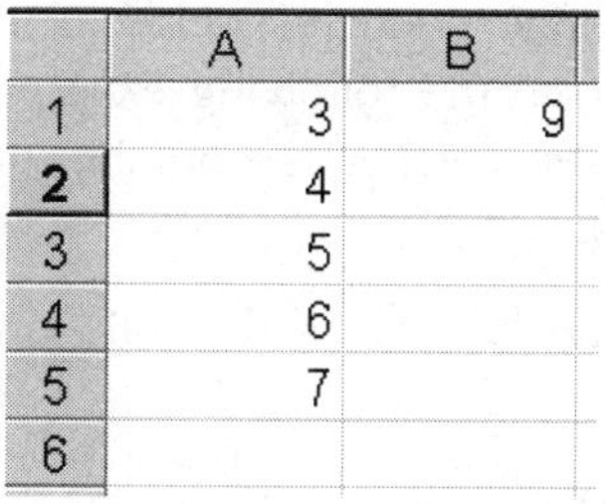

	A	B
1	3	9
2	4	
3	5	
4	6	
5	7	
6		

Figure 19-3. Worksheet to autofill range B1:B5

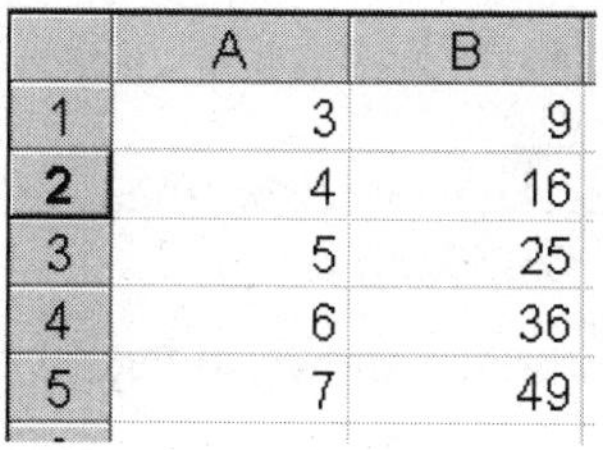

	A	B
1	3	9
2	4	16
3	5	25
4	6	36
5	7	49

Figure 19-4. Autofilling B1:B5 in Figure 19-3

with changes, to other cells. However, the *value* of the source cell is also copied, but *without changes*. Thus, if autocalculation is off, the formulas in the autofilled cells will be correct but the values will be incorrect. To fix this, just invoke the Calculate method.

AutoFilter Method

The AutoFilter method has two syntaxes, corresponding to two distinct functions. The syntax:

```
RangeObject.AutoFilter
```

simply toggles the display of the AutoFilter drop-down arrows for the columns that are involved in the range.

The syntax:

```
RangeObject.AutoFilter(Field, Criteria1, Operator, Criteria2)
```

displays the AutoFilter arrows and filters a list using the AutoFilter feature.

The optional *Field* parameter is the offset (as an integer, counting from the left) of the field on which the filter is based (the leftmost field is field one).

The optional *Criteria1* parameter is the criteria (as a string). We can use "=" to find blank fields, or "<>" to find nonblank fields. If this argument is omitted, the criteria is *All*. If *Operator* (see the following example) is set to xlTop10Items, then *Criteria1* specifies, as an integer, the number of items to display (this number need not be equal to 10).

The *Operator* parameter can be one of the following XlAutoFilterOperator constants:

```
Enum XlAutoFilterOperator
    xlAnd = 1
    xlOr = 2
    xlTop10Items = 3
    xlBottom10Items = 4
    xlTop10Percent = 5
    xlBottom10Percent = 6
End Enum
```

If this parameter is set to xlAnd or xlOr, then we must use *Criteria1* and *Criteria2* to construct the compound criteria.

To illustrate, consider the worksheet shown in Figure 19-5.

	A	B
1	Number	Year
2	1	1998
3	2	1996
4	3	1994
5	4	1997
6	5	1998
7	6	1994
8	7	1993
9	8	1994
10	9	1997
11	10	1998

Figure 19-5. A worksheet before autofiltering

The code:

```
Range("A1:B5").AutoFilter 2, "1997", xlOr, "1998"
```

will filter the range A1:B5 to show only those rows in that range for which the year is either 1997 or 1998. Note that it has no effect on the remaining rows of the worksheet. Hence, the result will be the worksheet in Figure 19-5 with rows 3 and 4 missing.

Recall that the AutoFilterMode property of the Worksheet object is **True** if the AutoFilter drop-down arrows are currently displayed on the worksheet. Note that we can set this property to **False** to remove the arrows, but we cannot set it to **True**. (To display the AutoFilter arrows, use the AutoFilter method.)

Recall also that the FilterMode property is **True** if the worksheet is in filter mode. Thus, for instance, if the AutoFilter arrows are displayed but no filtering has taken place, then AutoFilterMode is **True**, whereas FilterMode is **False**. Once filtering is actually performed, then FilterMode is **True**.

AutoFit Method

This method changes the width of the columns or the height of the rows (depending upon the type of range) to obtain the best fit for the range's contents. The syntax is:

```
RangeObject.AutoFit
```

where *RangeObject* refers to a Range object that consists of either one or more rows or one or more columns (but not both). Otherwise, the method generates an error. If the range consists of columns, then the column width is adjusted. If the range consists of rows, then the row height is adjusted.

AutoFormat Method

This method automatically formats a range using a predefined format. The syntax is:

```
RangeObject.AutoFormat(Format, Number, Font, _
    Alignment, Border, Pattern, Width)
```

All parameters of this method are optional. The *Format* parameter can be one of the following **XlRangeAutoFormat** constants:

```
Enum XlRangeAutoFormat
    xlRangeAutoFormatSimple = -4154
    xlRangeAutoFormatNone = -4142
    xlRangeAutoFormatClassic1 = 1          ' default
    xlRangeAutoFormatClassic2 = 2
    xlRangeAutoFormatClassic3 = 3
    xlRangeAutoFormatAccounting1 = 4
    xlRangeAutoFormatAccounting2 = 5
    xlRangeAutoFormatAccounting3 = 6
    xlRangeAutoFormatColor1 = 7
    xlRangeAutoFormatColor2 = 8
    xlRangeAutoFormatColor3 = 9
    xlRangeAutoFormatList1 = 10
    xlRangeAutoFormatList2 = 11
    xlRangeAutoFormatList3 = 12
    xlRangeAutoFormat3DEffects1 = 13
```

```
        xlRangeAutoFormat3DEffects2 = 14
        xlRangeAutoFormatLocalFormat1 = 15      ' not used
        xlRangeAutoFormatLocalFormat2 = 16      ' not used
        xlRangeAutoFormatAccounting4 = 17
        xlRangeAutoFormatLocalFormat3 = 19      ' not used
        xlRangeAutoFormatLocalFormat4 = 20      ' not used
        xlRangeAutoFormatReport1=21             ' Excel 9 only
        xlRangeAutoFormatReport2=22             ' Excel 9 only
        xlRangeAutoFormatReport3=23             ' Excel 9 only
        xlRangeAutoFormatReport4=24             ' Excel 9 only
        xlRangeAutoFormatReport5=25             ' Excel 9 only
        xlRangeAutoFormatReport6=26             ' Excel 9 only
        xlRangeAutoFormatReport7=27             ' Excel 9 only
        xlRangeAutoFormatReport8=28             ' Excel 9 only
        xlRangeAutoFormatReport9=29             ' Excel 9 only
        xlRangeAutoFormatReport10=30            ' Excel 9 only
        xlRangeAutoFormatClassicPivotTable=31   ' Excel 9 only
        xlRangeAutoFormatTable1=32              ' Excel 9 only
        xlRangeAutoFormatTable2=33              ' Excel 9 only
        xlRangeAutoFormatTable3=34              ' Excel 9 only
        xlRangeAutoFormatTable4=35              ' Excel 9 only
        xlRangeAutoFormatTable5=36              ' Excel 9 only
        xlRangeAutoFormatTable6=37              ' Excel 9 only
        xlRangeAutoFormatTable7=38              ' Excel 9 only
        xlRangeAutoFormatTable8=39              ' Excel 9 only
        xlRangeAutoFormatTable9=40              ' Excel 9 only
        xlRangeAutoFormatTable10=41             ' Excel 9 only
        xlRangeAutoFormatPTNone=42              ' Excel 9 only
    End Enum
```

Note that the constants marked as *not used* are not used in the U.S. English version of Excel.

The other parameters are Boolean and should be set to **True** (the default values) to include the corresponding format feature, as follows:

Number
> Include number formats

Font
> Include font formats

Alignment
> Include alignment

Border
> Include border formats

Pattern
> Include pattern formats

Width
> Include column width and row height in the autoformat

Note that if the range is a single cell, the AutoFormat method also formats the current region containing the cell. (The CurrentRegion property and the current region are discussed in detail later in this section.) Put another way, the following two statements are equivalent:

```
Cells("A1").AutoFormat
Cells("A1").CurrentRegion.AutoFormat
```

BorderAround Method

This method adds a border to a range and optionally sets the Color, LineStyle, and Weight properties for the border. The syntax is:

```
RangeObject.BorderAround(LineStyle, Weight, ColorIndex, Color)
```

The *LineStyle* parameter can be one of the following XlLineStyle constants (note that the Excel documentation refers to a nonexistent XlBorderLineStyle enum):

```
Enum XlLineStyle
    xlLineStyleNone = -4142
    xlDouble = -4119
    xlDot = -4118
    xlDash = -4115
    xlContinuous = 1          ' the default
    xlDashDot = 4
    xlDashDotDot = 5
    xlSlantDashDot = 13
End Enum
```

The optional *Weight* parameter specifies the border weight and can be one of the following XlBorderWeight constants:

```
Enum XlBorderWeight
    xlMedium = -4138
    xlHairline = 1
    xlThin = 2                ' the default
    xlThick = 4
End Enum
```

Note that the *Weight* property is ignored unless the *LineStyle* is xlContinuous or omitted.

The optional *ColorIndex* parameter specifies the border color, either as an index into the current color palette, or as one of the following XlColorIndex constants:

```
Enum XlColorIndex
    xlColorIndexNone = -4142
    xlColorIndexAutomatic = -4105
End Enum
```

The optional *Color* parameter also specifies the border color as an RGB value. Note that you should specify at most one of the color parameters.

The technique for clearing a border is a bit unexpected. For instance, suppose we have set a border with:

```
rng.BorderAround LineStyle:=xlDash
```

To clear this border, we might naturally try:

```
rng.BorderAround LineStyle:=xlLineStyleNone
```

but this does nothing. Instead, we must write:

```
rng.Borders.LineStyle = xlLineStyleNone
```

which clears the borders around each cell in the range separately.

Calculate Method

This method (which also applies to the Workbook and Worksheet objects) calculates all cells in the specified range. For instance, the code:

```
Worksheets(1).Rows(2).Calculate
```

will calculate all of the cells in the second row of the first worksheet.

Clear Methods

Excel has several clear methods. In particular, the Clear method clears all contents, formulas, and formatting from the cells in the given range. The ClearContents method clears only the contents (values and/or formulas) from the cells in the range, and leaves the formatting intact. The ClearFormats method clears only the formatting from the cells in the range.

ColumnDifferences and RowDifferences Methods

The ColumnDifferences method returns a Range object that represents all the cells in the range whose contents are different from certain comparison cells (there is one comparison cell in each column). The syntax is:

```
RangeObject.ColumnDifferences(ComparisonCell)
```

where *ComparisonCell* is a range object that represents a single cell. The purpose of *ComparisonCell* is simply to identify the *row* whose cells contain the comparison values.

To illustrate, consider the following code, whose results are shown in Figure 19-6:

```
Dim rng As Range, rng2 As Range
Set rng = Range("A1:D6")
Set rng2 = _
    rng.ColumnDifferences(Comparison:=Range("A1"))
rng2.Select
```

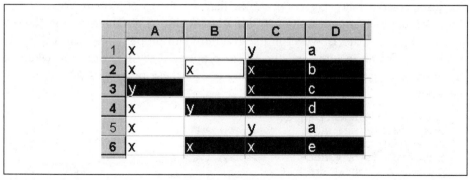

Figure 19-6. The result of the ColumnDifferences method

Since the *ComparisonCell* is cell A1, the first cell of each column in the range contains the comparison value. Thus, the cells that do not contain an "x" are selected in column A, the nonblank cells are selected in column B, the cells that do not contain a "y" are selected in column C and the cells that do not contain an "a" are selected in column D.

The RowDifferences method is the analog for rows of the ColumnDifferences method.

ColumnWidth and RowHeight Properties

The ColumnWidth property returns or sets the width of the columns in the specified range.

The return value is in units, each of which equals the width of one character in the Normal style. For proportional fonts, the width of the character "0" (zero) is used.

Note that if the columns in the range do not all have the same width, the Column-Width property returns Null.

The RowHeight property returns the height of all the rows in the range, measured in points. Note that if the rows in the range do not all have the same height, the RowHeight property returns Null.

Width, Height, Top, and Left Properties

These properties return values for the entire range, in points. For instance, the Top property returns the distance, in points, from the top of row 1 to the top of the first (leftmost) area of the range.

Note that when applied to a column, the Width property returns the width, in points, of the column. However, the relationship between Width and Column-Width can seem a bit strange at first.

For instance, the following code shows that a column of ColumnWidth 1 has Width 9.6 but a column of ColumnWidth 2 has Width 15. (In my case, the Normal style is 10 point Arial.) However, if the ColumnWidth property really measures the width of a column in units and the Width property really measures the width of the same column in points, then doubling one of these properties should double the other!

```
Columns("A").ColumnWidth = 1
MsgBox Columns("A").Width      ' Displays 9.6
Columns("A").ColumnWidth = 2
MsgBox Columns("A").Width      ' Displays 15
Columns("A").ColumnWidth = 10
MsgBox Columns("A").Width      ' Displays 58.2
```

Fortunately, a little high-school algebra reveals the truth here. It appears that the Width property includes padding on the far right and the far left of the entire group of characters (next to the column boundaries). To support this conclusion, let's do a little algebra, which you can skip if it upsets you.

Assume for a moment that the Width property includes not just the sum of the widths of the ColumnWidth characters, but also an additional p points of padding on each side of the entire group of characters. Thus, the formula for Width is:

```
Width = 2*p + ColumnWidth*w
```

where w is the true width of a single "0" character, in points. Thus, plugging in the values from the first two examples in the previous code gives:

```
9.6 = 2*p + 1*w
15 = 2*p + 2*w
```

Subtracting the first equation from the second gives:

```
5.4 = w
```

Substituting this into the first equation and solving for p gives:

```
p = 2.1
```

Thus, the formula for a Normal style of 10 point Arial is:

```
Width = 4.2 + ColumnWidth*5.4
```

Now, for a ColumnWidth of 10, this gives:

```
Width = 4.2 + 10*5.4 = 58.2
```

Eureka! (Check the third example in the previous code.)

Thus, we have verified (but not really proved) that the Width property measures not just the width of each character but includes some padding on the sides of the column—in this case 2.1 points of padding on each side.

Consolidate Method

This method combines (or consolidates) data from multiple ranges (perhaps on multiple worksheets) into a single range on a single worksheet. Its syntax is:

```
RangeObject.Consolidate(Sources, Function, _
    TopRow, LeftColumn, CreateLinks)
```

Sources is the source of the consolidation. It must be an array of references in R1C1-style notation. The references must include the full path of the ranges to be consolidated. (See the following example.)

Function is the function used to combine the data. It can be one of the following XlConsolidationFunction constants. (The default value is **xlAverage**.)

```
Enum XlConsolidationFunction
     xlVarP = -4165
     xlVar = -4164
     xlSum = -4157
     xlStDevP = -4156
     xlStDev = -4155
     xlProduct = -4149
     xlMin = -4139
     xlMax = -4136
     xlCountNums = -4113
     xlCount = -4112
     xlAverage = -4106
End Enum
```

TopRow should be set to **True** to consolidate the data based on column titles in the top row of the consolidation ranges. Set the parameter to **False** (the default) to consolidate data by position. In other words, if *TopRow* is **True**, Excel will combine columns with the same heading, even if they are not in the same position.

LeftColumn should be set to **True** to consolidate the data based on row titles in the left column of the consolidation ranges. Set the parameter to **False** (the default) to consolidate data by position.

CreateLinks should be set to **True** to have the consolidation use worksheet links. Set the parameter to **False** (the default) to have the consolidation copy the data.

To illustrate, consider the worksheets in Figure 19-7 and Figure 19-8 (note the order of the columns).

The code:

```
Worksheets("Sheet1").Range("A1").Consolidate _
   Sources:=Array("Sheet2!R1C1:R3C3", _
   "Sheet3!R1C1:R3C3"), Function:=xlSum
```

will produce the results shown in Figure 19-9 (on Sheet1).

	A	B	C
1	John	Mary	Henry
2	1	2	3
3	4	5	6
4			

Figure 19-7. Sheet2 before consolidation

	A	B	C
1	John	Henry	Mary
2	10	20	30
3	40	50	60
4			

Figure 19-8. Sheet3 before consolidation

	A	B	C
1			
2	11	22	33
3	44	55	66
4			

Figure 19-9. Sheet1 after consolidation with TopRow set to False

On the other hand, setting the TopRow property to **True**:

```
Worksheets("Sheet1").Range("A1").Consolidate _
    Sources:=Array("Sheet2!R1C1:R3C3", _
    "Sheet3!R1C1:R3C3"), Function:=xlSum, _
    TopRow:=True
```

produces the results shown in Figure 19-10, since the data is combined based on the names in the first row.

Copy and Cut Methods

As applied to the Range object, the Copy method has the syntax:

```
RangeObject.Copy(Destination)
```

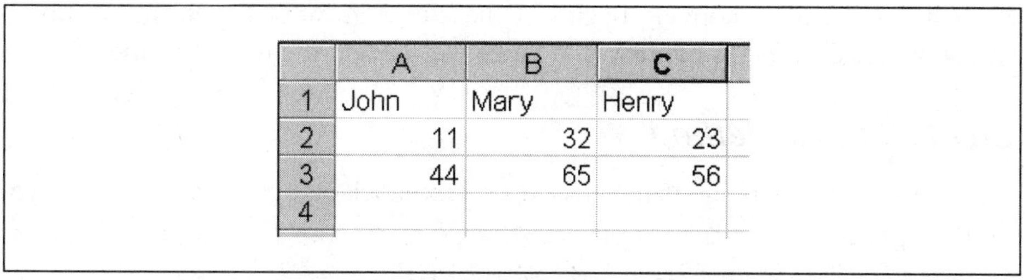

	A	B	C
1	John	Mary	Henry
2	11	32	23
3	44	65	56
4			

Figure 19-10. Sheet1 with TopRow set to True

where *Destination* is a Range object that specifies the new range to which the specified range will be copied. If this argument is omitted, Excel will copy the range to the Clipboard.

For instance, the code:

```
Range("A1:C3").Copy Range("D5")
```

copies the range A1:C3 to a range of like size whose upper-left corner is cell D5. Note that the same rules apply here as when copying using Excel's user interface. In particular, if the destination is more than a single cell, then it must have the same dimensions as the source range or else an error will occur.

The Cut method has similar syntax:

```
RangeObject.Cut(Destination)
```

and cuts the range rather than copying it.

CopyFromRecordset Method

For those readers familiar with DAO, CopyFromRecordset is a very powerful method that copies the contents of a DAO Recordset object onto a worksheet, beginning at the upper-left corner of the specified range. Note that if the Recordset object contains fields with OLE objects in them, this method fails.

To illustrate, consider the following code, which requires that a reference to Microsoft DAO is set in the References dialog box in the Excel VBA Tools menu:

```
Dim rs As Recordset
Set rs = _
  DBEngine.OpenDatabase("d:\excel\excel.mdb"). _
  OpenRecordset("Objects")
Range("A1").CopyFromRecordset(rs, 10, 10)
```

This code opens an Access database named *d:\excel\excel.mdb*, creates a recordset based on the table named Objects, and then copies the first 10 columns of the first 10 rows of the recordset to the current worksheet, starting at cell A1.

Note that, in general, copying begins at the current row of the Recordset object (which in our example is the first row, since we opened the recordset anew).

CreateNames Method

This method creates range names based on text labels in specified cells. The syntax is:

```
RangeObject.CreateNames(Top, Left, Bottom, Right)
```

The parameters are optional and have the default value of **False**. If one of the parameters is set to **True**, then the corresponding row (*Top* or *Bottom*) or column (*Left* or *Right*) is used to supply the names for the named ranges. If all of the parameters are **False**, then Excel tries to guess the location of the names. (I would generally advise against letting an application guess at anything.)

To illustrate, the following code, when applied to the sheet in Figure 19-8, will define three named ranges:

```
Range("A1:C3").CreateNames Top:=True
```

For instance, the range A2:A3 will be named John.

CurrentRegion Property

This useful property returns a Range object that represents the current region, which is the region bounded by the closest empty rows and columns. To illustrate, the following code, when applied to the sheet in Figure 19-11, selects the rectangular region A2:C4:

```
ActiveCell.CurrentRegion.Select
```

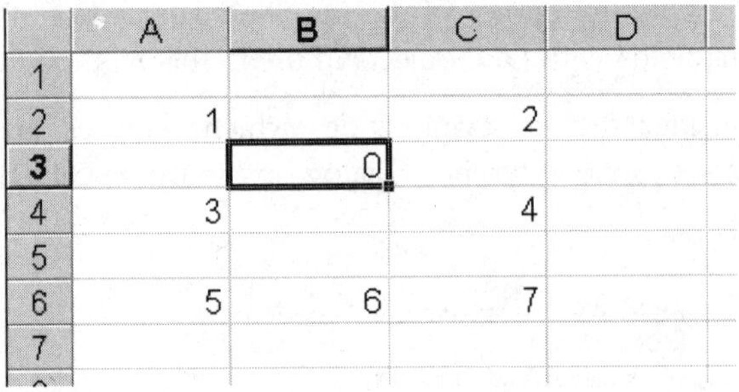

Figure 19-11. Illustrating CurrentRegion

Delete Method

This method deletes the cells in the range. Its syntax is:

```
RangeObject.Delete(Shift)
```

The optional *Shift* parameter specifies how to shift cells to replace the deleted cells. It can be one of the following constants:

```
Enum XlDeleteShiftDirection
    xlShiftUp = -4162
    xlShiftToLeft = -4159
End Enum
```

If this argument is omitted, then Excel guesses based on the shape of the range. In view of this, I would advise always including the argument. (Applications should not guess!)

Dependents and DirectDependents Properties

The Dependents property returns a Range object that represents all cells containing all the dependents of a cell. To illustrate, consider Figure 19-12, where we have displayed the underlying formulas in each cell.

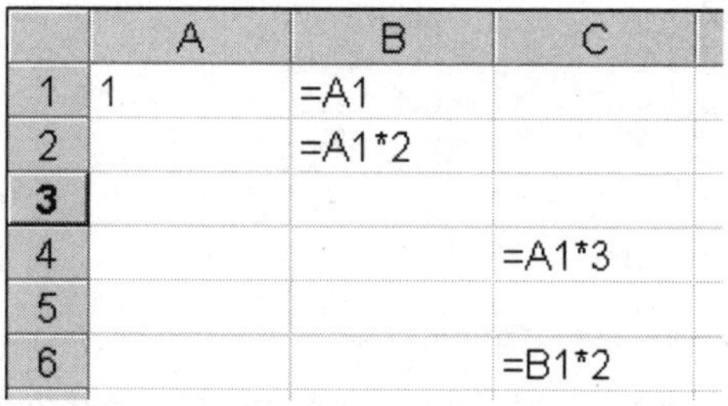

	A	B	C
1	1	=A1	
2		=A1*2	
3			
4			=A1*3
5			
6			=B1*2

Figure 19-12. Illustrating the Dependents property

The following code selects cells B1, B2, C4, and C6:

```
Range("A1").Dependents.Select
```

Note that C6 is not a direct dependent of A1.

By contrast, the following line selects the direct dependents of cell A1, which are cells B1, B2, and C4:

```
Range("A1").DirectDependents.Select
```

Precedents and DirectPrecedents Properties

These properties work just like the Dependents and DirectDependents properties, but in the reverse direction. For instance, referring to Figure 19-12, the line:

```
Range("C6").Precedents.Select
```

selects the cells B1 and A1, whereas the line:

```
Range("C6").DirectPrecedents.Select
```

selects the cell B1.

End Property

This property returns a Range object that represents the cell at the "end" of the region that contains the source range by mimicking a keystroke combination (see the following code). The syntax is:

```
RangeObject.End(Direction)
```

where *RangeObject* should be a reference to a single cell and *Direction* is one of the following constants. (The keystroke combination is also given in the following code.)

```
Enum XlDirection
    xlUp = -4162            ' Ctrl-Up
    xlToRight = -4161       ' Ctrl-Right
    xlToLeft = -4159        ' Ctrl-Left
    xlDown = -4121          ' Ctrl-Down
End Enum
```

Thus, for instance, the code:

```
Range("C4").End(xlToRight).Select
```

selects the rightmost cell in Row 4 for which all cells between that cell and cell C4 are nonempty (that is, the cell immediately to the left of the first empty cell in row 4 following cell C4).

EntireColumn and EntireRow Properties

The EntireColumn property returns a Range object that represents the column or columns that contain the specified range. The EntireRow property returns a Range object that represents the row or rows that contain the specified range.

For instance, the code:

```
Range("A1:A3").EntireRow.Select
```

selects the first three rows of the current worksheet.

Fill Methods

The Excel object model has four Fill methods: FillDown, FillUp, FillLeft, and Fill-Right. As expected, these methods work similarly, so we will describe only Fill-Down.

The FillDown method fills down from the top cell or cells in the specified range to the bottom of the range. The contents, formulas, and formatting of the cell or cells in the top row of a range are copied into the rest of the rows in the range. The syntax is:

```
RangeObject.FillDown
```

For instance, the code:

```
Range("B3:D5").FillDown
```

will duplicate the values of cells B3 through B5 in cells C3 through C5 and D3 through D5.

Find Method

The Find method returns the first cell in a given range that satisfies a criterion. Note that the Find method returns **Nothing** if no match is found. In any case, it does not affect the selection or the active cell.

The syntax of the Find method is:

```
RangeObject.Find(What, After, LookIn, LookAt, _
    SearchOrder, SearchDirection, MatchCase, MatchByte)
```

Note that all of the parameters except *What* are optional.

The *What* parameter is the data to search for and can be a string or any other valid Excel data type (number, date, etc.).

The *After* parameter is the cell after which the search should begin. (This would be the active cell when doing a search from the user interface.) Thus, the cell referred to by *After* is the last cell searched. If the *After* argument is omitted, the search starts after the cell in the upper-left corner of the range.

The *LookIn* parameter is one of the following constants:

```
Enum XlFindLookIn
    xlValues = -4163
    xlComments = -4144
    xlFormulas = -4123
End Enum
```

The *LookAt* parameter is one of the following constants that determines whether the What value must match the cell's entire contents or just any part of the cell's contents:

```
Enum XlLookAt
    xlWhole = 1
    xlPart = 2
End Enum
```

The *SearchOrder* parameter is one of the following `XlSearchOrder` constants:

```
Enum XlSearchOrder
    xlByRows = 1
    xlByColumns = 2
End Enum
```

The *SearchDirection* parameter is one of the following `XlSearchDirection` constants:

```
Enum XlSearchDirection
    xlNext = 1              ' Default
    xlPrevious = 2
End Enum
```

The *MatchCase* parameter should be set to **True** to do a case-sensitive search; otherwise, the search will be case-insensitive. (The *MatchByte* parameter is used only in the Far East version of Microsoft Excel. See the help documentation for details.)

There are several things to note about the Find method:

- The values of the *LookIn*, *LookAt*, *SearchOrder*, *MatchCase*, and *MatchByte* parameters (but not the *SearchDirection* parameter) are saved each time the Find method is invoked and are then reused for the next call to this method. Note also that setting these arguments changes the corresponding settings in Excel's Find dialog box, and conversely, changing the settings in the Find dialog box changes the values of these parameters. This implies that we cannot rely on the values of these parameters, since the user may have changed them through the Find dialog box. Hence, it is important to specify *each* of these arguments for each call to the Find method.

- The FindNext and FindPrevious methods (described in the next section) can be used to repeat a search.

- When a search reaches the end of the specified search range, it wraps around to the beginning of the range. If you do not want this behavior, consider using a different range.

- To find cells that match more complicated search criteria, such as those involving wildcard matches, we must use a more manual approach, such as cycling through the cells in the range with a **For Each** loop and using the

Like operator. For instance, the following code searches for all cells in the range A1:C5 whose contents begin with an "A" and sets the font for these cells to bold (note the use of the evaluation operator to denote the range A1:C5):

```
Dim c As Range
For Each c In [A1:C5]
    If c.Value Like "A*" Then
        c.Font.Bold = True
    End If
Next
```

FindNext and FindPrevious Methods

The FindNext method continues a search that was started with the Find method, returning the next cell that matches the criteria. The syntax is:

> *RangeObject*.FindNext(*After*)

The *After* parameter must be specified or the search will begin at the upper-left corner of the range. Thus, FindNext is the same as Find, except that it uses all of the parameters (except *After*) that were set by the previous use of the Find method.

To continue the search from the last cell found, use that cell as the *After* argument. For instance, the following code searches for all cells in the top row that contain the value 0, and removes the value:

```
Dim c As Range
Dim sFirstHit As String    ' Address of first hit
With Rows(1)
    Set c = .Find(0, LookIn:=xlValues)
    If Not c Is Nothing Then
        sFirstHit = c.Address
        Do
            ' Change cell contents
            c.Value = ""
            ' find next cell
            Set c = .FindNext(c)
        Loop While Not c Is Nothing
    End If
End With
```

The FindPrevious method has the syntax:

> *RangeObject*.FindPrevious(*Before*)

and works just like the FindNext method, but searches backward in the range starting with the cell *before* the cell referred to by the *Before* parameter (with wrap around from the beginning of the range to the end).

Formula and FormulaR1C1 Properties

The Formula property returns or sets the formula or value for each cell in the range. The formula must be expressed in A1-style notation, and must include a leading equal sign.

For instance, the line:

```
Range("A1").Formula = "=Sum(A2:A3)"
```

sets the formula in cell A1. The line:

```
Range("A1:C1").Formula = "=Sum(A2:A3)"
```

places the formula in cells A1:C1, but because the formula uses relative references, these references will be altered as usual. If we want to put the exact same formula in each cell, we must use an array, as in:

```
Range("A1:C1").Formula = _
  Array("=Sum(A2:A3)", "=Sum(A2:A3)", "=Sum(A2:A3)")
```

We can also return an array using the Formula property. To illustrate, consider the worksheet in Figure 19-13. The code:

```
Dim a As Variant
a = Range("A1:C2").Formula
```

sets the Variant variable *a* to an array, so that, for instance, $a(2,3) = 7$. Note that the Formula property returns a Variant, so that *a* must be declared as a Variant.

	A	B	C
1	2	3	4
2	5	6	7
3			

Figure 19-13. Illustrating the Formula property

If a cell contains a constant, the Formula property returns that constant. We can also assign a constant to a cell by writing, for example:

```
Range("A1").Formula = 1
```

If the cell is empty, then the Formula property returns an empty string. If the cell contains a formula, then the Formula method returns the formula as a string, as it would be displayed in the formula bar (including the equal sign).

If we set the Formula property (or the Value property) of a cell to a date, then Excel checks to see whether that cell is already formatted with one of the date or time formats. If not, Excel uses the default short date format.

The FormulaR1C1 property is the analog to the Formula property but accepts and returns formulas in R1C1 style.

FormulaArray Property

The FormulaArray property returns or sets an array formula, which must be in R1C1 style, for a range. To illustrate, consider the worksheet shown in Figure 19-14. The code:

```
Range("A9:C11").FormulaArray = "=A1:C3 + A5:C7"
```

produced the values in cells A9:C11 in Figure 19-14. The formula on the left says to add the contents of each cell in the uppermost 3-by-3 array to the corresponding cell in the middle 3-by-3 array, and place the result in the corresponding cell in the lower 3-by-3 array.

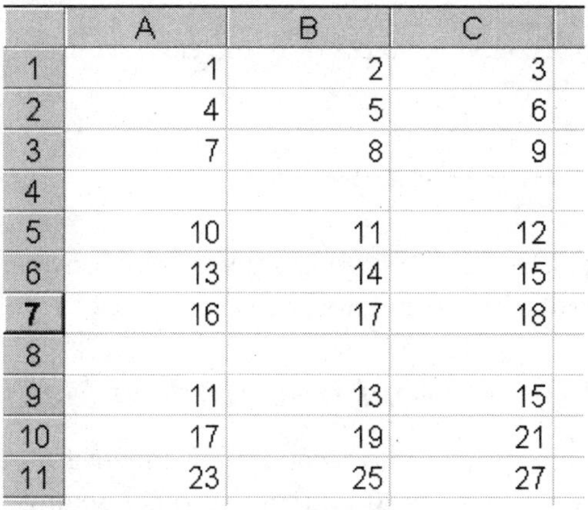

	A	B	C
1	1	2	3
2	4	5	6
3	7	8	9
4			
5	10	11	12
6	13	14	15
7	16	17	18
8			
9	11	13	15
10	17	19	21
11	23	25	27

Figure 19-14. Illustrating the FormulaArray property

Note also that the code:

```
Debug.Print Range("A9").FormulaArray
```

prints the array formula:

```
=A1:C3 + A5:C7
```

FormulaHidden Property (R/W Boolean)

This property returns or sets the Hidden state (**True** or **False**) for the formula in the cell to which it is applied. This is equivalent to setting the Hidden check box in the Protection tab of the Format Cells dialog.

Note that this is not the same as the Hidden property, which applies to ranges that consist of entire rows (or entire columns) and determines whether or not those rows (or columns) are hidden from view.

HasFormula Property (Read-Only)

This property returns `True` if all cells in the range contain formulas; it returns `False` if none of the cells in the range contains a formula, and `Null` otherwise.

HorizontalAlignment Property

The HorizontalAlignment property returns or sets the horizontal alignment of all cells in the range. The value can be one of the following constants:

```
Enum XlHAlign
    xlHAlignRight = -4152
    xlHAlignLeft = -4131
    xlHAlignJustify = -4130
    xlHAlignDistributed = -4117       'for Far East Excel
    xlHAlignCenter = -4108
    xlHAlignGeneral = 1
    xlHAlignFill = 5
    xlHAlignCenterAcrossSelection = 7
End Enum
```

Note especially the `xlHAlignCenterAcrossSelection` constant, which is very useful for aligning a title across multiple cells.

IndentLevel Property and InsertIndent Method

The IndentLevel property returns or sets the left indent for each cell in the range and can be any integer between 0 and 15. All other settings cause an error. Presumably, indents are useful for aligning the contents of cells or for formatting text.

For instance, to set the indent level of cell A1 to 10, we can write:

```
Range("A1").IndentLevel = 10
```

Unfortunately, the documentation does not specify how big an indent unit is, but we can still use indent units in a relative way. Presumably, an indent level of 2 is twice that of an indent level of 1.

An alternative is to use the InsertIndent method, with the syntax:

```
RangeObject.InsertIndent(InsertAmount)
```

where *InsertAmount* is an integer between 0 and 15. However, in this case, the InsertAmount parameter specifies the amount to *change* the current indent for the range.

Insert Method

This method inserts a cell or range of cells into the worksheet, shifting existing cells to make room. The syntax is:

```
RangeObject.Insert(Shift)
```

where *Shift* can be one of the **XlInsertShiftDirection** constants:

```
Enum XlInsertShiftDirection
    xlShiftToRight = -4161
    xlShiftDown = -4121
End Enum
```

If the *Shift* argument is omitted, Excel will decide upon the shift direction based on the shape of the range. (As with other cases when Excel will guess, I recommend against allowing it to do so.)

Locked Property

This property returns the Locked status of the cells in the range, or can be used to lock the range. The property returns **Null** if the range contains both locked and unlocked cells.

Merge-Related Methods and Properties

It is quite common to create a merged cell (that is, a single cell created by combining several adjacent cells) for use as a title or heading, for instance.

The Merge method creates a merged cell from the specified range. The syntax is:

```
RangeObject.Merge(Across)
```

where *Across* is an optional Variant that should be set to **True** to merge the cells in each row of the range into a single cell per row or **False** (the default) to merge all cells in all rows into a *single* cell. Note that when the individual cells contain data, the merged cell will contain only the data from the upper-left cell. Hence, the data in all other cells will be lost.

The UnMerge method separates a merged area into individual cells. Its syntax is:

```
RangeObject.UnMerge
```

Note that as long as *RangeObject* contains any of the cells within a merged range even if it does not contain all merged cells or if it contains additional cells not in the merged area, the method will unmerge the merged range. Note that calling the UnMerge method on a range that does not contain merged cells has no effect, and does *not* produce a runtime error.

The MergeArea property applies only to ranges that consist of a single cell (otherwise an error occurs). The property returns a Range object representing the merged range containing that cell (or the cell itself if it is not part of a merged range).

The MergeCells property returns **True** if the specified range is contained within a merged range of cells. The property returns **Null** if the specified range contains cells that are within a merged range as well as cells that lie outside the merged range.

Next and Previous Properties

When applied to a Range object, the Next property returns the cell that would be made active by striking the **TAB** key, although it does not actually select that cell. Thus, on an unprotected sheet, this property returns the cell immediately to the right of the upper-left cell in the range. On a protected sheet, this property returns the next *unlocked* cell.

Similarly, the Previous property emulates the Shift-Tab key by returning the appropriate cell (also without selecting the cell).

NumberFormat Property

This property returns or sets the number-formatting string for the cells in the range. Note that the property will return **Null** if the cells in the range do not all have the same number format.

One of the simplest ways to determine the desired formatting string is to record an Excel macro and use the Format dialog. You can then inspect the macro code for the correct formatting string.

Parse Method

This method parses the data in a column (or portion thereof) and distributes the contents of the range to fill adjacent columns. The syntax is:

```
RangeObject.Parse(ParseLine, Destination)
```

where *RangeObject* can be no more than one column wide.

The *ParseLine* parameter is a string containing left and right brackets to indicate where the data in the cells in the column should be split. For example, the string:

```
[xxx] [xxx]
```

causes the Parse method to insert the first three characters from each cell into the first column of the destination range, skip the fourth character and then insert the next three characters into the second column. Any additional characters (beyond the first six) are not included in the destination. This makes the Parse method most useful for parsing fixed-length data (each cell has data of the same length).

The *Destination* parameter is a Range object that represents the upper-left corner of the destination range for the parsed data. If this argument is omitted, Excel will parse the data in place; that is, it will use the source column as the first destination column.

PasteSpecial Method

This method pastes data from the Clipboard into the specified range. The syntax is:

```
RangeObject.PasteSpecial(Paste, Operation, SkipBlanks, Transpose)
```

The *Paste* parameter indicates what will be pasted and is one of the following XlPasteType constants:

```
Enum XlPasteType
    xlPasteValues = -4163
    xlPasteComments = -4144
    xlPasteFormulas = -4123
    xlPasteFormats = -4122
    xlPasteAll = -4104              ' Default
    xlPasteAllExceptBorders = 6
End Enum
```

The optional *Operation* parameter specifies a paste operation and can be one of the following XlPasteSpecialOperation constants:

```
Enum XlPasteSpecialOperation
    xlPasteSpecialOperationNone = -4142      ' Default
    xlPasteSpecialOperationAdd = 2
    xlPasteSpecialOperationSubtract = 3
    xlPasteSpecialOperationMultiply = 4
    xlPasteSpecialOperationDivide = 5
End Enum
```

The *SkipBlanks* parameter should be set to **True** to skip pasting blank cells from the Clipboard. To illustrate, suppose that the cell on the Clipboard that is destined to be pasted into cell D5 is blank. If *SkipBlanks* is **False** (the default), then whatever is in D5 before the paste operation will be overwritten when the blank cell is pasted, so D5 will then be empty. However, if *SkipBlank* is **True**, the blank cell will not be pasted into D5 and so the contents of D5 will not be disturbed.

The optional *Transpose* parameter can be set to **True** to transpose rows and columns when the range is pasted. The default value is **False**.

PrintOut Method

The PrintOut method prints a range. (This method applies to a host of other objects as well, such as Worksheet, Workbook, and Chart.) The syntax is:

```
RangeObject.PrintOut(From, To, Copies, Preview, _
    ActivePrinter, PrintToFile, Collate)
```

Note that all of the parameters to this method are optional.

The *From* parameter specifies the page number of the first page to print, and the *To* parameter specifies the last page to print. If omitted, the entire object (range, worksheet, etc.) is printed.

The *Copies* parameter specifies the number of copies to print. The default is 1.

Set *Preview* to `True` to invoke print preview rather than printing immediately. The default is `False`.

ActivePrinter sets the name of the active printer.

Setting *PrintToFile* to `True` causes Excel to print to a file. Excel will prompt the user for the name of the output file. (Unfortunately, there is no way to specify the name of the output file in code!)

The *Collate* parameter should be set to `True` to collate multiple multipage copies.

PrintPreview Method

This method invokes Excel's print preview feature for the given range (this method applies to the same list of objects as the PrintOut method). Its syntax is:

```
RangeObject.PrintPreview
```

Replace Method

This method finds and replaces specified data in all cells in a range. It has no effect on the selection or the active cell. The syntax is:

```
RangeObject.Replace(What, Replacement, LookAt, _
    SearchOrder, MatchCase, MatchByte)
```

The *What* parameter is the data to search for, and the *Replacement* parameter is the replacement data. These data can be strings or any other valid Excel data types (numbers, dates, etc.).

The *LookAt* parameter is one of the following constants that determines whether the *What* value must match the cell's entire contents or just any part of the cell's contents:

```
Enum XlLookAt
    xlWhole = 1
    xlPart = 2
End Enum
```

The *SearchOrder* parameter is one of the following **XlSearchOrder** constants:

```
Enum XlSearchOrder
    xlByRows = 1
    xlByColumns = 2
End Enum
```

The *MatchCase* parameter should be set to **True** to do a case-sensitive search (the default is **False**). The *MatchByte* parameter is used only in the Far East version of Microsoft Excel. See the help documentation for details.

Note that the values of the *LookAt*, *SearchOrder*, *MatchCase*, and *MatchByte* parameters are saved each time the Find method is invoked and then reused for the next call to this method. Note also that setting these arguments changes the corresponding settings in Excel's Find dialog box, and conversely, changing the settings in the Find dialog box changes the values of these parameters. This implies that we cannot rely on the values of these parameters, since the user may have changed them through the Find dialog box. Hence, it is important to specify *each* of these arguments for each call to the Find method.

If the contents of the *What* argument are found at least once, the Replace method returns **True**.

Select Method

This method selects the given range. Actually, the Select method applies to a whopping 81 different Excel objects. For the Range object, its syntax is:

```
RangeObject.Select
```

Note that this method selects a range of cells, whereas the Activate method activates a single cell.

ShrinkToFit Property

This property can be set to **True** to tell Excel to shrink the font size of all text in the range so that the text fits the available column width. It also returns **True** if ShrinkToFit is set for all cells in the range, **False** if it is turned off for all cells in the range, or **Null** if some cells have ShrinkToFit turned on and others have ShrinkToFit turned off.

Sort Method

This method sorts a range or the current region when the specified range contains only one cell. It can also be used to sort a pivot table. The syntax is:

```
RangeObject.Sort(Key1, Order1, Key2, Type, Order2, Key3, Order3, _
    Header, OrderCustom, MatchCase, Orientation, SortMethod, _
    IgnoreControlCharacters, IgnoreDiacritics, IgnoreKashida)
```

Sorting can take place based on up to three keys, denoted by *Key1*, *Key2*, and *Key3*. These parameters can be expressed as text (a range name) or a Range object. The corresponding *Order* parameter can be set to one of the following values:

```
Enum XlSortOrder
    xlAscending = 1          ' Default
    xlDescending = 2
End Enum
```

The optional *Type* parameter is used only when sorting pivot tables.

The optional *Header* parameter specifies whether the first row contains headers, in which case they are not included in the sort. The *Header* parameter can be one of the following values:

```
Enum XlYesNoGuess
    xlGuess = 0
    xlYes = 1
    xlNo = 2                 ' Default
End Enum
```

The optional *OrderCustom* parameter is an integer offset into the list of custom sort orders. However, Microsoft seems not to have documented this further, so it seems best to simply omit this argument, in which case it is assumed to be Normal (which sounds good).

The optional *MatchCase* parameter should be set to **True** to do a case-sensitive sort and **False** (the default) to do a sort that is not case-sensitive. For instance, suppose that cell A1 contains the text "AAA" and cell A2 contains the text "aaa." The code:

```
Range("A1:A2").Sort Key1:=Cells(1, 1), MatchCase:=True
```

will swap the contents of these two cells, but the code:

```
Range("A1:A2").Sort Key1:=Cells(1, 1), MatchCase:=False
```

will not.

The optional *Orientation* parameter determines whether the sort is done by row or by column. It can assume either of the values in the following enum:

```
Enum XlSortOrientation
    xlSortColumns = 1
```

```
        xlSortRows = 2
    End Enum
```

For instance:

```
    Range("A1:B2").Sort Key1:=Rows(1), Orientation:=xlSortColumns
```

sorts the columns in the range A1:B2 using the first row for the sort key.

The rest of the parameters are not used in the U.S. English version of Excel. The *SortMethod* parameter is not documented, but it has a default value xlPinYin, whatever that means.

SpecialCells Method

This method returns a Range object that represents all the cells that match a specified type and value. The syntax is:

```
    RangeObject.SpecialCells(Type, Value)
```

The *Type* parameter specifies the type of cells to include from *RangeObject*. It can be one of the following XlCellType constants:

```
Enum XlCellType
    xlCellTypeComments = -4144    'Cells with comments
    xlCellTypeFormulas = -4123    'Cells with formulas
    xlCellTypeConstants = 2       'Cells with constants
    xlCellTypeBlanks = 4          'Blank cells
    xlCellTypeLastCell = 11       'Last cell in range
    xlCellTypeVisible = 12        'All visible cells
End Enum
```

For instance, the code:

```
    Range("A1:D10").SpecialCells(xlCellTypeBlanks).Select
```

selects all blank cells in the range A1:D10.

The optional *Value* parameter applies when the *Type* parameter is either xlCellTypeConstants or xlCellTypeFormulas and identifies more specifically the type of cell to return. In these cases, the *Value* parameter can be set to one of, or a sum of, the following constants:

```
Enum XlSpecialCellsValue
    xlNumbers = 1
    xlTextValues = 2
    xlLogical = 4
    xlErrors = 16
End Enum
```

For instance, the code:

```
    Range("A1:D10").SpecialCells(xlCellTypeConstants, xlTextValues).Select
```

selects only the cells with text (as opposed to numbers) within the range A1:D10.

TextToColumns Method

This method parses a column (or columns) of cells that contain text into several columns. The syntax is:

```
RangeObject.TextToColumns(Destination, DataType, _
    TextQualifier, ConsecutiveDelimiter, Tab, Semicolon, _
    Comma, Space, Other, OtherChar, FieldInfo)
```

Note that all of the parameters to this method are optional.

The *Destination* parameter is a Range object that specifies where to put the results of the conversion. If the Range object represents more than a single cell, then the starting point for the destination is the upper-left cell in that range.

The *DataType* parameter specifies the format of the text to be split into columns. It can be one of the following **XlTextParsingType** constants:

```
Enum XlTextParsingType
    xlDelimited = 1           ' Default
    xlFixedWidth = 2
End Enum
```

The *TextQualifier* parameter is the text qualifier. It can be one of the following **XlTextQualifier** constants:

```
Enum XlTextQualifier
    xlTextQualifierNone = -4142
    xlTextQualifierDoubleQuote = 1    ' Default
    xlTextQualifierSingleQuote = 2
End Enum
```

The *ConsecutiveDelimiter* parameter should be set to **True** to have Excel consider consecutive delimiters as one delimiter. The default value is **False**.

There are several parameters that require that the *DataType* be **xlDelimited** and, when set to **True**, indicate that Excel should use the corresponding character as the text delimiter. They are described in the following list (all default values are **False**):

Tab
    Set to **True** to use the tab character as delimiter.

Semicolon
    Set to **True** to use a semicolon as delimiter.

Comma
    Set to **True** to use a comma as delimiter.

Space
    Set to **True** to use a space as delimiter.

Other

> Set to **True** to use a character that is specified by the *OtherChar* argument as delimiter.

When *Other* is **True**, *OtherChar* specifies the delimiter character. If *OtherChar* contains more than one character, only the first character is used.

The *FieldInfo* parameter is an array containing parse information for the individual source columns. The interpretation of *FieldInfo* depends on the value of *DataType*.

When *DataType* is xlDelimited, the *FieldInfo* argument should be an array whose size is the same as (or smaller than—see Table 19-3) the number of columns of converted data. The first element of a two-element array is the column number (starting with the number 1), and the second element is one of the numbers in Table 19-3 that specifies how the column is parsed.

Table 19-3. FieldInfo Values for xlDelimited Text

Code	Description
1	General
2	Text
3	MDY date
4	DMY date
5	YMD date
6	MYD date
7	DYM date
8	YDM date
9	Skip the column

If a two-element array for a given column is missing, then the column is parsed with the General setting. For instance, the following value for *FieldInfo* causes the first column to be parsed as text and the third column to be skipped:

```
Array(Array(1, 2), Array(3, 9))
```

All other columns will be parsed as general data.

To illustrate, consider the sheet shown in Figure 19-15. The code:

```
Range("A1:A3").TextToColumns _
   Destination:=Range("B1"), _
   DataType:=xlDelimited, _
   ConsecutiveDelimiter:=True, Comma:=True, _
   FieldInfo:=Array(Array(1, 2), Array(2, 3))
```

produces the second and third columns of Figure 19-15. Note that the cells in column C are formatted as dates.

	A	B	C
1	book, 12/4/98	book	12/4/98
2	record, 1/17/98	record	1/17/98
3	car, 11/2/98	car	11/2/98

Figure 19-15. A worksheet with text to be parsed in A1:A3

On the other hand, if *DataType* is **xlFixedWidth**, the first element of each two-element array specifies the starting character position in the column (0 being the first character) and the second element specifies the parse option (1–9) for the resulting column, as described previously.

To illustrate, consider the worksheet in Figure 19-16. The code:

```
Range("A1:A3").TextToColumns _
    Destination:=Range("B1"), _
    DataType:=xlFixedWidth, _
    FieldInfo:=Array(Array(0, 2), _
      Array(1, 9), Array(2, 2), Array(5, 9), _
      Array(6, 2))
```

parses the first column of Figure 19-16 into the remaining columns. (Note how we included arrays to skip the hyphens.)

	A	B	C	D
1	1-234-567	1	234	567
2	2-435-678	2	435	678
3	5-444-666	5	444	666

Figure 19-16. A worksheet with fixed-width data to be parsed in A1:A3

Value Property

The Value property returns the value of the specified cell. If the cell is empty, Value returns an empty string. This can be tested in either of the following ways:

```
If Range("A1") = "" Then . . .
```

or:

```
If IsEmpty(Range("A1")) Then . . .
```

If the Range object contains more than one cell, the *Value* property returns a two-dimensional array. For instance, referring to Figure 19-16, the code:

```
Dim v As Variant
v = Range("A1:A3").Value
Debug.Print IsArray(v)
Debug.Print v(2, 1)        ' row 2, col 1
```

will print:

```
True
2-435-678
```

WrapText Property

This property returns or sets the value that tells Excel whether to wrap text in the cells. It will return Null if the specified range contains some cells that wrap text and others that do not. Note that Excel will change the row height of the range, if necessary, to accommodate the text when wrapped.

Children of the Range Object

The children of the Range object are shown in Figure 19-17.

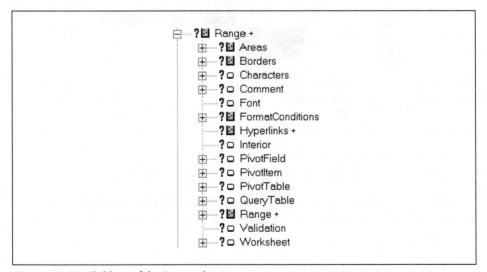

Figure 19-17. Children of the Range object

Corresponding to each of these children is a property of the Range object that returns the child. For instance, the PivotField property of the Range object returns a PivotField child object.

Let us take a look at the children of the Range object.

The Areas Collection

An *area* is a contiguous (that is, connected) block of cells in a worksheet. There is no Area object in the Excel object model. Instead, areas are Range objects.

However, every range is made up of one or more areas, and the collection of all Range objects that represent these areas is the Areas collection for the range. To illustrate, consider Figure 19-18, which is the result of calling the following code:

```
Dim rng As Range
Set rng = ActiveSheet.Cells.SpecialCells( _
   xlCellTypeConstants, xlNumbers)
rng.Select
```

Note that three distinct areas are selected.

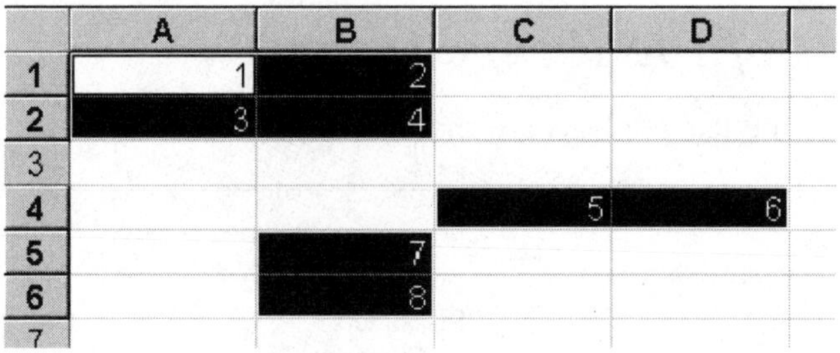

Figure 19-18. A range with three areas

We can clear the second area by writing:

```
rng.Areas(2).Clear
```

This will clear the cells C4 and D4. (**Areas** is a 1-based collection.)

It strikes me as a bit risky to refer to an individual area by index. However, it is perfectly safe to cycle through all areas using a **For** loop such as:

```
Dim rng As Range, r As Range
Set rng = ActiveSheet.Cells.SpecialCells( _
   xlCellTypeConstants, xlNumbers)
For Each r In rng.Areas
   Debug.Print r.Cells.Count
Next
```

The Borders Collection

Every range has a set of borders. For instance, the bottom border consists of the bottom borders of all of the cells that one would encounter by looking up at the range from the bottom of the worksheet. (Imagine moving up each column of the sheet until you encounter a cell in the range.)

For example, the bottom border of the range:

```
Range("a1:b4, d2:e2")
```

is shown as a dark line in Figure 19-19.

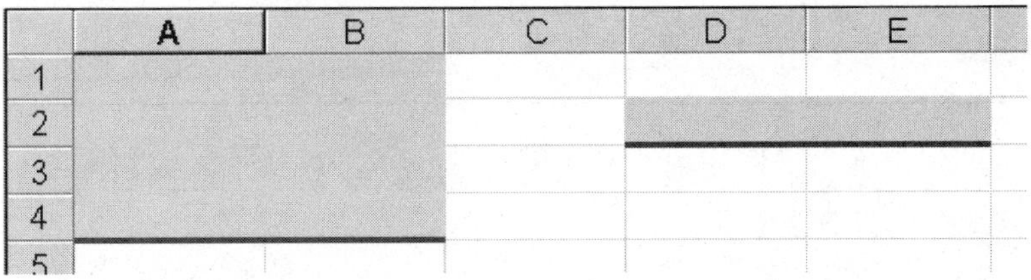

Figure 19-19. Illustrating the Border object

The Borders property of the Range object returns a Borders collection for the range. This collection contains several Border objects, indexed by the following constants:

```
Enum XlBordersIndex
      xlDiagonalDown = 5
      xlDiagonalUp = 6
      xlEdgeLeft = 7
      xlEdgeTop = 8
      xlEdgeBottom = 9
      xlEdgeRight = 10
      xlInsideVertical = 11
      xlInsideHorizontal = 12
End Enum
```

(The Excel help documentation refers to these as **XlBorderType** constants.)

To illustrate, the following code sets the interior color of the range shown in Figure 19-19 to a gray scale and sets the bottom border to thick red (shown as black in the figure). Note the use of nested **With** statements:

```
With Range("a1:b4, d2:e2")
   .Interior.Color = RGB(196, 196, 196)
   With .Borders(xlEdgeBottom)
     .Weight = xlThick
     .Color = RGB(255, 0, 0)
   End With
End With
```

Figure 19-20 shows the results of changing the constant **xlEdgeBottom** to **xlDiagonalDown**, while Figure 19-21 shows the results of changing the constant to **xlInsideVertical**.

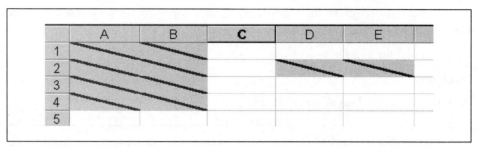

Figure 19-20. The xlDiagonalDown constant

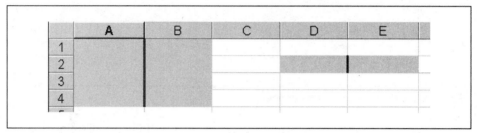

Figure 19-21. The xlInsideVertical constant

The Border Object

The most interesting properties and methods of the Border object are described in this section.

Color property

This property returns or sets the primary color of the border. It can also be applied to the Borders collection to set all vertical and horizontal lines for the borders at the same time. (The property also applies to Font objects and Interior objects.)

For instance, the following code has the effect shown in Figure 19-22:

```
With Range("a1:b4, d2:e2")
  .Interior.Color = RGB(196, 196, 196)
  With .Borders
    .Weight = xlThick
    .Color = RGB(255, 0, 0)
  End With
End With
```

To set a color value, we use the *RGB* color function, which has the form:

```
RGB(red, green, blue)
```

where *red*, *green*, and *blue* are integers between 0 and 255, inclusive, that represent the strength of the respective color component. Table 19-4 gives some common color values.

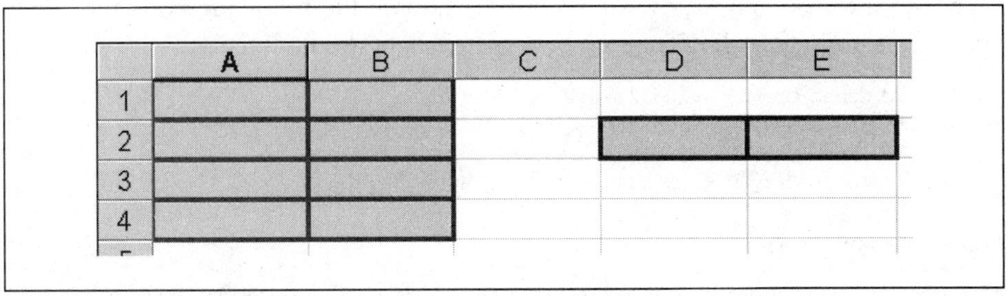

Figure 19-22. Assigning the Colors property of the Borders collection

Table 19-4. Some Common Colors

Color	Red	Green	Blue
Black	0	0	0
Blue	0	0	255
Green	0	255	0
Cyan	0	255	255
Red	255	0	0
Magenta	255	0	255
Yellow	255	255	0
White	255	255	255

To use a grayscale, set the red, green, and blue components equally. For instance:

```
RGB(196, 196, 196)
```

will produce a 25 percent grayscale. (The larger the numbers, the closer to white.) Unfortunately, Excel rounds all grayscale settings to one of the following:

- 0% (white)

- 25%

- 40%

- 50%

- 80%

- 100% (black)

You can see this by running the following code:

```
Dim r As Integer
For r = 1 To 25
  Cells(r, 1).Interior.Color = _
     RGB(255 - 10 * r, 255 - 10 * r, 255 - 10 * r)
  Cells(r, 2).Value = 255 - 10 * r
Next
```

If you want to use grayscales often, consider adding the following constant declarations to a code module. (The numbers on the right are RGB values.)

```
Public Const Gray25 = 12632256
Public Const Gray40 = 9868950
Public Const Gray50 = 8421504
Public Const Gray80 = 3355443
```

ColorIndex property

This property sets the color by using an index into a color palette. There is no way
to do justice to this in a black and white book, so I suggest you take a look at this
property in Excel's help documentation, where there is a color picture. However,
you can set this property to one of the following **XlColorIndex** constants as well:

```
Enum XlColorIndex
    xlColorIndexNone = -4142          ' no interior fill
    xlColorIndexAutomatic = -4105     ' automatic fill
End Enum
```

LineStyle property

The LineStyle property returns or sets the line style for the border. It can be one of
the following **XlLineStyle** constants:

```
Enum XlLineStyle
    xlLineStyleNone = -4142
    xlDouble = -4119
    xlDot = -4118
    xlDash = -4115
    xlContinuous = 1
    xlDashDot = 4
    xlDashDotDot = 5
    xlSlantDashDot = 13
End Enum
```

These values speak pretty much for themselves.

Weight property

The Weight property returns or sets the weight of the border. It can be one of the
following **XlBorderWeight** constants:

```
Enum XlBorderWeight
    xlMedium = -4138
    xlHairline = 1
    xlThin = 2
    xlThick = 4
End Enum
```

The Characters Object

The Characters object represents a contiguous sequence of text characters. The main purpose of the Characters object is to modify a *portion* of a text string. The syntax is:

```
RangeObject.Characters(start, length)
```

where *start* is the start character number and *length* is the number of characters. To illustrate, the following code boldfaces the first word in a cell:

```
Dim rng As Range
Set rng = Range("A1")
rng.Characters(1, InStr(rng.Value, " ") - 1).Font.Bold = True
```

The results are shown in Figure 19-23.

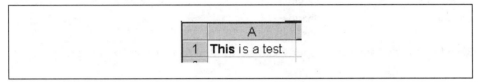

Figure 19-23. Boldfacing the first word of a cell

The Comment Object

Recall that the AddComment method of the Range object is used to add a comment to a range. Once the comment has been added, a corresponding Comment object is created. Each comment object belongs to the Comments collection of the Worksheet object.

To illustrate, the following code creates a comment in cell A1 if it does not already exist. It then sets the text and makes the comment visible for approximately three seconds. Note the use of the **DoEvents** statement to ensure that Windows has the opportunity to display the comment before entering the **Do** loop. (You might want to try this code without the **DoEvents** statement. On my system, the comment is not displayed.) Note also that the *Timer* function returns the number of seconds since midnight (so there is a potential problem if the three-second interval happens to occur at midnight).

```
Dim tm As Single
tm = Timer
If Range("A1").Comment Is Nothing Then
   Range("A1").AddComment "comment"
End If
Range("A1").Comment.Text "Created: " & Now
Range("A1").Comment.Visible = True
DoEvents
Do: Loop Until Timer - tm > 3
Range("A1").Comment.Visible = False
```

The Font Object

The Font property of a Range object returns a Font object. Font objects are used to control the characteristics of the font (font name, size, color, and so on) used in the range.

The properties of the Font object are shown in Table 19-5.

Table 19-5. Properties of the Font Object

Application	FontStyle	Size
Background	Italic	Strikethrough
Bold	Name	Subscript
Color	OutlineFont	Superscript
ColorIndex	Parent	Underline
Creator	Shadow	

Recall that the Characters property can be used to format *portions* of text.

The FormatConditions Collection

Excel allows us to apply *conditional formatting* to a cell (or a range of cells). A *conditional format* is a format that is applied if and only if certain conditions are met by the contents of the cell. For instance, we may want to make a number red if it is negative, black if it is positive, or green if it is 0. This requires three conditional formats.

The FormatConditions property of a Range object returns a FormatConditions collection that can contain up to three FormatCondition objects, each of which represents a conditional format.

The Add method of the FormatConditions collection is used to add FormatCondition objects to the collection. However, attempting to add more than three such objects will generate an error. The syntax for the Add method is:

```
FormatConditionsObject.Add(Type, Operator, Formula1, Formula2)
```

The required *Type* parameter specifies whether the conditional format is based on the value in the cell or an expression. It can be either of the following **XlFormatConditionType** constants:

```
Enum XlFormatConditionType
    xlCellValue = 1
    xlExpression = 2
End Enum
```

When *Type* is xlCellValue, the *Operator* parameter specifies the operator to use with that value. If *Type* is xlExpression, the *Operator* argument is ignored. The value of *Operator* is one of the following constants:

```
Enum XlFormatConditionOperator
    xlBetween = 1
    xlNotBetween = 2
    xlEqual = 3
    xlNotEqual = 4
    xlGreater = 5
    xlLess = 6
    xlGreaterEqual = 7
    xlLessEqual = 8
End Enum
```

If *Type* is xlCellValue, then *Formula1* and *Formula2* give the comparison values used with *Operator* and the cell value. Note that *Formula2* is used only with the xlBetween and xlNotBetween constants.

For example, the following code sets the interior color of a cell in the range A1:C4 to 25 percent grayscale if the number is between 0 and 10 (inclusive) and to white otherwise. The results are shown in Figure 19-24. Note that we first cleared all conditional formatting before creating new FormatCondition objects. Note also that an empty cell is treated as if it contains a 0.

```
Dim rng As Range
Dim i As Integer
Set rng = Range("A1:C4")
' Clear all existing formats
For i = rng.FormatConditions.Count To 1 Step -1
    rng.FormatConditions(i).Delete
Next
With rng
    .FormatConditions.Add xlCellValue, xlBetween, 0, 10
    .FormatConditions(1).Interior.Color = RGB(196, 196, 196)
    .FormatConditions.Add xlCellValue, xlNotBetween, 0, 10
    .FormatConditions(2).Interior.Color = RGB(255, 255, 255)
End With
```

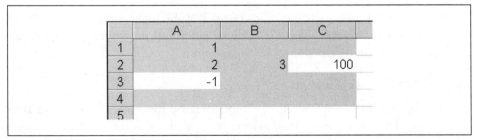

Figure 19-24. A conditionally formatted range

When *Type* is xlExpression, *Formula2* is ignored, and *Formula1* gives the formula or expression that determines the condition. This parameter can be a constant, a string, a cell reference, or a formula. To illustrate, the following code sets the interior color based on whether cells A1 and A2 contain the same value:

```
Dim rng As Range
Dim i As Integer
Set rng = Range("A1:A2")
' Clear all existing formats
For i = rng.FormatConditions.Count To 1 Step -1
  rng.FormatConditions(i).Delete
Next
With rng
  .FormatConditions.Add xlExpression, , _
      Range("A1").Value = Range("A2").Value
  .FormatConditions(1).Interior.Color = _
      RGB(0, 0, 255)
  .FormatConditions.Add xlExpression, , _
      Range("A1").Value <> Range("A2").Value
  .FormatConditions(2).Interior.Color = _
      RGB(255, 0, 0)
End With
```

As the previous examples show, the actual formatting is done by setting some of the properties of children of the FormatCondition object. In particular, the Borders, Font, and Interior properties return child objects of the same name, whose properties can be set to indicate the desired formatting.

Note finally that an existing FormatCondition object can be deleted using the Delete method of the FormatConditions collection, and it can be changed using the Modify method of the FormatCondition object. The Modify method has the syntax:

```
FormatConditionObject.Modify(Type, Operator, Formula1, Formula2)
```

where the parameters are identical to those of the Add method.

The Interior Object

The Interior object represents the characteristics of the interior region of a cell (or range of cells). The Interior object has only a handful of properties (and no methods), as described in this section.

Color and ColorIndex properties

These properties are analogous to the properties by the same name of the Borders object, discussed earlier. They set the interior of a cell (or cells) to the color specified.

Pattern property

This property returns or sets the interior pattern. It can be one of the following `XlPattern` constants:

```
Enum XlPattern
      xlPatternVertical = -4166
      xlPatternUp = -4162
      xlPatternNone = -4142
      xlPatternHorizontal = -4128
      xlPatternGray75 = -4126
      xlPatternGray50 = -4125
      xlPatternGray25 = -4124
      xlPatternDown = -4121
      xlPatternAutomatic = -4105
      xlPatternSolid = 1
      xlPatternChecker = 9
      xlPatternSemiGray75 = 10
      xlPatternLightHorizontal = 11
      xlPatternLightVertical = 12
      xlPatternLightDown = 13
      xlPatternLightUp = 14
      xlPatternGrid = 15
      xlPatternCrissCross = 16
      xlPatternGray16 = 17
      xlPatternGray8 = 18
End Enum
```

Note that this provides another way to access grayscales.

PatternColor and PatternColorIndex properties

These properties set the color (or color index) of the pattern used to fill the interior of a cell. For more on setting color and color indexes, please see the discussion of the Color and ColorIndex properties of the Border object.

The PivotField, PivotItem, and PivotTable Objects

These objects relate to PivotTable objects and will be discussed in Chapter 20, *Pivot Tables*.

The QueryTable Object

A QueryTable object represents a worksheet table that is built from data returned from an external data source, such as Microsoft SQL Server or a Microsoft Access database. We will not discuss QueryTable objects in this book. (There are better ways to retrieve data from an external source.)

The Validation Object

A Validation object is used to enforce data validation on a cell or range of cells. The Validation property of the Range object returns a Validation object, whose properties can be returned or set. Note that there is no Validations collection.

Data validation involves three parts: the actual validation, an input message that can be displayed when a cell is activated, and an error message that can be displayed if the data entered is invalid.

The methods of the Validation object are Add, Delete, and Modify. To add validation to a range, use the Add method, whose syntax is:

```
ValidationObject.Add(Type, AlertStyle, Operator, Formula1, Formula2)
```

Note the similarity between the parameters of the Add method of the Validation object and the Add method of the FormatConditions object.

The required *Type* parameter specifies the type of data allowed and can be one of the following XlDVType constants:

```
Enum XlDVType
    xlValidateInputOnly = 0
    xlValidateWholeNumber = 1
    xlValidateDecimal = 2
    xlValidateList = 3
    xlValidateDate = 4
    xlValidateTime = 5
    xlValidateTextLength = 6
    xlValidateCustom = 7
End Enum
```

The xlValidateInputOnly constant causes Excel to treat all data as valid. This value should be used when we want to display an input message (described later in this section), but not invoke data validation.

The optional *AlertStyle* parameter specifies the buttons that will appear on the error dialog box that is displayed if the data entered is invalid. It can be one of the following XlDVAlertStyle constants:

```
Enum XlDVAlertStyle
    xlValidAlertStop = 1
    xlValidAlertWarning = 2
    xlValidAlertInformation = 3
End Enum
```

The meanings of these constants are as follows:

xlValidAlertInformation
    OK and Cancel buttons

xlValidAlertStop
    Retry and Cancel buttons

xlValidAlertWarning

    Yes, No, and Cancel buttons

The optional *Operator* parameter is the operator used in the validation, and can be any one of the **XlFormatConditionOperator** constants:

```
Enum XlFormatConditionOperator
    xlBetween = 1
    xlNotBetween = 2
    xlEqual = 3
    xlNotEqual = 4
    xlGreater = 5
    xlLess = 6
    xlGreaterEqual = 7
    xlLessEqual = 8
End Enum
```

The *Formula1* parameter specifies the first part of the data-validation equation, and *Formula2* specifies the second part when *Operator* is **xlBetween** or **xlNotBetween**.

To understand this rather complex object, it is best to look at the corresponding dialog boxes in the Excel user interface. Figure 19-25 shows the Settings tab of the Validation dialog box.

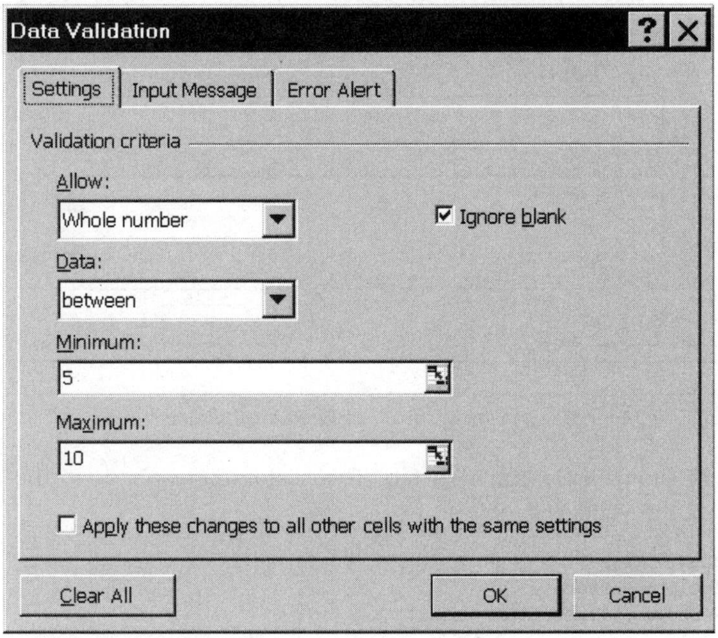

Figure 19-25. The Settings tab of the Data Validation dialog

This dialog corresponds to setting:

```
Type:=xlValidateWholeNumber
Operator:=xlBetween
Formula1:="5"
Formula2:="10"
IgnoreBlank = True
```

You can learn more about the *Type* constants by clicking on the ? button in the Data Validation dialog and then clicking on the Allow drop-down list box. Note that the other controls on the tab in Figure 19-25 will change depending upon the value selected in the Allow drop-down box.

The Input Message tab is shown in Figure 19-26. The values in this dialog correspond to properties of the Validation object. In particular, we have:

```
ShowInput = True
InputTitle = "Input:"
InputMessage = "Input a number"
```

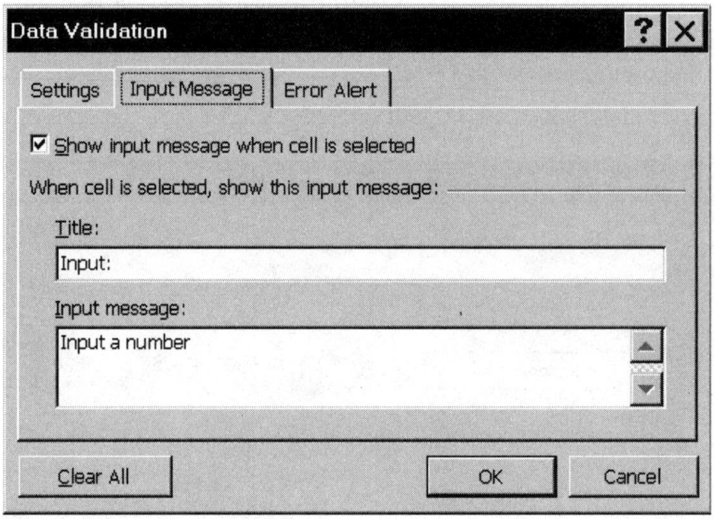

Figure 19-26. The Input Message tab of the Data Validation dialog

Figure 19-27 shows the Error Alert tab. This dialog corresponds to the following properties of the Validation object:

```
ShowError = True
ErrorTitle = "Error:"
ErrorMessage = "This is an error"
```

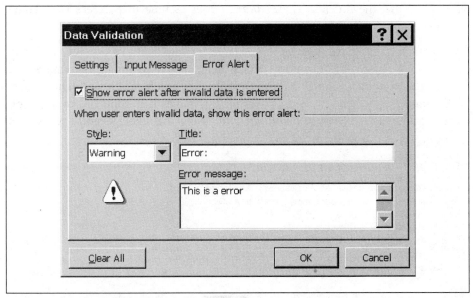

Figure 19-27. The Error Alert tab of the Data Validation dialog

We can now put all of the pieces together to show how to set up data validation for a range of cells. Note that the first order of business is to delete any old validation:

```
With Range("A1:D4").Validation
   .Delete
   .Add Type:=xlValidateWholeNumber, _
       AlertStyle:=xlValidAlertStop, _
       Operator:=xlBetween, _
       Formula1:="5", Formula2:="10"
   .IgnoreBlank = True
   .ShowInput = True
   .InputTitle = "Input:"
   .InputMessage = "Input a number"
   .ShowError = True
   .ErrorTitle = "Error:"
   .ErrorMessage = "This is a error"
End With
```

Example: Getting the Used Range

As we mentioned in Chapter 18, *The Worksheet Object*, the UsedRange method seems to have some problems, in that it does not always return what we would consider to be the *currently* used range, that is the smallest rectangular region of cells that contains all cells that currently have data. In any case, if you too have trouble with the UsedRange method, the following function can be used in its place. Note that the function *GetUsedRange* does assume that Excel's UsedRange method returns a superset of the correct used range.

The operation of *GetUsedRange* is straightforward. As its source code in Example 19-1 shows, the function starts with Excel's used range, determines the coordinates (row and column numbers) of the upper-left and lower-right corners of this range, and then proceeds to shrink this range if it contains rows or columns that are blank. This is determined by using the Excel *CountA* worksheet function, which counts the number of nonempty cells.

Example 19-1. The GetUsedRange Function

```
Function GetUsedRange(ws As Worksheet) As Range
' Assumes that Excel's UsedRange gives a superset
' of the real used range.
Dim s As String, x As Integer
Dim rng As Range
Dim r1Fixed As Integer, c1Fixed As Integer
Dim r2Fixed As Integer, c2Fixed As Integer
Dim i As Integer
Dim r1 As Integer, c1 As Integer
Dim r2 As Integer, c2 As Integer

Set GetUsedRange = Nothing

' Start with Excel's used range
Set rng = ws.UsedRange

' Get bounding cells for Excel's used range
' That is, Cells(r1,c1) to Cells(r2,c2)
r1 = rng.Row
r2 = rng.Rows.Count + r1 - 1
c1 = rng.Column
c2 = rng.Columns.Count + c1 - 1

' Save existing values
r1Fixed = r1
c1Fixed = c1
r2Fixed = r2
c2Fixed = c2

' Check rows from top down for all blanks.
' If found, shrink rows.
For i = 1 To r2Fixed - r1Fixed + 1
    If Application.CountA(rng.Rows(i)) = 0 Then
        ' empty row -- reduce
        r1 = r1 + 1
    Else
        ' nonempty row, get out
        Exit For
    End If
Next
```

Example 19-1. The GetUsedRange Function (continued)

```
' Repeat for columns from left to right
For i = 1 To c2Fixed - c1Fixed + 1
    If Application.CountA(rng.Columns(i)) = 0 Then
        c1 = c1 + 1
    Else
        Exit For
    End If
Next

' Reset the range
Set rng = _
    ws.Range(ws.Cells(r1, c1), ws.Cells(r2, c2))

' Start again
r1Fixed = r1
c1Fixed = c1
r2Fixed = r2
c2Fixed = c2

' Do rows from bottom up
For i = r2Fixed - r1Fixed + 1 To 1 Step -1
    If Application.CountA(rng.Rows(i)) = 0 Then
        r2 = r2 - 1
    Else
        Exit For
    End If
Next

' Repeat for columns from right to left
For i = c2Fixed - c1Fixed + 1 To 1 Step -1
    If Application.CountA(rng.Columns(i)) = 0 Then
        c2 = c2 - 1
    Else
        Exit For
    End If
Next

Set GetUsedRange = _
    ws.Range(ws.Cells(r1, c1), ws.Cells(r2, c2))

End Function
```

Example: Selecting Special Cells

The Excel user interface does not have a built-in method for selecting worksheet cells based on various criteria. For instance, there is no way to select all cells whose value is between 0 and 100, or all cells that contain a date later than January 1, 1998. There is also no way to select only those cells in a given column whose value is different from the value of the preceding cell. This can be very useful when you have a sorted column and want to extract a set of *unique* values, as shown in Figure 19-28.

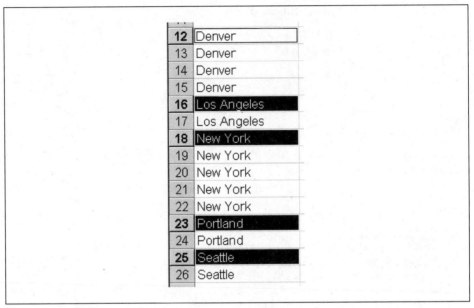

Figure 19-28. Selecting unique values

We will develop a small utility (and add it to the SRXUtils application) that can make a selection based on some simple criteria. You may want to enhance this utility by adding more criteria.

The first step is to augment the DataSheet for SRXUtils by adding a new row for the new utility, as shown in Figure 19-29. (The order of the rows in this DataSheet is based on the order in which we want the items to appear in the custom menu.)

	A	B	C	D	E	F	G	H
1	Utility	OnAction Proc	Procedure	In Workbook	Menu Item	SubMenu Item	On Wks Menu	On Chart Menu
2	Activate Sheet	RunUtility	ActivateSheet	ThisWorkbook	&Activate Sheet		TRUE	TRUE
3	Print Charts	RunUtility	PrintCharts	Print.utl	&Print	Embedded &Charts	TRUE	TRUE
4	Print Pivot Tables	RunUtility	PrintPivotTables	Print.utl		&Pivot Tables	TRUE	TRUE
5	Print Sheets	RunUtility	PrintSheets	Print.utl		&Sheets	TRUE	TRUE
6	Select Special	RunUtility	SelectSpecial	ThisWorkbook	S&elect Special		TRUE	FALSE
7	Sort Sheets	RunUtility	SortSheets	ThisWorkbook	&Sort Sheets		TRUE	TRUE

Figure 19-29. Augmenting the DataSheet worksheet

Designing the Utility

To keep our utility relatively simple, we will implement the following selection criteria:

- Select cell if preceding cell is different
- Select cell if preceding cell is the same
- Select empty cells
- Select nonempty cells

The search range for the selection operation, that is, the area to which the selection criteria will be applied, is the current selection on the active worksheet. Note that we will need to verify that this is a selection of worksheet cells and not, say, a chart. For the first two criteria, this range must be either a single row or a single column or a portion thereof. For the last two criteria, the search range can be any selection of cells.

As a courtesy to the user, if the current selection is just a single cell, the utility will default to the used range for the last two criteria (empty or nonempty) and to the used portion of the *column* containing the active cell for the first two criteria (same and different).

As a bonus, we also include a feature that enlarges the current selection by including the entire row (or column) containing each selected cell. For instance, applying this to the worksheet in Figure 19-28 will select rows 12, 16, 18, 23, and 25.

Designing the Dialog

Now that our game plan has be mapped out, we can design and construct the dialog. The final product is shown in Figure 19-30. It is a UserForm called *dlgSelectSpecial*, and its Caption property should be set to "Select Special."

As to the operation of the utility, the user will first select one of the mutually exclusive options under Select Cells If. The actual search range is displayed at the bottom of the dialog.

Here are some of the highlights of this form design. We suggest you read on before creating your own form.

The Frame control

A frame control is used to group other controls. This is often done just to group controls that have a similar purpose. However, in the case of option buttons, it has a more profound effect. Namely, the option buttons in a single frame are *mutually exclusive*, which means that if the user selects one option button, the others are automatically unselected.

To ensure that the option buttons are really inside the frame and not merely on top of it, make sure the frame is selected when you click on the *OptionButton* control icon in the Toolbox. Then create the option button inside the frame. Also,

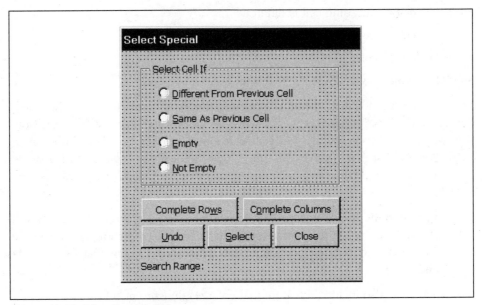

Figure 19-30. Select Special dialog

if you decide to copy and paste the additional option buttons, make sure that the frame is selected when you choose the Paste command.

Control names

The control names were chosen to conform to my naming convention. Their names are:

- *fraType* (frame)
- *optDifferent*
- *optSame*
- *optEmpty*
- *cmdSelect*
- *cmdCancel*
- *cmdUndo*
- *cmdCompleteRows*
- *cmdCompleteColumns*
- *lblSearchRange*

You will not need to set many control properties beyond the Name property and the Accelerator property (indicated for each control in Figure 19-30 by an underscore in its caption). Be sure to set the WordWrap property of the *lblSearch-*

Range label to `False` so that the label will occupy only a single line. Also, set the TabStop property of *lblSearchRange* to `False`.

Tab Order

It is important whenever designing a custom dialog to set the tab order of all controls properly. There is nothing less professional than having the focus jump around randomly when the user repeatedly hits the Tab key! The simplest way to set the correct tab order is to use the Tab Order dialog box, available from the View menu and shown in Figure 19-31. You can use this dialog to get an overall view of the current tab order and to change that order if desired. Remember that the control with tab order 0 will receive the focus when the dialog is first displayed. You will need to display the Tab Order dialog twice: once while the entire dialog is selected and once while the frame control is selected (to see the tab orders of the option buttons).

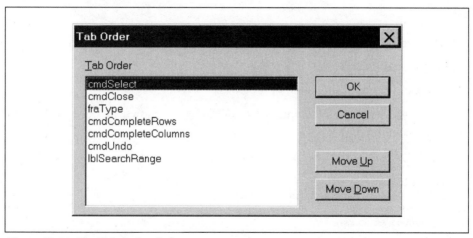

Figure 19-31. The Tab Order dialog

Some final tips

We should remark that the VB editor's Format menu has some very useful items for aligning and resizing controls on a UserForm to give your forms a more professional look. You should definitely do some exploration of this menu. Another useful trick is to copy and paste controls. This produces controls of identical size and preserves other properties as well. (Of course, some properties, such as the Name property or the position properties, are not preserved.)

Writing the Code

Now that the dialog is created, we can start writing the code.

In the *basMain* standard module, place the code that displays the Select Special dialog box. However, it is possible that the current selection in the active worksheet is not a collection of cells. It could be a drawing object or chart, for instance. In this case, we want to issue a message stating that the current selection is inappropriate for the *SelectSpecial* utility, and not to bother displaying the dialog. The code in Example 19-2 (which should be stored in *basMain*) will do the job.

Example 19-2. The SelectSpecial Procedure

```
Sub SelectSpecial()

' Check for valid selection
If TypeName(Selection) <> "Range" Then
  MsgBox "Selection must be a range of worksheet cells.", vbCritical
Else
  dlgSelectSpecial.Show
End If

End Sub
```

Note that we use the *TypeName* function. When applied to an object, as in:

```
    TypeName(ObjectVariable)
```

the function will return the name of the object.

Next, we need a couple of module-level declarations, shown in Example 19-3, in the form's code module.

Example 19-3. dlgSelectSpecial Module-Level Declarations

```
Option Explicit
' These are used by more than one procedure
Dim rngSearch As Range
Dim rngForUndo As Range
```

The Initialize event of the form is the place to initialize the controls. As Example 19-4 shows, we first want to disable some command buttons and fill the *lblSearchRange* label. We also can set the module-level variables here.

Example 19-4. The Initialize Event Procedure

```
Private Sub UserForm_Initialize()

cmdSelect.Enabled = False
cmdUndo.Enabled = False
lblSearchRange.Caption = "Search Range: Nothing"

Set rngSearch = Selection
Set rngForUndo = rngSearch

End Sub
```

The Close button simply unloads the form; its source code is shown in Example 19-5.

Example 19-5. The cmdClose_Click Event Procedure

```
Private Sub cmdClose_Click()
  Unload Me
End Sub
```

Incidentally, you can test out your progress so far (and later) by running the Initialize event. Just place the cursor in this event and hit F5.

The Undo button returns the selection to its original state, which is saved in the module-level variable *rngForUndo*. Its source code is shown in Example 19-6.

Example 19-6. The cmdUndo_Click Event Procedure

```
Private Sub cmdUndo_Click()
  If Not rngForUndo Is Nothing Then
    rngForUndo.Select
    cmdUndo.Enabled = False
  End If
End Sub
```

The first thing the user will do after the dialog is displayed is choose an option from the frame at the top. This choice will determine in part the search range. Also, some choices require a more restrictive search range. To react to the user's choice, we call a procedure called *GetSearchRange* whenever an option button is selected. The code to handle the option buttons is shown in Example 19-7.

Example 19-7. Event Handlers for the Option Buttons

```
Private Sub optDifferent_Click()
  GetSearchRange
End Sub

Private Sub optEmpty_Click()
  GetSearchRange
End Sub

Private Sub optNotEmpty_Click()
  GetSearchRange
End Sub

Private Sub optSame_Click()
  GetSearchRange
End Sub
```

The *GetSearchRange* procedure is shown in Example 19-8.

Example 19-8. The GetSearchRange Procedure

```
Private Sub GetSearchRange()

' Set search range based on choice of search type.
' If Different or Same, validate range
' If single cell, change to:
'  - used column for Different or Same match
'  - used range for Empty or Not Empty match
' We know that rngSearch is a range of cells.
' Disables Select button if not a valid range.

Dim cColumns As Integer, cRows As Integer

cmdSelect.Enabled = True   ' May be temporary

If optDifferent Or optSame Then

   ' Search range must be (portion of)
   ' a single row or column

   cColumns = rngSearch.Columns.Count
   cRows = rngSearch.Rows.Count

   If rngSearch.Areas.Count > 1 Or _
   (cColumns <> 1 And cRows <> 1) Then
     lblSearchRange.Caption = "Requires (portion of) single column or row."
     cmdSelect.Enabled = False
     Exit Sub
   End If

   ' If single cell then expand to used portion of column
   If cColumns = 1 And cRows = 1 Then
     Set rngSearch = Application.Intersect( _
        rngSearch.EntireColumn, ActiveSheet.UsedRange)
   End If

ElseIf optEmpty Or optNotEmpty Then

   ' If selection is single cell then expand to used range
   If rngSearch.Cells.Count = 1 Then
     Set rngSearch = ActiveSheet.UsedRange
   End If

End If

lblSearchRange.Caption = "Search Range: " & _
     rngSearch.Address(RowAbsolute:=False, ColumnAbsolute:=False)

End Sub
```

When the user hits the Select button, the action begins, based on the user's selection. Thus, we should call a different procedure based on which option button is selected. After the new selection is made, the Select button is disabled. Since the CompleteRows and CompleteColumns features are still available, however, we do not want to dismiss the main dialog. The code to handle the Select button is shown in Example 19-9.

Example 19-9. The cmdSelect_Click Event Procedure

```
Private Sub cmdSelect_Click()

' Read option buttons and
' call appropriate procedure
If optDifferent Then
   SelectIfDifferent
ElseIf optSame Then
   SelectIfSame
ElseIf optEmpty Then
   SelectIfEmpty
ElseIf optNotEmpty Then
   SelectIfNotEmpty
End If

cmdSelect.Enabled = False

End Sub
```

The *SelectIfDifferent* procedure is shown in Example 19-10. It basically searches through the **rngSearch** range, looking for cells whose contents differ from the previous cell. Since we do not know whether the range is a column or row (or portion thereof), it is easier to use a double **For** loop. However, it would be a bit more efficient to split the code into two cases (**cColumns** = 1 and **cRows** = 1). Note that the first cell needs a bit of special attention, since we want to include it in the selection. The selection is accumulated in a Range object variable called **rngMatch**, using the *Union* function. However, we always need to consider the possibility that **rngMatch** is currently equal to **Nothing**, in which case the *Union* function will (unfortunately) return **Nothing**. In other words:

```
    Application.Union(Something, Nothing) = Nothing
```

Example 19-10. The SelectIfDifferent Procedure

```
Private Sub SelectIfDifferent()

Dim rngMatch As Range
Dim vCellValue As Variant
Dim vPreviousCellValue As Variant
Dim cMatches As Integer
Dim oCell As Object
Dim cRows As Integer, cColumns As Integer
```

Example 19-10. The SelectIfDifferent Procedure (continued)

```
Dim r As Integer, c As Integer

' Get row and column count (one of which is 1)
cColumns = rngSearch.Columns.Count
cRows = rngSearch.Rows.Count

' Start search
cMatches = 0
Set rngMatch = Nothing

For r = 1 To cRows
  For c = 1 To cColumns

    Set oCell = rngSearch.Cells(r, c)
    vCellValue = oCell.Value
    vCellValue = CStr(vCellValue)

    If r = 1 And c = 1 Then
      ' Include first cell
      If rngMatch Is Nothing Then
          Set rngMatch = oCell
        Else
          Set rngMatch = Application.Union(rngMatch, oCell)
        End If
      cMatches = cMatches + 1
      ' Save value for next comparison
      vPreviousCellValue = vCellValue
    Else
        ' Do comparison with previous cell
      vCellValue = rngSearch.Cells(r, c).Value
      vCellValue = CStr(vCellValue)
      If vCellValue <> vPreviousCellValue Then
        If rngMatch Is Nothing Then
          Set rngMatch = oCell
        Else
          Set rngMatch = Application.Union(rngMatch, oCell)
        End If
        cMatches = cMatches + 1
      End If
      ' Save value for next comparion
      vPreviousCellValue = vCellValue
    End If
  Next ' column
Next   ' row

' Select the range
If cMatches > 0 Then
  rngMatch.Select
  cmdUndo.Enabled = False
Else
  MsgBox "No matching cells. Selection will not be changed.", vbInformation
  cmdUndo.Enabled = False
```

Example 19-10. The SelectIfDifferent Procedure (continued)

```
End If

End Sub
```

The *SelectIfSame* procedure, which is shown in Example 19-11, is very similar to the *SelectIfDifferent* procedure. One significant difference is that we do not include the first cell.

Example 19-11. The SelectIfSame Procedure

```
Private Sub SelectIfSame()

Dim rngMatch As Range
Dim vCellValue As Variant
Dim vPreviousCellValue As Variant
Dim cMatches As Integer
Dim oCell As Object
Dim cRows As Integer, cColumns As Integer
Dim r As Integer, c As Integer

' Get row and column count (one of which is 1)
cColumns = rngSearch.Columns.Count
cRows = rngSearch.Rows.Count

' Start search
cMatches = 0
Set rngMatch = Nothing

  For r = 1 To cRows
    For c = 1 To cColumns

      Set oCell = rngSearch.Cells(r, c)
      vCellValue = oCell.Value
      vCellValue = CStr(vCellValue)

      If r = 1 And c = 1 Then
        ' Save first value for next comparion
        vPreviousCellValue = vCellValue
      Else
        ' Do comparison with previous cell
        vCellValue = rngSearch.Cells(r, c).Value
        vCellValue = CStr(vCellValue)
        If vCellValue = vPreviousCellValue Then
          If rngMatch Is Nothing Then
            Set rngMatch = oCell
          Else
            Set rngMatch = Application.Union(rngMatch, oCell)
          End If
          cMatches = cMatches + 1
        End If
        ' Save value for next comparion
        vPreviousCellValue = vCellValue
```

Example 19-11. The SelectIfSame Procedure (continued)

```
      End If
    Next ' column
  Next  ' row


' Select the range
If cMatches > 0 Then
  rngMatch.Select
  cmdUndo.Enabled = False
Else
  MsgBox "No matching cells. Selection will not be changed.", vbInformation
  cmdUndo.Enabled = False
End If

End Sub
```

The *SelectIfEmpty* and *SelectIfNotEmpty* procedures are almost identical. *SelectIfEmpty* is shown in Example 19-12.

Example 19-12. The SelectIfEmpty Procedure

```
Private Sub SelectIfEmpty()

Dim rngMatch As Range
Dim cMatches As Integer
Dim oCell As Object
Dim cRows As Integer, cColumns As Integer
Dim r As Integer, c As Integer

' Get row and column count (one of which is 1)
cColumns = rngSearch.Columns.Count
cRows = rngSearch.Rows.Count

' Start search
cMatches = 0
Set rngMatch = Nothing

  For r = 1 To cRows
    For c = 1 To cColumns

      Set oCell = rngSearch.Cells(r, c)

      If IsEmpty(oCell) Then
        If rngMatch Is Nothing Then
          Set rngMatch = oCell
        Else
          Set rngMatch = Application.Union(rngMatch, oCell)
        End If
        cMatches = cMatches + 1
      End If

    Next ' column
  Next  ' row
```

Example 19-12. The SelectIfEmpty Procedure (continued)

```
' Select the range
If cMatches > 0 Then
  rngMatch.Select
  cmdUndo.Enabled = False
Else
  MsgBox "No matching cells. Selection will not be changed.", vbInformation
  cmdUndo.Enabled = False
End If

End Sub
```

To get the *SelectIfNotEmpty* procedure, just change the line:

```
    If IsEmpty(oCell) Then
```

to:

```
    If Not IsEmpty(oCell) Then
```

Finally, the *CompleteColumns* and *CompleteRows* procedures are called from the corresponding command-button Click events and are very similar. *Complete-Columns* is shown in Example 19-13.

Example 19-13. The cmdCompleteColumns_Click Procedure

```
Private Sub cmdCompleteColumns_Click()

' For each selected cell, select the entire column

Dim oCell As Object
Dim rngNew As Range

Set rngNew = Nothing

For Each oCell In Selection
  If rngNew Is Nothing Then
    Set rngNew = oCell.EntireColumn
  Else
    Set rngNew = Union(rngNew, oCell.EntireColumn)
  End If
Next

rngNew.Select
cmdUndo.Enabled = True

End Sub
```

To get *CompleteRows*, just replace EntireColumn by EntireRow in two places.

20

Pivot Tables

In this chapter, we take a look at pivot tables and how to create and format them using code.

Pivot Tables

While we are assuming that the reader is familiar with the basics of Excel, it probably would not hurt to quickly review the concept of a pivot table (or PivotTable).

PivotTables are one of the most powerful features in Excel. They are designed to accomplish three main tasks:

- Import external data
- Aggregate data; for example, sum, count, or average the data
- Display the data in interesting ways

PivotTables can use data from external sources, as well as from one or more Excel tables. For instance, the data for a PivotTable can come from an Access database. However, setting up Excel to import external data requires that the appropriate data source drivers be installed on the user's computer. Moreover, there are significant limitations on Excel's ability to import data through PivotTables. For instance, all strings are limited to a length of 255 characters, which makes using SQL to define a data source much more difficult.

All in all, importing data using a PivotTable can be problematic. Furthermore, we always have the option of importing the required data directly to an Excel worksheet (using a variety of more sophisticated methods, such as DAO and the GetRows method) and then creating the PivotTable from the worksheet. Accordingly, we will restrict our discussion to using Excel data as the PivotTable source.

Table 20-1, which represents sales from a fictitious fast food company that has both company and franchise stores, shows the first half of the data that we will use to build our pivot table. The actual source table is an Excel worksheet that contains twice the number of rows as Table 20-1, the additional rows being the analogous data for the year 1997. (Thus, the first column in the remainder of the table contains the year 1997.)

Table 20-1. Source Data for Pivot Table (for 1998)

Year	Period	Store Code	Store City	Store Type	Transactions	Sales
1998	1	BO-1	BOSTON	Company	3881	$6,248.00
1998	1	BO-2	BOSTON	Company	3789	$5,722.00
1998	1	BO-3	BOSTON	Company	3877	$6,278.00
1998	1	BO-4	BOSTON	Company	3862	$6,123.00
1998	1	BO-5	BOSTON	Franchise	4013	$6,861.00
1998	1	BO-6	BOSTON	Franchise	3620	$5,039.00
1998	2	BO-1	BOSTON	Company	3948	$6,468.00
1998	2	BO-2	BOSTON	Company	3878	$6,301.00
1998	2	BO-3	BOSTON	Company	3911	$6,390.00
1998	2	BO-4	BOSTON	Company	3926	$6,438.00
1998	2	BO-5	BOSTON	Franchise	3990	$6,767.00
1998	2	BO-6	BOSTON	Franchise	3615	$5,091.00
1998	3	BO-1	BOSTON	Company	3936	$6,307.00
1998	3	BO-2	BOSTON	Company	3857	$6,153.00
1998	3	BO-3	BOSTON	Company	3898	$6,319.00
1998	3	BO-4	BOSTON	Company	3949	$6,453.00
1998	3	BO-5	BOSTON	Franchise	3617	$5,052.00
1998	3	BO-6	BOSTON	Franchise	3624	$5,111.00
1998	4	BO-1	BOSTON	Company	3853	$6,021.00
1998	4	BO-2	BOSTON	Company	3891	$6,333.00
1998	4	BO-3	BOSTON	Company	3892	$6,289.00
1998	4	BO-4	BOSTON	Company	3966	$6,571.00
1998	4	BO-5	BOSTON	Franchise	3595	$4,945.00
1998	4	BO-6	BOSTON	Franchise	3611	$5,051.00
1998	1	LA-1	LOS ANGELES	Franchise	8259	$29,267.00
1998	1	LA-2	LOS ANGELES	Company	9140	$31,947.00
1998	1	LA-3	LOS ANGELES	Company	9727	$35,405.00
1998	1	LA-4	LOS ANGELES	Franchise	9494	$33,830.00
1998	1	LA-5	LOS ANGELES	Franchise	10644	$39,971.00
1998	1	LA-6	LOS ANGELES	Franchise	10649	$40,077.00

Table 20-1. Source Data for Pivot Table (for 1998) (continued)

Year	Period	Store Code	Store City	Store Type	Transactions	Sales
1998	2	LA-1	LOS ANGELES	Franchise	9066	$32,595.00
1998	2	LA-2	LOS ANGELES	Company	9789	$35,217.00
1998	2	LA-3	LOS ANGELES	Company	9814	$35,455.00
1998	2	LA-4	LOS ANGELES	Franchise	9917	$35,926.00
1998	2	LA-5	LOS ANGELES	Franchise	10617	$39,424.00
1998	2	LA-6	LOS ANGELES	Franchise	10190	$38,387.00
1998	3	LA-1	LOS ANGELES	Franchise	9531	$33,966.00
1998	3	LA-2	LOS ANGELES	Company	9698	$34,419.00
1998	3	LA-3	LOS ANGELES	Company	9771	$34,494.00
1998	3	LA-4	LOS ANGELES	Franchise	10232	$37,315.00
1998	3	LA-5	LOS ANGELES	Franchise	10561	$39,141.00
1998	3	LA-6	LOS ANGELES	Franchise	10924	$41,938.00
1998	4	LA-1	LOS ANGELES	Franchise	9310	$33,202.00
1998	4	LA-2	LOS ANGELES	Company	9496	$33,910.00
1998	4	LA-3	LOS ANGELES	Company	9596	$34,500.00
1998	4	LA-4	LOS ANGELES	Franchise	10050	$37,274.00
1998	4	LA-5	LOS ANGELES	Franchise	10440	$38,304.00
1998	4	LA-6	LOS ANGELES	Franchise	10778	$40,965.00
1998	1	NY-1	NEW YORK	Company	6390	$19,890.00
1998	1	NY-2	NEW YORK	Franchise	7016	$22,229.00
1998	1	NY-3	NEW YORK	Franchise	7293	$24,077.00
1998	1	NY-4	NEW YORK	Company	7037	$22,704.00
1998	1	NY-5	NEW YORK	Franchise	7815	$26,962.00
1998	1	NY-6	NEW YORK	Franchise	6935	$22,925.00
1998	2	NY-1	NEW YORK	Company	6954	$22,389.00
1998	2	NY-2	NEW YORK	Franchise	7531	$25,324.00
1998	2	NY-3	NEW YORK	Franchise	7486	$24,753.00
1998	2	NY-4	NEW YORK	Company	7285	$24,112.00
1998	2	NY-5	NEW YORK	Franchise	7749	$26,325.00
1998	2	NY-6	NEW YORK	Franchise	6881	$23,123.00
1998	3	NY-1	NEW YORK	Company	7256	$23,330.00
1998	3	NY-2	NEW YORK	Franchise	7330	$24,258.00
1998	3	NY-3	NEW YORK	Franchise	7212	$23,386.00
1998	3	NY-4	NEW YORK	Company	7480	$24,619.00
1998	3	NY-5	NEW YORK	Franchise	6771	$22,189.00
1998	3	NY-6	NEW YORK	Franchise	6954	$23,188.00

Table 20-1. Source Data for Pivot Table (for 1998) (continued)

Year	Period	Store Code	Store City	Store Type	Transactions	Sales
1998	4	NY-1	NEW YORK	Company	7086	$22,703.00
1998	4	NY-2	NEW YORK	Franchise	7275	$24,245.00
1998	4	NY-3	NEW YORK	Franchise	7121	$23,025.00
1998	4	NY-4	NEW YORK	Company	7562	$25,329.00
1998	4	NY-5	NEW YORK	Franchise	6569	$20,845.00
1998	4	NY-6	NEW YORK	Franchise	6973	$23,220.00

The Period column in Table 20-1 is the time period. For simplicity, we consider only four time periods. The Store Code column gives the store code, used to uniquely identify a store. The Store City gives the city in which the store is located. The Store Type column indicates whether the store is owned by the company or is franchised. The Transactions column gives the number of transactions for that time period. The Sales column gives the total sales for that store during that period.

Note that there is one and only one row for each time period/store code. (In database language, the time period/store code forms a *key* for the data.)

Our goal is to create a PivotTable from the data in Table 20-1. Of course, before creating a PivotTable, we need to identify the type of aggregate data in which we are interested. Clearly, we want total sales and transaction counts. The question is: "Over what groupings?"

The best approach is to first identify the *most refined* (or *smallest*) grouping for the aggregate data. In this case, it is store type/store location/time period. For example, we want the total sales for all company stores in New York during period 1.

In addition, we will want aggregates for larger groupings—for example, total sales for all company stores in New York over all periods, and total sales for New York.

Finally, we want separate totals for the years 1998 and 1997.

The PivotTable Wizard

Let us first walk through the PivotTable wizard to create our PivotTable. Then we will create the same PivotTable using code.

The first step is to select the source data and start the wizard by selecting Pivot-Table Report under the Data menu. This will produce the first wizard dialog, as shown in Figure 20-1.

Note that this dialog allows us to select the data source for the PivotTable data. Clicking the Next button produces the dialog in Figure 20-2.

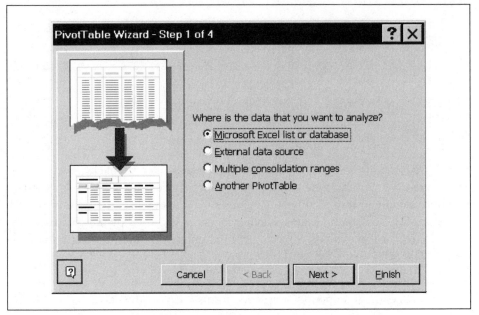

Figure 20-1. Step 1 in the PivotTable wizard

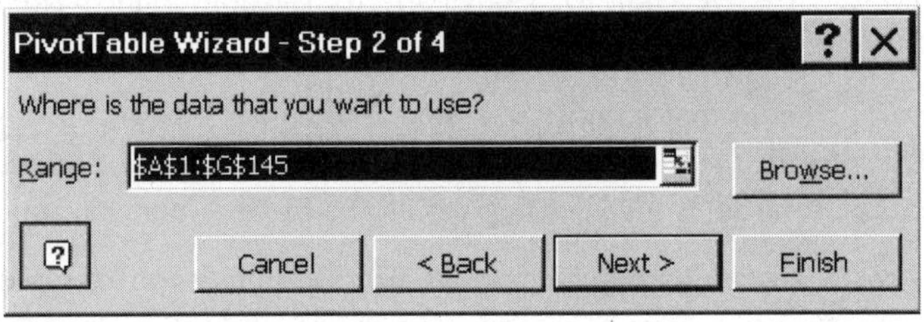

Figure 20-2. Step 2 in the PivotTable wizard

Since we selected the correct source range before starting the wizard, Excel has correctly identified that range in Figure 20-2, so we can simply hit the Next button, which produces the dialog in Figure 20-3.

This dialog is where we format the PivotTable by deciding which columns of the original source table become pages in the PivotTable, which become rows, which become columns, and which become data (for aggregation). The procedure is to drag the buttons on the right to the proper location—row, column, page, or data. (We want one page for each of the two years.)

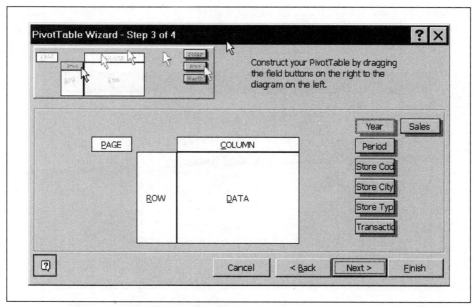

Figure 20-3. Step 3 in the PivotTable wizard

For our example, we drag the buttons to the locations shown in Figure 20-4. Note that the only button not used is Store Code. This field is the *aggregate* field, that is, we will sum over all store codes.

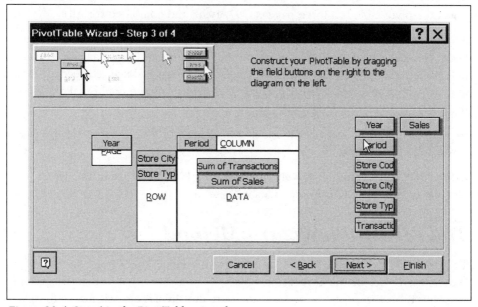

Figure 20-4. Step 4 in the PivotTable wizard

Clicking the Next button takes us to the dialog in Figure 20-5, where we choose the location for the PivotTable. We choose a new worksheet.

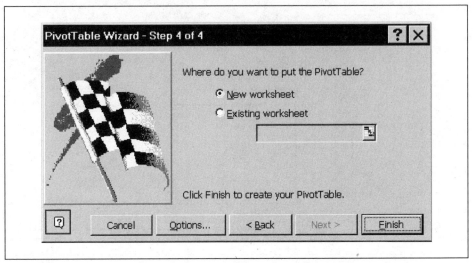

Figure 20-5. Step 5 in the PivotTable wizard

Clicking the Finish button produces the PivotTable in Figure 20-6.

Note that the page button is labeled Year. Selecting one of All, 1998, or 1997 from the drop-down list box next to this button will confine the data to that selection. Thus, the pivot table has three pages: 1997, 1998, and combined (or All).

Note also that the columns are labeled by periods and the rows are labeled by both Store City and Store Type, as requested. In addition, Excel has created a new field called Data that is used as row labels. In this case, Excel correctly guessed that we want sums, but if Excel had guessed incorrectly we could make a change manually.

In summary, we can see that the main components of a pivot table are the pages, rows, columns, and data fields.

Rather than pursue further development of this PivotTable using the Excel interface, let us now switch to using code.

The PivotTableWizard Method

To create a PivotTable through code, we use the PivotTableWizard method of the Worksheet object or the PivotTable object. Contrary to what you might assume, the PivotTableWizard method does not start the PivotTable wizard. Rather, it is

	A	B	C	D	E	F	G	H
1	Year	(All) ▼						
2								
3				Period				
4	Store City	Store Type	Data	1	2	3	4	Grand Total
5	BOSTON	Company	Sum of Transactions	28248	28714	28672	28602	114236
6			Sum of Sales	44678	46927	46256	46223	184084
7		Franchise	Sum of Transactions	13993	13942	13275	13210	54420
8	.		Sum of Sales	21816	21739	18632	18325	80512
9	BOSTON Sum of Transactions			42241	42656	41947	41812	168656
10	BOSTON Sum of Sales			66494	68666	64888	64548	264596
11	LOS ANGE	Company	Sum of Transactions	34588	35938	35692	35001	141219
12			Sum of Sales	123478	129564	126340	125418	504800
13		Franchise	Sum of Transactions	71583	72947	75619	74392	294541
14			Sum of Sales	262431	268274	279325	274531	1084561
15	LOS ANGELES Sum of Transactions			106171	108885	111311	109393	435760
16	LOS ANGELES Sum of Sales			385909	397838	405665	399949	1589361
17	NEW YOR	Company	Sum of Transactions	24616	26104	27015	26854	104589
18			Sum of Sales	78089	85251	87905	88058	339303
19		Franchise	Sum of Transactions	53273	54351	51822	51218	210664
20			Sum of Sales	176353	182461	170537	167446	696797
21	NEW YORK Sum of Transactions			77889	80455	78837	78072	315253
22	NEW YORK Sum of Sales			254442	267712	258442	255504	1036100
23	Total Sum of Transactions			226301	231996	232095	229277	919669
24	Total Sum of Sales			706845	734216	728995	720001	2890057

Figure 20-6. The PivotTable

used to create a PivotTable when applied to the Worksheet object or to modify an existing PivotTable when applied to the PivotTable object.

The syntax is:

```
expression.PivotTableWizard(SourceType, SourceData, TableDestination, _
    TableName, RowGrand, ColumnGrand, SaveData, HasAutoFormat, _
    AutoPage, Reserved, BackgroundQuery, OptimizeCache, _
    PageFieldOrder, ageFieldWrapCount, ReadData, Connection)
```

where *expression* returns either a Worksheet object or a PivotTable object. As you might expect, the parameters of the PivotTableWizard method correspond to settings in the PivotTable wizard. On the other hand, the PivotTableWizard method cannot do everything that the PivotTable wizard can do. For instance, it cannot be used to specify the row, column, and data fields. (We will see how to do that a bit later.) Put another way, the PivotTableWizard method sets the properties of an *empty* PivotTable.

Let us go over some of the more important parameters to the PivotTableWizard method.

The optional *SourceType* parameter specifies the source of the PivotTable data and can be one of the following `XlPivotTableSourceType` constants:

```
Enum XlPivotTableSourceType
    xlPivotTable = -4148
    xlDatabase = 1
    xlExternal = 2
    xlConsolidation = 3
End Enum
```

These directly correspond to the first dialog of the PivotTable wizard, as shown in Figure 20-1.

If we specify a value for *SourceType*, then we must also specify a value for *SourceData*. If we specify neither, Excel uses the source type **xlDatabase**, and the source data from a named range called **Database**. If this named range does not exist, Excel uses the current region if the current selection is in a range of more than 10 cells that contain data. Otherwise, the method will fail. All in all, this rule is sufficiently complicated to warrant always specifying these parameters.

The *SourceData* parameter specifies the data for the PivotTable. It can be a Range object, an array of ranges, or a text constant that represents the name of another PivotTable. For external data, this must be a two-element array, the first element of which is the connection string specifying the ODBC source for the data, and the second element of which is the SQL query string used to get the data.

The *TableDestination* parameter is a Range object specifying where the Pivot-Table should be placed. It can include a worksheet qualifier to specify the worksheet upon which to place the pivot table as well.

The *TableName* parameter is a string that specifies the name of the new Pivot-Table.

The *RowGrand* parameter should be set to **True** to show grand totals for rows in the PivotTable. Similarly, the *ColumnGrand* parameter should be set to **True** to show grand totals for columns in the PivotTable.

The *SaveData* parameter should be set to **True** to save data with the PivotTable. If it is **False**, then only the PivotTable definition is saved.

HasAutoFormat is set to **True** to have Excel automatically format the PivotTable whenever it is refreshed or whenever any fields are moved.

The *PageFieldOrder* and *PageFieldWrapCount* parameters are meaningful only when there is more than one page field, in which case these parameters specify where the page field buttons and concomitant drop-down list boxes are placed relative to one another. The *PageFieldOrder* parameter can be either **xlDown–**

`ThenOver` (the default) or `xlOverThenDown`. For instance, if there were three page fields, then the setting:

```
PageFieldOrder = xlDownThenOver
PageFieldWrapCount = 2
```

would arrange the page fields as in Figure 20-7. This pivot table is only for illustration of the page field order. It was created from the original pivot table by moving the row fields to page fields. Note also that setting *PageFieldOrder* to **xlOverThenDown** would simply reverse the positions of Store City and Store Type.

	A	B	C	D	E	F
1						
2	Year	(All) ▼		Store Type	(All) ▼	
3	Store City	(All) ▼				
4						
5		Period				
6	Data	1	2	3	4	Grand Total
7	Sum of Transactions	226301	231996	232095	229277	919669
8	Sum of Sales	706845	734216	728995	720001	2890057

Figure 20-7. Illustrating page field order

The following code ostensibly creates the PivotTable in Figure 20-6 at the location of the active cell:

```
ActiveSheet.PivotTableWizard _
    SourceType:=xlDatabase, _
    SourceData:="'Source'!R1C1:R145C7", _
    TableName:="Sales&Trans"
```

In fact, the results of executing this code are shown in Figure 20-8. The reason nothing much seems to have happened is that, as we mentioned earlier, the PivotTableWizard method does not allow us to specify which fields are page, row, column, and data fields. The table in Figure 20-8 is an empty PivotTable.

	A	B
1		Total
2	Total	

Figure 20-8. An empty PivotTable

The PivotTable Object

To understand better what must be done next, we must discuss the PivotTable object and its various child collection objects.

Invoking the PivotTableWizard method has created a PivotTable object named Sales&Trans for us. All PivotTable objects have a PivotFields collection, accessed through the PivotFields property. Thus, the code:

```
Dim pf As PivotField
For Each pf In _
  ActiveSheet.PivotTables("Sales&Trans").PivotFields
     Debug.Print pf.Name
Next
```

produces the following list of pivot fields:

```
Year
Period
Store Code
Store City
Store Type
Transactions
Sales
```

Now, each PivotField object can have a designation that specifies whether this field is to be used as a row field, a column field, a page field, or a data field. This designation is referred to as its *orientation*.

It turns out that there is more than one way to set the orientation of a pivot field. One approach is to set the pivot field's Orientation property, and another approach is to use the AddFields method. Unfortunately, neither of these methods is sufficiently documented, so some experimentation is in order.

As to the Orientation property approach, consider the code in Example 20-1, which sets both the Orientation and Position properties. We will discuss the subtleties of this code after you have looked at it.

Example 20-1. The CreatePivotFields Procedure

```
Sub CreatePivotFields()
With ActiveSheet.PivotTables("Sales&Trans")

  Debug.Print "Before all:"
  ShowFields

  .PivotFields("Year").Orientation = xlPageField
  .PivotFields("Year").Position = 1

  .PivotFields("Store City").Orientation =   xlRowField
  .PivotFields("Store City").Position = 1
```

Example 20-1. The CreatePivotFields Procedure (continued)

```
   .PivotFields("Store Type").Orientation = xlRowField
   .PivotFields("Store Type").Position = 2

   .PivotFields("Period").Orientation = xlColumnField
   Debug.Print "Before data fields:"
   ShowFields

   With .PivotFields("Transactions")
      .Orientation = xlDataField
      .Position = 1
   End With
   With .PivotFields("Sales")
      .Orientation = xlDataField
      .Position = 2
   End With
   Debug.Print ""
   Debug.Print "After data fields:"
   ShowFields
   .PivotFields("Data").Orientation = xlRowField
   .PivotFields("Data").Position = 3
End With
End Sub
```

The *ShowFields* procedure used in *CreatePivotFields* is shown in Example 20-2; it simply prints (to the Immediate window) a list of all pivot fields and is very useful for experimenting or debugging.

Example 20-2. The ShowFields Procedure

```
Sub ShowFields()
Dim pf As PivotField
Debug.Print "*PivotFields:"
For Each pf In _
 ActiveSheet.PivotTables("Sales&Trans").PivotFields
   Debug.Print pf.Name
Next
Debug.Print "*RowFields:"
For Each pf In _
 ActiveSheet.PivotTables("Sales&Trans").RowFields
   Debug.Print pf.Name
Next
Debug.Print "*ColFields:"
For Each pf In _
 ActiveSheet.PivotTables("Sales&Trans").ColumnFields
   Debug.Print pf.Name
Next
Debug.Print "*DataFields:"
For Each pf In _
 ActiveSheet.PivotTables("Sales&Trans").DataFields
   Debug.Print pf.Name
Next
End Sub
```

Running *CreatePivotFields* results in the following display to the Immediate window:

```
Before all:
*PivotFields:
Year
Period
Store Code
Store City
Store Type
Transactions
Sales
*RowFields:
*ColFields:
*DataFields:

Before data fields:
*PivotFields:
Year
Period
Store Code
Store City
Store Type
Transactions
Sales
*RowFields:
Store City
Store Type
*ColFields:
Period
*DataFields:

After data fields:
*PivotFields:
Year
Period
Store Code
Store City
Store Type
Transactions
Sales
Data
*RowFields:
Store City
Store Type
Data
*ColFields:
Period
*DataFields:
Sum of Transactions
Sum of Sales
```

The first thing we notice from this list is that the special pivot field called Data is created by Excel *only after* the Transactions and Sales fields are assigned the `xlDataField` orientation. This statement is further supported by the fact that if we move the last two lines of code:

```
.PivotFields("Data").Orientation = xlRowField
.PivotFields("Data").Position = 3
```

to just before the **With** block related to the Transactions field, Excel will issue an error message when we try to run the code, stopping at the line:

```
.PivotFields("Data").Orientation = xlRowField
```

because it cannot set the Orientation property of the nonexistent Data field.

Next, we observe that, with respect to Row, Column, and Page fields, Excel simply adds the pivot fields to the appropriate collections. However, with respect to Data fields, Excel creates *new* field objects called Sum of Transactions and Sum of Sales that are considered data fields but not pivot-table fields!

Naming Data Fields

We should make a few remarks about naming data fields. It is important to note that if the name of a data field has not been changed but we make a change to the aggregate function, say from *Sum* to *Average*, then Excel will automatically rename the data field, in this case from **Sum of Sales** to **Average of Sales**. However, once we set a new name for the data field, Excel will not rename it when we change the aggregate function.

We can rename a data field simply by setting its Name property. However, even though Data fields do not seem to belong to the PivotFields collection, we cannot use the name of a pivot field for a data field. For instance, we cannot rename **Sum of Transactions** to **Transactions**, since this is already taken by the pivot field. (Trying to do so will produce an error.) Thus, in designing the source table for the pivot table, we should choose a column heading that we do not want to use in the pivot table!

The Complete Code

For reference, let us put together the code required to create the pivot table in Figure 20-6; it is shown in Example 20-3.

Example 20-3. The CreatePivot Procedure

```
Sub CreatePivot()

' Create pivot table at active cell
' Assumes that the source table is in sheet called Source

ActiveSheet.PivotTableWizard _
    SourceType:=xlDatabase, _
```

Example 20-3. The CreatePivot Procedure (continued)

```
    SourceData:="'Company Both'!R1C1:R145C7", _
    TableName:="Sales&Trans"

' Assign field orientations and data fields
With ActiveSheet.PivotTables("Sales&Trans")

  .PivotFields("Year").Orientation = xlPageField
  .PivotFields("Year").Position = 1

  .PivotFields("Store City").Orientation = _
      xlRowField
  .PivotFields("Store City").Position = 1

  .PivotFields("Store Type").Orientation = _
      xlRowField
  .PivotFields("Store Type").Position = 2

  .PivotFields("Period").Orientation = _
      xlColumnField
  With .PivotFields("Transactions")
    .Orientation = xlDataField
    .Position = 1
  End With
  With .PivotFields("Sales")
    .Orientation = xlDataField
    .Position = 2
  End With
  .PivotFields("Data").Orientation = xlRowField
  .PivotFields("Data").Position = 3
End With
End Sub
```

Another approach to assigning orientation for the pivot fields is to use the AddFields method of the PivotTable object. We can use this method for all but data fields. The syntax is:

```
    PivotTableObject.AddFields(RowFields, _
        ColumnFields, PageFields, AddToTable)
```

The optional *RowFields* parameter can specify either a single pivot-field name or an array of pivot-field names to be added as rows, and similarly for the *ColumnFields* and *PageFields* parameters.

It is important to note that any invocation of the AddFields method will *replace* all existing fields of the given type (row, column, or page) with the fields designated by the parameters of the method. To increment rather than replace existing fields, we must set the *AddToTable* parameter to **True**.

The alternative to *CreatePivot* shown in Example 20-4 uses the AddFields method for row, column, and page fields. Note that this is shorter than the previous procedure. (It is also the approach taken by Excel itself when we record a macro that creates this pivot table.)

Example 20-4. Creating a Pivot Table Using the AddFields Method

```
Sub CreatePivot2()

' Create pivot table at active cell
' Assumes that the source table is in sheet called Source

ActiveSheet.PivotTableWizard _
    SourceType:=xlDatabase, _
    SourceData:="'Source'!R1C1:R145C7", _
    TableName:="Sales&Trans2"

ActiveSheet.PivotTables("Sales&Trans2").AddFields _
    RowFields:=Array("Store City", "Store Type"), _
    ColumnFields:="Period", _
    PageFields:="Year"
With ActiveSheet.PivotTables("Sales&Trans2")

  With .PivotFields("Transactions")
    .Orientation = xlDataField
    .Position = 1
  End With
  With .PivotFields("Sales")
    .Orientation = xlDataField
    .Position = 2
  End With
End With
End Sub
```

Properties and Methods of the PivotTable Object

The members of the PivotTable object are shown in Table 20-2. We'll discuss the most important of these members by their function.

Table 20-2. Members of the PivotTable Object

AddFields	InnerDetail	RefreshDate
Application	ListFormulas	RefreshName
CacheIndex	ManualUpdate	RefreshTable
CalculatedFields	MergeLabels	RowFields
ColumnFields	Name	RowGrand
ColumnGrand	NullString	RowRange
ColumnRange	PageFieldOrder	SaveData
Creator	PageFields	SelectionMode

Table 20-2. Members of the PivotTable Object (continued)

DataBodyRange	PageFieldStyle	ShowPages
DataFields	PageFieldWrapCount	SourceData
DataLabelRange	PageRange	SubtotalHiddenPageItems
DisplayErrorString	PageRangeCells	TableRange1
DisplayNullString	Parent	TableRange2
EnableDrilldown	PivotCache	TableStyle
EnableFieldDialog	PivotFields	Tag
EnableWizard	PivotFormulas	Update
ErrorString	PivotSelect	VacatedStyle
GetData	PivotSelection	Value
HasAutoFormat	PivotTableWizard	VisibleFields
HiddenFields	PreserveFormatting	

Returning a Fields Collection

Several of the members of the PivotTable object are designed to return a fields collection.

ColumnFields property

This property returns the collection of all column fields, using the syntax:

```
PivotTableObject.ColumnFields
```

Alternatively, we can return selected column fields using the syntax:

```
PivotTableObject.ColumnFields(Index)
```

where *Index* is either a single index (the index number of the desired field) or an array of indexes.

DataFields property

This property returns the collection of all data fields, using the syntax:

```
PivotTableObject.DataFields
```

Alternatively, we can return selected data fields using the syntax:

```
PivotTableObject.DataFields(Index)
```

where *Index* is either a single index (the index number of the desired field) or an array of indexes.

HiddenFields property

As we will see, a pivot field can be hidden by setting its orientation to **xlHidden**. The HiddenFields property returns the collection of all hidden fields, using the syntax:

```
PivotTableObject.HiddenFields
```

Alternatively, we can return selected hidden fields using the syntax:

```
PivotTableObject.HiddenFields(Index)
```

where *Index* is either a single index (the index number of the desired field) or an array of indexes.

PageFields property

The PageFields property returns the collection of all page fields, using the syntax:

```
PivotTableObject.PageFields
```

Alternatively, we can return selected page fields using the syntax:

```
PivotTableObject.PageFields(Index)
```

where *Index* is either a single index (the index number of the desired field) or an array of indexes.

PivotFields property

The PivotFields property returns the collection of all pivot fields, using the syntax:

```
PivotTableObject.PivotFields
```

Alternatively, we can return selected pivot fields using the syntax:

```
PivotTableObject.PivotFields(Index)
```

where *Index* is either a single index (the index number of the desired field) or an array of indexes.

RowFields property

The RowFields property returns the collection of all row fields, using the syntax:

```
PivotTableObject.RowFields
```

Alternatively, we can return selected row fields using the syntax:

```
PivotTableObject.RowFields(Index)
```

where *Index* is either a single index (the index number of the desired field) or an array of indexes.

VisibleFields property

The VisibleFields property returns the collection of all visible fields, using the syntax:

```
PivotTableObject.VisibleFields
```

Alternatively, we can return selected visible fields using the syntax:

```
PivotTableObject.VisibleFields(Index)
```

where *Index* is either a single index (the index number of the desired field) or an array of indexes.

Totals-Related Members

The PivotTable object has two properties that affect the display of totals.

ColumnGrand property (R/W Boolean)

When this property is **True**, the PivotTable shows grand column totals.

RowGrand property (R/W Boolean)

When this property is **True**, the PivotTable shows grand row totals.

To illustrate, referring to the pivot table in Figure 20-6, the code:

```
ActiveSheet.PivotTables("Sales&Trans"). _
    ColumnGrand = False
ActiveSheet.PivotTables("Sales&Trans"). _
    RowGrand = False
```

produces the pivot table in Figure 20-9, with no grand totals.

We can also suppress the display of individual pivot-field totals, such as the totals for Store City in Figure 20-9. This is a property of the particular PivotField object, so we will discuss it when we discuss this object later in the chapter. As a preview, however, the display of field totals is governed by the Subtotals property of the PivotField object. For instance, the following code turns off all field totals in Figure 20-9:

```
Dim i As Integer
For i = 1 To 12
  ActiveSheet.PivotTables("Sales&Trans"). _
  PivotFields("Store City").Subtotals(i) = False
Next
```

(There are 12 types of totals, and we must turn them all off.) This produces the pivot table in Figure 20-10.

	Store City	Store Type	Data	Period			
1	Year	(All) ▼					
2							
3				Period			
4	Store City	Store Type	Data	1	2	3	4
5	BOSTON	Company	Sum of Transactions	28248	28714	28672	28602
6			Sum of Sales	44678	46927	46256	46223
7		Franchise	Sum of Transactions	13993	13942	13275	13210
8			Sum of Sales	21816	21739	18632	18325
9	BOSTON Sum of Transactions			42241	42656	41947	41812
10	BOSTON Sum of Sales			66494	68666	64888	64548
11	LOS ANGE	Company	Sum of Transactions	34588	35938	35692	35001
12			Sum of Sales	123478	129564	126340	125418
13		Franchise	Sum of Transactions	71583	72947	75619	74392
14			Sum of Sales	262431	268274	279325	274531
15	LOS ANGELES Sum of Transactions			106171	108885	111311	109393
16	LOS ANGELES Sum of Sales			385909	397838	405665	399949
17	NEW YOR	Company	Sum of Transactions	24616	26104	27015	26854
18			Sum of Sales	78089	85251	87905	88058
19		Franchise	Sum of Transactions	53273	54351	51822	51218
20			Sum of Sales	176353	182461	170537	167446
21	NEW YORK Sum of Transactions			77889	80455	78837	78072
22	NEW YORK Sum of Sales			254442	267712	258442	255504

Figure 20-9. No grand totals

	A	B	C	D	E	F	G
1	Year	(All) ▼					
2							
3				Period			
4	Store City	Store Type	Data	1	2	3	4
5	BOSTON	Company	Sum of Transactions	28248	28714	28672	28602
6			Sum of Sales	44678	46927	46256	46223
7		Franchise	Sum of Transactions	13993	13942	13275	13210
8			Sum of Sales	21816	21739	18632	18325
9	LOS ANGE	Company	Sum of Transactions	34588	35938	35692	35001
10			Sum of Sales	123478	129564	126340	125418
11		Franchise	Sum of Transactions	71583	72947	75619	74392
12			Sum of Sales	262431	268274	279325	274531
13	NEW YOR	Company	Sum of Transactions	24616	26104	27015	26854
14			Sum of Sales	78089	85251	87905	88058
15		Franchise	Sum of Transactions	53273	54351	51822	51218
16			Sum of Sales	176353	182461	170537	167446

Figure 20-10. No totals at all

Returning a Portion of a PivotTable

Several of the members of the PivotTable object are designed to return a portion of the pivot table as a Range object. They are as follows.

ColumnRange property

This property returns a Range object that represents the column area in the pivot table. Figure 20-11 illustrates the column range.

	A	B	C	D	E	F	G
1	Year	(All) ▼					
2							
3				Period			
4	Store City	Store Type	Data	1	2	3	4
5	BOSTON	Company	Sum of Transactions	28248	28714	28672	28602
6			Sum of Sales	44678	46927	46256	46223
7		Franchise	Sum of Transactions	13993	13942	13275	13210
8			Sum of Sales	21816	21739	18632	18325
9	LOS ANGE	Company	Sum of Transactions	34588	35938	35692	35001
10			Sum of Sales	123478	129564	126340	125418
11		Franchise	Sum of Transactions	71583	72947	75619	74392
12			Sum of Sales	262431	268274	279325	274531
13	NEW YOR	Company	Sum of Transactions	24616	26104	27015	26854
14			Sum of Sales	78089	85251	87905	88058
15		Franchise	Sum of Transactions	53273	54351	51822	51218
16			Sum of Sales	176353	182461	170537	167446

Figure 20-11. The ColumnRange range

DataBodyRange property

This property returns a Range object that represents the PivotTable's data area. Figure 20-12 shows the results of selecting the DataBodyRange.

DataLabelRange property

This read-only property returns a Range object that represents the labels for the PivotTable data fields. Figure 20-13 illustrates DataLabelRange.

PageRange and PageRangeCells properties

The PageRange property returns a Range object that represents the PivotTable's page area. This is the smallest rectangular region containing all page field-related cells.

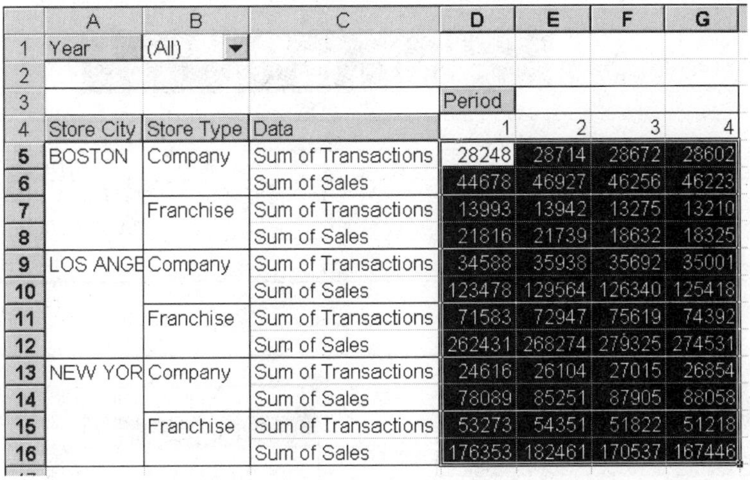

Figure 20-12. The DataBodyRange range

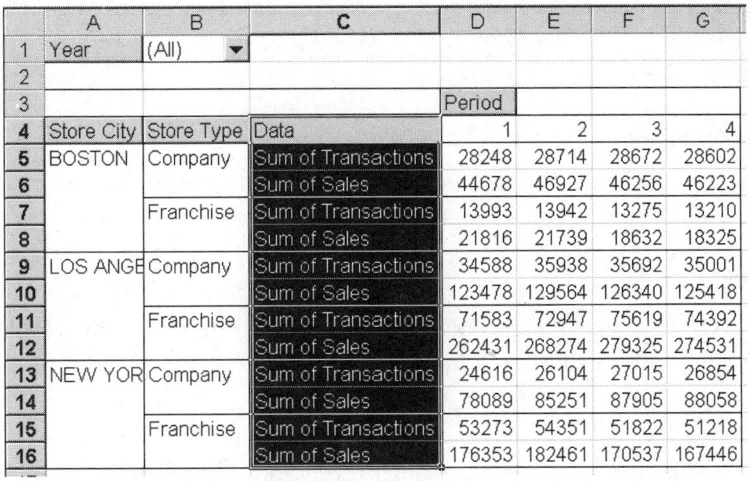

Figure 20-13. The DataLabelRange range

The PageRangeCells property returns a Range object that represents just the cells in the PivotTable containing the page-field buttons and item drop-down lists. Figure 20-14 and Figure 20-15 illustrate the difference.

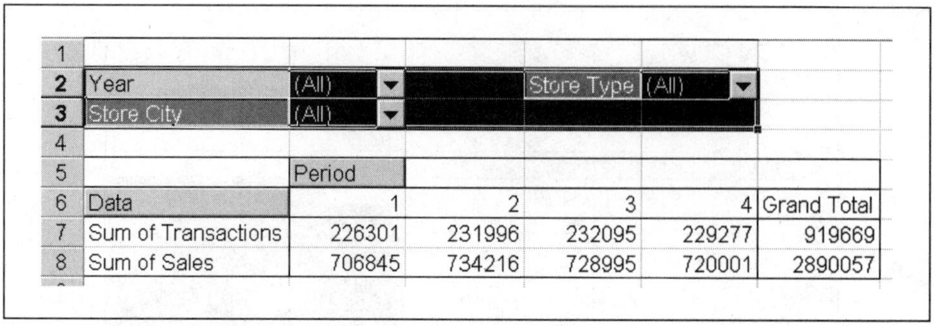

1					
2	Year	(All) ▼		Store Type (All) ▼	
3	Store City	(All) ▼			
4					
5		Period			
6	Data	1	2	3	4 Grand Total
7	Sum of Transactions	226301	231996	232095	229277 919669
8	Sum of Sales	706845	734216	728995	720001 2890057

Figure 20-14. The PageRange range

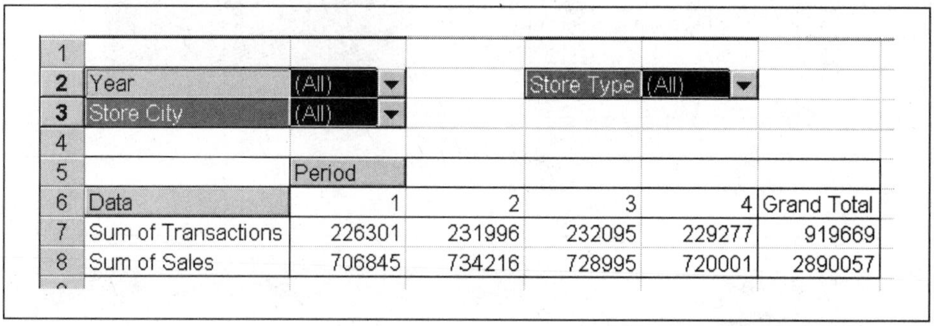

1					
2	Year	(All) ▼		Store Type (All) ▼	
3	Store City	(All) ▼			
4					
5		Period			
6	Data	1	2	3	4 Grand Total
7	Sum of Transactions	226301	231996	232095	229277 919669
8	Sum of Sales	706845	734216	728995	720001 2890057

Figure 20-15. The PageRangeCells range

RowRange property

This property returns a Range object that represents the PivotTable's row area. Figure 20-16 illustrates the row area.

TableRange1 property

This property returns a Range object that represents the entire PivotTable except the page fields. This is illustrated in Figure 20-17.

TableRange2 property

This property returns a Range object that represents the entire PivotTable, including the page fields. This is illustrated in Figure 20-18.

	A	B	C	D	E	F	G
1	Year	(All) ▼					
2							
3				Period			
4	Store City	Store Type	Data	1	2	3	4
5	BOSTON	Company	Sum of Transactions	28248	28714	28672	28602
6			Sum of Sales	44678	46927	46256	46223
7		Franchise	Sum of Transactions	13993	13942	13275	13210
8			Sum of Sales	21816	21739	18632	18325
9	LOS ANGE	Company	Sum of Transactions	34588	35938	35692	35001
10			Sum of Sales	123478	129564	126340	125418
11		Franchise	Sum of Transactions	71583	72947	75619	74392
12			Sum of Sales	262431	268274	279325	274531
13	NEW YOR	Company	Sum of Transactions	24616	26104	27015	26854
14			Sum of Sales	78089	85251	87905	88058
15		Franchise	Sum of Transactions	53273	54351	51822	51218
16			Sum of Sales	176353	182461	170537	167446

Figure 20-16. The RowRange range

	A	B	C	D	E	F	G
1	Year	(All) ▼					
2							
3				Period			
4	Store City	Store Type	Data	1	2	3	4
5	BOSTON	Company	Sum of Transactions	28248	28714	28672	28602
6			Sum of Sales	44678	46927	46256	46223
7		Franchise	Sum of Transactions	13993	13942	13275	13210
8			Sum of Sales	21816	21739	18632	18325
9	LOS ANGE	Company	Sum of Transactions	34588	35938	35692	35001
10			Sum of Sales	123478	129564	126340	125418
11		Franchise	Sum of Transactions	71583	72947	75619	74392
12			Sum of Sales	262431	268274	279325	274531
13	NEW YOR	Company	Sum of Transactions	24616	26104	27015	26854
14			Sum of Sales	78089	85251	87905	88058
15		Franchise	Sum of Transactions	53273	54351	51822	51218
16			Sum of Sales	176353	182461	170537	167446

Figure 20-17. The TableRange1 range

	A	B	C	D	E	F	G
1	Year	(All) ▼					
2							
3				Period			
4	Store City	Store Type	Data	1	2	3	4
5	BOSTON	Company	Sum of Transactions	28248	28714	28672	28602
6			Sum of Sales	44678	46927	46256	46223
7		Franchise	Sum of Transactions	13993	13942	13275	13210
8			Sum of Sales	21816	21739	18632	18325
9	LOS ANGE	Company	Sum of Transactions	34588	35938	35692	35001
10			Sum of Sales	123478	129564	126340	125418
11		Franchise	Sum of Transactions	71583	72947	75619	74392
12			Sum of Sales	262431	268274	279325	274531
13	NEW YOR	Company	Sum of Transactions	24616	26104	27015	26854
14			Sum of Sales	78089	85251	87905	88058
15		Franchise	Sum of Transactions	53273	54351	51822	51218
16			Sum of Sales	176353	182461	170537	167446

Figure 20-18. The TableRange2 range

PivotSelect and PivotSelection

The PivotSelect method selects part of a PivotTable. The syntax is:

```
PivotTableObject.PivotSelect(Name, Mode)
```

The *Mode* parameter specifies the selection mode and can be one of the following XlPTSelectionMode constants:

```
Enum XlPTSelectionMode
    xlDataAndLabel = 0
    xlLabelOnly = 1
    xlDataOnly = 2
    xlOrigin = 3
    xlBlanks = 4
    xlButton = 15
    xlFirstRow = 256      ' Excel 9 only
End Enum
```

The *Name* parameter specifies the selection in what Microsoft refers to as "standard PivotTable selection format." Unfortunately, the documentation does not tell us what this means, saying instead, "A string expression used to specify part of a PivotTable. The easiest way to understand the required syntax is to turn on the macro recorder, select cells in the PivotTable, and then study the resulting code." There is more on this, and we refer the reader to the Excel VBA help documentation (start by looking up the PivotSelect topic).

So let us consider some examples, all of which are based on the pivot table in Figure 20-10. However, to illustrate the Name property and to shorten the figures a bit, we will rename the data field "Sum of Transactions" to "Trans" and "Sum of Sales" to "Sale" using the following code:

```
Sub Rename()

' To shorten the names of the data fields

ActiveSheet.PivotTables("Sales&Trans"). _
    DataFields("Sum of Transactions").Name = "Trans"

ActiveSheet.PivotTables("Sales&Trans"). _
    DataFields("Sum of Sales").Name = "Sale"

End Sub
```

This also emphasizes a point we made earlier. Namely, we would like to rename the "Sum of Sales" field to "Sales" but there is a column in the source table by that name, so Excel will not let us use the name for a data field. Thus, we are stuck with "Sale." Now back to business.

The following code selects the entire pivot table:

```
ActiveSheet.PivotTables("Sales&Trans"). _
    PivotSelect "", xlDataAndLabel
```

The following code selects the Store Type label area (pivot-field label and pivot-item labels):

```
ActiveSheet.PivotTables("Sales&Trans"). _
    PivotSelect "'Store Type'[All]", xlLabelOnly
```

The following code selects all data and labels related to the Company pivot item:

```
ActiveSheet.PivotTables("Sales&Trans"). _
    PivotSelect "Company", xlDataAndLabel
```

The following code selects the cells shown in Figure 20-19:

```
ActiveSheet.PivotTables("Sales&Trans"). _
    PivotSelect "Company BOSTON", xlDataAndLabel
```

On the other hand, by reversing the words Company and BOSTON:

```
ActiveSheet.PivotTables("Sales&Trans"). _
    PivotSelect "BOSTON Company", xlDataAndLabel
```

we get the selection in Figure 20-20, which does not include the Company label!

The following code selects cell E12 of the pivot table in Figure 20-10:

```
ActiveSheet.PivotTables("Sales&Trans").PivotSelect _
    "'LOS ANGELES' Franchise 'Sale' '2'", xlDataOnly
```

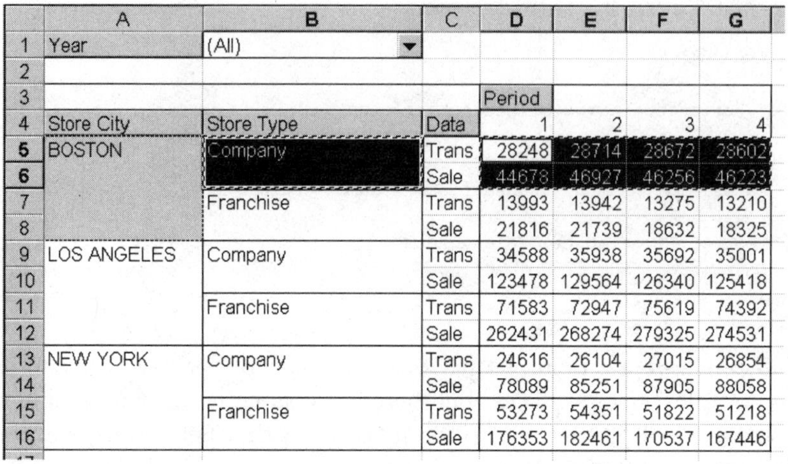

Figure 20-19. Selecting the company label and data for Boston

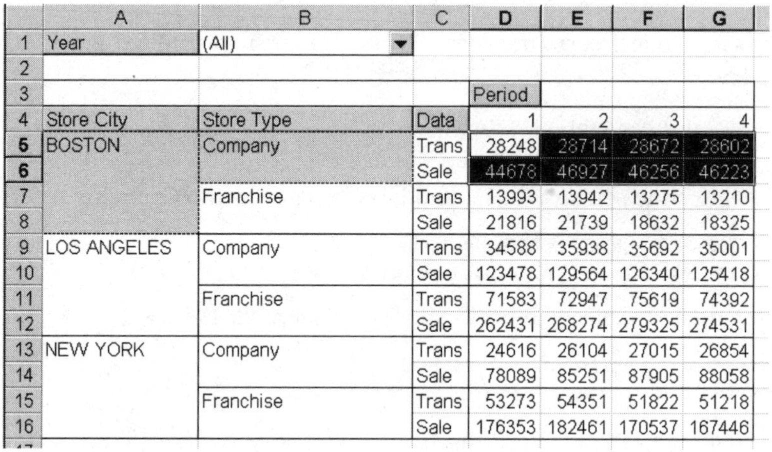

Figure 20-20. Reversing the word order to select company data for Boston only

The following code selects the labels and data for Boston and New York:

```
ActiveSheet.PivotTables("Sales&Trans"). _
    PivotSelect  "'Store City'[BOSTON,'NEW YORK']", xlDataAndLabel
```

If we replace the comma with a colon:

```
ActiveSheet.PivotTables("Sales&Trans"). _
    PivotSelect  "'Store City'[BOSTON:'NEW YORK']", xlDataAndLabel
```

then all items from Boston to New York (that is, all items) are selected.

The PivotSelection property returns or sets the PivotTable selection, again in standard PivotTable selection format. Setting this property is equivalent to calling the PivotSelect method with the *Mode* argument set to xlDataAndLabel.

Additional Members of the PivotTable Object

Let us take a look at some additional members of the PivotTable object.

AddFields method

We have seen this method in action earlier in this chapter.

CalculatedFields method

It is possible to add *calculated fields* to a pivot table. These are fields that are not part of the original source data, but instead are calculated from source fields using a formula.

The CalculatedFields method returns the CalculatedFields collection of all calculated fields. To add a new calculated field, we use the Add method of the CalculatedFields collection. The syntax is:

```
CalculatedFieldsObject.Add(Name, Formula)
```

where *Name* is the name of the field and *Formula* is the formula for the field.

To illustrate, the following code creates a calculated field and displays it in the pivot table from Figure 20-10. The results are shown in Figure 20-21.

```
With ActiveSheet.PivotTables("Sales&Trans"). _
   CalculatedFields.Add("Average", _
   "= Sales/Transactions")
      .Orientation = xlDataField
      .Name = "Avg Check"
      .NumberFormat = "##.#"
End With
```

We should make a brief remark about the arithmetic of the calculated field. The calculated field is computed directly from the data in the pivot table. The source data is not involved *directly*. This is why we did not specify an aggregate function for the calculated field. (Such a function would have been ignored.) Thus, for instance, the value in cell D7 is obtained by dividing the value in cell D6 by the value in cell D5.

Finally, we note that the ListFormulas method can be used to create a list of all calculated fields on a separate worksheet.

	A	B	C	D	E	F	G
1	Year	(All) ▼					
2							
3				Period			
4	Store City	Store Type	Data	1	2	3	4
5	BOSTON	Company	Trans	28248	28714	28672	28602
6			Sale	44678	46927	46256	46223
7			Avg Check	1.6	1.6	1.6	1.6
8		Franchise	Trans	13993	13942	13275	13210
9			Sale	21816	21739	18632	18325
10			Avg Check	1.6	1.6	1.4	1.4
11	LOS ANGE	Company	Trans	34588	35938	35692	35001
12			Sale	123478	129564	126340	125418
13			Avg Check	3.6	3.6	3.5	3.6
14		Franchise	Trans	71583	72947	75619	74392
15			Sale	262431	268274	279325	274531
16			Avg Check	3.7	3.7	3.7	3.7
17	NEW YOR	Company	Trans	24616	26104	27015	26854
18			Sale	78089	85251	87905	88058
19			Avg Check	3.2	3.3	3.3	3.3
20		Franchise	Trans	53273	54351	51822	51218
21			Sale	176353	182461	170537	167446
22			Avg Check	3.3	3.4	3.3	3.3
23							

Figure 20-21. Illustrating a calculated field

Errors-related properties

When the DisplayErrorString property is **True**, the PivotTable displays a custom error string in cells that contain errors. (The default value is **False**.) As the Excel help file observes, this property is particularly useful for suppressing divide-by-zero errors.

The ErrorString property can be used to set the string that is displayed in cells that contain errors when DisplayErrorString is **True**. (The default value is an empty string.)

Null-related properties

When the DisplayNullString property is **True**, the PivotTable displays a custom string in cells that contain null values. (The default value is **True**.)

The NullString property can be used to set the custom string for such cells. (The default value is an empty string.)

EnableDrillDown property

One of the features of a PivotTable is the *DrillDown* feature. To illustrate, if we double-click on a data cell, such as cell D5 in the pivot table of Figure 20-10, Excel will create a new worksheet, as shown in Figure 20-22. This worksheet shows the original source rows that contribute to the value in the double-clicked cell D5. (Note that the rows are complete, although the Sales column does not contribute to cell D5.)

	A	B	C	D	E	F	G
1	Year	Period	Store Code	Store City	Store Type	Transactions	Sales
2	1998	1	BO-1	BOSTON	Company	3881	6248
3	1998	1	BO-2	BOSTON	Company	3789	5722
4	1998	1	BO-3	BOSTON	Company	3877	6278
5	1998	1	BO-4	BOSTON	Company	3862	6123
6	1997	1	BO-4	BOSTON	Company	3218	5102
7	1997	1	BO-3	BOSTON	Company	3230	5231
8	1997	1	BO-2	BOSTON	Company	3157	4768
9	1997	1	BO-1	BOSTON	Company	3234	5206

Figure 20-22. Illustrating DrillDown

By now you have probably guessed that the read-write Boolean property Enable-DrillDown is used to enable or disable this feature for the pivot table.

Formatting properties and methods

The read-write HasAutoFormat property is **True** (its default value) if the Pivot-Table is automatically formatted when it is refreshed or when some of its fields are moved.

The labels for the rows, columns, subtotals, and totals in Figure 20-6 are not merged with adjacent blank cells. (The borders are adjusted so it may appear so, however.) To merge the labels with adjacent blank cells, we can set the Merge-Labels property to **True**.

The read-write PreserveFormatting property is **True** (its default value) if Pivot-Table formatting is preserved when the PivotTable is refreshed or recalculated by operations such as pivoting, sorting, or changing page-field items.

The TableStyle property returns or sets the style name (as a string) used in the PivotTable body. The default value is a null string, so no style is applied.

Refreshing a pivot table

When the ManualUpdate property is **True**, the PivotTable is recalculated only at the user's request. The default value is **False**.

The RefreshTable method refreshes the PivotTable from the original source data. The method returns **True** if it is successful.

The RefreshDate property returns the date on which the PivotTable or pivot cache was last refreshed. It is read-only.

The RefreshName property returns the user name of the person who last refreshed the PivotTable data or pivot cache.

PageField-related properties

As discussed earlier in the chapter, the PageFieldOrder property returns or sets the order in which page fields are added to the PivotTable layout. It can be one of the following XlOrder constants: **xlDownThenOver** or **xlOverThenDown**. The default constant is **xlDownThenOver**.

Recall also that the PageFieldWrapCount property returns or sets the number of PivotTable page fields in each column or row.

The PageFieldStyle property returns or sets the style used in the page field area.

Name property

This property returns or sets the name of the pivot table as a string.

SaveData property (R/W Boolean)

When this property is **True**, its default value, data for the PivotTable is saved with the workbook. If it is **False**, only the PivotTable definition is saved.

ShowPages method

This method creates a new PivotTable for each item in the specified page field. Each new PivotTable is created on a new worksheet. The syntax is:

```
PivotTableObject.ShowPages(PageField)
```

For instance, if we apply this method to the pivot table in Figure 20-10 with the code:

```
ActiveSheet.PivotTables("Sales&Trans").ShowPages "Year"
```

we will get two new worksheets. One worksheet, named 1997, will contain the original pivot table, but with the Year page field set to 1997. The other worksheet will contain the same pivot table with the Year field set to 1998. (We can still change the Year field on any of the pivot tables. In other words, each pivot table contains the data for all of the Year field values.)

SourceData property

This read-only property returns the data source for the PivotTable. For instance, when that source is a single Excel worksheet, the SourceData method returns a string describing the source range. The code:

```
debug.print ActiveSheet.PivotTables("Sales&Trans").SourceData
```

returns the string:

```
'Company Both'!R1C1:R145C7
```

Children of the PivotTable Object

The children of the PivotTable object are shown in Figure 20-23.

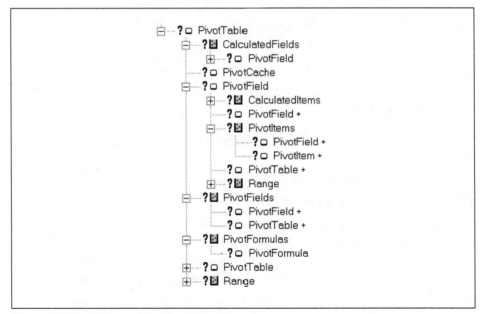

Figure 20-23. Children of the PivotTable object

The PivotField Object

The properties and methods of the PivotField object are shown in Table 20-3.

Table 20-3. Members of the PivotField Object

Application	CurrentPage	NumberFormat
AutoShow	DataRange	Orientation
AutoShowCount	DataType	Parent
AutoShowField	Delete	ParentField
AutoShowRange	DragToColumn	ParentItems
AutoShowType	DragToHide	PivotItems
AutoSort	DragToPage	Position
AutoSortField	DragToRow	ServerBased
AutoSortOrder	Formula	ShowAllItems
BaseField	Function	SourceName
BaseItem	GroupLevel	Subtotals
CalculatedItems	HiddenItems	TotalLevels
Calculation	IsCalculated	Value
ChildField	LabelRange	VisibleItems
ChildItems	MemoryUsed	NumberFormat
Creator	Name	

Let us take a look at some of these members.

AutoShow-Related Members

The AutoShow method is used to restrict the display of pivot items for a given pivot field. The syntax is:

```
PivotFieldObject.AutoShow(Type, Range, Count, Field)
```

All parameters are required for this method.

The *Type* parameter has two possible values: xlAutomatic activates the remaining parameters and thereby causes the restrictions to take effect, and xlManual disables the remaining parameters and causes Excel to remove any restrictions caused by a previous call to this method with *Type* equal to xlAutomatic.

The other parameters can be described by the following sentence: Restrict pivot items to the top (*Range*=xlTop) or bottom (*Range*=xlBottom) *Count* pivot items based on the value in pivot field *Field*.

Thus, for instance, referring to Figure 20-10, the code:

```
ActiveSheet.PivotTables("Sales&Trans"). _
   PivotFields("Store Type").AutoShow _
   xlAutomatic, xlTop, 1, "Sale"
```

shows the top (*Range*=xlTop and *Count*=1) Store Type based on the value of Sale. The result is shown in Figure 20-24.

	A	B	C	D	E	F	G
1	Year	(All) ▼					
2							
3				Period			
4	Store City	**Store Type**	Data	1	2	3	4
5	BOSTON	Company	Trans	28248	28714	28672	28602
6			Sale	44678	46927	46256	46223
7	LOS ANGELES	Franchise	Trans	71583	72947	75619	74392
8			Sale	262431	268274	279325	274531
9	NEW YORK	Franchise	Trans	53273	54351	51822	51218
10			Sale	176353	182461	170537	167446

Figure 20-24. Illustrating AutoShow

As you can see, the top sales in Boston are from the company stores, whereas the top sales in the other cities are in franchise stores.

The same code as the previous but with *Type* set to **xlManual** will remove the restrictions and restore the original pivot table:

```
ActiveSheet.PivotTables("Sales&Trans"). _
   PivotFields("Store Type").AutoShow _
   xlManual, xlTop, 1, "Sale"
```

The following properties are associated with AutoShow:

AutoShowCount property

The read-only AutoShowCount property returns the number of items that are automatically shown in the pivot field (this is the *Count* parameter of the AutoShow method).

AutoShowField property

This read-only property returns the name of the data field used to determine which items are shown (this is the *Field* parameter of the *AutoShow* method).

AutoShowRange property

This read-only property returns **xlTop** or **xlBottom**. This is the value of the *Range* parameter of the AutoShow method.

AutoShowType property

This read-only property returns **xlAutomatic** if AutoShow is enabled for the pivot field and **xlManual** if AutoShow is disabled.

Sorting Pivot Fields

The AutoSort method sets the *automatic* field-sorting rules for the pivot field. The syntax is:

```
PivotFieldObject.AutoSort(Order, Field)
```

The *Order* parameter specifies the sort order and is one of the following constants:

```
Enum XlSortOrder
    xlAscending = 1
    xlDescending = 2
End Enum
```

It can also be set to **xlManual** to disable automatic sorting. The *Field* parameter is the name of the field to use as the sort key.

For instance, referring to Figure 20-10, the code:

```
ActiveSheet.PivotTables("Sales&Trans"). _
    PivotFields("Store Type").AutoSort _
    xlAscending, "Sale"
```

sorts by Sale and produces the results shown in Figure 20-25. Note the order of the Store Type items for Boston as compared to the other cities.

	A	B	C	D	E	F	G
1	Year	(All)					
2							
3				Period			
4	Store City	Store Type	Data	1	2	3	4
5	BOSTON	Franchise	Trans	13993	13942	13275	13210
6			Sale	21816	21739	18632	18325
7		Company	Trans	28248	28714	28672	28602
8			Sale	44678	46927	46256	46223
9	LOS ANGELES	Company	Trans	34588	35938	35692	35001
10			Sale	123478	129564	126340	125418
11		Franchise	Trans	71583	72947	75619	74392
12			Sale	262431	268274	279325	274531
13	NEW YORK	Company	Trans	24616	26104	27015	26854
14			Sale	78089	85251	87905	88058
15		Franchise	Trans	53273	54351	51822	51218
16			Sale	176353	182461	170537	167446

Figure 20-25. Illustrating AutoSort

The read-only AutoSortField property returns the name of the key field and the AutoSortOrder property returns the sort order of the pivot field (**xlAscending**, **xlDescending**, or **xlManual**).

The Fundamental Properties

The PivotField object has a handful of basic properties that you will almost always want to set.

Function property

This property applies only to data fields and returns or sets the aggregate function used to summarize the pivot field. It can be one of the following XlConsolidationFunction constants:

```
Enum XlConsolidationFunction
      xlVarP = -4165
      xlVar = -4164
      xlSum = -4157
      xlStDevP = -4156
      xlStDev = -4155
      xlProduct = -4149
      xlMin = -4139
      xlMax = -4136
      xlCountNums = -4113
      xlCount = -4112
      xlAverage = -4106
      xlUnknown = 1000      ' Excel 9 only
End Enum
```

NumberFormat property

This property applies only to data fields and returns or sets the formatting string for the object. Note that it will return Null if all cells in the specified range do not have the same number format. This is a read-write string property.

Orientation property

This property returns or sets the orientation of the pivot field. It can be set to one of the following values:

```
Enum XlPivotFieldOrientation
      xlHidden = 0
      xlRowField = 1
      xlColumnField = 2
      xlPageField = 3
      xlDataField = 4
End Enum
```

Position property

This read-write property returns or sets the position of the pivot field among all pivot fields in the same area (row, column, page, or data).

Selecting Ranges

The PivotField object has two properties related to selecting portions of the pivot table related to the field.

DataRange property

This property returns a Range object representing the value area associated with the given PivotField. To illustrate, the code:

```
ActiveSheet.PivotTables("Sales&Trans"). _
   PivotFields("Store Type"). _
   DataRange.Select
```

results in Figure 20-26.

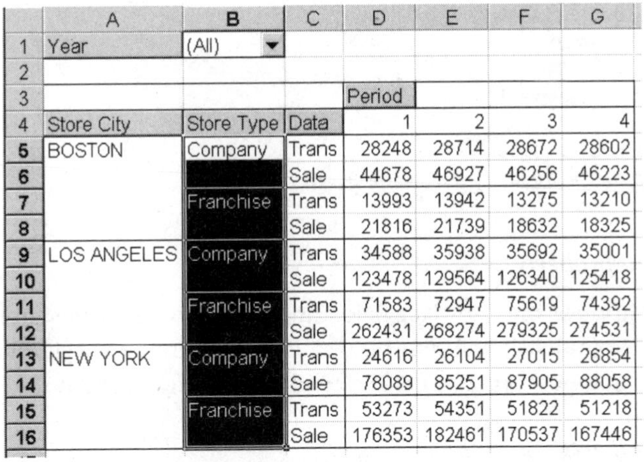

	A	B	C	D	E	F	G
1	Year	(All) ▼					
2							
3				Period			
4	Store City	Store Type	Data	1	2	3	4
5	BOSTON	Company	Trans	28248	28714	28672	28602
6			Sale	44678	46927	46256	46223
7		Franchise	Trans	13993	13942	13275	13210
8			Sale	21816	21739	18632	18325
9	LOS ANGELES	Company	Trans	34588	35938	35692	35001
10			Sale	123478	129564	126340	125418
11		Franchise	Trans	71583	72947	75619	74392
12			Sale	262431	268274	279325	274531
13	NEW YORK	Company	Trans	24616	26104	27015	26854
14			Sale	78089	85251	87905	88058
15		Franchise	Trans	53273	54351	51822	51218
16			Sale	176353	182461	170537	167446

Figure 20-26. DataRange for Store Type

LabelRange property

The LabelRange property returns a Range object that represents the label cells for the PivotField. To illustrate, the code:

```
ActiveSheet.PivotTables("Sales&Trans"). _
   PivotFields("Store Type"). _
   LabelRange.Select
```

will select just the cell containing the button labeled Store Type in Figure 20-26.

Dragging Pivot Fields

The PivotField object has some properties that can prevent the user from moving the field. They are as follows (all default values are **True**):

DragToColumn property
> Set to **False** to prevent the field from being dragged to the column area.

DragToHide property
> Set to **False** to prevent the field from being hidden by being dragged off of the pivot table.

DragToPage property
> Set to **False** to prevent the field from being dragged to the page field area.

DragToRow property
> Set to **False** to prevent the field from being dragged to the row field area.

Name, Value, and SourceName Properties

The read-write Name property returns or sets the name of the PivotField. This is the value that appears in the label for that field. The Value property is the same as the Name property.

The read-only SourceName property returns the name of the field in the original source data. This may differ from the value of the Name property if the Name property has been changed.

Grouping

Excel also lets us group (and ungroup) the data for a selection of pivot items into a single new pivot item. This is done using the Group and Ungroup methods of the Range object. Note that these methods apply to the Range object, not the PivotField or PivotItem objects.

The Group method has two syntaxes, but we will look at only the more flexible of the two. (For all of the details on the Group method, we refer the interested reader to the Excel help documentation.)

Let us look at an example. Referring as usual to the pivot table in Figure 20-10, the following code selects all labels and data for Boston and New York and then groups this data into a single group. The group is then renamed Eastern. The results are shown in Figure 20-27. Observe that Excel creates both a new pivot field and a new pivot item. The pivot field is called Store City2 and contains the existing Los Angeles pivot item along with a new pivot item, which would have been given the name Group1 by Excel if we had not specified the name Eastern.

```
With ActiveSheet.PivotTables("Sales&Trans")
  .PivotSelect "'Store City'[BOSTON,'New York']", xlDataAndLabel
  Set rng = Selection
  rng.Group
  .PivotFields("Store City2").PivotItems(1). Name = "Eastern"
  .PivotSelect "Eastern", xlDataAndLabel
End With
```

	A	B	C	D	E	F	G	H
1	Year	(All) ▼						
2								
3					Period			
4	Store City2	Store City	Store	Data	1	2	3	4
5	Eastern	BOSTON	Comp	Trans	28248	28714	28672	28602
6				Sale	44678	46927	46256	46223
7			Franc	Trans	13993	13942	13275	13210
8				Sale	21816	21739	18632	18325
9		NEW YORK	Comp	Trans	24616	26104	27015	26854
10				Sale	78089	85251	87905	88058
11			Franc	Trans	53273	54351	51822	51218
12				Sale	176353	182461	170537	167446
13	LOS ANGELES	LOS ANGEL	Comp	Trans	34588	35938	35692	35001
14				Sale	123478	129564	126340	125418
15			Franc	Trans	71583	72947	75619	74392
16				Sale	262431	268274	279325	274531

Figure 20-27. Illustrating the Group method

Data Field Calculation

Normally, data fields show a value based on the Function property of the field. On the other hand, Excel also permits us to change the *meaning* of the value that is displayed in a data field.

Calculation property

This is done by setting the Calculation property for the data field. (The property applies only to data fields.) The possible values of this property are given by the following enum:

```
Enum XlPivotFieldCalculation
    xlNoAdditionalCalculation = -4143
    xlDifferenceFrom = 2
    xlPercentOf = 3
    xlPercentDifferenceFrom = 4
    xlRunningTotal = 5
    xlPercentOfRow = 6
    xlPercentOfColumn = 7
    xlPercentOfTotal = 8
    xlIndex = 9
End Enum
```

As you can see from these constants, the idea is to replace the raw value in the data field by a type of relative value. (We will see an example in a moment.)

Note that for some values of Calculation, additional information is required. In particular, if Calculation is equal to `xlDifferenceFrom`, `xlPercentDifferenceFrom`, or `xlPercentOf`, then we must specify the following two properties:

BaseField property

This property, which applies only to data fields, returns or sets the field upon which the data field calculation is based.

BaseItem property

This property, which applies only to data fields, returns or sets the item in the base data field used for the calculation.

Calculations not requiring a BaseField/BaseItem

The Calculation values that do not require a BaseField/BaseItem pair are:

`xlRunningTotal`

Keeps a running total of all values, going down the rows of the table.

`xlPercentOfRow`

Each cell is replaced by that cell's percentage of the sum of the values in that cell's row (for the given data field).

`xlPercentOfColumn`

Each cell is replaced by that cell's percentage of the sum of the values in that cell's column (for the given data field).

`xlPercentOfTotal`

Each cell is replaced by that cell's percentage of the sum of the values in the entire table (for the given data field).

The formula to compute the value in a cell is:

```
new value = (current value * grand total) / (row total * column total)
```

Figures 20-28 through 20-31 illustrate these calculations, starting with the pivot table in Figure 20-10. Note that the percent calculations require that the grand row and column totals be displayed.

The code for Figure 20-28 is:

```
ActiveSheet.PivotTables("Sales&Trans"). _
    PivotFields("Sale").Calculation = xlRunningTotal
```

Referring to Figure 20-28, cell D6 contains sales for Boston, cell D10 contains total sales for Boston and Los Angeles, and cell D14 contains total sales for Boston, Los Angeles, and New York. (I have had reports that the Calculation property does not always work properly. For some reason, it may simply cause the relevant cells to fill with Excel's infamous #N/A symbols. Indeed, I have had this same experience at times, but I have not been able to figure out why.)

	A	B	C	D	E	F	G
1	Year	(All) ▼					
2							
3				Period			
4	Store	Store Type	Data	1	2	3	4
5	BOST	Company	Trans	28248	28714	28672	28602
6			Sale	44678	46927	46256	46223
7		Franchise	Trans	13993	13942	13275	13210
8			Sale	21816	21739	18632	18325
9	LOS	Company	Trans	34588	35938	35692	35001
10			Sale	168156	176491	172596	171641
11		Franchise	Trans	71583	72947	75619	74392
12			Sale	284247	290013	297957	292856
13	NEW	Company	Trans	24616	26104	27015	26854
14			Sale	246245	261742	260501	259699
15		Franchise	Trans	53273	54351	51822	51218
16			Sale	460600	472474	468494	460302

Figure 20-28. Calculation = xlRunningTotal

The code for Figure 20-29 is:

```
ActiveSheet.PivotTables("Sales&Trans"). _
    PivotFields("Sale").Calculation = xlPercentOfRow
```

	A	B	C	D	E	F	G	H
1	Year	(All) ▼						
2								
3				Period				
4	Store City	Store Type	Data	1	2	3	4	Grand Total
5	BOSTON	Franchise	Trans	13993	13942	13275	13210	54420
6			Sale	27.10%	27.00%	23.14%	22.76%	100.00%
7		Company	Trans	28248	28714	28672	28602	114236
8			Sale	24.27%	25.49%	25.13%	25.11%	100.00%
9	LOS ANGELES	Company	Trans	34588	35938	35692	35001	141219
10			Sale	24.46%	25.67%	25.03%	24.85%	100.00%
11		Franchise	Trans	71583	72947	75619	74392	294541
12			Sale	24.20%	24.74%	25.75%	25.31%	100.00%
13	NEW YORK	Company	Trans	24616	26104	27015	26854	104589
14			Sale	23.01%	25.13%	25.91%	25.95%	100.00%
15		Franchise	Trans	53273	54351	51822	51218	210664
16			Sale	25.31%	26.19%	24.47%	24.03%	100.00%

Figure 20-29. Calculation = xlPercentOfRow

The code for Figure 20-30 is:

```
ActiveSheet.PivotTables("Sales&Trans"). _
    PivotFields("Sale").Calculation = xlPercentOfColumn
```

	A	B	C	D	E	F	G	H
1	Year	(All) ▼						
2								
3				Period				
4	Store	Store Type	Data	1	2	3	4	Grand Total
5	BOS	Company	Trans	28248	28714	28672	28602	114236
6			Sale	6.32%	6.39%	6.35%	6.42%	6.37%
7		Franchise	Trans	13993	13942	13275	13210	54420
8			Sale	3.09%	2.96%	2.56%	2.55%	2.79%
9	LOS	Company	Trans	34588	35938	35692	35001	141219
10			Sale	17.47%	17.65%	17.33%	17.42%	17.47%
11		Franchise	Trans	71583	72947	75619	74392	294541
12			Sale	37.13%	36.54%	38.32%	38.13%	37.53%
13	NEW	Company	Trans	24616	26104	27015	26854	104589
14			Sale	11.05%	11.61%	12.06%	12.23%	11.74%
15		Franchise	Trans	53273	54351	51822	51218	210664
16			Sale	24.95%	24.85%	23.39%	23.26%	24.11%
17	Total Trans			226301	231996	232095	229277	919669
18	Total Sale			100.00%	100.00%	100.00%	100.00%	100.00%

Figure 20-30. Calculation = xlPercentOfColumn

The code for Figure 20-31 is:

```
ActiveSheet.PivotTables("Sales&Trans"). _
    PivotFields("Sale").Calculation = xlPercentOfTotal
```

Calculations requiring a BaseField/BaseItem

The procedure for making calculations with a BaseField/BaseItem is not explained very well in the documentation, so let us see if we can clear it up by first considering an example. Consider the code:

```
With ActiveSheet.PivotTables("Sales&Trans"). _
  PivotFields("Sale")
    .Calculation = xlDifferenceFrom
    .BaseField = "Store City"
    .BaseItem = "Boston"
End With
```

Referring to Figure 20-32, we have reproduced our usual pivot table (from Figure 20-10) with several changes. First, we removed the Trans values, since they are not relevant to our example. We have also replaced the Sale values for the given BaseField and BaseItem by symbols (b1–b8). Finally, we replaced the other Sale values with number signs, since we do not care about the actual values.

	A	B	C	D	E	F	G	H
1	Year	(All) ▼						
2								
3				Period				
4	Store	Store Type	Data	1	2	3	4	Grand Total
5	BOST	Company	Trans	28248	28714	28672	28602	114236
6			Sale	1.55%	1.62%	1.60%	1.60%	6.37%
7		Franchise	Trans	13993	13942	13275	13210	54420
8			Sale	0.75%	0.75%	0.64%	0.63%	2.79%
9	LOS ,	Company	Trans	34588	35938	35692	35001	141219
10			Sale	4.27%	4.48%	4.37%	4.34%	17.47%
11		Franchise	Trans	71583	72947	75619	74392	294541
12			Sale	9.08%	9.28%	9.67%	9.50%	37.53%
13	NEW	Company	Trans	24616	26104	27015	26854	104589
14			Sale	2.70%	2.95%	3.04%	3.05%	11.74%
15		Franchise	Trans	53273	54351	51822	51218	210664
16			Sale	6.10%	6.31%	5.90%	5.79%	24.11%
17	Total Trans			226301	231996	232095	229277	919669
18	Total Sale			24.46%	25.40%	25.22%	24.91%	100.00%

Figure 20-31. Calculation = xlPercentOfTotal

	A	B	C	D	E	F	G
1				Period			
2	Store City	Store Type	Data	1	2	3	4
3	BOSTON	Company	Trans				
4			Sale	b1	b2	b3	b4
5		Franchise	Trans				
6			Sale	b5	b6	b7	b8
7	LOS ANGE	Company	Trans				
8			Sale	#	#	#	#
9		Franchise	Trans				
10			Sale	#	#	#	#
11	NEW YOR	Company	Trans				
12			Sale	#	#	#	#
13		Franchise	Trans				
14			Sale	#	#	#	#

Figure 20-32. Illustrating a calculation

Now, the trick in seeing how the calculations are made is to fix a value for the fields other than the base field—in our case the Store Type and Period. Consider, for instance, the values:

```
Store Type = "Company"
Period = 1
```

The Sale data cells corresponding to these values are grayed in Figure 20-32. One of these cells (cell D4) is the base item cell. For this Store Type/Period combination, a calculation is made using the value in this cell as the base value. In our case, it is the **xlDifferenceFrom** calculation that is being made. Hence, the base value is subtracted from the values in all three grayed cells. This gives the table in Figure 20-33. Note that the base value is even subtracted from itself, giving 0. This is done for each Store Type/Period combination, as shown in Figure 20-33.

	A	B	C	D	E	F	G
1				Period			
2	Store City	Store Type	Data	1	2	3	4
3	BOSTON	Company	Trans				
4			Sale	0	0	0	0
5		Franchise	Trans				
6			Sale	0	0	0	0
7	LOS ANGE	Company	Trans				
8			Sale	#-b1	#-b2	#-b3	#-b4
9		Franchise	Trans				
10			Sale	#-b5	#-b6	#-b7	#-b8
11	NEW YOR	Company	Trans				
12			Sale	#-b1	#-b2	#-b3	#-b4
13		Franchise	Trans				
14			Sale	#-b5	#-b6	#-b7	#-b8

Figure 20-33. The finished calculation

The formulas for the Calculation property that require BaseField/BaseItem values are:

xlDifferenceFrom
> # – base value

xlPercentOf
> #/base value (expressed as a percent)

xlPercentDifferenceFrom
> (# – base value)/base value (expressed as a percent)

To illustrate, Figure 20-34 shows the actual effect of the earlier code on Figure 20-10:

```
With ActiveSheet.PivotTables("Sales&Trans"). _
  PivotFields("Sale")
    .Calculation = xlDifferenceFrom
    .BaseField = "Store City"
    .BaseItem = "Boston"
End With Figure 20-10.
```

	A	B	C	D	E	F	G
1	Year	(All) ▼					
2							
3				Period			
4	Store	Store Type	Data	1	2	3	4
5	BOS	Company	Trans	28248	28714	28672	28602
6			Sale				
7		Franchise	Trans	13993	13942	13275	13210
8			Sale				
9	LOS	Company	Trans	34588	35938	35692	35001
10			Sale	78800	82637	80084	79195
11		Franchise	Trans	71583	72947	75619	74392
12			Sale	240615	246535	260693	256206
13	NEW	Company	Trans	24616	26104	27015	26854
14			Sale	33411	38324	41649	41835
15		Franchise	Trans	53273	54351	51822	51218
16			Sale	154537	160722	151905	149121

Figure 20-34. Illustrating the Calculation property

CurrentPage Property

This property returns or sets the current page. It is only valid for page fields. Note that the property should be set either to the name of the page field or to "All" to show all pages.

DataType Property

This read-only property returns a constant that describes the type of data in the pivot field. It can be one of the following **XlPivotFieldDataType** constants:

```
Enum XlPivotFieldDataType
      xlText = -4158
      xlNumber = -4145
      xlDate = 2
End Enum
```

HiddenItems and VisibleItems Properties

The HiddenItems property returns the PivotItems collection of all hidden Pivot-Item objects, using the syntax:

```
PivotFieldObject.HiddenItems
```

It can also return a single or array of hidden PivotItem objects using the syntax:

```
PivotFieldObject.HiddenItems(Index)
```

where *Index* is a single index or an array of indexes.

Similarly, the VisibleItems property returns a PivotItems collection of all visible PivotItem objects or a single or array of such objects. The syntax is the same as for the HiddenItems property.

MemoryUsed Property

This read-only property returns the amount of memory currently being used by the PivotField (it also applies to PivotItem objects) as a Long integer.

ServerBased Property

This read-write Boolean property applies to page fields only and is used with (generally very large) external data sources. It is **True** when the PivotTable's data source is external and only the items matching the page-field selection are retrieved.

By setting this property to **True**, the pivot cache (discussed later in the chapter) needs to accommodate only the data for a single page field. This may be important, or even necessary, when the external data source is large. The trade-off is that each time the page field is changed, there may be a delay while Excel requeries the original source data to retrieve data on the new page field.

Note that there are some circumstances under which this property cannot be set to **True**:

- The field is grouped.
- The data source is not external.
- The cache is used by more than one PivotTable.
- The field has a data type that cannot be server-based (such as a memo field or an OLE object).

ShowAllItems Property

This read-write Boolean property is **True** if all items in the PivotTable are displayed. The default value is **False**, in which case the pivot items that do not contribute to the data fields are not displayed. Note that this property corresponds to the "Show items with no data" check box on Excel's PivotTable Field dialog box.

To illustrate, suppose we add a single row to our source table:

```
1998   1   BO-1   BOSTON   AStoreType   1000   $10000.00
```

This row creates a new store type but adds data only for Boston. The resulting pivot table will have the default appearance shown in Figure 20-35. Since Show-

AllItems is `False`, there are no rows for the new store type corresponding to Los Angeles or New York.

	A	B	C	D	E	F	G
1	Year	(All) ▼					
2							
3				Period			
4	Store	Store Type	Data	1	2	3	4
5	BOST	AStoreType	Trans	1000			
6			Sale	10000			
7		Company	Trans	28248	28714	28672	28602
8			Sale	44678	46927	46256	46223
9		Franchise	Trans	13993	13942	13275	13210
10			Sale	21816	21739	18632	18325
11	LOS	Company	Trans	34588	35938	35692	35001
12			Sale	123478	129564	126340	125418
13		Franchise	Trans	71583	72947	75619	74392
14			Sale	262431	268274	279325	274531
15	NEW	Company	Trans	24616	26104	27015	26854
16			Sale	78089	85251	87905	88058
17		Franchise	Trans	53273	54351	51822	51218
18			Sale	176353	182461	170537	167446
19							

Figure 20-35. ShowAllItems = False

On the other hand, the code:

```
ActiveSheet.PivotTables("Sales&Trans"). _
    PivotFields("Store Type").ShowAllItems = True
```

will produce the pivot table shown in Figure 20-36.

Subtotals Method

This method returns or sets the display of a particular type of subtotal for the specified pivot field. It is valid for all fields other than data fields. The syntax is:

```
PivotFieldObject.Subtotals(Index)
```

where the optional Index parameter indicates the type of subtotal and is a number from Table 20-4.

Figure 20-36. ShowAllItems = True

Table 20-4. Values for the Subtotals Method's Index Parameter

Index	Subtotal Type
1	Automatic
2	Sum
3	Count
4	Average
5	Max
6	Min
7	Product
8	Count Nums
9	StdDev
10	StdDevp
11	Var
12	Varp

For instance, the following code requests a display of subtotals for both Sum and Count:

```
ActiveSheet.PivotTables("Sales&Trans"). _
    PivotFields("Store City").Subtotals(2) = True
```

```
ActiveSheet.PivotTables("Sales&Trans"). _
    PivotFields("Store City").Subtotals(3) = True
```

We can also set the Subtotals property to an array of 12 Boolean values to set multiple subtotals. For instance, the following code displays all subtotals:

```
ActiveSheet.PivotTables("Sales&Trans"). _
    PivotFields("Store City"). _
    Subtotals = Array(False, True, True, True, True, _
    True, True, True, True, True, True, True)
```

Note that we set Automatic to **False** in this array, since if Automatic is set to **True**, then all other values are set to **False** (thus providing a quick way to set all subtotals to **False**).

If this argument is omitted, the Subtotals method returns an array containing a Boolean value for each subtotal.

The PivotCache Object

Pivot tables can manipulate the source data in a variety of ways, and this can require a great deal of processing power. For maximum efficiency, the data for a pivot table is first stored in memory in what is referred to as a *pivot cache*. The pivot table itself actually provides various views of the pivot cache. This allows manipulation of the data without the need to further access the original source which might, after all, be an external data source.

The PivotCache object represents a pivot table's cache. It is returned by the Pivot-Cache method of the PivotTable object. Let us take a look at some of the main properties and methods of the PivotCache object.

Refreshing a Pivot Cache

The Refresh method refreshes both the pivot cache and the pivot table.

However, we can prevent a pivot table from being refreshed, either through the user interface (the Refresh data menu item on the PivotTable menu) or through code, by setting the EnableRefresh property to **False**.

The read-write Boolean RefreshOnFileOpen property is **True** if the PivotTable cache is automatically updated each time the workbook is opened by the user. The default value is **False**. Note that this property is ignored if the EnableRefresh property is set to **False**. Note also that the PivotTable cache is not automatically refreshed when the workbook is opened through code, even if RefreshOn-FileOpen is **True**.

The RefreshDate property returns the date on which the pivot cache was last refreshed, and the RefreshName property returns the name of the user who last refreshed the cache.

MemoryUsed Property

The read-only MemoryUsed property applies to either a *PivotCache* object or a PivotField object and returns the amount of memory currently being used by the cache, in bytes.

OptimizeCache Property

Cache optimization is used with large or complex source data. It will slow the initial construction of the cache. This read-write Boolean property can be used to set cache optimization. Unfortunately, the precise consequences of cache optimization are not made clear in the documentation, leaving us to use trial and error to decide whether it should be employed. Perhaps the best strategy is to leave this property set to its default (**False**) unless performance seems to be a problem.

RecordCount Property

This read-only property returns the number of records in the PivotTable cache.

SourceData Property

This property returns the data source for the PivotTable, as we discussed in the section on the PivotTable object.

Sql Property

This read-write string property returns or sets the SQL query string used with an ODBC data source.

The PivotItem Object

A PivotItem is a unique value of a PivotField. To illustrate, consider the following code:

```
Dim pi As PivotItem
For Each pi In _
  ActiveSheet.PivotTables("Sales&Trans"). _
  PivotFields("Store City").PivotItems
    Debug.Print pi.Name
Next
```

That code will print the list:

```
BOSTON
LOS ANGELES
NEW YORK
```

which contains the distinct Store City values from the Store City pivot field.

The PivotItems method of the PivotField object returns PivotItem objects. The syntax:

```
PivotFieldObject.PivotItems
```

returns the collection of all PivotItem objects for that PivotField. The syntax:

```
PivotFieldObject.PivotItems(Index)
```

can return a single PivotItem object or an array of PivotItem objects (by setting *Index* to an array of indexes).

Table 20-5 shows the properties and methods of the PivotItem object. Let us take a look at some of these members. Note that several of the members of the Pivot-Field object also apply to the PivotItem object.

Table 20-5. Members of the PivotItem Object

Application	IsCalculated	Position
ChildItems	LabelRange	RecordCount
Creator	Name	ShowDetail
DataRange	Parent	SourceName
Delete	ParentItem	Value
Formula	ParentShowDetail	Visible

DataRange Property

This property returns a Range object representing the data area associated with the given PivotItem. To illustrate, the code:

```
ActiveSheet.PivotTables("Sales&Trans"). _
    PivotFields("Store Type"). _
    PivotItems("Company").DataRange.Select
```

results in Figure 20-37.

LabelRange Property

The LabelRange property returns a Range object that represents the label cells for the PivotItem. Figure 20-38 illustrates the results of the code:

```
ActiveSheet.PivotTables("Sales&Trans"). _
    PivotFields("Store Type"). _
    PivotItems("Company").LabelRange.Select
```

	A	B	C	D	E	F	G
1	Year	(All) ▼					
2							
3				Period			
4	Store City	Store Type	Data	1	2	3	4
5	BOSTON	Company	Trans	28248	28714	28672	28602
6			Sale	44678	46927	46256	46223
7		Franchise	Trans	13993	13942	13275	13210
8			Sale	21816	21739	18632	18325
9	LOS ANGELES	Company	Trans	34588	35938	35692	35001
10			Sale	123478	129564	126340	125418
11		Franchise	Trans	71583	72947	75619	74392
12			Sale	262431	268274	279325	274531
13	NEW YORK	Company	Trans	24616	26104	27015	26854
14			Sale	78089	85251	87905	88058
15		Franchise	Trans	53273	54351	51822	51218
16			Sale	176353	182461	170537	167446

Figure 20-37. DataRange for Store Type = Company

	A	B	C	D	E	F	G
1	Year	(All) ▼					
2							
3				Period			
4	Store City	Store Type	Data	1	2	3	4
5	BOSTON	Company	Trans	28248	28714	28672	28602
6			Sale	44678	46927	46256	46223
7		Franchise	Trans	13993	13942	13275	13210
8			Sale	21816	21739	18632	18325
9	LOS ANGELES	Company	Trans	34588	35938	35692	35001
10			Sale	123478	129564	126340	125418
11		Franchise	Trans	71583	72947	75619	74392
12			Sale	262431	268274	279325	274531
13	NEW YORK	Company	Trans	24616	26104	27015	26854
14			Sale	78089	85251	87905	88058
15		Franchise	Trans	53273	54351	51822	51218
16			Sale	176353	182461	170537	167446

Figure 20-38. LabelRange for Store Type = Company

IsCalculated Property

This property returns **True** if the pivot item is a calculated item. We discuss calculated items later in the chapter.

Name, Value, and SourceName Properties

The read-write Name property returns or sets the name o the PivotItem. This is the value that appears in the label for that item. The Value property is the same as the Name property.

The read-only SourceName property returns the name of the item in the original source data. This may differ from the value of the Name property if the Name property has been changed.

Position Property

The Position property returns or sets the position of the pivot item. For instance, the code:

```
ActiveSheet.PivotTables("Sales&Trans"). _
    PivotFields("Store Type"). _
    PivotItems("Franchise").Position
```

returns the number 2, since Franchise is the second pivot item in the pivot table (see Figure 20-10). Moreover, we can reverse the positions of Company and Franchise by setting the Position of the Franchise pivot item to 1, as follows:

```
ActiveSheet.PivotTables("Sales&Trans"). _
    PivotFields("Store Type"). _
    PivotItems("Franchise").Position = 1
```

RecordCount Property

This read-only property returns the number of records in the PivotTable cache that contain the pivot item. For instance, the code:

```
ActiveSheet.PivotTables("Sales&Trans"). _
    PivotFields("Store Type"). _
    PivotItems("Franchise").RecordCount
```

will return the number 80 because there are 80 rows in the source table (and hence the pivot cache) that involve the Franchise store type.

ShowDetail Property

When this read-write property is set to **True**, the pivot item is shown in detail; if it is **False**, the PivotItem is hidden. To illustrate, consider as usual the pivot table in Figure 20-10. The code:

```
ActiveSheet.PivotTables("Sales&Trans"). _
    PivotFields("Store City"). _
    PivotItems("Boston").ShowDetail = False
```

results in the pivot table in Figure 20-39. As we can see, the Transactions and Sales for Boston are summed over all (both) store types (Company and Franchise).

	A	B	C	D	E	F	G
1	Year	(All) ▼					
2							
3				Period			
4	Store City	Store Type	Data	1	2	3	4
5	BOSTON		Trans	42241	42656	41947	41812
6			Sale	66494	68666	64888	64548
7	LOS ANGELES	Company	Trans	34588	35938	35692	35001
8			Sale	123478	129564	126340	125418
9		Franchise	Trans	71583	72947	75619	74392
10			Sale	262431	268274	279325	274531
11	NEW YORK	Company	Trans	24616	26104	27015	26854
12			Sale	78089	85251	87905	88058
13		Franchise	Trans	53273	54351	51822	51218
14			Sale	176353	182461	170537	167446

Figure 20-39. Illustrating ShowDetail

Unfortunately, there seems to be a problem when the ShowDetail method is applied to inner pivot items. For instance, the code:

```
ActiveSheet.PivotTables("Sales&Trans"). _
   PivotFields("Store Type"). _
   PivotItems("Company").ShowDetail = False
```

does seem to set the ShowDetail property to **False**, as can be verified by the code:

```
MsgBox ActiveSheet.PivotTables("Sales&Trans"). _
   PivotFields("Store Type"). _
   PivotItems("Company").ShowDetail
```

However, the pivot table does not reflect this change! (At least this happens on the two systems on which I have run this code. You should check this carefully on any system on which you intend to run this code. A similar problem occurs with the Subtotals property as well.)

As another example, the following code toggles the display of details for the Boston pivot item:

```
With ActiveSheet.PivotTables("Sales&Trans"). _
   PivotFields("Store City").PivotItems("Boston")
      .ShowDetail = Not .ShowDetail
End With
```

The ShowDetail property also applies to the Range object, even when the range lies inside a pivot table. To illustrate, the following code will also produce the pivot table in Figure 20-39:

```
ActiveSheet.PivotTables("Sales&Trans"). _
    PivotSelect "Boston", xlDataAndLabel
Selection.ShowDetail = False
```

The following code toggles the display of the Boston details:

```
Dim rng As Range
ActiveSheet.PivotTables("Sales&Trans"). _
    PivotSelect "Boston", xlDataAndLabel
Set rng = Selection.Cells(1, 1)
rng.ShowDetail = Not rng.ShowDetail
```

Note that *rng* refers only to the first cell in the range representing the Boston data and labels; that is, we have:

```
Set rng = Selection.Cells(1, 1)
```

This is done because, when applied to the Range object, the ShowDetail property will return a value *only* when the range is a single cell.

As another illustration, the following code will hide the details for the entire Store City pivot field:

```
ActiveSheet.PivotTables("Sales&Trans"). _
    PivotSelect "'Store City'", xlDataAndLabel
Selection.ShowDetail = False
ActiveSheet.PivotTables("Sales&Trans"). _
    PivotSelect "'Store City'", xlDataAndLabel
```

(Replacing `False` by `True` will unhide the details.)

We must conclude by suggesting that since the ShowDetails property is very poorly documented, you should experiment carefully and completely before relying on this property to perform in a certain way.

Visible Property

This property determines whether or not the pivot item is visible in the pivot table.

Calculated Items and Calculated Fields

We have seen that it is possible to add a calculated field to a pivot table. A calculated field is special type of PivotField object that is not part of the original source data, but instead is calculated from source fields using a formula. Note that there is no such thing as a CalculatedField object, but there is a CalculatedFields collection.

As we have seen, to create a new calculated field, we use the Add method of the CalculatedFields collection of the PivotTable object. The syntax is:

```
CalculatedFieldsObject.Add(Name, Formula)
```

where *Name* is the name of the field and *Formula* is the formula for the field.

On the other hand, a *calculated item* is a special type of PivotItem object associated with a given PivotField object. (There is no such thing as a CalculatedItem object, but there is a CalculatedItems collection.) The values of this item are calculated by using a formula.

The PivotField object has a CalculatedItems collection of all calculated items for that pivot field. To create a new calculated item, we use the Add method of the CalculatedItems object. This method has the same syntax as the Add method of the CalculatedFields object:

```
CalculatedItemsObject.Add(Name, Formula)
```

where *Name* is the name of the field and *Formula* is the formula for the field.

To illustrate, the following code adds a new calculated item to the Store Type pivot field:

```
ActiveSheet.PivotTables("Sales&Trans"). _
   PivotFields("Store Type").CalculatedItems. _
   Add "CompanyX2", "='Store Type'Company*2"
```

The results are shown in Figure 20-40, where the calculated item is CompanyX2. The value in each of the CompanyX2 cells is twice the value in the corresponding Company cell.

For comparison, let us add a calculated field to the pivot table in Figure 20-40. We will add the same calculated field that we added when we discussed the CalculatedFields method earlier in the chapter:

```
With ActiveSheet.PivotTables("Sales&Trans"). _
   CalculatedFields.Add("Average", _
   "= Sales/Transactions")
      .Orientation = xlDataField
      .Name = "Avg Check"
      .NumberFormat = "##.#"
End With
```

The result is shown in Figure 20-41.

Note that the ListFormulas method of the PivotTable object will produce a list (on a separate worksheet) of all formulas in the pivot table. The outcome for the pivot table in Figure 20-41 is shown in Figure 20-42.

Let us conclude by recalling that the read-only IsCalculated property can be used to determine whether or not a pivot field or pivot item is calculated.

	A	B	C	D	E	F	G
1	Year	(All) ▼					
2							
3				Period			
4	Store City	Store Type	Data	1	2	3	4
5	BOSTON	Company	Trans	28248	28714	28672	28602
6			Sale	44678	46927	46256	46223
7		Franchise	Trans	13993	13942	13275	13210
8			Sale	21816	21739	18632	18325
9		CompanyX2	Trans	56496	57428	57344	57204
10			Sale	89356	93854	92512	92446
11	LOS ANGELES	Company	Trans	34588	35938	35692	35001
12			Sale	123478	129564	126340	125418
13		Franchise	Trans	71583	72947	75619	74392
14			Sale	262431	268274	279325	274531
15		CompanyX2	Trans	69176	71876	71384	70002
16			Sale	246956	259128	252680	250836
17	NEW YORK	Company	Trans	24616	26104	27015	26854
18			Sale	78089	85251	87905	88058
19		Franchise	Trans	53273	54351	51822	51218
20			Sale	176353	182461	170537	167446
21		CompanyX2	Trans	49232	52208	54030	53708
22			Sale	156178	170502	175810	176116

Figure 20-40. Illustrating a calculated item (CompanyX2)

Example: Printing Pivot Tables

Now we can implement the PrintPivotTables feature of the SRXUtils application. A complex Excel workbook may have a large number of pivot tables scattered on various worksheets. A simple utility for printing these pivot tables can be useful. (I have often been asked to write such a utility in my consulting practice.)

Our application displays a dialog box, as shown in Figure 20-43. The list box contains a list of all pivot tables. Each entry includes the pivot table's name, followed by the name of the worksheet. The user can select one or more pivot tables and hit the print button to print these tables.

The following are the steps to create the print utility. All the action takes place in the *Print.xls* workbook, so open this workbook. When the changes are finished, you will need to save *Print.xls* as *Print.utl* as well. If *Print.utl* is loaded, the only way to unload it is to unload the add-in *SRXUtils.xla* (if it is loaded) and close the workbook *SRXUtils.xls* (if it is open).

	A	B	C	D	E	F	G
1	Year	(All) ▼					
2							
3				Period			
4	Store City	Store Type	Data	1	2	3	4
5	BOSTON	Company	Trans	28248	28714	28672	28602
6			Sale	44678	46927	46256	46223
7			Avg Check	1.6	1.6	1.6	1.6
8		Franchise	Trans	13993	13942	13275	13210
9			Sale	21816	21739	18632	18325
10			Avg Check	1.6	1.6	1.4	1.4
11		CompanyX2	Trans	56496	57428	57344	57204
12			Sale	89356	93854	92512	92446
13			Avg Check	1.6	1.6	1.6	1.6
14	LOS ANGELES	Company	Trans	34588	35938	35692	35001
15			Sale	123478	129564	126340	125418
16			Avg Check	3.6	3.6	3.5	3.6
17		Franchise	Trans	71583	72947	75619	74392
18			Sale	262431	268274	279325	274531
19			Avg Check	3.7	3.7	3.7	3.7
20		CompanyX2	Trans	69176	71876	71384	70002
21			Sale	246956	259128	252680	250836
22			Avg Check	3.6	3.6	3.5	3.6
23	NEW YORK	Company	Trans	24616	26104	27015	26854
24			Sale	78089	85251	87905	88058
25			Avg Check	3.2	3.3	3.3	3.3
26		Franchise	Trans	53273	54351	51822	51218
27			Sale	176353	182461	170537	167446
28			Avg Check	3.3	3.4	3.3	3.3
29		CompanyX2	Trans	49232	52208	54030	53708
30			Sale	156178	170502	175810	176116
31			Avg Check	3.2	3.3	3.3	3.3

Figure 20-41. Illustrating a calculated field and calculated item

	A	B	C	D	E	
1	*Calculated Field*					
2	**Solve Order**	**Field**	**Formula**			
3	1	Average	=Sales /Transactions			
4						
5	*Calculated Item*					
6	**Solve Order**	**Item**	**Formula**			
7	1	CompanyX2	=Company*2			
8						
9						
10	**Note:**		When a cell is updated by more than one formula,			
11			the value is set by the formula with the last solve order.			
12						
13			To change formula solve orders,			
14			use the Solve Order command on the PivotTable command bar.			
15						

Figure 20-42. The output of ListFormulas

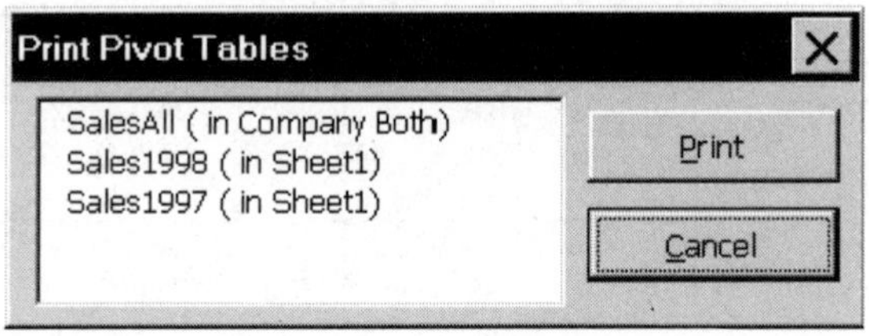

Figure 20-43. Print pivot tables

Create the UserForm

Create the dialog shown in Figure 20-43 in the *Print.xls* workbook. Name the dialog `dlgPrintPivotTables`, change its Caption property to "Print Pivot Tables," and change the PrintPivotTables procedure as shown in Example 20-5.

Example 20-5. The PrintPivotTables Procedure

```
Public Sub PrintPivotTables()
  dlgPrintPivotTables.Show
End Sub
```

The *dlgPrintPivotTables* dialog has two command buttons and one list box.

List box

Place a list box on the form as in Figure 20-43. Using the Properties window, set the following properties:

Property	Value
Name	lstPTs
TabIndex	0
MultiSelect	frmMultiSelectExtended

When the Cancel property of the *cmdCancel* button is set to **True**, the button is "clicked" when the user hits the Escape key. Thus, the Escape key will dismiss the print dialog.

The MultiSelect property is set to **frmMultiSelectExtended** so that the user can use the Control key to select multiple (possibly nonconsecutive) entries and the Shift key to select multiple consecutive entries.

The TabIndex property determines not only the order in which the controls are visited as the user hits the Tab key, but also determines which control has the initial focus. Since we want the initial focus to be on the list box, we set its tab index to 0.

Print button

Place a command button on the form as in Figure 20-43. Using the Properties window, set the following properties:

Property	Value
Name	cmdPrint
Accelerator	P
Caption	Print
TabIndex	1

Cancel button

Place another command button on the form as in Figure 20-43. Using the Properties window, set the following properties:

Property	Value
Name	cmdCancel
Accelerator	C
Caption	Cancel

Property	Value
TabIndex	2
Cancel	True

Create the Code Behind the UserForm

Now it is time to create the code behind these controls.

The Declarations section

The Declarations section should contain declarations of the module-level variables as shown in Example 20-6.

Example 20-6. Module-Level Variables in the User Form's Declarations Section

```
Dim cPTs As Integer
Dim sPTNames() As String
Dim sSheets() As String
```

Cancel button code

The Cancel button code is shown in Example 20-7.

Example 20-7. The cmdCancel_Click Event Procedure

```
Private Sub cmdCancel_Click()
    Unload Me
End Sub
```

Print button code

The Print button calls the main print procedure and then unloads the form; its event code is shown in Example 20-8.

Example 20-8. The cmdPrint_Click Event Procedure

```
Private Sub cmdPrint_Click()
    PrintSelectedPTs
    Unload Me
End Sub
```

The Form's Initialize event

The user form's Initialize event is the place to fill the list box with a list of pivot tables. Our application uses two module-level arrays: one to hold the worksheet names and one to hold the pivot-table names. There is also a module-level variable to hold the pivot-table count. We fill these arrays in the Initialize event, as shown in Example 20-9, and then use the arrays to fill the list. These arrays are used again in the main print procedure, which is why we have declared them at the module level.

Note the use of the `ReDim` statement to redimension the arrays. This is necessary since we do not know at the outset how many pivot tables there are in the workbook.

Example 20-9. The Initialize Event

```
Private Sub UserForm_Initialize()
' Fill lstPTs with the list of pivot tables
Dim ws As Worksheet
Dim PT As PivotTable
ReDim sPTNames(1 To 10) As String
ReDim sSheets(1 To 10) As String
lstPTs.Clear
cPTs = 0
For Each ws In ActiveWorkbook.Worksheets
  For Each PT In ws.PivotTables
    ' Update PT count
    cPTs = cPTs + 1
    ' Redimension arrays if necessary
    If UBound(sSheets) < cPTs Then
      ReDim Preserve sSheets(1 To cPTs + 5)
      ReDim Preserve sPTNames(1 To cPTs + 5)
    End If
    ' Save name of pivot table and ws
    sPTNames(cPTs) = PT.Name
    sSheets(cPTs) = ws.Name
    ' Add item to list box
    lstPTs.AddItem PT.Name & " ( in " & _
      sSheets(cPTs) & ")"
  Next
Next
End Sub
```

PrintPTs procedure

The main printing procedure is shown in Example 20-10. Note that we have been careful to deal with two special cases. First, there may not be any pivot tables in the workbook. Second, the user may hit the Print button without selecting any pivot tables in the list box. Note also that list boxes are 0-based, meaning that the first item is item 0. However, our arrays are 1-based (the first item is item 1), so we must take this into account when we move from a selection to an array member; to wit, selection *i* corresponds to array index *i+1*.

Example 20-10. The PrintSelectedPTs Procedure

```
Sub PrintSelectedPTs()
' Print the selected pivot tables in lstPTs
Dim i As Integer
Dim bNoneSelected As Boolean
bNoneSelected = True
If cPTs = 0 Then
  MsgBox "No pivot tables in this workbook.", _
```

Example 20-10. The PrintSelectedPTs Procedure (continued)

```
        vbExclamation
    Exit Sub
Else
  For i = 0 To lstPTs.ListCount - 1
    If lstPTs.Selected(i) Then
      bNoneSelected = False
      ' List box is 0-based, arrays are 1-based
      Worksheets(sSheets(i + 1)). _
          PivotTables(sPTNames(i + 1)). _
          TableRange2.PrintOut
    End If
  Next
End If
If bNoneSelected Then
  MsgBox "No pivot tables have been selected.", _
      vbExclamation
End If
End Sub
```

21

The Chart Object

Excel charts are represented by Chart objects in the Excel object model. Since charts are quite complex, the Chart object is one of the most complicated in the object model.

To set the terminology, Figure 21-1 shows a typical chart that has been labeled with some of the commonly used chart-related terms.

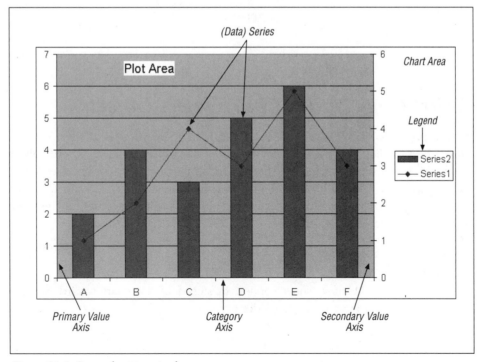

Figure 21-1. Some chart terminology

Figure 21-2 shows the Chart object and its immediate children.

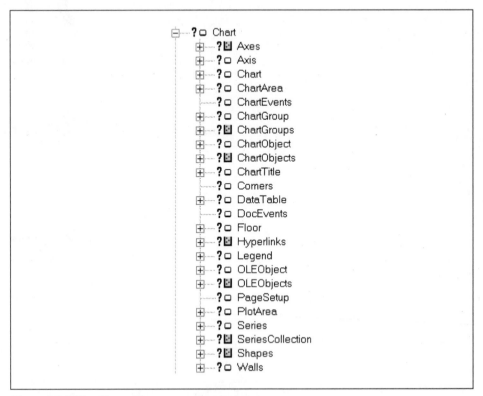

Figure 21-2. The Chart object

Chart Objects and ChartObject Objects

As you probably know, Excel charts can reside in a special type of sheet called a *chart sheet* or they can be embedded in an ordinary worksheet. Accordingly, a Chart object can represent a chart sheet (standalone chart) or an embedded chart. In the latter case, the Chart object is not contained directly in a worksheet. Rather, the worksheet contains a ChartObject object that acts as a *container* for the Chart object.

Thus, for instance, if we create a new chart using the chart wizard, the fourth step in the wizard displays the dialog shown in Figure 21-3.

If we choose the "As new sheet" option in step 4 of the chart wizard, we can access the resulting chart using the code:

```
Dim c as Chart
Set c = ThisWorkbook.Charts("Chart1")
```

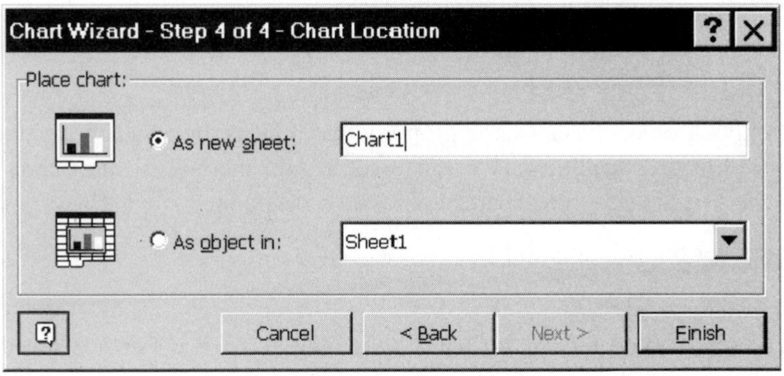

Figure 21-3. Step 4 in the Chart Wizard

On the other hand, choosing the "As object in" option in step 4 of the chart wizard, we access the chart using the code:

```
Dim c As Chart
Set c = Worksheets("Sheet1").ChartObjects("Chart 1").Chart
```

Note the space between the word Chart and the number 1 in the name of the ChartObject object, but not in the name of the Chart object.

We emphasize that there is no ChartSheet object. The Charts property of the Application object returns a so-called Sheets collection containing one Chart object for each chart sheet. It does not contain Chart objects for the embedded charts.

Creating a Chart

We have seen that a PivotTable is created and added to the PivotTables collection by invoking the PivotTableWizard method. On the other hand, creating a new chart requires a different approach, since it depends upon whether the chart is standalone (a chart sheet) or embedded in a worksheet (and thus contained in a ChartObject object).

Also, unlike the PivotTableWizard method, the ChartWizard method does not create a chart; it merely formats an existing chart. Accordingly, there are three steps required to create a meaningful chart:

- Decide whether to create a standalone chart (a chart sheet) or an embedded chart.

- Create the standalone chart or embedded chart as described in the following section.

- Format the chart using either the ChartWizard method or using individual properties and methods of the chart object.

Creating Chart Sheets

The Workbook object has a Charts property that returns the Charts collection of all *chart sheets* in the workbook. We can use the Add method of the Charts collection to create and add a new chartsheet to the workbook.

The syntax for the Add method is:

```
ChartsObject.Add(Before, After, Count)
```

As usual, this method returns a Chart object. The *Before* parameter specifies the sheet before which the new sheet is added, and the *After* parameter specifies the sheet after which the new sheet is added. Only one of these parameters can be specified at one time or an error will result. If neither is set, the new chart is inserted before the active sheet.

The optional *Count* parameter is an integer that specifies the number of sheets to be added. The default value is 1.

For example, the following code creates a new chart sheet named "Sales":

```
Dim ch As Chart
Set ch = ThisWorkbook.charts.Add()
ch.Name = "Sales"
```

The Add method cannot be used to format the chart. As mentioned earlier, this must be done using the various properties of the Chart object or the ChartWizard method, discussed later in the chapter.

Creating Embedded Charts

The Worksheet object also has a ChartObjects property that returns a ChartObjects collection, which is the collection of all ChartObjects in the worksheet. As we have mentioned, a ChartObject object is a container for a Chart object—that is, an embedded chart.

The ChartObjects collection has an Add method that is used to create a new embedded chart. The syntax is:

```
ChartsObjectObject.Add(Left, Top, Width, Height)
```

where the required *Left* and *Top* parameters give the coordinates of the upper-left corner of the chart (in points) relative to the upper-left corner of cell A1 on the worksheet, and *Width* and *Height* specify the initial size of the chart (also in points). Recall that the InchesToPoints method can be used to convert inches to points.

Note that the Add method returns a ChartObject object, rather than a Chart object. This is a bit confusing, since the method creates both a ChartObject object *and* the contained Chart object. The code in Example 21-1 creates a new ChartObject object called ExampleChart along with its contained Chart object. It positions the chart so that its upper-left corner is three columns from the left edge of the sheet and 1/2 row down from the top of the sheet. The dimensions of the chart are 8 columns wide and 20 rows high.

Example 21-1. Creating an Embedded Chart

```
Sub CreateAChart()

' Create an embedded chart

Dim co As ChartObject
Dim cw As Long, rh As Long

' Get data for positioning chart
cw = Columns(1).Width
rh = Rows(1).Height

' Position chart using column width and row height units
Set co = ActiveSheet.ChartObjects.Add(cw * 3, rh * 0.5, cw * 8, rh * 20)

' Name it
co.Name = "ChartExample"

Debug.Print co.Name
Debug.Print co.Chart.Name

' Set chart type
co.Chart.ChartType = xlLine

End Sub
```

The output of the Debug.Print statements are:

```
    ChartExample
    Sheet1 Chart 1
```

The chart appears as in Figure 21-4. (Yes, the chart is empty.)

You may have noticed that the chart in Figure 21-4 is a trifle uninteresting. We will need to use the various properties and methods of the Chart object (or the ChartWizard method) to create a useful chart.

Note that, although the documentation does not discuss the matter, experimentation shows that the Name property of the Chart object appears to be read-only. Indeed, the code:

```
    co.Chart.Name = "AChart"
```

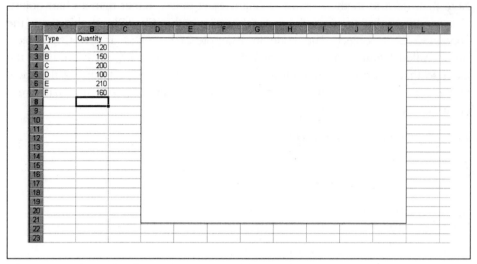

Figure 21-4. The results of creating an embedded chart object

results in the error message: "Method Name of object _Chart failed."

Note also that we can run the *CreateAChart* procedure multiple times without error and this will produce multiple ChartObject objects with the same name! Thus, the name property seems to be of little use for both ChartObject objects and embedded Chart objects. In fact, after running the *CreateAChart* procedure twice and getting two charts named ExampleChart, the code:

```
Debug.Print ActiveSheet.ChartObjects(1).Name
Debug.Print ActiveSheet.ChartObjects(2).Name
ActiveSheet.ChartObjects("ChartExample").Left = 600
```

actually produces the output:

```
ChartExample
ChartExample
```

and moves one of the charts to the new position specified by the Left property!

An Example of Chart Creation

As we have said, creating a useful chart from scratch requires using the properties and methods of the Chart object. As we will see, this object is quite complex, with a great many properties, methods, and children. Before plunging into a discussion of these items, we want to give an example of chart creation. This will put our future discussion into some perspective. In fact, we will have several occasions to make reference to this code in the sequel.

So, the *CreateChart* procedure shown in Example 21-2 produces the chart in Figure 21-5. It may not be pretty, but it does illustrate much of the chart making process.

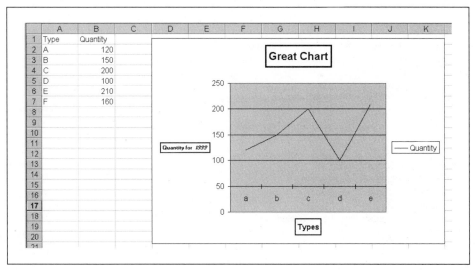

Figure 21-5. The results of CreateChart

Example 21-2. The CreateChart Procedure

```
Sub CreateChart()

' Create an embedded chart

Dim co As ChartObject
Dim cw As Long, rh As Long

' Temporary
If ActiveSheet.ChartObjects.Count > 0 Then
   ActiveSheet.ChartObjects(1).Delete
End If

' Get data for positioning chart
cw = Columns(1).Width
rh = Rows(1).Height

' Position chart using column width and row height units
Set co = ActiveSheet.ChartObjects.Add(cw * 3, rh * 0.5, cw * 8, rh * 20)

' Name it
co.Name = "ChartExample"

' Set chart type
co.Chart.ChartType = xlLine

' Add data series
```

Example 21-2. The CreateChart Procedure (continued)

```
co.Chart.SeriesCollection.Add _
   Source:=ActiveSheet.Range("A1:B6"), _
   Rowcol:=xlColumns, SeriesLabels:=True, _
   Categorylabels:=True

' Add axes
' (This is actually the default setting,
'    but is added here for illustration)
With co.Chart
   .HasAxis(xlCategory, xlPrimary) = True
   .HasAxis(xlCategory, xlSecondary) = False
   .HasAxis(xlValue, xlPrimary) = True
   .HasAxis(xlValue, xlSecondary) = False
End With

' Axis title formatting
With co.Chart.Axes(xlCategory)
  .HasTitle = True
  .AxisTitle.Caption = "Types"
  .AxisTitle.Border.Weight = xlMedium
End With
With co.Chart.Axes(xlValue)
  .HasTitle = True
  With .AxisTitle
    .Caption = "Quantity for 1999"
    .Font.Size = 6
    .Orientation = xlHorizontal
    .Characters(14, 4).Font.Italic = True
    .Border.Weight = xlMedium
  End With
End With

' Change the category names (Types) to lower case
' (On the worksheet they are in upper case)
co.Chart.Axes(xlCategory).CategoryNames = _
  Array("a", "b", "c", "d", "e")

' Set the crossing point on the (primary) value axis at 50
co.Chart.Axes(xlValue).CrossesAt = 50

' Horizontal but no vertical gridlines
co.Chart.Axes(xlValue).HasMajorGridlines = True
co.Chart.Axes(xlCategory).HasMajorGridlines = False

' Outside Tickmarks on category axis
co.Chart.Axes(xlCategory).MajorTickMark = xlTickMarkCross

' Move tick labels to below chart area
co.Chart.Axes(xlCategory).TickLabelPosition = _
        xlTickLabelPositionNextToAxis

' Set chart area fill to solid white
```

Example 21-2. The CreateChart Procedure (continued)

```
co.Chart.ChartArea.Interior.Color = RGB(255, 255, 255)

' Set plot area fill to gray
co.Chart.PlotArea.Interior.ColorIndex = 15

' Format chart title
With co.Chart.ChartTitle
  .Caption = "Great Chart"
  .Font.Size = 14
  .Font.Bold = True
  .Border.Weight = xlThick
End With

End Sub
```

Z-Order and ChartObject Objects

Before looking at the main properties, methods, and children of the Chart object, we can get one simple but important item out of the way.

Namely, it is possible for two or more embedded charts to overlap, which raises the question of how to control which chart object appears on the top. Every Chart-Object object has an order, called its *z-order*, that indicates the object's relative position with respect to an imaginary z-axis that comes directly out of the monitor at right angles, towards the user, as pictured in Figure 21-6.

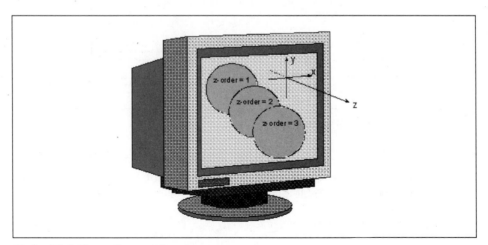

Figure 21-6. Illustrating z-order

The ChartObject object has a read-only ZOrder property that is used to return the z-order of the ChartObject. It also has BringToFront and SendToBack methods for changing the z-order. These properties can be used to shuffle the order of Chart-Object objects.

Chart Types

Each Excel chart has either a *standard* chart type or a *custom* chart type. In addition, there are two types of custom chart types: built-in and user-defined. All chart types are accessible by the user through the Chart Type dialog box shown in Figure 21-7 (right-click a chart and choose Chart Type).

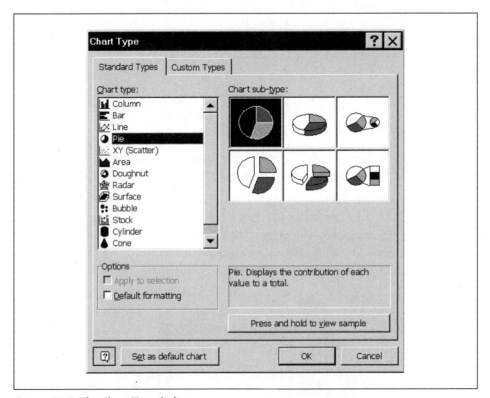

Figure 21-7. The Chart Type dialog

ChartType property

The ChartType property is a read-write property that can be set to any one of the **XlChartType** constants in Table 21-1.

Table 21-1. ChartType Constants

Type	Description	Constant(Value)
Area	3D Area	xl3DArea(-4098)
	3D Stacked Area	xl3DAreaStacked(78)
	3D 100% Stacked Area	xl3DAreaStacked100(79)
	Area	xlArea(1)

Table 21-1. ChartType Constants (continued)

Type	Description	Constant(Value)
	Stacked Area	xlAreaStacked(76)
	100% Stacked Area	xlAreaStacked100(77)
Bar	3D Clustered Bar	xl3DBarClustered(60)
	3D Stacked Bar	xl3DBarStacked(61)
	3D 100% Stacked Bar	xl3DBarStacked100(62)
	Clustered Bar	xlBarClustered(57)
	Stacked Bar	xlBarStacked(58)
	100% Stacked Bar	xlBarStacked100(59)
Bubble	Bubble	xlBubble(15)
	Bubble with 3D effects	xlBubble3DEffect(87)
Column	3D Column	xl3DColumn(-4100)
	3D Clustered Column	xl3DColumnClustered(54)
	3D Stacked Column	xl3DColumnStacked(55)
	3D 100% Stacked Column	xl3DColumnStacked100(56)
	Clustered Column	xlColumnClustered(51)
	Stacked Column	xlColumnStacked(52)
	100% Stacked Column	xlColumnStacked100(53)
Cone	Clustered Cone Bar	xlConeBarClustered(102)
	Stacked Cone Bar	xlConeBarStacked(103)
	100% Stacked Cone Bar	xlConeBarStacked100(104)
	3D Cone Column	xlConeCol(105)
	Clustered Cone Column	xlConeColClustered(99)
	Stacked Cone Column	xlConeColStacked(100)
	100% Stacked Cone Column	xlConeColStacked100(101)
Cylinder	Clustered Cylinder Bar	xlCylinderBarClustered(95)
	Stacked Cylinder Bar	xlCylinderBarStacked(96)
	100% Stacked Cylinder Bar	xlCylinderBarStacked100(97)
	3D Cylinder Column	xlCylinderCol(98)
	Clustered Cylinder Column	xlCylinderColClustered(92)
	Stacked Cylinder Column	xlCylinderColStacked(93)
	100% Stacked Cylinder Column	xlCylinderColStacked100(94)
Doughnut	Doughnut	xlDoughnut(-4120)
	Exploded Doughnut	xlDoughnutExploded(80)
Line	3D Line	xl3DLine(-4101)
	Line	xlLine(4)
	Line with Markers	xlLineMarkers(65)

Table 21-1. ChartType Constants (continued)

Type	Description	Constant(Value)
	Stacked Line with Markers	xlLineMarkersStacked(66)
	100% Stacked Line with Markers	xlLineMarkersStacked100(67)
	Stacked Line	xlLineStacked(63)
	100% Stacked Line	xlLineStacked100(64)
Pie	3D Pie	xl3DPie(-4102)
	Exploded 3D Pie	xl3DPieExploded(70)
	Bar of Pie	xlBarOfPie(71)
	Pie	xlPie(5)
	Exploded Pie	xlPieExploded(69)
	Pie of Pie	xlPieOfPie(68)
Pyramid	Clustered Pyramid Bar	xlPyramidBarClustered(109)
	Stacked Pyramid Bar	xlPyramidBarStacked(110)
	100% Stacked Pyramid Bar	xlPyramidBarStacked100(111)
	3D Pyramid Column	xlPyramidCol(112)
	Clustered Pyramid Column	xlPyramidColClustered(106)
	Stacked Pyramid Column	xlPyramidColStacked(107)
	100% Stacked Pyramid Column	xlPyramidColStacked100(108)
Radar	Radar	xlRadar(-4151)
	Filled Radar	xlRadarFilled(82)
	Radar with Data Markers	xlRadarMarkers(81)
Stock Quotes	High-Low-Close	xlStockHLC(88)
	Open-High-Low-Close	xlStockOHLC(89)
	Volume-High-Low-Close	xlStockVHLC(90)
	Volume-Open-High-Low-Close	xlStockVOHLC(91)
Surface	3D Surface	xlSurface(83)
	Surface (Top View)	xlSurfaceTopView(85)
	Surface (Top View) wireframe)	xlSurfaceTopViewWireframe(86)
	3D Surface (wireframe)	xlSurfaceWireframe(84)
XY (Scatter)	Scatter	xlXYScatter(-4169)
	Scatter with Lines	xlXYScatterLines(74)
	Scatter with Lines and No Data Markers	xlXYScatterLinesNoMarkers(75)
	Scatter with Smoothed Lines	xlXYScatterSmooth(72)
	Scatter with Smoothed Lines and No Data Markers	xlXYScatterSmoothNoMarkers(73)

In Example 21-3, at the end of the chapter, we present a macro that scrolls through the chart types in Table 21-1, allowing you to determine which chart type is appropriate for a particular purpose.

Note that it is possible that the return value of the ChartType property may not be one of the values in Table 21-1. For instance, the code:

```
MsgBox ActiveChart.ChartType
```

returns –4111 when applied to a chart with a particular user-defined chart type. This value actually occurs only once in the Excel object model. It is part of the **Constants** enum and is assigned the symbolic name **xlCombination**. (Since this seems not to be documented, I cannot say that this is the only value of ChartType that is not in Table 21-1.)

Note that each individual data series can have a chart type; that is, the Series object also has a ChartType property. In this way, if a chart has two data series, each series can have a different chart type. For instance, one series can be plotted as a line graph and the other as a column graph. (We will discuss Series objects later in the chapter.)

ApplyCustomType method

Contrary to its name, the ApplyCustomType method can apply either a standard or a custom chart type to a chart. The syntax is:

```
ChartObject.ApplyCustomType(ChartType, TypeName)
```

The *ChartType* parameter is either a standard chart type constant from Table 21-1 or one of the following **XlChartGallery** constants:

```
Enum XlChartGallery
    xlBuiltIn = 21
    xlUserDefined = 22
    xlAnyGallery = 23
End Enum
```

(The term ChartGallery does not seem to appear in the Excel documentation. However, in the Word object model, the term ListGallery refers to the objects that represent the three tabs in the Bullets and Numbering dialog box. Extrapolating to Excel, we might surmise that the term ChartGallery refers to the two tabs in the Chart Type dialog box in Figure 21-8.)

If ChartType is an **XlChartGallery** constant, then the optional *TypeName* parameter specifies the name of the custom chart type.

For instance, the following code:

```
ActiveChart.ApplyCustomType _
    ChartType:=xlBuiltIn, TypeName:="Blue Pie"
```

applies the built-in chart type called Blue Pie. This is equivalent to selecting Blue Pie in the Excel dialog box shown in Figure 21-8.

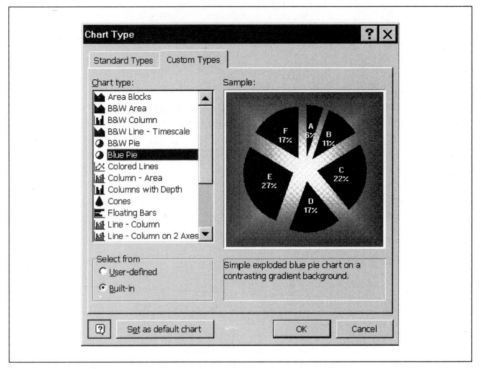

Figure 21-8. Illustrating ApplyCustomType

As another example, the following code sets the chart type to a user-defined type named DefaultXY:

```
ActiveChart.ApplyCustomType _
    ChartType:=xlUserDefined, TypeName:="DefaultXY"
```

Children of the Chart Object

Figure 21-9 shows the children of the Chart object.

An Excel chart has several components: axes, the chart area, a chart title, a data table, a floor (for a 3-D-chart), a plot area, and one or more data series (with data labels and data values). These components are represented by the children of the Chart object, which we now examine.

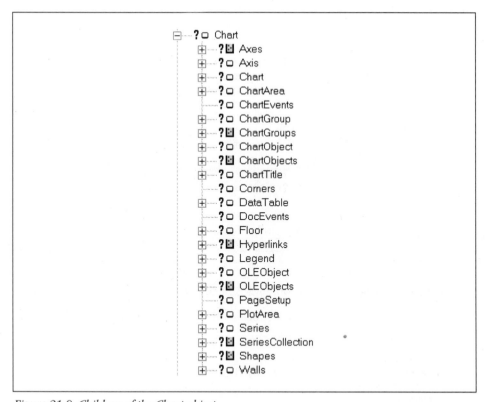

Figure 21-9. Children of the Chart object

The Axes Collection

Figure 21-10 shows the portion of the Excel object model that relates to chart axes.

The Chart object has an Axes collection that contains an Axis object for each axis in the chart. The Axes method returns either a single axis or the Axes collection for a chart. To return the Axes collection for a chart, use the syntax:

```
ChartObject.Axes
```

To return a specific Axis object, use the syntax:

```
ChartObject.Axes(Type, AxisGroup)
```

Here the optional *Type* parameter specifies the axis to return. It can be one of the following **XlAxisType** constants:

```
Enum XlAxisType
    xlCategory = 1
    xlValue = 2
    xlSeriesAxis = 3
End Enum
```

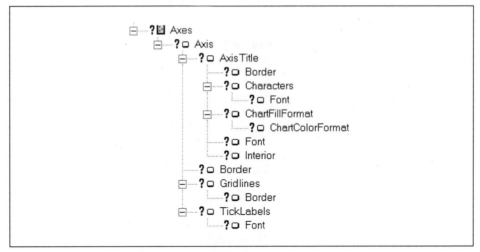

Figure 21-10. Axes-related objects

Note that `xlSeriesAxis` is valid only for 3-D charts.

The optional *AxisGroup* parameter specifies the axis group. It can be one of the following `XlAxisGroup` constants:

```
Enum XlAxisGroup
    xlPrimary = 1           ' The default
    xlSecondary = 2
End Enum
```

A secondary axis is a second vertical or horizontal axis upon which a second value series (vertical case) or category series (horizontal case) is plotted (see Figure 21-1). If this argument is omitted, the primary group is used. Note that 3-D charts have only one axis group.

The Chart object has a read-write property named HasAxis that determines whether or not the chart *displays* various types of axes. However, it is important to note that this method will fail if the chart does not yet have the corresponding data series. For instance, if you are creating a chart from scratch, it might be natural to add the code to create a category axis before adding the category data that will be plotted against that axis. *This not to do* (to quote Hamlet)!

In fact, referring to the *CreateChart* example procedure earlier in the chapter, if we reverse the data series code and the axes-related code, changing this:

```
' Add data series using data on the sheet itself
co.Chart.SeriesCollection.Add _
    Source:=ActiveSheet.Range("A1:B6"), _
    Rowcol:=xlColumns, SeriesLabels:=True, _
    Categorylabels:=True
```

```
' Add axes
With co.Chart
   .HasAxis(xlCategory, xlPrimary) = True
   .HasAxis(xlCategory, xlSecondary) = False
   .HasAxis(xlValue, xlPrimary) = True
   .HasAxis(xlValue, xlSecondary) = False
End With
```

to this:

```
' Add axes
With co.Chart
   .HasAxis(xlCategory, xlPrimary) = True
   .HasAxis(xlCategory, xlSecondary) = False
   .HasAxis(xlValue, xlPrimary) = True
   .HasAxis(xlValue, xlSecondary) = False
End With

' Add data series using data on the sheet itself
co.Chart.SeriesCollection.Add _
   Source:=ActiveSheet.Range("A1:B6"), _
   Rowcol:=xlColumns, SeriesLabels:=True, _
   Categorylabels:=True
```

Excel will issue the completely useless error message: "Method 'HasAxis' of object '_Chart' has failed." (Unfortunately, as is all too often the case, the documentation does not discuss this issue at all.)

The syntax for the HasAxis property is:

```
ChartObject.HasAxis(Index1, Index2)
```

where the parameters, despite their generic names, correspond directly to the *Type* and *AxisGroup* parameters of the Axes method. For instance, the following code displays a primary category axis and both primary and secondary value axes for the active chart:

```
With ActiveChart
   .HasAxis(xlCategory, xlPrimary) = True
   .HasAxis(xlCategory, xlSecondary) = False
   .HasAxis(xlValue, xlPrimary) = True
   .HasAxis(xlValue, xlSecondary) = True
End With
```

The Axis Object

Table 21-2 shows the properties and methods of the Axis object. As you can see, Axis objects are fairly involved in their own right. Fortunately, most of the members in Table 21-2 are self-explanatory, so we consider them only briefly. Note that most of these members correspond to the myriad check boxes and edit boxes in the five tabs of the Excel Format Axis dialog box.

Table 21-2. Members of the Axis Object

Application	HasDisplayUnitLabel (Excel 9)	MinorTickMark
AxisBetweenCategories	HasMajorGridlines	MinorUnit
AxisGroup	HasMinorGridlines	MinorUnitIsAuto
AxisTitle	HasTitle	MinorUnitScale
BaseUnit	Height	Parent
BaseUnitIsAuto	Left	ReversePlotOrder
Border	MajorGridlines	ScaleType
CategoryNames	MajorTickMark	Select
CategoryType	MajorUnit	TickLabelPosition
Creator	MajorUnitIsAuto	TickLabels
Crosses	MajorUnitScale	TickLabelSpacing
CrossesAt	MaximumScale	TickMarkSpacing
Delete	MaximumScaleIsAuto	Top
DisplayUnit (Excel 9)	MinimumScale	Type
DisplayUnitCustom (Excel 9)	MinimumScaleIsAuto	Width
DisplayUnitLabel (Excel 9)	MinorGridlines	

AxisGroup Property

This read-only property returns the group for the specified axis. It can be either **xlPrimary** (=1) or **xlSecondary** (=2).

Axis Titles and Their Formatting

The AxisTitle property returns an AxisTitle object that represents the title of the specified axis.

HasTitle property (R/W Boolean)

Before we can format an axis title, we must tell Excel that the axis has a title using the HasTitle property:

```
AxisObject.HasTitle = True
```

The AxisTitle object has several properties, the most prominent of which are the following:

AutoScaleFont

When this property is **True**, the label text font size is scaled automatically when the chart size changes. The default value is **True**.

Border

    Returns a Border object that can be used to set the color, line style, and width of the border of the axis title.

Caption

    Used to set the text for the title.

Characters

    Used to return a Characters object, which is a range of characters in the caption. This allows us to format a *portion* of the text in the caption.

Fill

    Returns a ChartFillFormat object used to set fill-formatting properties for the axis title.

Font

    Returns a Font object that can be used to set the font characteristics of the labels.

HorizontalAlignment and VerticalAlignment

    Used to set the alignment of axis title text.

Interior

    Returns an Interior object that can be used to format the interior of the axis title area.

NumberFormat

    Used to set the number format code for the labels. This property returns `Null` if all labels do not have the same number format. Note that since the format codes are the same as those used by Excel to format worksheet cells, we can use the macro recorder to get appropriate format codes.

Orientation

    This returns or sets the orientation for the axis title. It can be any one of the following constants:

```
Enum XlOrientation
    xlUpward = -4171
    xlDownward = -4170
    xlVertical = -4166
    xlHorizontal = -4128
End Enum
```

Let us take a closer look at the Characters object. A Characters object represents a *contiguous* portion of text within a text string. The Characters property returns a Characters object. (Note that the Characters property also applies to the ChartTitle object and the Range object.)

The syntax of the Characters property is:

```
AxisTitleObject.Characters(start, length)
```

where *start* is the start character number and *length* is the number of characters to return in the Characters object. When start is missing, it is assumed to be equal to 1, and when length is missing, all characters after the starting character are included.

To illustrate, the following code creates a title for the primary value axis and italicizes the word "billions." (Note the setting of the HasTitle property, to avoid an error message.)

```
With ActiveChart.Axes(xlValue, xlPrimary)
    .HasTitle = True
    .AxisTitle.Text = "These are billions"
    .AxisTitle.Characters(11, 8).Font.Italic = True
End With
```

Of course, if we wanted to italicize the entire title, we could simply use the Font property of the AxisTitle object, as in:

```
ActiveChart.Axes(xlValue, xlPrimary). _
    AxisTitle.Font.Italic = True
```

The Border property and the Border object

This property returns a Border object that represents the border of the object. The Border object can be used to set the color, line style, and weight of the border of an object, such as an axis title.

The Border object has no methods. Its main properties are Color, ColorIndex, LineStyle, and Weight.

The Color property can be set to any RGB value. For instance, the following code sets the major axis color to blue:

```
ActiveChart.Axes(xlCategory, xlPrimary). _
    MajorGridlines.Border.Color = RGB(0, 0, 255)
```

The ColorIndex property can be used to set the color via a color palette. For more information, including the ColorIndex values, see the help documentation.

The LineStyle property can take on any of the following values:

```
Enum XlLineStyle
    xlLineStyleNone = -4142
    xlDouble = -4119
    xlDot = -4118
    xlDash = -4115
    xlContinuous = 1
    xlDashDot = 4
    xlDashDotDot = 5
    xlSlantDashDot = 13
End Enum
```

The Weight property can be set to one of the following **XLBorderWeight** constants:

```
Enum XlBorderWeight
      xlMedium = -4138
      xlHairline = 1
      xlThin = 2
      xlThick = 4
End Enum
```

To further illustrate axis-title formatting, here is the relevant code from the *Create-Chart* procedure:

```
' Axis formatting
With co.Chart.Axes(xlCategory)
  .HasTitle = True
  .AxisTitle.Caption = "Types"
  .AxisTitle.Border.Weight = xlMedium
End With

With co.Chart.Axes(xlValue)
  .HasTitle = True
  With .AxisTitle
    .Caption = "Quantity for 1999"
    .Font.Size = 6
    .Orientation = xlHorizontal
    .Characters(14, 4).Font.Italic = True
    .Border.Weight = xlMedium
  End With
End With
```

CategoryNames Property

This property returns or sets the category names for the axis. It can be set to either an array or a Range object that contains the category names.

For instance, the code:

```
ActiveChart.Axes(xlCategory, xlSecondary). _
    CategoryNames = Array("One", "Two", "Three", "Four", "Five", "Six")
```

changes the labels on the upper horizontal axis to "One," "Two," "Three," etc.

CategoryType Property and BaseUnit Property

The CategoryType property returns or sets the type for a category axis. (It applies only to category-type axes.) It can be one of the following **XlCategoryType** constants:

```
Enum XlCategoryType
      xlAutomaticScale = -4105
      xlCategoryScale = 2
      xlTimeScale = 3
```

```
End Enum
```

The default is `xlAutomaticScale`.

When the CategoryType property for the axis is set to `xlTimeScale`, the Base-Unit property returns or sets the base unit for the specified category axis. It can be one of the following `XlTimeUnit` constants:

```
Enum XlTimeUnit
    xlDays = 0
    xlMonths = 1
    xlYears = 2
End Enum
```

Note that the value of this property takes effect only when the CategoryType property for the axis is set to `xlTimeScale`, even though the value can be changed at any time.

Crosses and CrossesAt Properties

The Crosses property returns or sets the point on the specified axis at which the "other" axis crosses—that is (we surmise), the other axis that is in the *same axis group*. Thus, if the specified axis is a primary axis, so is the other axis. If the specified axis is a secondary axis, so is the other axis. For instance, the code:

```
ActiveChart.Axes(xlValue, xlPrimary).Crosses = xlAxisCrossesMaximum
```

instructs the primary category axis (the other axis) to cross the primary value axis (the specified axis) at the maximum point of the primary value axis (the specified axis).

The Crosses property can assume one of the following `XlAxisCrosses` constants:

```
Enum XlAxisCrosses
    xlAxisCrossesCustom = -4114
    xlAxisCrossesAutomatic = -4105
    xlAxisCrossesMaximum = 2
    xlAxisCrossesMinimum = 4
End Enum
```

When set to `xlAxisCrossesAutomatic`, Excel determines the crossing point. When set to `xlMinimum`, the other axis crosses at the minimum value when the specified axis is a value axis or the far-left category when the specified axis is a category axis. When set to `xlMaximum`, the other axis crosses at the maximum value when the specified axis is a value axis or the far-right category when the specified axis is a category axis. (Unfortunately, this property does not always seem to act as advertised. In particular, I have noticed that setting this property to `xlMinimum` does not always adjust the crossing point properly.)

Finally, the `xlAxisCrossesCustom` setting applies only to value axes, in which case when set to `xlAxisCrossesCustom`, the CrossesAt property determines the crossing point for the other (category) axis. Note that setting the CrossesAt property automatically sets the Crosses property to `xlAxisCrossesCustom`.

For instance, referring to the *CreateChart* procedure, the code:

```
co.Chart.Axes(xlValue).CrossesAt = 50
```

causes the category axis to cross the value axis at 50.

Finally, note that these properties do not apply to 3-D charts.

Display Units

New to Excel 9 are the display unit-related properties HasDisplayUnitLabel, DisplayUnitLabel, DisplayUnit, and DisplayUnitCustom, and the DisplayUnitLabel object. These properties can be used to display a unit's legend for a chart axis. This is useful when dealing with labels that contain very large numbers. For instance, if a series of labels has the form 1000000, 2000000, 3000000, and so on, we can create a legend with the word "millions" and then change the labels to 1, 2, 3, ...

As an example, the code:

```
Sub DisplayUnitLabel()
With ActiveChart.Axes(xlValue)
    .DisplayUnit = xlMillions
    .HasDisplayUnitLabel = True
    With .DisplayUnitLabel
        .Caption = "millions"
        .Font.Size = 14
    End With
End With
End Sub
```

produces the chart in Figure 21-11. Note that the value axis is labeled with millions as the legend indicates.

Gridline-Related Properties and the Gridline Object

The Axis object has several properties that relate to gridlines; they are described in the following list:

HasMajorGridlines

Set this read-write property to **True** to show major gridlines for the axis, or **False** to hide gridlines. Applies only to primary axes (not secondary axes).

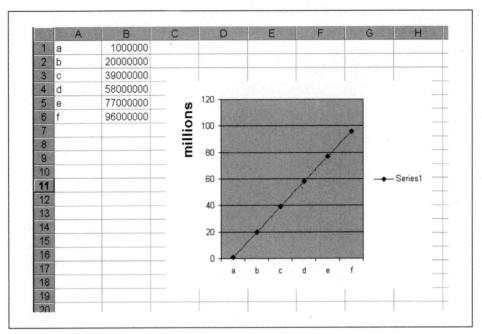

Figure 21-11. Display unit labels

HasMinorGridlines

Set this read-write property to **True** to show minor gridlines for the axis, or **False** to hide gridlines. Applies only to primary axes (not secondary axes).

MajorGridlines

This read-only property returns a Gridlines object that represents the major gridlines for the specified axis. Applies only to primary axes (not secondary axes).

MinorGridlines

This read-only property returns a Gridlines object that represents the minor gridlines for the specified axis. Applies only to primary axes (not secondary axes).

Note that the Gridlines object is not a collection object; that is, there is no Gridline object. Instead, the properties of the Gridlines object apply to all of the gridlines for the axis. For instance, the following code adds major gridlines to the category axis and formats these lines:

```
ActiveChart.Axes(xlCategory, xlPrimary). _
    HasMajorGridlines = True
With ActiveChart.Axes(xlCategory, xlPrimary). _
    MajorGridlines.Border
      .Color = RGB(0, 0, 255)
      .LineStyle = xlDot
```

```
        .Weight = xlThick
    End With
```

Position- and Dimension-Related Properties

The Axis object has the following properties related to its position and dimensions. These properties are read-only.

Height

Returns the height of the axis in points.

Width

Returns the width of the axis in points.

Left

Returns the distance from the left edge of the axis to the left edge of the chart area.

Top

Returns the distance from the top edge of the axis to the top of the chart area.

(Note that the width of a vertical axis is 0 and the height of a horizontal axis is 0.)

Tick Mark–Related Properties

The Axis object has several properties related to tick marks. The MajorTickMark property returns or sets the type of major tick mark for the specified axis, and the MinorTickMark property does the same for minor tick marks. Each of these properties can assume any value from the following enum:

```
Enum XlTickMark
    xlTickMarkNone = -4142
    xlTickMarkInside = 2
    xlTickMarkOutside = 3
    xlTickMarkCross = 4
End Enum
```

The TickMarkSpacing property returns or sets the number of categories or series between tick marks. This applies only to category and series axes (for 3-D charts). To set the tick mark spacing on a value axis, we can use the MajorUnit and MinorUnit properties (described later in this chapter).

There are also several properties related to tick-mark labels. The TickLabels property returns a TickLabels object that represents the tick-mark labels for the specified axis.

The TickLabelPosition property returns or sets the position of tick-mark labels on the specified axis. It can be one of the following **XlTickLabelPosition** constants:

```
Enum XlTickLabelPosition
    xlTickLabelPositionNone = -4142
    xlTickLabelPositionLow = -4134
    xlTickLabelPositionHigh = -4127
    xlTickLabelPositionNextToAxis = 4
End Enum
```

The TickLabelSpacing property returns or sets the number of categories or series between tick-mark labels. This property applies only to category and series axes (for 3-D charts). Note that Excel determines label spacing on all value axes.

The TickLabels object

The TickLabels object represents the set of tick-mark labels for an axis. Note that this is not a collection object; that is, there is no TickLabel object. Thus, the properties of the TickLabels object affect all of the labels for an axis simultaneously.

The TickLabels object has several properties, the most prominent of which are the following:

Font

> Returns a Font object that can be used to set the font characteristics of the labels.

AutoScaleFont

> When this property is **True**, the label text font size is scaled automatically when the chart size changes. The default value is **True**.

NumberFormat

> Used to set the number-format code for the labels. This property returns **Null** if all labels do not have the same number format. Note that since the format codes are the same as those used by Excel to format worksheet cells, we can use the macro recorder to get appropriate format codes.

Orientation

> Returns or sets the orientation for the labels and can be any one of the following constants:

```
Enum XlTickLabelOrientation
    xlTickLabelOrientationUpward = -4171
    xlTickLabelOrientationDownward = -4170
    xlTickLabelOrientationVertical = -4166
    xlTickLabelOrientationHorizontal = -4128
    xlTickLabelOrientationAutomatic = -4105
End Enum
```

Units-Related Properties

The Axis object has several properties related to setting units and the scale factor on the axis.

MajorUnit and MinorUnit

Returns or sets (as a Double) the major units or minor units for the specified axis. Setting this property sets the corresponding MajorUnitIsAuto or Minor-UnitsIsAuto property to `False`.

MajorUnitIsAuto and MinorUnitIsAuto

If `True`, Excel calculates the major units or minor units for the axis. These properties are read/write Boolean.

MajorUnitScale and MinorScaleUnit

Returns or sets the major unit scale value or minor unit scale value for the category axis when the CategoryType property is set to `xlTimeScale`. It can be one of the following `XlTimeUnit` constants:

```
Enum XlTimeUnit
    xlDays = 0
    xlMonths = 1
    xlYears = 2
End Enum
```

MaximumScale and MinimumScale

Returns or sets the maximum or minimum value on the axis as a Double.

MaximumScaleIsAuto and MinimumScaleIsAuto

If True, Excel calculates the maximum value or minimum value for the axis. This property is read/write Boolean.

ScaleType

Returns or sets the value axis scale type; this property applies only to value axes. It can be one of the following `XlScaleType` constants:

```
Enum XlScaleType
    xlScaleLogarithmic = -4133      'Common logarithm
    xlScaleLinear = -4132
End Enum
```

To illustrate, the following code:

```
With ActiveChart.Axes(xlValue, xlPrimary)
   .MajorUnit = 1
   .MaximumScale = 5
End With
```

will cause the axis to appear as on the left in Figure 21-12. On the other hand, the code:

```
With ActiveChart.Axes(xlValue, xlPrimary)
   .MajorUnit = 5
   .MaximumScale = 3
End With
```

results in the axis shown on the right in Figure 21-12.

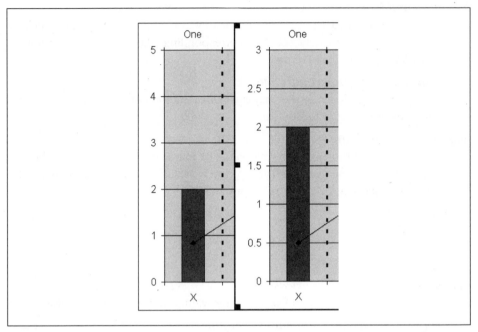

Figure 21-12. Axis units and scale

ReversePlotOrder Property

This read/write Boolean property can be set to **True** to have Excel reverse the direction of an axis (although the name is not very descriptive of the function). For instance, if the active chart is the chart in Figure 21-13, then the code:

```
ActiveChart.Axes(xlValue, xlPrimary).ReversePlotOrder = True
```

changes this chart to the one in Figure 21-14, where the primary axis data is plotted from the top down (so to speak).

Type Property

The Type property returns or sets the axis type. It can be one of the following **XlAxisType** constants:

```
Enum XlAxisType
    xlCategory = 1
    xlValue = 2
    xlSeriesAxis = 3
End Enum
```

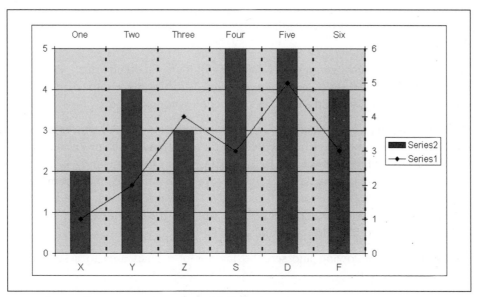

Figure 21-13. Illustrating ReversePlotOrder (before)

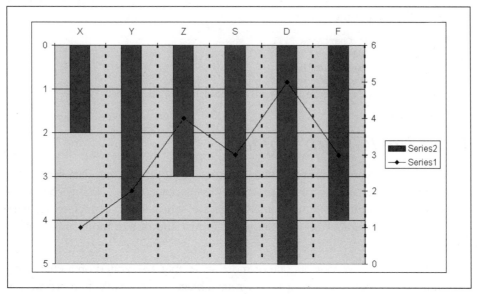

Figure 21-14. Illustrating ReversePlotOrder (after)

The ChartArea Object

The ChartArea object represents the chart area of a chart. As shown in Figure 21-1, the chart area on a 2-D chart contains essentially the entire chart: the axes, chart title, axis titles, and legend. On the other hand, the chart area on a 3-D chart contains the chart title and the legend but does not include the plot area, where the data is plotted.

The ChartArea object has several children—Border, ChartFillFormat, Font, and Interior—that can be used to set the characteristics of the entire chart. (These objects have been discussed earlier, in connection with axis titles.)

Unfortunately, the documentation does not clearly define the differences between the ChartFillFormat object (which represents fill formatting for chart elements) and its use and the Interior object and its use. Thus, some experimenting is in order. While both of these objects have a Pattern property in common, they seem generally to have different properties and methods. The ChartFillFormat object appears to relate more to gradient and texture fills, whereas the Interior object seems to relate more to solid fills and pattern fills.

To illustrate, the following line sets the interior of a chart area to a solid color (ColorIndex 3 is red):

```
ActiveChart.ChartArea.Interior.ColorIndex = 3
```

The following code creates a gradient pattern in the chart area, changing from red at the top to violet at the bottom:

```
With ActiveChart.ChartArea.Fill
   .Visible = True
   .ForeColor.SchemeColor = 3
   .BackColor.SchemeColor = 7
   .TwoColorGradient Style:=msoGradientHorizontal, Variant:=1
End With
```

The ChartGroup Object

As you no doubt know, an Excel chart can contain more than one data series. We have remarked that each series (that is, the Series object) has a ChartType property that can be used to set the chart type of the series. Thus, a single chart may have one or more series with a column-type format and one or more series with a line-type format.

A ChartGroup object represents one or more series that are plotted on a chart with the same chart type. Note that a ChartGroup object is not a collection. To access the individual Series objects represented by a ChartGroup, we must use the Series-Collection property (discussed later in this chapter).

The ChartGroup objects for a single chart are stored in the ChartGroups collection for the Chart object. This collection is accessed using the ChartGroups property.

The Excel object model provides a way to get "subcollections" of the ChartGroups collection that correspond to the major chart types (line, column, bar, etc.). To illustrate, the ColumnGroups method applies to a 2-D chart and returns the collection of all ChartGroup objects that correspond to the various column-type formats. The syntax is:

```
ChartObject.ColumnGroups
```

We can also access a single ChartGroup in this collection using the syntax:

```
ChartObject.ColumnGroups(Index)
```

Note, however, that there is no ColumnChartGroups collection per se. The ColumnGroups method actually returns a ChartGroups collection, but not the full collection that would be returned by:

```
ChartObject.ChartGroups
```

To illustrate, the chart in Figure 21-15 has two series. While each series has a line type, the subtypes are different. One series has been formatted with a line type with no data point markers, whereas the other has data markers. Accordingly, the code:

```
ActiveChart.LineGroups.Count
```

returns the value 2, since there are two distinct ChartGroup objects that fit in the LineGroups collection.

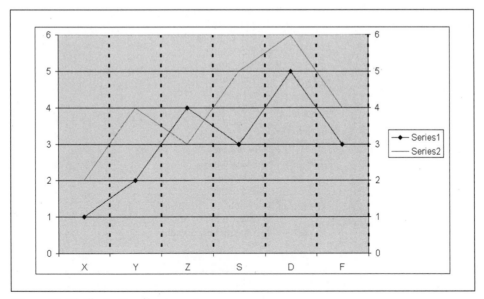

Figure 21-15. Illustrating chart groups

The Chart object has the following methods that return corresponding collections of ChartGroup objects:

- AreaGroups

- BarGroups

- ColumnGroups

- DoughnutGroups

- LineGroups

- PieGroups

- RadarGroups

- XYGroups

There are also some members of the Chart object that return chart groups for 3-D charts. They are: Area3DGroup, Bar3DGroup, Column3DGroup, Line3DGroup, Pie3DGroup, and SurfaceGroup. These members are singular because they return a single ChartGroup object.

The portion of the Excel object model that relates to ChartGroup objects is shown in Figure 21-16.

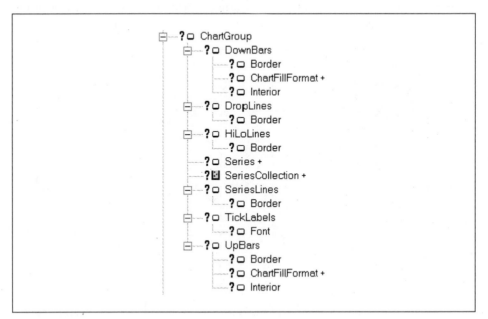

Figure 21-16. The ChartGroup object

UpBars and DownBars

UpBars and DownBars are shown in Figure 21-17. These bars are used to give a quick indication of the difference between data values in two different data series of line type. The UpBars are in white and DownBars are in black. The code to generate these bars is:

```
With ActiveChart.LineGroups(1)
    .HasUpDownBars = True
    .UpBars.Interior.Color = RGB(255, 255, 255)
    .DownBars.Interior.Color = RGB(0, 0, 0)
End With
```

Note that UpBars and DownBars apply only to 2-D line-type charts.

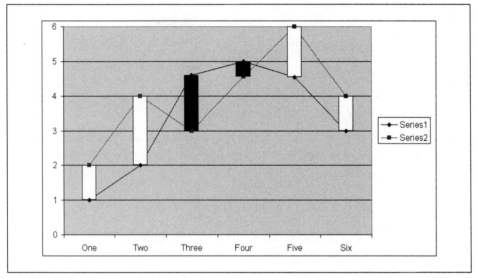

Figure 21-17. UpBars are in white and DownBars are in black

DropLines

DropLines are vertical lines that extend from the data markers on a line chart to the category axis. The HasDropLines property of the ChartGroup object can be set to **True** to display DropLines.

HiLoLines

HiLoLines are shown in Figure 21-18. The HasHiLoLines property of the Chart-Group object can be set to **True** to display HiLoLines. HiLoLines apply only to two-dimensional charts.

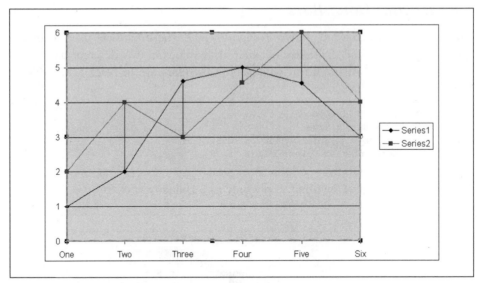

Figure 21-18. HiLoLines

SeriesCollection and Series Objects

The SeriesCollection property of a ChartGroup object returns the SeriesCollection collection of all Series objects that lie in that chart group. We will discuss Series objects later in the chapter.

SeriesLines

SeriesLines are shown in Figure 21-19. They apply only to stacked column or stacked bar chart groups. The HasSeriesLines property can be set to **True** to display series lines for a chart group.

The ChartTitle Object

A ChartTitle object represents a chart title. The ChartTitle object is shown in Figure 21-20.

As with several of the other chart-related objects, the ChartTitle object has Border, Characters, ChartFillFormat, Font, and Interior children that are used to format the corresponding portion of the chart title. We have discussed these objects before, so we will not comment further on them here.

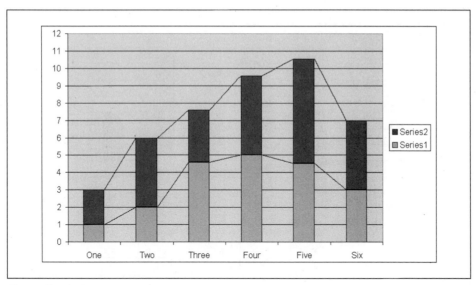

Figure 21-19. SeriesLines

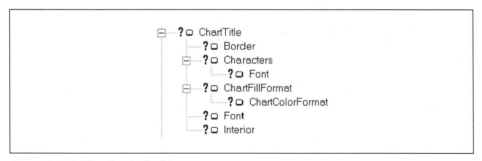

Figure 21-20. The ChartTitle object

The DataTable Object

Figure 21-21 shows a data table. Data tables are represented by DataTable objects.

The Chart object has a property called HasDataTable. Setting this property to **True** displays a data table, as in Figure 21-21. Indeed, the data table in Figure 21-21 was produced and given a border with the following code:

```
ActiveChart.HasDataTable = True
ActiveChart.DataTable.HasBorderOutline = True
```

The DataTable object has a variety of self-explanatory properties, such as AutoScaleFont, Border, Font, HasBorderHorizontal, HasBorderOutline, HasBorder-Vertical, and ShowLegendKey. (The ShowLegendKey property is responsible for the small squares on the far left portion of the data table in Figure 21-21.)

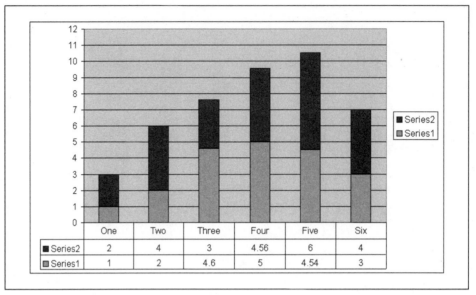

Figure 21-21. A data table

The Floor Object

The Floor object applies only to 3-D charts and represents the floor of the chart. For instance, the following code:

```
ActiveChart.Floor.Interior.Pattern = xlPatternChecker
```

sets the floor of the active 3-D chart to a checkered pattern, as shown in Figure 21-22. The Floor object has Border, ChartFillFormat, and Interior children.

The Legend Object

Legend objects represent legends. The Legend object and its children are shown in Figure 21-23.

The Chart object has a Legend property that returns the Legend object for that chart. As expected, the Legend object has Border, ChartFillFormat, Font, and Interior children that serve the same purpose here as they do for the ChartTitle, Axis-Title, ChartArea, and other objects.

The LegendEntry Object

Figure 21-1 shows a chart legend with two legend entries. Legend entries are represented by LegendEntry objects. The LegendEntry objects for a legend are kept in

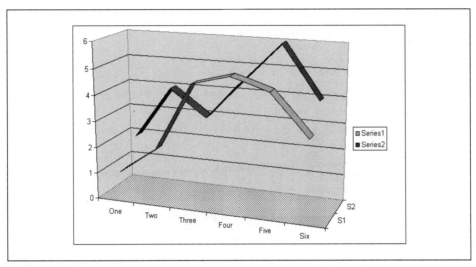

Figure 21-22. The floor of a 3-D chart (checkered)

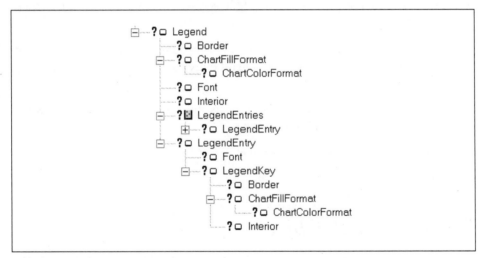

Figure 21-23. The Legend object

the LegendEntries collection object for the Legend object. This collection is accessed using the LegendEntries property of the Chart object.

Each legend entry has two parts: the text of the legend entry is the name of the series associated with that entry, and the *entry key* (also called an entry marker) is a small copy of the associated series and its formatting.

Note that the *text* of a legend entry cannot be changed. However, the LegendEntry object does have a Font property that can be used to change the font of the legend entry, as in:

```
ActiveChart.Legend.Font.Italic = True
```

In addition, LegendEntry objects can be deleted. However, after a legend entry has been deleted, the only way to restore it is to remove and recreate the entire legend by setting the HasLegend property for the chart first to **False** and then to **True**.

Also, no pattern formatting is allowed for legend entries, nor can a legend entry's position or size be changed.

Note finally that there is no direct way to return the series corresponding to a given legend entry.

The LegendKey Object

A legend key is represented by a LegendKey object. This object has Border, ChartFillFormat, and Interior children.

It is very important to note that formatting the LegendKey object will also automatically format the actual series that the legend entry represents. In other words, the series and its legend key *always* match.

Thus, for instance, the following code formats the first data series and its legend key with a red interior and a thick border:

```
With ActiveChart.Legend.LegendEntries(1).LegendKey
   .Interior.ColorIndex = 3
   .Border.Weight = xlThick
End With
```

The PageSetup Object

The PageSetup object represents all of the page formatting for a chart (or worksheet). The members of the PageSetup object are shown in Table 21-3.

Table 21-3. Members of the PageSetup Object

Application	FitToPagesWide	PrintGridlines
BlackAndWhite	FooterMargin	PrintHeadings
BottomMargin	HeaderMargin	PrintNotes
CenterFooter	LeftFooter	PrintQuality
CenterHeader	LeftHeader	PrintTitleColumns
CenterHorizontally	LeftMargin	PrintTitleRows

Table 21-3. Members of the PageSetup Object (continued)

CenterVertically	Order	RightFooter
ChartSize	Orientation	RightHeader
Creator	PaperSize	RightMargin
Draft	Parent	TopMargin
FirstPageNumber	PrintArea	Zoom
FitToPagesTall	PrintComments	

For instance, the following code sets the margins and then does a print preview for the active chart:

```
With ActiveChart.PageSetup
    .LeftMargin = Application.InchesToPoints(0.5)
    .RightMargin = Application.InchesToPoints(0.75)
    .TopMargin = Application.InchesToPoints(1.5)
    .BottomMargin = Application.InchesToPoints(1)
    .HeaderMargin = Application.InchesToPoints(0.5)
    .FooterMargin = Application.InchesToPoints(0.5)
End With
ActiveChart.PrintPreview
```

The PlotArea Object

The plot area of a chart (see Figure 21-1) is the area where the chart data is plotted. For a 2-D chart, it consists of the data markers, gridlines, data labels, trend lines, and optional chart items, but *not* the axes. For a 3-D chart, it also includes the walls, floor, axes, axis titles, and tick-mark labels in the chart. The plot area is surrounded by the chart area (which does contain the axes on a 2-D chart).

The PlotArea object has Border, ChartFillFormat, and Interior children used for the formatting of these items. The PlotArea object also has Top, Left, Height, and Width properties that can be used to set the size and position of the plot area within the chart area. Note that there are some restrictions on how these values can be set. For instance, it appears that Excel will not let us set the Top property in such a way that the bottom of the plot area would fall below the bottom of the chart area (which makes sense).

The Series Object

The Series object represents a data series in an Excel chart. The Series object and its children are shown in Figure 21-24.

The Series object has Border, ChartFillFormat, and Interior child object, which we have discussed before. Let us look at some of its other children.

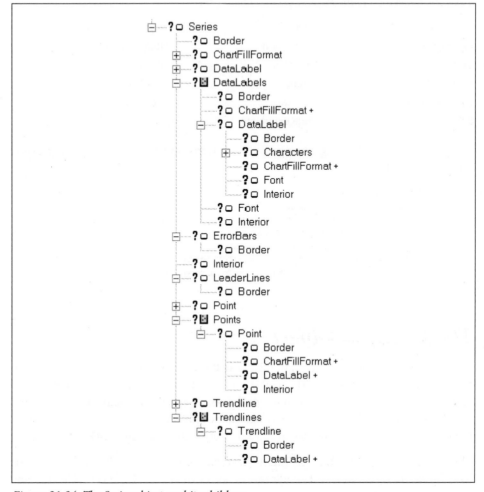

Figure 21-24. The Series object and its children

The Series objects for a chart are contained in a collection object named SeriesCollection. This collection is returned by the SeriesCollection method of the Chart object. (We will see examples later in this section.)

The members of the Series object are shown in Table 21-4.

Table 21-4. Members of the Series Object

Application	ErrorBars	MarkerForegroundColorIndex
ApplyCustomType	Explosion	MarkerSize
ApplyDataLabels	Fill	MarkerStyle
ApplyPictToEnd	Formula	Name
ApplyPictToFront	FormulaLocal	Parent

Table 21-4. Members of the Series Object (continued)

ApplyPictToSides	FormulaR1C1	Paste
AxisGroup	FormulaR1C1Local	PictureType
BarShape	Has3DEffect	PictureUnit
Border	HasDataLabels	PlotOrder
BubbleSizes	HasErrorBars	Points
ChartType	HasLeaderLines	Select
ClearFormats	Interior	Shadow
Copy	InvertIfNegative	Smooth
Creator	LeaderLines	Trendlines
DataLabels	MarkerBackgroundColor	Type
Delete	MarkerBackgroundColorIndex	Values
ErrorBar	MarkerForegroundColor	XValues

Adding a New Series

To add a new series to a chart, we use the Add method of the SeriesCollection object. The syntax is:

```
SeriesCollectionObject.Add(Source, Rowcol, _
    SeriesLabels, CategoryLabels, Replace)
```

The *Source* parameter specifies the new data as a Range object.

The optional *Rowcol* parameter specifies whether the data series are in rows or columns in the specified range. It can be one of the following XlRowCol constants:

```
Enum XlRowCol
    xlRows = 1
    xlColumns = 2         ' The default
End Enum
```

The optional *SeriesLabels* parameter applies only when *Source* is a range (not an array). It is **True** if the first row or column contains the name of the data series and **False** if the first row or column contains the first data point of the series. If this argument is omitted, Excel attempts to determine the location of the series name from the contents of the first row or column. (As I have stated several times before, my advice is to supply any values that you require, rather than letting Excel guess.)

Similarly, the optional *CategoryLabels* parameter applies only when *Source* is a range (not an array). It is **True** if the first row or column contains the name of the category labels and **False** if the first row or column contains the first data point of the series. If this argument is omitted, Excel attempts to determine the location of the category label from the contents of the first row or column.

The optional *Replace* parameter has the following meaning: If *CategoryLabels* is *True* and *Replace* is *True*, the specified categories replace the categories that currently exist for the series. If *Replace* is *False*, the existing categories will not be replaced. The default value is *False*.

To illustrate, consider the worksheet in Figure 21-25.

	A	B	C
1		Average	Std. Dev.
2	A	1.23	2
3	B	2	4
4	C	4.6	3
5	D	4.43	4.56
6	E	4.54	6
7	F	3	4

Figure 21-25. Illustrating the Add method: The data

The following code will create the chart in Figure 21-26:

```
Dim co As ChartObject
Set co = ActiveSheet.ChartObjects. _
    Add(100, 100, 300, 200)
co.Chart.ChartType = xlColumnClustered
co.Chart.SeriesCollection.Add _
    Source:=ActiveSheet.Range("A1:C7"), _
    Rowcol:=xlColumns, SeriesLabels:=True, _
    Categorylabels:=True
```

Note that the series labels are in the first row and the category labels are in the first column.

The DataLabel Object

A DataLabel object represents the data label of a chart data point (or trendline). (We discuss the Point object later in the chapter.) Each Series object has a DataLabels collection that contains one DataLabel object for each point in the series. The Data-Labels collection is returned by the DataLabels method, as in:

```
If ActiveChart.SeriesCollection(1). _
    HasDataLabels Then
        MsgBox ActiveChart.SeriesCollection(1)._
        DataLabels.Count
```

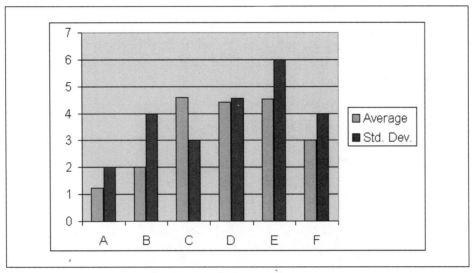

Figure 21-26. Illustrating the Add method: The chart

```
End If
```

Note that if there are no data labels for a given series, then the DataLabels method will generate an error; we should check this first before calling the method, using the HasDataLabels property of the Series object.

The *visibility* of a data label (not its existence) is governed by the HasDataLabel property of the corresponding Point object (discussed later). Thus, the code:

```
ActiveChart.SeriesCollection(1).Points(1).HasDataLabel = False
```

suppresses the display of a data label for the first data point in the series.

We can use the ApplyDataLabels method to display or hide data labels and to change the type of labels. The syntax for this method is:

```
expression.ApplyDataLabels(Type, LegendKey)
```

where **expression** can return either a Chart, Point, or Series object. When the method is applied to a Chart object, it affects the data labels for all series in the chart at the same time.

The **Type** parameter is the data-label type and can be one of the following **XlDataLabelsType** constants:

```
Enum XlDataLabelsType
    xlDataLabelsShowNone = -4142
    xlDataLabelsShowValue = 2
    xlDataLabelsShowPercent = 3
    xlDataLabelsShowLabel = 4
    xlDataLabelsShowLabelAndPercent = 5
```

```
    xlDataLabelsShowBubbleSizes = 6
End Enum
```

The optional *LegendKey* parameter can be set to **True** to show the legend key next to each data point. The default value is **False**. Figure 21-27 shows data point legends in action.

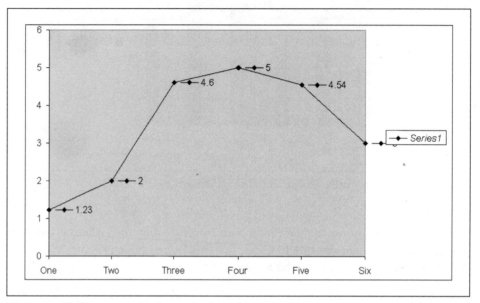

Figure 21-27. Illustrating the data point legend

The properties and methods of the DataLabel object are shown in Table 21-5.

Table 21-5. Members of the DataLabel Object

Application	Font	ReadingOrder
AutoScaleFont	HorizontalAlignment	Select
AutoText	Interior	Shadow
Border	Left	ShowLegendKey
Caption	Name	Text
Characters	NumberFormatLinked	Top
Creator	Orientation	Type
Delete	Parent	VerticalAlignment
Fill	Position	

Note that on a trendline (discussed later in this chapter), the DataLabel property returns the text shown with the trendline. This text can be the equation, the R-squared value, or both (if both are showing).

The Point Object

A Point object represents a single data point in a series. The Point object for the points in a given series are contained in the Points collection for the Series object. This collection is returned by the Points property of the Series object.

The Point object has the following children: Border, ChartFillFormat, DataLabel, and Interior. The members of the Point object are shown in Table 21-6. Most of these members are self-explanatory. Let us look briefly at some of the others.

Table 21-6. Members of the Point Object

Application	Delete	MarkerSize
ApplyDataLabels	Explosion	MarkerStyle
ApplyPictToEnd	Fill	Parent
ApplyPictToFront	HasDataLabel	Paste
ApplyPictToSides	Interior	PictureType
Border	InvertIfNegative	PictureUnit
ClearFormats	MarkerBackgroundColor	SecondaryPlot
Copy	MarkerBackgroundColorIndex	Select
Creator	MarkerForegroundColor	Shadow
DataLabel	MarkerForegroundColorIndex	

Explosion property

This property returns or sets the explosion value for a pie-chart or doughnut-chart slice. Figure 21-28 shows an explosion value of 20, the result of the following code:

```
ActiveChart.SeriesCollection(1).Points(2).Explosion = 20
```

Note that the Explosion property can be applied to a data series, in which case it "explodes" all of the segments. An explosion value of 0 corresponds to no explosion.

MarkerSize and MarkerStyle

The MarkerSize property returns or sets the size of a data point in points (as a Long). The property also applies to the Series object, in which case it sets all markers in the series at once.

The MarkerStyle property determines the style of the data point and can be one of the following values:

```
Enum XlMarkerStyle
    xlMarkerStyleX = -4168
    xlMarkerStylePicture = -4147
```

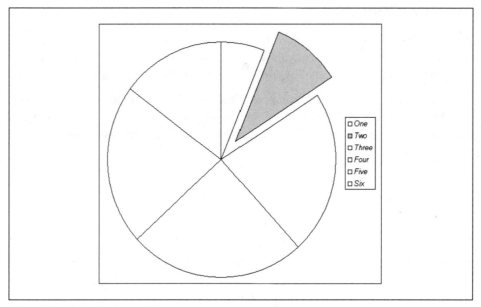

Figure 21-28. Explosion = 20

```
        xlMarkerStyleNone = -4142
        xlMarkerStyleDot = -4118
        xlMarkerStyleDash = -4115
        xlMarkerStyleAutomatic = -4105
        xlMarkerStyleSquare = 1
        xlMarkerStyleDiamond = 2
        xlMarkerStyleTriangle = 3
        xlMarkerStyleStar = 5
        xlMarkerStyleCircle = 8
        xlMarkerStylePlus = 9
    End Enum
```

To illustrate, the following code produces the rather odd-looking chart in Figure 21-29.

```
With ActiveChart.SeriesCollection(1)
   .MarkerSize = 10
   .MarkerStyle = xlMarkerStyleDiamond
   With .Points(2)
     .MarkerSize = 20
     .MarkerStyle = xlMarkerStyleCircle
   End With
End With
```

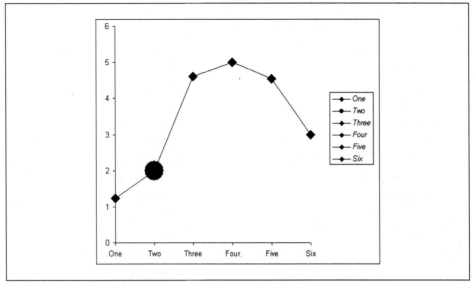

Figure 21-29. Illustrating MarkerSize and MarkerStyle

Properties and Methods of the Chart Object

The 91 properties and methods of the Chart object are shown in Table 21-7.

Table 21-7. Members of the Chart Object

Activate	DoughnutGroups	Previous
Application	Elevation	PrintOut
ApplyCustomType	Evaluate	PrintPreview
ApplyDataLabels	Export	Protect
Area3DGroup	Floor	ProtectContents
AreaGroups	GapDepth	ProtectData
AutoScaling	GetChartElement	ProtectDrawingObjects
Axes	HasAxis	ProtectFormatting
Bar3DGroup	HasDataTable	ProtectGoalSeek
BarGroups	HasLegend	ProtectionMode
BarShape	HasTitle	ProtectSelection
ChartArea	HeightPercent	RadarGroups
ChartGroups	Hyperlinks	Refresh
ChartObjects	Index	RightAngleAxes
ChartTitle	Legend	Rotation

Table 21-7. Members of the Chart Object (continued)

ChartType	Line3DGroup	SaveAs
ChartWizard	LineGroups	Select
CheckSpelling	Location	SeriesCollection
CodeName	Move	SetBackgroundPicture
Column3DGroup	Name	SetSourceData
ColumnGroups	Next	Shapes
Copy	OLEObjects	ShowWindow
CopyPicture	PageSetup	SizeWithWindow
Corners	Parent	SurfaceGroup
CreatePublisher	Paste	Unprotect
Creator	Perspective	Visible
DataTable	Pie3DGroup	Walls
Delete	PieGroups	WallsAndGridlines2D
DepthPercent	PlotArea	XYGroups
Deselect	PlotBy	
DisplayBlanksAs	PlotVisibleOnly	

Table 21-8 shows the members of the Chart object that return children of the Chart object, along with the objects that they return. Note that several members can return a single object or a collection of objects.

Table 21-8. Members that Return Children

Name	Return Type
Application	Application
Area3DGroup	ChartGroup
AreaGroups	ChartGroup(s)
Axes	Axis/Axes
Bar3DGroup	ChartGroup
BarGroups	ChartGroup(s)
ChartArea	ChartArea
ChartGroups	ChartGroup(s)
ChartObjects	ChartObject(s)
ChartTitle	ChartTitle
Column3DGroup	ChartGroup
ColumnGroups	ChartGroup(s)
Corners	Corners
DataTable	DataTable
DoughnutGroups	ChartGroup(s)

Table 21-8. Members that Return Children (continued)

Name	Return Type
Floor	Floor
Hyperlinks	Hyperlinks
Legend	Legend
Line3DGroup	ChartGroup
LineGroups	ChartGroup(s)
Location	Chart
OLEObjects	OLEObject(s)
PageSetup	PageSetup
Pie3DGroup	ChartGroup
PieGroups	ChartGroup(s)
PlotArea	PlotArea
RadarGroups	ChartGroup(s)
SeriesCollection	Series/SeriesCollection
Shapes	Shapes
SurfaceGroup	ChartGroup
Walls	Walls
XYGroups	ChartGroup(s)

Let us discuss a few of the members of the Chart object. (We have encountered many of these members in connection with other chart-related objects.)

ChartWizard Method

The ChartWizard method modifies the properties of a chart. Note that unlike the PivotTable wizard, the ChartWizard method does not create a chart. The ChartWizard method is useful for applying several formatting properties to a chart at one time. The method changes only the properties that are specified by the parameters that are included in the call to the method.

The syntax for the ChartWizard method is:

```
ChartObject.ChartWizard(Source, Gallery, Format, _
    PlotBy, CategoryLabels, SeriesLabels, HasLegend, _
    Title, CategoryTitle, ValueTitle, ExtraTitle)
```

Note that all parameters are optional.

The *Source* parameter is the range that contains the source data for the chart. If *Source* is omitted, then Excel will use the selected embedded chart or the active chart sheet. If no embedded chart is selected and no chart sheet is active, then an error will result.

The *Gallery* parameter is used to specify a general chart type and can be one of the following XlChartType constants: xlArea, xlBar, xlColumn, xlLine, xlPie, xlRadar, xlXYScatter, xlCombination, xl3DArea, xl3DBar, xl3DColumn, xl3DLine, xl3DPie, xl3DSurface, xlDoughnut, or xlDefaultAutoFormat.

The *Format* parameter is used to specify the specific chart type, given the value of *Gallery*. The value of Format can be a number from 1 through 10, depending on the gallery type. Note that this value corresponds to the chart types in the Chart Format dialog. If this argument is omitted, Excel will select a value based on the gallery type and data source.

The *PlotBy* parameter specifies whether the data for each series is in rows or columns. It can be one of the values xlRows or xlColumns.

The *CategoryLabels* parameter is an integer that specifies the number of rows or columns within the source range that contain category labels. It can be any value from 0 through one less than the maximum number of categories or series.

Similarly, *SeriesLabels* is an integer that specifies the number of rows or columns within the source range that contain series labels. It can be any value from 0 through one less than the maximum number of categories or series.

The *HasLegend* parameter should be set to **True** to include a chart legend.

The *Title* parameter should be set to the chart title text. Similarly, *CategoryTitle* is the category axis title text, *ValueTitle* is the value axis title text, and *ExtraTitle* is the series axis title for 3-D charts or the second value axis title for 2-D charts with a second value axis.

To illustrate, imagine that the chart in Figure 21-30 is the active chart. The following code reformats the chart in Figure 21-30, as shown in Figure 21-31:

```
ActiveChart.ChartWizard Gallery:=xlLine, _
    Format:=1, HasLegend:=True, Title:="Averages", _
    CategoryTitle:="Grades", ValueTitle:="Average"
```

Export Method

The *Export* method exports a chart in a graphic format. The syntax is:

```
ChartObject.Export(FileName, FilterName, Interactive)
```

Here *FileName* is the name of the graphic file to create. *FilterName* is the name of the graphic filter as it appears in the registry. Microsoft does not say *where* in the registry, but it seems likely to be the key:

```
HKEY_LOCAL_MACHINE\Software\Microsoft\Shared Tools\Graphics Filters\Export
```

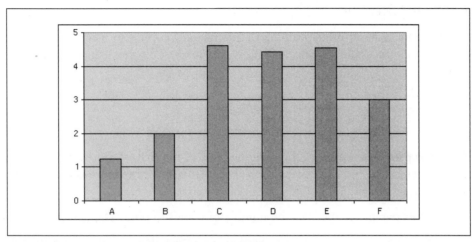

Figure 21-30. Illustrating the ChartWizard method

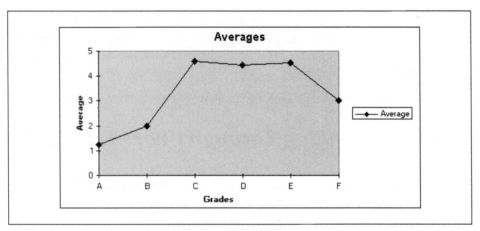

Figure 21-31. Results of the ChartWizard method

The *Interactive* parameter can be set to **True** to display the dialog box that contains filter-specific options. If this argument is **False** (the default), Excel uses the default values for the filter.

To illustrate, the following code creates three graphic files from the active chart:

```
ActiveChart.Export "d:\excel\test.png", "PNG"
ActiveChart.Export "d:\excel\test.jpg", "JPEG"
ActiveChart.Export "d:\excel\test.gif", "GIF"
```

Note that in these cases, setting *Interactive* to **True** seems to have no effect. Note also that any file of the name *FileName* will be overwritten without warning.

PrintOut Method

The PrintOut method prints the chart. This method applies to a variety of other objects, such as Charts, Worksheet(s), Workbook(s) and the Range object. The syntax is:

```
ChartObject.PrintOut(from, To, Copies, Preview, _
    ActivePrinter, PrintToFile, Collate)
```

Note that all of the parameters to this method are optional.

The *From* parameter specifies the page number of the first page to print, and the *To* parameter specifies the last page to print. If omitted, the entire object (range, worksheet, etc.) is printed.

The *Copies* parameter specifies the number of copies to print. The default is 1.

Set *Preview* to `True` to invoke print preview rather than printing immediately. The default is `False`.

ActivePrinter sets the name of the active printer. On the other hand, setting *PrintToFile* to `True` causes Excel to print to a file. Excel will prompt the user for the name of the output file. (Unfortunately, there is no way to specify the name of the output file in code.)

The *Collate* parameter should be set to `True` to collate multiple copies.

Example: Scrolling Through Chart Types

There are a total of 73 distinct chart types. This is too many to easily look at examples of each type by hand. However, a bit of coding can produce a simple application that scrolls through the various chart types, so that we can determine which chart type is most appropriate for a particular purpose.

Start by creating a chart (with some data such as that in Figure 21-6) in a chartsheet. Then add the code in Example 21-3 to the chart sheet's code module.

Example 21-3. Code in the Chart Sheet's Code Module

```
Option Explicit

Dim bPause As Boolean

Sub ScrollChartTypes()
Dim iType As Integer, sName As String
Dim fr As Integer
fr = FreeFile
Open ThisWorkbook.Path & _
    "\charttypes.txt" For Input As #fr
Do While Not EOF(fr)
```

Example 21-3. Code in the Chart Sheet's Code Module (continued)

```
  Input #fr, iType, sName
  On Error Resume Next
  ActiveChart.ChartType = iType
  ActiveChart.HasTitle = True
  ActiveChart.ChartTitle.Text = _
    iType & " -- " & sName
  Delay 2
  If bPause Then
    Do
      DoEvents
    Loop Until bPause = False
  End If
Loop
Close fr
End Sub


'-----


Sub Delay(rTime As Single)
'Delay rTime seconds (min=.01, max=300)
Dim OldTime As Variant
'Safty net
If rTime < 0.01 Or rTime > 300 Then rTime = 1
OldTime = Timer
Do
    DoEvents
Loop Until Timer - OldTime >= rTime
End Sub


'-----


Private Sub Chart_MouseDown(ByVal Button As Long, ByVal Shift As Long, ByVal X As
Long, ByVal Y As Long)
  If Button = xlPrimaryButton Then _
    bPause = Not bPause
End Sub
```

This code contains three procedures. The main procedure is *ScrollChartTypes*, which sets the chart type and adjusts the chart's title accordingly. The procedure uses a text file, *ChartTypes.txt*, that contains a list of all chart types and their names. The contents of that text file are shown in Example 21-4. This file will need to be in the same directory as the workbook.

Example 21-4. The ChartTypes.txt File

```
-4169    XYScatter
-4151    Radar
-4120    Doughnut
-4102    3DPie
-4101    3DLine
-4100    3DColumn
-4098    3DArea
```

Example 21-4. The ChartTypes.txt File (continued)

```
1       Area
4       Line
5       Pie
15      Bubble
51      ColumnClustered
52      ColumnStacked
53      ColumnStacked100
54      3DColumnClustered
55      3DColumnStacked
56      3DColumnStacked100
57      BarClustered
58      BarStacked
59      BarStacked100
60      3DBarClustered
61      3DBarStacked
62      3DBarStacked100
63      LineStacked
64      LineStacked100
65      LineMarkers
66      LineMarkersStacked
67      LineMarkersStacked100
68      PieOfPie
69      PieExploded
70      3DPieExploded
71      BarOfPie
72      XYScatterSmooth
73      XYScatterSmoothNoMarkers
74      XYScatterLines
75      XYScatterLinesNoMarkers
76      AreaStacked
77      AreaStacked100
78      3DAreaStacked
79      3DAreaStacked100
80      DoughnutExploded
81      RadarMarkers
82      RadarFilled
83      Surface
84      SurfaceWireframe
85      SurfaceTopView
86      SurfaceTopViewWireframe
87      Bubble3DEffect
88      StockHLC
89      StockOHLC
90      StockVHLC
91      StockVOHLC
92      CylinderColClustered
93      CylinderColStacked
94      CylinderColStacked100
95      CylinderBarClustered
96      CylinderBarStacked
97      CylinderBarStacked100
98      CylinderCol
```

Example 21-4. The ChartTypes.txt File (continued)

```
99    ConeColClustered
100   ConeColStacked
101   ConeColStacked100
102   ConeBarClustered
103   ConeBarStacked
104   ConeBarStacked100
105   ConeCol
106   PyramidColClustered
107   PyramidColStacked
108   PyramidColStacked100
109   PyramidBarClustered
110   PyramidBarStacked
111   PyramidBarStacked100
112   PyramidCol
```

Note the use of the **On Error** line in *ScrollChartTypes*, which resumes execution in case we try to set the chart type to a value that is not acceptable for the particular chart.

The *Delay* procedure simply waits for the prescribed number of seconds. Finally, the MouseDown event is used to change the state of the module level Boolean variable *bPause*. When the left mouse button is clicked, scrolling is paused until the mouse button is clicked again. To stop the procedure completely, just hit Ctrl-Break.

Example: Printing Embedded Charts

We can now implement the *PrintCharts* feature of our SRXUtils application. This is designed to provide a list of the embedded charts in the active workbook, so the user can select from this list and print the selected charts. (To print a chart sheet, use the *PrintSheets* utility.)

Implementing the *PrintCharts* utility is similar to implementing the *PrintSheets* and *PrintPivotTables* utilities, which we did earlier in the book. At the present time, this print utility, located in the *Print.utl* add-in, simply displays a message box. To implement this feature, we want the utility to first display a dialog box, as shown in Figure 21-32.

The list box contains a list of all embedded charts in the active workbook. The user can select one or more charts and hit the Print button.

The following are the steps to create the print utility. All the action takes place in the *Print.xls* workbook, so open this workbook. When the changes are finished, you will need to save *Print.xls* as *Print.utl* as well. If *Print.utl* is loaded, the only way to unload it is to unload the add-in *SRXUtils.xla* (if it is loaded) and close the workbook *SRXUtils.xls* (if it is open).

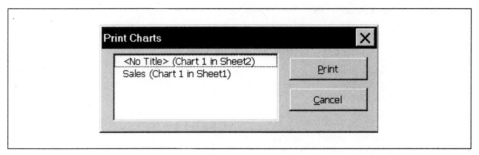

Figure 21-32. Print Charts dialog

Create the UserForm

Create the dialog shown in Figure 21-32 in the *Print.xls* workbook. Name the dialog *dlgPrintCharts*, change its caption to "Print Charts," and change the *Print-Charts* procedure to:

```
Public Sub PrintCharts()
    dlgPrintCharts.Show
End Sub
```

The *dlgPrintCharts* dialog has two command buttons and one list box.

List box

Place a list box on the form as in Figure 21-32. Using the Properties window, set the properties shown in Table 21-9.

Table 21-9. Nondefault Properties of the ListBox Control

Property	Value
Name	lstCharts
TabIndex	0
MultiSelect	frmMultiSelectExtended

The MultiSelect property is set to **frmMultiSelectExtended** so that the user can use the Control key to select multiple (possibly nonconsecutive) entries and the Shift key to select multiple consecutive entries.

The TabIndex property determines not only the order in which the controls are visited as the user hits the Tab key, but also determines which control has the initial focus. Since we want the initial focus to be on the list box, we set its tab index to 0.

Print button

Place a command button on the form as in Figure 21-32. Using the Properties window, set the properties shown in Table 21-10.

Table 21-10. Nondefault Properties of the Print Button

Property	Value
Name	cmdPrint
Accelerator	P
Caption	Print
TabIndex	1

Cancel button

Place another command button on the form as in Figure 21-32. Using the Properties window, set the properties shown in Table 21-11.

Table 21-11. Nondefault Properties of the Cancel Button

Property	Value
Name	cmdCancel
Accelerator	C
Caption	Cancel
TabIndex	2
Cancel	True

When the Cancel property of the **cmdCancel** button is set to **True**, the button is "clicked" when the user hits the Escape key. Thus, the Escape key will dismiss the print dialog.

Create the Code Behind the UserForm

Now it is time to create the code behind these controls.

The Declarations section

The Declarations section of the UserForm should contain declarations of the module-level variables, as shown in Example 21-5.

Example 21-5. Module-Level Declarations in the UserForm's Declarations Section

```
Option Explicit
Dim cCharts As Integer
Dim sChartObjNames() As String
Dim sSheets() As String
```

Cancel button code

The Cancel button code is shown in Example 21-6.

Example 21-6. The Cancel Button's Click Event Handler

```
Private Sub cmdCancel_Click()
   Unload Me
End Sub
```

Print button code

The Print button calls the main print procedure and then unloads the form, as shown in Example 21-7.

Example 21-7. The cmdPrint_Click Procedure

```
Private Sub cmdPrint_Click()
PrintSelectedCharts
Unload Me
End Sub
```

The Form's Initialize event

The UserForm's Initialize event, which is shown in Example 21-8, is the place to fill the list box with a list of embedded charts. Our application uses a module-level array to hold the chart names, a module-level array to hold the ChartObject object names, and a module-level integer variable to hold the chart count. We fill these variables in the Initialize event and then use the arrays to fill the list. The variables are used again in the main print procedure, which is why we have declared them at the module level.

Note the use of the ReDim statement to redimension the arrays. This is necessary since we do not know at the outset how many embedded charts there are in the workbook.

Example 21-8. The UserForm's Initialize Event Procedure

```
Private Sub UserForm_Initialize()

' Fill lstCharts with the list of embedded charts

Dim ws As Worksheet
Dim chObj As ChartObject
ReDim sChartObjNames(1 To 10) As String
ReDim sSheets(1 To 10) As String

lstCharts.Clear
cCharts = 0
For Each ws In ActiveWorkbook.Worksheets
  For Each chObj In ws.ChartObjects
    ' Update chart count
```

Example 21-8. The UserForm's Initialize Event Procedure (continued)

```
        cCharts = cCharts + 1
        ' Redimension arrays if necessary
        If UBound(sSheets) < cCharts Then
          ReDim Preserve sSheets(1 To cCharts + 5)
          ReDim Preserve sChartObjNames(1 To cCharts + 5)
        End If
        ' Save name of chart and ws
        sChartObjNames(cCharts) = chObj.Name
        sSheets(cCharts) = ws.Name
        ' Add item to list box
        If chObj.Chart.HasTitle Then
          lstCharts.AddItem chObj.Chart.ChartTitle.Text & " (" & _
                  sChartObjNames(cCharts) & " in " & sSheets(cCharts) & ")"
        Else
          lstCharts.AddItem "<No Title> (" & sChartObjNames(cCharts) & " in " & _
                  sSheets(cCharts) & ")"
        End If
    Next
  Next
End Sub
```

The PrintCharts procedure

The main printing procedure is shown in Example 21-9. Note that we have been careful to deal with two special cases. First, there may not be any embedded charts in the workbook. Second, the user may hit the Print button without selecting any charts in the list box.

It is important to note also that list boxes are 0-based, meaning that the first item is item 0. However, our arrays are 1-based (the first item is item 1), so we must take this into account when we move from a selection to an array member; to wit, selection *i* corresponds to array index *i+1*.

Example 21-9. The PrintSelectedCharts Procedure

```
Sub PrintSelectedCharts()
' Print the selected charts in lstCharts
Dim i As Integer
Dim bNoneSelected As Boolean

bNoneSelected = True

If cCharts = 0 Then
  MsgBox "No embedded charts in this workbook.", vbExclamation
  Exit Sub
Else
  For i = 0 To lstCharts.ListCount - 1
    If lstCharts.Selected(i) Then
      bNoneSelected = False
      ' List box is 0-based, arrays are 1-based
      Worksheets(sSheets(i + 1)). _
```

Example 21-9. The PrintSelectedCharts Procedure (continued)

```
            ChartObjects(sChartObjNames(i + 1)).Chart.PrintOut
    End If
  Next
End If

If bNoneSelected Then
  MsgBox "No charts have been selected from the list box.", vbExclamation
End If
End Sub
```

Example: Setting Data Series Labels

As you may know, data labels can be edited individually by clicking twice (paus-ing in between clicks) on a data label. This places the label in edit mode, as shown in Figure 21-33.

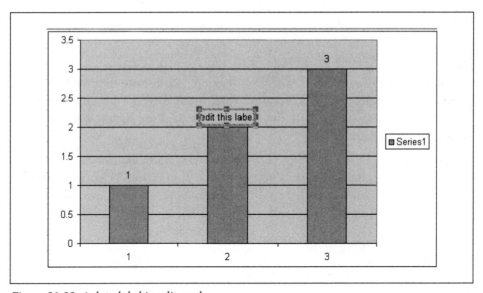

Figure 21-33. A data label in edit mode

Once in edit mode, we can change the text of a data label (which breaks any links) or set a new link to a worksheet cell. For instance, the code:

```
    ActiveChart.SeriesCollection(1).DataLabels(2).Text = "=MyChartSheet!R12C2"
```

sets the data label for the second data point to the value of cell B12. Note that the formula must be in R1C1 notation. Unfortunately, however, Excel does not pro-vide a way to associate all of the data labels for a data series with a worksheet range in a simple way (beyond doing this one data label at a time). So let us write a utility for this purpose and add it to SRXUtils.

When the utility is invoked, it presents a dialog (see Figure 21-34) with a list of all the data series for the selected chart. The user can select a data series and then define a range to which the data labels will be linked or from which the values will be copied. If the cell values are copied, no link is established and so changes made to the range are not reflected in the chart. There is also an option with regard to whether formatting is linked or copied.

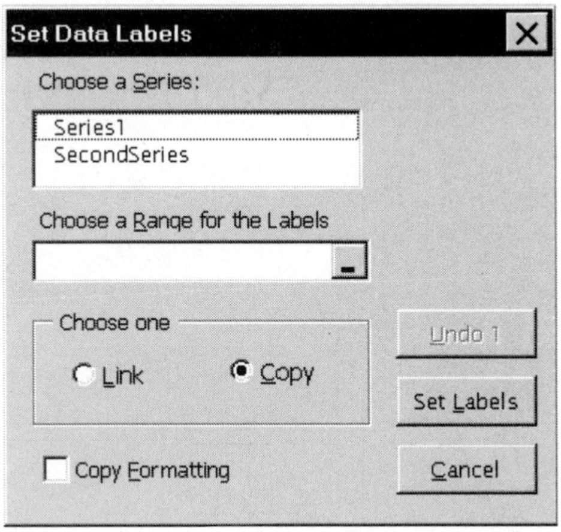

Figure 21-34. Set Data Labels dialog

We begin by augmenting the DataSheet sheet by adding a row for the new utility, as in Figure 21-35 (the new utility is listed in row 2).

	A	B	C	D	E	F	G	H
1	Utility	OnAction Proc	Procedure	In Workbook	Menu Item	SubMenu Item	On Wks Menu	On Chart Menu
2	Activate Sheet	RunUtility	ActivateSheet	ThisWorkbook	&Activate Sheet		TRUE	TRUE
3	Label Data Series	RunUtility	LabelDataSeries	ThisWorkbook	&Label Data Series		TRUE	TRUE
4	Print Charts	RunUtility	PrintCharts	Print.utl	&Print	Embedded &Charts	TRUE	TRUE
5	Print Pivot Tables	RunUtility	PrintPivotTables	Print.utl		&Pivot Tables	TRUE	TRUE
6	Print Sheets	RunUtility	PrintSheets	Print.utl		&Sheets	TRUE	TRUE
7	Select Special	RunUtility	SelectSpecial	ThisWorkbook	S&elect Special		TRUE	FALSE
8	Sort Sheets	RunUtility	SortSheets	ThisWorkbook	&Sort Sheets		TRUE	TRUE

Figure 21-35. DataSheet

Next, create the dialog shown in Figure 21-34. We have used the RefEdit control, which simulates the Excel feature of choosing a range using the mouse. Unfortunately, this control is not documented in the help files. (You can get a list of its properties, methods, and events in the Microsoft Object Browser, but no help.) In any case, we are interested in only one or two properties, as shown in the upcoming code.

The *LabelDataSeries* procedure, which is called when the menu item is selected, should be placed in a new standard code module called *basDataLabels*. The Declarations section of the code module has some module-level declarations, which are shown in Example 21-10.

Example 21-10. The Declarations Section of the basDataLabels Code Module

```
Option Explicit

Private Type utDataLabels
  HasDataLabel As Boolean
  Label As String
  FontName As String
  FontSize As Single
  Color As Long
  Bold As Boolean
  Italic As Boolean
End Type

Public LabelsForUndo() As utDataLabels
Public DataSeries As Series
Public cPoints As Integer
Public bCopyFormatting As Boolean
Public oChart As Chart
Dim cSeries as Long
```

Note in particular the user-defined type declaration. This is used to save the original data labels for a possible Undo operation. It can hold not only the data label's text, but also the formatting options that can be set using this utility.

The *LabelDataSeries* procedure, which is shown in Example 21-11, first verifies that a chart sheet or embedded chart is selected. Then it sets the global variable *oChart* to refer to this chart. This variable will be used by the dialog, so it needs to be public. Next, it sets the global variable *cSeries* to the number of data series in the chart. If the chart has no data series, a message is displayed. If everything is satisfactory, the Set Data Labels dialog is displayed.

Example 21-11. The LabelDataSeries Procedure

```
Public Sub LabelDataSeries()

' Verify that a chart sheet or
' an embedded chart is active.
' If so, set it to oChart.

Set oChart = Nothing

If ActiveWorkbook.Sheets.Count = 0 Then
  MsgBox "Active workbook has no charts. Exiting.", vbInformation
  Exit Sub
End If
```

Example 21-11. The LabelDataSeries Procedure (continued)

```
On Error GoTo NoChartActive
Set oChart = ActiveChart
If Not oChart Is Nothing Then
  ' Check for data series
  cSeries = oChart.SeriesCollection.Count
  If cSeries = 0 Then
    MsgBox "Active chart has no data series.", vbInformation
    Exit Sub
  End If
  ' If so, display dialog
  dlgDataLabels.Show
Else
  MsgBox "This utility requires that a chart be selected.", vbInformation
End If

Exit Sub

NoChartActive:
  MsgBox "This utility requires that a chart be selected.", vbInformation
Exit Sub

End Sub
```

After creating *basDataLabels*, you should create the dialog in Figure 21-34, name it *dlgDataLabels*, and assign the string "Set Data Labels" to its Caption property. We have created several custom dialogs earlier in the book, so we will not go into any details here. (You can design your dialog differently if you wish. There is nothing sacred about my design.) The control names are:

CmdCancel
: For the Cancel button

CmdSetLabels
: For the Set Labels button

cmdUndo
: For the Undo button

LblSeries
: For the "Choose a Series:" label

LstSeries
: For the list box

LblRange
: For the "Choose a Range for the Labels" label

reditLabels
: For the Reference Editor control

fraOptions
> For the frame

OptLink
> For the Link option button

OptCopy
> For the Copy option button

chkOption
> For the Copy Formatting check box

You should not have any trouble determining which name goes with which control (which is a benefit of using a naming convention, after all).

Most of the code behind the dialog is pretty straightforward. The Initialize event, shown in Example 21-12, first fills the list box (*lstSeries*) with a list of all of the data series in the chart *oChart*. Then it initializes some of the other controls.

Example 21-12. The Initialize Event Procedure

```
Private Sub UserForm_Initialize()

' oChart is set to refer to the active chart
' cSeries has count of series

Dim ds As Series

' Fill the lstSeries
For Each ds In oChart.SeriesCollection
  lstSeries.AddItem ds.Name
Next

optCopy.Value = True
chkOption.Caption = "Copy Formatting"
chkOption.Accelerator = "F"
cmdUndo.Enabled = False

End Sub
```

We want the caption (and accelerator key) of the check box at the bottom of the dialog to change based on the choice of option button (Link or Copy). Hence, we need some code in the appropriate Click events, as shown in Example 21-13.

Example 21-13. The Option Buttons' Click Events

```
Private Sub optCopy_Click()

' Set correct check box label and enable
chkOption.Caption = "Copy Formatting"
chkOption.Accelerator = "F"
chkOption.Enabled = True
```

Example 21-13. The Option Buttons' Click Events (continued)

```
End Sub


Private Sub optLink_Click()

' Set correct check box label and enable
chkOption.Caption = "Link Number Format"
chkOption.Accelerator = "N"
chkOption.Enabled = True

End Sub
```

As usual, the command buttons' Click events are short. They are shown in Example 21-14.

Example 21-14. The cmdCancel and cmdSetLabels Click Events

```
Private Sub cmdCancel_Click()
  Unload Me
End Sub

Private Sub cmdSetLabels_Click()
  DoDataLabels
End Sub
```

The main portion of the code, the *DoDataLabels* procedure shown in Example 21-15 (and housed in the UserForm module), checks to see if a data series and label range have been selected and compares their sizes, which must match or else an error message is displayed.

Example 21-15. The DoDataLabels Procedure

```
Sub DoDataLabels()

Dim i As Integer
Dim rngLabels As Range
Dim fnt As Font

' Is a data series selected? Get its size.
If lstSeries.ListIndex = -1 Then
  MsgBox "You must select a data series.", vbInformation
  Exit Sub
Else
  Set DataSeries = oChart.SeriesCollection(lstSeries.ListIndex + 1)
    ' There will be an error if the chart does not support data points
    On Error Resume Next
    cPoints = DataSeries.Points.Count
    If Err.Number <> 0 Then
      MsgBox "Charts of the selected type do not support data labels.", _
             vbCritical
      Unload Me
      Exit Sub
```

Example 21-15. The DoDataLabels Procedure (continued)

```
    End If
End If


' Get the labels range
Set rngLabels = Range(reditLabels.Value)
If rngLabels Is Nothing Then
  MsgBox "You must select a range of cells equal in number to " & _
        "the number of data points in the series.", vbInformation
  Exit Sub
End If


' Check counts
If cPoints <> rngLabels.Count Then
  MsgBox "The number of label cells (" & rngLabels.Count & _
        ") does not equal the number of data points (" & cPoints & _
        ") in the selected series.", vbInformation
  Exit Sub
End If


' Check for existing labels and save them
If DataSeries.HasDataLabels Then
  ' Dimension the array
  ReDim LabelsForUndo(1 To cPoints)
  ' Fill array
  For i = 1 To cPoints
    LabelsForUndo(i).HasDataLabel = DataSeries.Points(i).HasDataLabel
    If LabelsForUndo(i).HasDataLabel Then
      ' Save the label text
      LabelsForUndo(i).Label = DataSeries.Points(i).DataLabel.Text
      ' Save the formatting
      With DataSeries.Points(i).DataLabel.Font
        LabelsForUndo(i).FontName = .Name
        LabelsForUndo(i).FontSize = .Size
        LabelsForUndo(i).Color = .Color
        LabelsForUndo(i).Bold = .Bold
        LabelsForUndo(i).Italic = .Italic
      End With
    End If
  Next
  cmdUndo.Enabled = True
End If


' Now do data labels based on options
If optLink Then
  For i = 1 To cPoints
    DataSeries.Points(i).HasDataLabel = True
    DataSeries.Points(i).DataLabel.Text = "=" & rngLabels.Parent.Name _
      & "!" & rngLabels.Cells(i).Address(ReferenceStyle:=xlR1C1)
    If chkOption Then
      ' Set number format link
      DataSeries.Points(i).DataLabel.NumberFormatLinked = True
    End If
```

Example 21-15. The DoDataLabels Procedure (continued)

```
      Next
Else
  For i = 1 To cPoints
    DataSeries.Points(i).HasDataLabel = True
    DataSeries.Points(i).DataLabel.Text = rngLabels.Cells(i).Value
    If chkOption Then
      bCopyFormatting = True
      With DataSeries.Points(i).DataLabel.Font
        .Name = rngLabels.Cells(i).Font.Name
        .Size = rngLabels.Cells(i).Font.Size
        .Bold = rngLabels.Cells(i).Font.Bold
        .Italic = rngLabels.Cells(i).Font.Italic
        .Color = rngLabels.Cells(i).Font.Color
      End With
      DataSeries.Points(i).DataLabel.NumberFormat = _
                rngLabels.Cells(i).NumberFormat
    Else
      bCopyFormatting = False
    End If
  Next
End If

End Sub
```

The Undo command button's Click event, which is shown in Example 21-16, restores the original data labels that are saved in the *DoDataLabels* procedure.

Example 21-16. The cmdUndo_Click Event Procedure

```
Private Sub cmdUndo_Click()

' Restore labels for DataSeries

Dim i As Integer

For i = 1 To cPoints
  If LabelsForUndo(i).HasDataLabel Then
    DataSeries.Points(i).HasDataLabel = True
    DataSeries.Points(i).DataLabel.Text = LabelsForUndo(i).Label
    If bCopyFormatting Then
      ' Restore formatting
      With DataSeries.Points(i).DataLabel.Font
        .Name = LabelsForUndo(i).FontName
        .Size = LabelsForUndo(i).FontSize
        .Color = LabelsForUndo(i).Color
        .Bold = LabelsForUndo(i).Bold
        .Italic = LabelsForUndo(i).Italic
      End With
    End If
  Else
    DataSeries.Points(i).HasDataLabel = False
  End If
Next
```

Example 21-16. The cmdUndo_Click Event Procedure (continued)

```
cmdUndo.Enabled = False

End Sub
```

IV

Appendixes

The Shape Object

Now we want to take a brief look at the issue of drawing pictures using VBA code. Since this subject is not fundamental to Excel VBA programming, we will be very brief, but hopefully this introduction will give you the necessary background for further study using the VBA help files.

What Is the Shape Object?

Each Excel sheet (chartsheet or worksheet) and each Excel chart has a *drawing layer* upon which we can place drawing objects. A drawing object is represented by a Shape object.

As usual, the Shape objects for a sheet are stored in a Shapes collection. The Chart object and the Worksheet object both have a Shapes property that returns the collection of all Shape objects drawn on the chart or worksheet.

There is also a ShapeRange object that is used to hold a collection of selected Shape objects, much as a Range object can contain a collection of selected cells. The ShapeRange object allows us to set the properties of a subcollection of all Shape objects.

The Shape-related objects are shown in Figure A-1.

Z-Order

Every Shape object has an order, called its *z-order*, that indicates the object's relative position with respect to an imaginary z-axis that comes directly out of the monitor at right angles, towards the user, as pictured in Figure A-2.

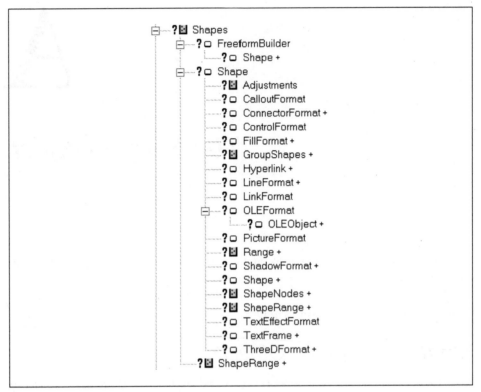

Figure A-1. The Shape-related objects

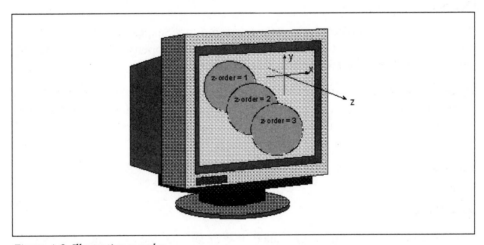

Figure A-2. Illustrating z-order

The read-only ZOrderPosition property of a Shape object reports the current z-order of the object which, incidentally, is the same as the object's index within the

Shapes collection. Shape objects with a larger z-order appear on top of objects with a smaller z-order. Hence, the Shape object with z-order equal to 1 is Shapes(1) and lies at the bottom of the pile!

The ZOrder method sets the z-order of a Shape object *relative* to other objects. Note that the method does not set the absolute z-order. The syntax is:

```
ShapeObject.ZOrder(ZOrderCmd)
```

where *ZOrderCmd* is one of the constants in the following enum (from the Microsoft Office object model):

```
Enum MsoZOrderCmd
    msoBringToFront = 0
    msoSendToBack = 1
    msoBringForward = 2
    msoSendBackward = 3
End Enum
```

Thus, the z-order can only be set in the following ways:

- Move the object to the front of the z-order.

- Move the object to the back of the z-order.

- Move the object one forward in the z-order; that is, increase its index by 1.

- Move the object one backward in the z-order; that is, decrease its index by 1.

Incidentally, as we have seen, the ChartObject object has a read-only ZOrder property that is used to return the z-order of the ChartObject. It also has BringTo-Front and SendToBack methods for changing the z-order.

Creating Shapes

An AutoShape is a Shape object that represents a built-in drawing. To add a new AutoShape object, we use the AddShape method, whose syntax is:

```
ShapesObject.AddShape(Type, Left, Top, Width, Height)
```

The parameter *Type* is the type of AutoShape to create. It can be any one of the **MsoAutoShapeType** constants in Table A-1.

The required parameters *Left* and *Top* specify the position (in points as a Single) of the upper-left corner of the bounding box for the AutoShape object, measured relative to the upper-left corner of the container object (chart, chart sheet, or worksheet).

The *Width* and *Height* parameters specify the width and height (in points as a Single) of the bounding box for the AutoShape. Note that the type of a Shape object can be changed by setting the AutoShapeType property.

Table A-1. MsoAutoShapeType Constants (and Values)

msoShape16pointStar (94)	msoShapeFlowchartCard (75)	msoShapeLineCallout2-BorderandAccentBar (122)
msoShape24pointStar (95)	msoShapeFlowchartCollate (79)	msoShapeLineCallout2No-Border (118)
msoShape32pointStar (96)	msoShapeFlowchartCon-nector (73)	msoShapeLineCallout3 (111)
msoShape4pointStar (91)	msoShapeFlowchartData (64)	msoShapeLineCallout3-AccentBar (115)
msoShape5pointStar (92)	msoShapeFlowchartDeci-sion (63)	msoShapeLineCallout3-BorderandAccentBar (123)
msoShape8pointStar (93)	msoShapeFlowchartDelay (84)	msoShapeLineCallout3No-Border (119)
msoShapeActionButton-BackorPrevious (129)	msoShapeFlowchartDirect-AccessStorage (87)	msoShapeLineCallout4 (112)
msoShapeActionButton-Beginning (131)	msoShapeFlowchart-Display (88)	msoShapeLineCallout4-AccentBar (116)
msoShapeActionButton-Custom (125)	msoShapeFlowchartDocu-ment (67)	msoShapeLineCallout4-BorderandAccentBar (124)
msoShapeActionButton-Document (134)	msoShapeFlowchartExtract (81)	msoShapeLineCallout4No-Border (120)
msoShapeActionButtonEnd (132)	msoShapeFlowchartInter-nalStorage (66)	msoShapeMixed (-2)
msoShapeActionButtonFor-wardorNext (130)	msoShapeFlowchartMag-neticDisk (86)	msoShapeMoon (24)
msoShapeActionButton-Help (127)	msoShapeFlowchart-ManualInput (71)	msoShapeNoSymbol (19)
msoShapeActionButton-Home (126)	msoShapeFlowchart-ManualOperation (72)	msoShapeNotchedRight-Arrow (50)
msoShapeActionButton-Information (128)	msoShapeFlowchartMerge (82)	msoShapeNotPrimitive (138)
msoShapeActionButton-Movie (136)	msoShapeFlowchartMulti-document (68)	msoShapeOctagon (6)
msoShapeActionButton-Return (133)	msoShapeFlowchart-OffpageConnector (74)	msoShapeOval (9)
msoShapeActionButton-Sound (135)	msoShapeFlowchartOr (78)	msoShapeOvalCallout (107)
msoShapeArc (25)	msoShapeFlowchart-PredefinedProcess (65)	msoShapeParallelogram (2)
msoShapeBalloon (137)	msoShapeFlowchartPrepa-ration (70)	msoShapePentagon (51)

Table A-1. MsoAutoShapeType Constants (and Values) (continued)

msoShapeBentArrow (41)	msoShapeFlowchart-Process (61)	msoShapePlaque (28)
msoShapeBentUpArrow (44)	msoShapeFlowchart-PunchedTape (76)	msoShapeQuadArrow (39)
msoShapeBevel (15)	msoShapeFlowchartSe-quentialAccessStorage (85)	msoShapeQuadArrow-Callout (59)
msoShapeBlockArc (20)	msoShapeFlowchartSort (80)	msoShapeRectangle (1)
msoShapeCan (13)	msoShapeFlowchartStored-Data (83)	msoShapeRectangular-Callout (105)
msoShapeChevron (52)	msoShapeFlowchartSum-mingJunction (77)	msoShapeRegularPentagon (12)
msoShapeCircularArrow (60)	msoShapeFlowchartTermi-nator (69)	msoShapeRightArrow (33)
msoShapeCloudCallout (108)	msoShapeFoldedCorner (16)	msoShapeRightArrow-Callout (53)
msoShapeCross (11)	msoShapeHeart (21)	msoShapeRightBrace (32)
msoShapeCube (14)	msoShapeHexagon (10)	msoShapeRightBracket (30)
msoShapeCurvedDown-Arrow (48)	msoShapeHorizontalScroll (102)	msoShapeRightTriangle (8)
msoShapeCurvedDown-Ribbon (100)	msoShapeIsoscelesTriangle (7)	msoShapeRounded-Rectangle (5)
msoShapeCurvedLeftArrow (46)	msoShapeLeftArrow (34)	msoShapeRoundedRectan-gularCallout (106)
msoShapeCurvedRight-Arrow (45)	msoShapeLeftArrowCallout (54)	msoShapeSmileyFace (17)
msoShapeCurvedUpArrow (47)	msoShapeLeftBrace (31)	msoShapeStripedRight-Arrow (49)
msoShapeCurvedUp-Ribbon (99)	msoShapeLeftBracket (29)	msoShapeSun (23)
msoShapeDiamond (4)	msoShapeLeftRightArrow (37)	msoShapeTrapezoid (3)
msoShapeDonut (18)	msoShapeLeftRightArrow-Callout (57)	msoShapeUpArrow (35)
msoShapeDoubleBrace (27)	msoShapeLeftRightUp-Arrow (40)	msoShapeUpArrowCallout (55)
msoShapeDoubleBracket (26)	msoShapeLeftUpArrow (43)	msoShapeUpDownArrow (38)
msoShapeDoubleWave (104)	msoShapeLightningBolt (22)	msoShapeUpDownArrow-Callout (58)
msoShapeDownArrow (36)	msoShapeLineCallout1 (109)	msoShapeUpRibbon (97)

Table A-1. MsoAutoShapeType Constants (and Values) (continued)

msoShapeDownArrow-Callout (56)	msoShapeLineCallout1-AccentBar (113)	msoShapeUTurnArrow (42)
msoShapeDownRibbon (98)	msoShapeLineCallout1-BorderandAccentBar (121)	msoShapeVerticalScroll (101)
msoShapeExplosion1 (89)	msoShapeLineCallout1No-Border (117)	msoShapeWave (103)
msoShapeExplosion2 (90)	msoShapeLineCallout2 (110)	
msoShapeFlowchartAlter-nateProcess (62)	msoShapeLineCallout2-AccentBar (114)	

The short program in Example A-1 will display each AutoShape, along with its AutoShapeType, for 0.5 seconds. (It should be run on a blank worksheet. You can interrupt this program at any time by striking Ctrl-Break.) The Delay subroutine that it calls is shown in Example A-2.

Example A-1. Displaying Each AutoShape

```
Sub DisplayAutoShapes()

Dim sh As Shape
Dim i As Integer
Set sh = ActiveSheet.Shapes.AddShape(1, 100, 100, 72, 72)
For i = 1 To 138
    sh.AutoShapeType = i
    sh.Visible = True
    ActiveSheet.Cells(1, 1).Value = sh.AutoShapeType
    Delay 0.5
Next i

End Sub
```

Example A-2. The Delay Procedure

```
Public Sub Delay(rTime As Single)
'Delay rTime seconds (min=.01, max=300)
Dim OldTime As Variant
'Safty net
If rTime < 0.01 Or rTime > 300 Then rTime = 1
OldTime = Timer
Do
    DoEvents
Loop Until Timer - OldTime >= rTime
End Sub
```

The TextFrame Object

Each Shape object has a text frame associated with it that holds any text associated with the object. The TextFrame property returns this TextFrame object.

The TextFrame object has a Characters property that returns a Characters collection. This collection can be used to set the text in the text frame. For instance, the code in Example A-3 adds a rectangle to the active sheet and also adds text to the rectangle and sets the alignment for the text frame.

Example A-3. The AddRectangle Procedure

```
Sub AddRectangle()

With ActiveSheet.Shapes.AddShape(msoShapeRectangle, 10, 10, 200, 100).TextFrame
    .Characters.Text = "This is a rectangle"
    .HorizontalAlignment = xlHAlignCenter
    .VerticalAlignment = xlVAlignCenter
End With

End Sub
```

The FillFormat Object

The FillFormat object is used to set various formatting for a Shape object. It is accessed using the Fill property of the Shape object. Among the properties of the FillFormat object are the BackColor, ForeColor, Pattern, and Visible properties. To set one of the color properties, we use the RGB color model, as in the following example:

```
sh.Fill.ForeColor.RGB = RGB(0, 0, 255)
```

Examples

To illustrate the use of *AutoShapes*, Example A-4 inserts a dampened sine curve of small stars in the drawing layer.

Example A-4. DrawSine2, to Generate a Dampened Sine Curve of Small Stars

```
Sub DrawSine2()
' Dampened sine wave of small stars
Const pi = 3.1416
Dim i As Integer
Dim x As Single, y As Single
Dim rng As Range      ' For starting point
Dim n As Single       ' Cycle length in inches
Dim k As Integer      ' k stars
Dim ScaleY As Single ' Vertical scaling
Dim sSize As Single  ' Star size
Dim sDamp1 As Single  ' Dampening factor
Dim sDamp2 As Single  ' Dampening factor
Dim cCycles As Integer   ' Number of cycles
Dim sh As Shape
Dim StartLeft As Integer
Dim StartTop As Integer
```

Example A-4. DrawSine2, to Generate a Dampened Sine Curve of Small Stars (continued)

```
' Starting position
StartLeft = ActiveCell.Left
StartTop = ActiveCell.Top

cCycles = 3
sDamp1 = 1
sDamp2 = 0.2
n = 2
k = 20
ScaleY = 0.5
sSize = Application.InchesToPoints(0.1)
' Loop for first curve with phase shift
For i = 1 To cCycles * k
    x = n * i / k
    y = ScaleY * Sin((2 * pi * i) / k + n) * _
        (sDamp1 / (x + sDamp2))
    y = Application.InchesToPoints(y)
    x = Application.InchesToPoints(x)
    Set sh = ActiveSheet.Shapes.AddShape _
        (msoShape5pointStar, StartLeft + x, StartTop + y, sSize, sSize)
    sh.Fill.ForeColor.RGB = RGB(192, 192, 192)    ' 25% gray
    sh.Fill.Visible = msoTrue
Next i
End Sub
```

The output from this code is shown in Figure A-3.

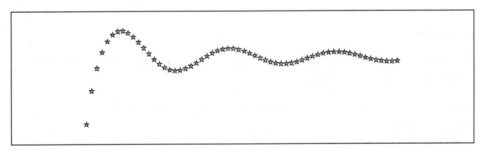

Figure A-3. A dampened sine wave of stars

The code in Example A-5 produces a random series of stars, each containing a single letter that together spells a name. Note that each time the program is run, the pattern is different.

Example A-5. Code to Produce a Random Series of Stars

```
Sub DrawName()

' Random placement of large stars with name
Const pi = 3.1416
Dim i As Integer
Dim x As Single, y As Single
```

Example A-5. Code to Produce a Random Series of Stars (continued)

```
Dim z As Single
Dim rng As Range      ' For starting point
Dim n As Single       ' Cycle length in inches
Dim k As Integer      ' k stars
Dim sSize As Single   ' Star size
Dim sh As Shape
Dim sName As String   ' Name to display
Dim StartLeft As Integer
Dim StartTop As Integer

' Starting position
StartLeft = ActiveCell.Left
StartTop = ActiveCell.Top

sName = "Steven Roman"
n = 5
k = Len(sName)
sSize = Application.InchesToPoints(0.5)

Randomize Timer
z = 0#
' Loop for first curve with phase shift
For i = 1 To k
    If Mid(sName, i, 1) <> " " Then
        x = n * i / k
        x = Application.InchesToPoints(x)

        ' Get random 0 or 1. Go up or down accordingly.
        If Int(2 * Rnd) = 0 Then
            z = z + 0.2
        Else
            z = z - 0.2
        End If
        y = Application.InchesToPoints(z)
        Set sh = ActiveSheet.Shapes.AddShape _
            (msoShape5pointStar, StartLeft + x, StartTop + y, sSize, sSize)

        ' Add shading
        sh.Fill.ForeColor.RGB = RGB(230, 230, 230)
        sh.Fill.Visible = msoTrue

        ' Add text
        sh.TextFrame.Characters.Text = Mid(sName, i, 1)
        sh.TextFrame.Characters.Font.Size = 10
        sh.TextFrame.Characters.Font.Name = "Arial"
        sh.TextFrame.Characters.Font.Bold = True

    End If
Next i
End Sub
```

The output from this code is shown in Figure A-4.

Figure A-4. Random stars spelling a name

Example A-6 prints a hypocycloid. (It may take a few minutes to complete.)

Example A-6. The DrawHypocycloid Procedure

```
Sub DrawHypocycloid()

' Draw hypocycloid of small stars
Const pi = 3.1416
Dim t As Single
Dim i As Integer
Dim x As Single, y As Single
Dim rng As Range      ' For starting point
Dim n As Single
Dim k As Integer
Dim sSize As Single  ' Star size
Dim r As Integer
Dim r0 As Integer
Dim R1 As Integer
Dim sh As Shape
Dim sc As Single
Dim StartLeft As Integer
Dim StartTop As Integer

' Starting position
StartLeft = ActiveCell.Left
StartTop = ActiveCell.Top

r = 1
r0 = 3 * r
R1 = 8 * r
n = 400
k = 4
sc = 0.1
sSize = Application.InchesToPoints(0.03)
' Start curve at insertion point
Set rng = ActiveCell
For i = 1 To n
    t = k * pi * i / n
    x = (R1 - r) * Cos(t) + r0 * Cos(t * (R1 - r) / r)
    y = (R1 - r) * Sin(t) - r0 * Sin(t * (R1 - r) / r)
    x = sc * x
```

Example A-6. The DrawHypocycloid Procedure (continued)

```
    y = sc * y
    x = Application.InchesToPoints(x)
    y = Application.InchesToPoints(y)
    Set sh = ActiveSheet.Shapes.AddShape _
            (msoShape5pointStar, StartLeft + x, StartTop + y, sSize, sSize)
Next i
End Sub
```

The results are shown in Figure A-5. (The small vertical bar in Figure A-5 indicates the left edge of the active cell.

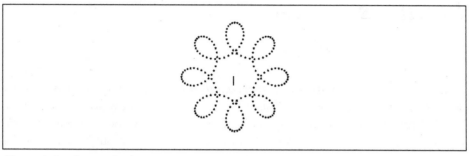

Figure A-5. A hypocycloid

B

Getting the Installed Printers

As discussed in Chapter 10, *Excel Applications*, the ActivePrinter property can be used to set the active printer. This raises the issue of how to determine the installed printers on a given computer. Unfortunately, VBA does not seem to provide a way to do this. (Visual Basic has a Printers collection, but Visual Basic for Applications does not.)

In this appendix, we describe a program for getting this printer information. As mentioned in Chapter 10, this program uses the Windows API. To use this program, just type it into your own code, as described here.

The first step is to declare some special constants in the Declarations section of a standard module:

```
Public Const KEY_ENUMERATE_SUB_KEYS = &H8
Public Const HKEY_LOCAL_MACHINE = &H80000002
Public Const SUCCESS = 0&
```

Next, we need to declare a *user-defined type*. We have not discussed these data structures in this book, but a user-defined type is essentially just a custom data type. Enter the following code into the Declarations section:

```
Type FILETIME
   dwLowDateTime As Long
   dwHighDateTime As Long
End Type
```

Then we need to declare three API functions. As you can see, these are relatively complicated functions as VBA functions go, but not as API functions go. Enter the following in the Declarations section:

```
Declare Function RegOpenKeyEx Lib "advapi32.dll" Alias _
    "RegOpenKeyExA" (ByVal hKey As Long, ByVal lpSubKey As _
    String, ByVal ulOptions As Long, ByVal samDesired As _
```

```
        Long, phkResult As Long) As Long
    Declare Function RegEnumKeyEx Lib "advapi32.dll" Alias _
        "RegEnumKeyExA" (ByVal hKey As Long, ByVal dwIndex As _
        Long, ByVal lpName As String, lpcbName As Long, ByVal _
        lpReserved As Long, ByVal lpClass As String, lpcbClass _
        As Long, lpftLastWriteTime As FILETIME) As Long
    Declare Function RegCloseKey Lib "advapi32.dll" _
        (ByVal hKey As Long) As Long
```

We are now ready for the main procedure, shown in Example B-1, which will extract the names of the installed printers from the Windows registry.

Example B-1. The GetInstalledPrinters Procedure

```
Public Sub GetInstalledPrinters(ByRef sPrinters() As _
    String, ByRef cPrinters As Long)
' Sets cPrinters to the number of installed printers.
' Sizes and fills sPrinters array with the names
' of these printers.
Dim ft As FILETIME
Dim KeyHandle As Long
Dim KeyName As String
Dim KeyLen As Long
Dim Response As Long
On Error GoTo ERR_INSTALLED_PRINTERS
ReDim sPrinters(1 To 5)
cPrinters = 0
' Open registry key whose subkeys are installed printers
Response = RegOpenKeyEx(HKEY_LOCAL_MACHINE, _
    "SYSTEM\CurrentControlSet\Control\Print\Printers", _
    0, KEY_ENUMERATE_SUB_KEYS, KeyHandle)
' If Error display message and exit
If Response <> SUCCESS Then
    MsgBox "Could not open the registry key."
    Exit Sub
End If
' Loop to get subkeys
Do
    KeyLen = 1000   ' Plenty of room for printer name
    KeyName = String(KeyLen, 0)   ' Fill with 0s

    Response = RegEnumKeyEx(KeyHandle, cPrinters, _
        KeyName, KeyLen, 0&, vbNullString, 0&, ft)

    ' If unsuccessful, then exit
    If Response <> SUCCESS Then Exit Do

    ' Next free index
    cPrinters = cPrinters + 1

    ' Make room if necessary
    If UBound(sPrinters) < cPrinters Then
        ReDim Preserve sPrinters(1 To cPrinters + 5)
    End If
```

Example B-1. The GetInstalledPrinters Procedure (continued)

```
    ' Add to array
    sPrinters(cPrinters) = Left(KeyName, KeyLen)

Loop
RegCloseKey KeyHandle
Exit Sub
ERR_INSTALLED_PRINTERS:
    MsgBox Err.Description
    Exit Sub
End Sub
```

The *GetInstalledPrinters* procedure has two parameters: a String array named **sPrinters** and a Long named **cPrinters**. The procedure will set the value of **cPrinters** to the number of installed printers and resize and fill the **sPrinters** array with the names of the printers.

Example B-2 shows how to use the *GetInstalledPrinters* subroutine. It simply gathers the printer names in a single String variable and displays that variable.

Example B-2. Calling the GetInstalledPrinters Procedure

```
Sub DisplayInstalledPrinters()
Dim sPrinters() As String
Dim cPrinters As Long
Dim i As Integer
Dim msg As String
' Get the installed printers
GetInstalledPrinters sPrinters(), cPrinters
' Create the message and display it
msg = ""
For i = 1 To cPrinters
    msg = msg & sPrinters(i) & vbCrLf
Next i
MsgBox msg, , cPrinters & " Printers"
End Sub
```

The output of this macro on my system is shown in Figure B-1.

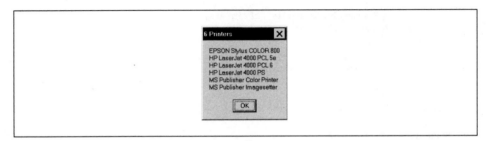

Figure B-1. Installed printers

One word of caution: Before executing the *GetInstalledPrinters* subroutine for the *first* time (through the *DisplayInstalledPrinters* macro or any by other means), be sure to save *all* of your work in *all* of your open applications. If you have made an error in typing in this program, the result may be a system-wide computer crash, in which case you will loose all unsaved work!

C

Command Bar
Controls

In this appendix, we present a list of built-in command-bar controls, along with their ID numbers for use with the Add method of the CommandBarControls object.

Built-in Command-Bar Controls

Table C-1. Command-Bar Controls and Their Corresponding ID Numbers

<Custom>	1	AutoFormat	107
&Spelling	2	&Format Painter	108
&Save	3	Print Pre&view	109
&Print	4	Custom	112
&New	18	&Bold	113
&Copy	19	&Italic	114
Cu&t	21	&Underline	115
&Paste	22	&Custom	117
Open	23	&Dark Shading	118
Can't Repeat	37	&Align Left	120
&Microsoft Word	42	&Align Right	121
Clear Contents	47	&Center	122
Custom	51	&Justify	123
&Piggy Bank	52	What's &This?	124
Custom	59	Custom	126
&Double Underline	60	&Undo	128
Custom	67	&Redo	129
Custom	68	&Line	130
&Close	106	Te&xt Box	139

Table C-1. Command-Bar Controls and Their Corresponding ID Numbers (continued)

&Find File	140	Page Set&up	247
&Top Border	145	&Style	254
&Bottom Border	146	Routing Slip	259
&Left Border	147	Microsoft &Mail	262
&Right Border	148	Microsoft &Access	264
Apply Inside Borders	149	Microsoft &Schedule+	265
&Outside Borders	150	Microsoft Visual &FoxPro	266
Clear Border	151	Microsoft &PowerPoint	267
&Group	164	Microsoft P&roject	269
&Ungroup	165	Custom	270
Bring to Fron&t	166	Custom	271
Send to Bac&k	167	Custom	272
Bring &Forward	170	Custom	273
Send &Backward	171	Custom	274
F&ull Screen	178	Custom	275
&Select Objects	182	Custom	276
&Record New Macro	184	Custom	278
&Macros	186	Custom	279
Step Macro	187	&Camera	280
Resume Macro	189	Custom	281
Flip &Horizontal	196	&Button	282
Flip &Vertical	197	Custom	283
Rotate &Right	198	Custom	286
Rotate &Left	199	&Strikethrough	290
&Freeform	200	Delete	292
&Borders	203	Delete &Rows	293
&Drawing	204	Delete &Columns	294
&Edit Points	206	C&ells	295
Sort &Ascending	210	&Rows	296
Sort Des&cending	211	&Columns	297
&Edit Box	219	&Arrange	298
&Check Box	220	&Split	302
&Combo Box	221	&New Window	303
Control Properties	222	&Accept or Reject Changes	305
Lock Cell	225	R&eplace	313
&AutoSum	226	Regr&oup	338
&Arrow	243	&3-D	339

Table C-1. Command-Bar Controls and Their Corresponding ID Numbers (continued)

Se&nd	363	&Rotate Text Up	406
&Set Print Area	364	&Rotate Text Down	407
&Insert MS Excel 4.0 Macro	365	Distribute &Horizontally	408
&Clear Formatting	368	&Scribble	409
&Paste Formatting	369	Custom	417
&Paste Values	370	&Area Chart	418
&Right	371	&Bar Chart	419
&Down	372	&Column Chart	420
&Equal Sign	373	&Stacked Column Chart	421
&Plus Sign	374	&Line Chart	422
&Minus Sign	375	&Pie Chart	423
&Multiplication Sign	376	&3-D Area Chart	424
&Division Sign	377	&3-D Bar Chart	425
&Exponentiation Sign	378	&3-D Clustered Column Chart	426
&Left Parenthesis	379	&3-D Column Chart	427
&Right Parenthesis	380	&3-D Line Chart	428
&Colon	381	&3-D Pie Chart	429
&Comma	382	&(XY) Scatter Chart	430
&Percent Sign	383	&3-D Surface Chart	431
&Dollar Sign	384	&Radar Chart	432
Paste Function	385	&Volume/High-Low-Close Chart	434
&Constrain Numeric	387	&Default Chart	435
&XL Left Border	389	&Chart Wizard	436
&XL Right Border	390	&Value Axis Gridlines	437
&XL Top Border	391	&Category Axis Gridlines	438
&Light Shading	393	&Legend	439
&Shadow	394	&Show Outline Symbols	440
&Currency Style	395	&Select Visible Cells	441
&Percent Style	396	&Select Current Region	442
&Comma Style	397	&Freeze Panes	443
&Increase Decimal	398	&Zoom In	444
&Decrease Decimal	399	&Zoom Out	445
&Font Color	401	&Option Button	446
&Merge and Center	402	&Scroll Bar	447
&Increase Font Size	403	&List Box	448
&Decrease Font Size	404	&Doughnut Chart	449
&Vertical Text	405	&Remove Dependent Arrows	450

Table C-1. Command-Bar Controls and Their Corresponding ID Numbers (continued)

Trace &Dependents	451	H&eight	541
&Remove Precedent Arrows	452	&Width	542
Remove &All Arrows	453	&Object	546
&Attach Note	454	Control T&oolbox	548
&Update File	455	To &Grid	549
&Toggle Read Only	456	C&ancel	569
&Wizard	457	&More Controls	642
Auto&Filter	458	Align &Left	664
&Refresh Data	459	Align &Right	665
&Field	460	Align &Top	666
Show &Pages	461	Align &Bottom	667
&Show Detail	462	Align &Center	668
Trace &Error	463	Align &Middle	669
&Hide Detail	464	&Clip Art	682
Distribute &Vertically	465	Free Ro&tate	688
&Group Box	467	&Line Style	692
&Spinner	468	&Dash Style	693
Ta&b Order	469	&Arrow Style	694
&Run Dialog	470	&Organization Chart	702
&Combination List-Edit	471	&Normal	723
&Combination Drop-Down Edit	475	&Page Break Preview	724
&Label	476	&Crop	732
Custom	477	Save &As	748
Custom	478	Propert&ies	750
Custom	479	E&xit	752
Custom	480	Paste &Special	755
Custom	481	&Go To	757
Custom	482	Lin&ks	759
Custom	483	&Header and Footer	762
Custom	484	&AutoFormat	786
Toggle Grid	485	&AutoCorrect	793
&Trace Precedents	486	&Customize	797
&Code	488	&Merge Cells	798
&Dialog	489	Unmerge Cells	800
Page &Break	509	T&ext to Columns	806
&Options	522	Assign &Macro	825
Para&meters	537	&Window Name Goes Here	830

Table C-1. Command-Bar Controls and Their Corresponding ID Numbers (continued)

&Recent File Name Goes Here	831	&Hide	883
&Create Microsoft Outlook Task	837	&Unhide	884
Mi&nimize	838	&AutoFit Selection	885
&Restore	839	&Hide	886
&Close	840	&Unhide	887
&Move	841	&Standard Width	888
&Size	842	&Rename	889
Ma&ximize	843	&Hide	890
Save &Workspace	846	&Unhide	891
De&lete Sheet	847	&Show Auditing Toolbar	892
&Move or Copy Sheet	848	&Protect Sheet	893
&Formula Bar	849	Protect &Workbook	894
&Status Bar	850	Relative Reference	896
&Worksheet	852	Auto&Filter	899
C&ells	855	&Show All	900
&Goal Seek	856	&Advanced Filter	901
Sc&enarios	857	&Auto Outline	904
Assig&n Macro	859	&Clear Outline	905
F&orm	860	S&ettings	906
Su&btotals	861	&Series	907
&Table	862	Sized with &Window	908
Co&nsolidate	863	Add T&rendline	914
&Hide	865	&Selected Object	917
&Unhide	866	Chart &Type	918
&Up	867	3-D &View	919
&Left	868	&Zoom	925
&Across Worksheets	869	&About Microsoft Excel	927
&Series	870	&Sort	928
&Justify	871	&Label	932
&Formats	872	&Lotus 1-2-3 Help	936
&Contents	873	&Answer Wizard	937
Co&mments	874	&Exchange Folder	938
&Define	878	Add-&Ins	943
&Paste	879	&Insert	945
&Create	880	&Select All Sheets	946
&Apply	881	Custom &Views	950
&AutoFit	882	&Background	952

Table C-1. Command-Bar Controls and Their Corresponding ID Numbers (continued)

&Source Data	954	&Elbow Connector	1043
&Location	955	C&urved Connector	1044
Chart &Options	956	&Callouts	1047
&Sheet List	957	&Flowchart	1048
&Calculate Now	960	Block &Arrows	1049
&Object	961	&Stars and Banners	1050
C&ells	962	&More Fill Colors	1051
&Contents and Index	983	&More Line Colors	1052
Microsoft Excel &Help	984	&Patterned Lines	1053
&Data Table	987	&More Lines	1054
Series in &Columns	988	&More Arrows	1055
Series in &Rows	989	&Shadow Settings	1056
&Enable Selection	991	&3-D Settings	1057
&List Formulas	992	&WordArt Shape	1058
&Data	993	&WordArt Alignment	1059
Label &and Data	994	&WordArt Character Spacing	1060
&Label	995	&WordArt Vertical Text	1061
&Fill Effects	1006	&WordArt Same Letter Heights	1063
&Angle Text Upward	1013	&More Contrast	1064
&Angle Text Downward	1014	&Less Contrast	1065
&Open	1015	&More Brightness	1066
&Start Page	1016	&Less Brightness	1067
&Back	1017	&Nudge Shadow Up	1068
&Forward	1018	&Nudge Shadow Down	1069
&Stop Current Jump	1019	&Nudge Shadow Left	1070
&Refresh Current Page	1020	&Nudge Shadow Right	1071
Open &Favorites	1021	&More Shadow Colors	1072
&Add to Favorites	1022	&More 3-D Colors	1073
&Show Only Web Toolbar	1023	&Left Align	1108
&WordArt	1031	&Center	1109
Rerou&te Connectors	1033	&Line Callout 4 (Border and Accent Bar)	1110
&Up	1035		
&Down	1036	&Rectangle	1111
&Left	1037	&Parallelogram	1112
&Right	1038	&Trapezoid	1113
&Curve	1041	&Diamond	1114
St&raight Connector	1042	&Rounded Rectangle	1115
		&Octagon	1116

Table C-1. Command-Bar Controls and Their Corresponding ID Numbers (continued)

&Isosceles Triangle	1117	&Striped Right Arrow	1154
&Right Triangle	1118	&Notched Right Arrow	1155
&Oval	1119	&Pentagon	1156
&Hexagon	1120	&Chevron	1157
&Cross	1121	&Circular Arrow	1158
&Cube	1122	&Curved Right Arrow	1160
&Plaque	1123	&Curved Left Arrow	1161
&Regular Pentagon	1124	&Curved Up Arrow	1162
&Wave	1125	&Curved Down Arrow	1163
&Can	1126	&Right Arrow Callout	1164
&Vertical Scroll	1127	&Left Arrow Callout	1165
&Horizontal Scroll	1128	&Up Arrow Callout	1166
&Folded Corner	1129	&Down Arrow Callout	1167
&Bevel	1130	&Left-Right Arrow Callout	1168
&Smiley Face	1131	&Up-Down Arrow Callout	1169
&Donut	1132	&Quad Arrow Callout	1170
&"No" Symbol	1133	&Rectangular Callout	1172
&Block Arc	1134	&Rounded Rectangular Callout	1173
&Left Bracket	1135	&Oval Callout	1174
&Right Bracket	1136	&Cloud Callout	1175
&Left Brace	1137	&Line Callout 2	1176
&Right Brace	1138	&Line Callout 3	1177
&Arc	1139	&Line Callout 4	1178
&Lightning Bolt	1140	&Down Ribbon	1179
&Heart	1141	&Up Ribbon	1180
&Right Arrow	1142	&Curved Down Ribbon	1181
&Left Arrow	1143	&Curved Up Ribbon	1182
&Up Arrow	1144	&5-Point Star	1183
&Down Arrow	1145	&8-Point Star	1184
&Left-Right Arrow	1146	&16-Point Star	1185
&Up-Down Arrow	1147	&24-Point Star	1186
&Quad Arrow	1148	&32-Point Star	1187
&Left-Right-Up Arrow	1149	&Explosion 1	1188
&Left-Up Arrow	1150	&Explosion 2	1189
&Bent-Up Arrow	1151	&Flowchart: Process	1190
&Bent Arrow	1152	&Flowchart: Alternate Process	1191
&U-Turn Arrow	1153	&Flowchart: Decision	1192

Table C-1. Command-Bar Controls and Their Corresponding ID Numbers (continued)

Control	ID	Control	ID
&Flowchart: Data	1193	&Line Callout 2 (Border and Accent Bar)	1229
&Flowchart: Predefined Process	1194		
&Flowchart: Internal Storage	1195	&Line Callout 3 (Border and Accent Bar)	1230
&Flowchart: Document	1196		
&Flowchart: Multidocument	1197	&Right Align	1352
&Flowchart: Terminator	1198	Le&tter Justify	1353
&Flowchart: Preparation	1199	&Word Justify	1354
&Flowchart: Manual Input	1200	&Stretch Justify	1355
&Flowchart: Manual Operation	1201	Very T&ight	1356
&Flowchart: Connector	1202	&Tight	1357
&Flowchart: Off-page Connector	1203	&Normal	1358
&Flowchart: Card	1204	&Loose	1359
&Flowchart: Punched Tape	1205	&Very Loose	1360
&Flowchart: Summing Junction	1206	&Kern Character Pairs	1361
&Flowchart: Or	1207	&Reset Picture	1362
&Flowchart: Collate	1208	&Automatic	1365
&Flowchart: Sort	1209	&Grayscale	1366
&Flowchart: Extract	1210	&Black && White	1367
&Flowchart: Merge	1211	&Watermark	1368
&Flowchart: Stored Data	1213	&3-D On/Off	1374
&Flowchart: Sequential Access Storage	1214	&Tilt Down	1375
		&Tilt Up	1376
&Flowchart: Magnetic Disk	1215	&Tilt Left	1377
&Flowchart: Direct Access Storage	1216	&Tilt Right	1378
		&Depth	1379
&Flowchart: Display	1217	&Direction	1380
&Flowchart: Delay	1218	&Lighting	1382
&Line Callout 1	1219	&Surface	1383
&Line Callout 1 (Accent Bar)	1220	&0 pt.	1384
&Line Callout 2 (Accent Bar)	1221	&36 pt.	1385
&Line Callout 3 (Accent Bar)	1222	&72 pt.	1386
&Line Callout 4 (Accent Bar)	1223	&144 pt.	1387
&Line Callout 1 (No Border)	1224	&288 pt.	1388
&Line Callout 2 (No Border)	1225	&Infinity	1389
&Line Callout 3 (No Border)	1226	&Perspective	1390
&Line Callout 4 (No Border)	1227	P&arallel	1391
&Line Callout 1 (Border and Accent Bar)	1228	&Bright	1392
		&Normal	1393

Table C-1. Command-Bar Controls and Their Corresponding ID Numbers (continued)

&Dim	1394	Open in New &Window	1574
&Matte	1395	&Copy Hyperlink	1575
&Plastic	1396	Hyperl&ink	1576
Me&tal	1398	Edit &Hyperlink	1577
&Wire Frame	1399	&Select Hyperlink	1578
Edit Te&xt	1401	&Add to Print Area	1583
To &Shape	1402	&Clear Print Area	1584
&Image Control	1403	Reset All Page &Breaks	1585
&Basic Shapes	1405	&Exclude From Print Area	1586
&Callouts	1406	Insert Page &Break	1588
&Flowchart	1407	Co&mment	1589
Block &Arrows	1408	&Previous Comment	1590
&Stars and Banners	1409	&Next Comment	1591
Show WordArt Toolba&r	1410	Delete Co&mment	1592
&Exit Rotate Mode	1412	Sh&ow Comment	1593
Show Picture Toolba&r	1413	Hide All Comments	1594
&Add Point	1415	Calculated &Field	1597
De&lete Point	1416	Calculated &Item	1598
&Straight Segment	1417	Entire &Table	1600
&Curved Segment	1418	[[TBTIP_SxUpdateM]]	1601
Close C&urve	1420	&Options	1604
Au&to Point	1421	&Design Mode	1605
&Smooth Point	1422	&WordArt Gallery	1606
St&raight Point	1423	&Chart Type	1616
&Corner Point	1424	&Pattern	1617
Exit &Edit Point	1425	&Border	1618
&No Color	1453	&Chart Objects:	1622
&Color Scheme	1455	&Navigate Circular Reference:	1623
&Standard Colors	1456	&Bubble Chart	1635
&Automatic Color	1459	&3-D Cylinder Chart	1636
&Color Scheme	1460	&3-D Pyramid Chart	1637
&Standard Colors	1461	&3-D Cone Chart	1638
&Color Scheme	1465	&Double Arrow	1639
&Standard Colors	1466	&Fill Color	1691
&Color Scheme	1470	&Line Color	1692
&Standard Colors	1471	&Shadow Color	1693
&View Code	1561	&3-D Color	1694

Table C-1. Command-Bar Controls and Their Corresponding ID Numbers (continued)

&Visual Basic Editor	1695	&Cancel Refresh	1953
&Bottom Double Border	1699	&Refresh Status	1954
&Font:	1728	C&hart	1957
&Font Size:	1731	&Add Data	1963
&Style:	1732	&All	1964
&Zoom:	1733	&<verb>	1965
&Scenario:	1737	Pic&k From List	1966
&Address:	1740	Con&vert	1967
M&ap	1741	&Ungroup Sheets	1968
&Merge Across	1742	&Pattern	1988
From &Scanner	1764	&None	2012
&Inside Horizontal Border	1840	&Average	2013
&Inside Vertical Border	1841	&Count	2014
&Diagonal Down Border	1842	C&ount Nums	2015
&Diagonal Up Border	1843	&Max	2016
&Check Box	1848	M&in	2017
&Find	1849	&Sum	2018
&Text Box	1850	&Copy Cells	2019
&Command Button	1851	Fill &Series	2020
&Option Button	1852	Fill &Formats	2021
&List Box	1853	Fill &Values	2022
&Combo Box	1854	Fill &Days	2023
&Toggle Button	1855	Fill &Weekdays	2024
&Spin Button	1856	Fill &Months	2025
&Scroll Bar	1857	Fill &Years	2026
&Label	1858	&Linear Trend	2027
&Semitransparent Shadow	1859	&Growth Trend	2028
Search the &Web	1922	S&eries	2029
&Automatic Color	1926	Insert Co&mment	2031
&Color Scheme	1927	Va&lidation	2034
&Color	1928	Circle Invalid Data	2035
&Color Scheme	1929	R&eset Print Area	2038
&Color	1930	S&hare Workbook	2040
Run &Web Query	1948	&Highlight Changes	2042
Run &Database Query	1949	Merge &Workbooks	2044
&Edit Query	1950	&Copy Here	2045
D&ata Range Properties	1951	&Move Here	2046
Refresh &All	1952	Copy Here as &Formats Only	2047

Table C-1. Command-Bar Controls and Their Corresponding ID Numbers (continued)

Copy Here as &Values Only	2048	&Curved Arrow Connector	2644
&Shift Down and Copy	2049	&Curved Double-Arrow Connector	2645
Shif&t Right and Copy	2050		
Shift &Down and Move	2051	&Fill Effects	2668
Shift &Right and Move	2052	De&lete Segment	2692
Create &New Query	2054	Open C&urve	2693
&Clear Validation Circles	2055	Paste as &Hyperlink	2787
&Image	2089	&Set Transparent Color	2827
&Straight Connector	2091	&Solve Order	2914
&Elbow Connector	2092	&PivotTable Report	2915
C&urved Connector	2093	&Web Toolbar	2934
Edit Te&xt	2094	&Custom Menu Item	2949
&Link Here	2158	&Custom Button	2950
Create &Hyperlink Here	2159	&Free Stuff	3021
&Shadow On/Off	2175	&Product News	3022
Set AutoShape &Defaults	2179	Frequently Asked &Questions	3023
Stop &Recording	2186	Online &Support	3024
&Mail Recipient	2188	&Web Help 5	3025
&New	2520	&Web Help 6	3026
Print (HP LaserJet 4000 Series PS)	2521	&Web Help 7	3027
Ch&art Window	2571	&Web Help 8	3028
&From File	2619	Microsoft &Office Home Page	3029
&AutoShapes	2630	Send Feedbac&k	3030
&Lines	2631	&Best of the Web	3031
&Basic Shapes	2632	Search the &Web	3032
Co&nnectors	2633	Web &Tutorial	3033
&Sun	2634	&Web Help 14	3034
&Moon	2635	&Web Help 15	3035
&Double Bracket	2636	&Web Help 16	3036
&Double Brace	2637	Con&ditional Formatting	3058
&4-Point Star	2638	Protect and &Share Workbook	3059
&Double Wave	2639	Microsoft &Home Page	3091
&Straight Arrow Connector	2640	Clear Co&ntents	3125
&Straight Double-Arrow Connector	2641	&Automatic Color	3141
&Elbow Arrow Connector	2642	&Group	3159
&Elbow Double-Arrow Connector	2643	&Ungroup	3160
		&Increase Indent	3161
		&Decrease Indent	3162

D

Face IDs

The FaceID property of a CommandBarButton object defines the icon that's displayed on the button's face. (For an example of using the FaceID property to define the image on a button's face, see the section "Example: Creating a Toolbar," in Chapter 12, *Custom Menus and Toolbars.*)

Figures D-1 through D-5 show the icons that are available from Visual Basic, along with their corresponding faceIDs. Each figure shows 400 icons whose beginning and ending faceIDs are shown in the figure caption of the image. In addition, to make identifying a particular faceID easier, a numbered grid has been superimposed on the image. The column numbers indicate the one's digit; the row numbers indicate all other significant digits. For example, the faceID of the F icon in Figure D-1 is 85, because it's in row 8x (the row containing faceIDs 80–89) and in column x5 (the column containing faceIDs whose one's digit is 5).

Note that some numbers aren't used as faceIDs; in these cases, no icon is displayed in that faceID's grid in Figures D-1 through D-5.

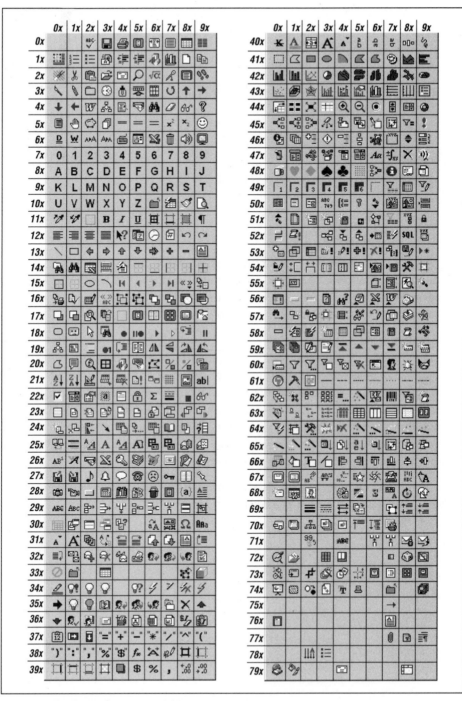

Figure D-1. FaceIDs for icons 0–799

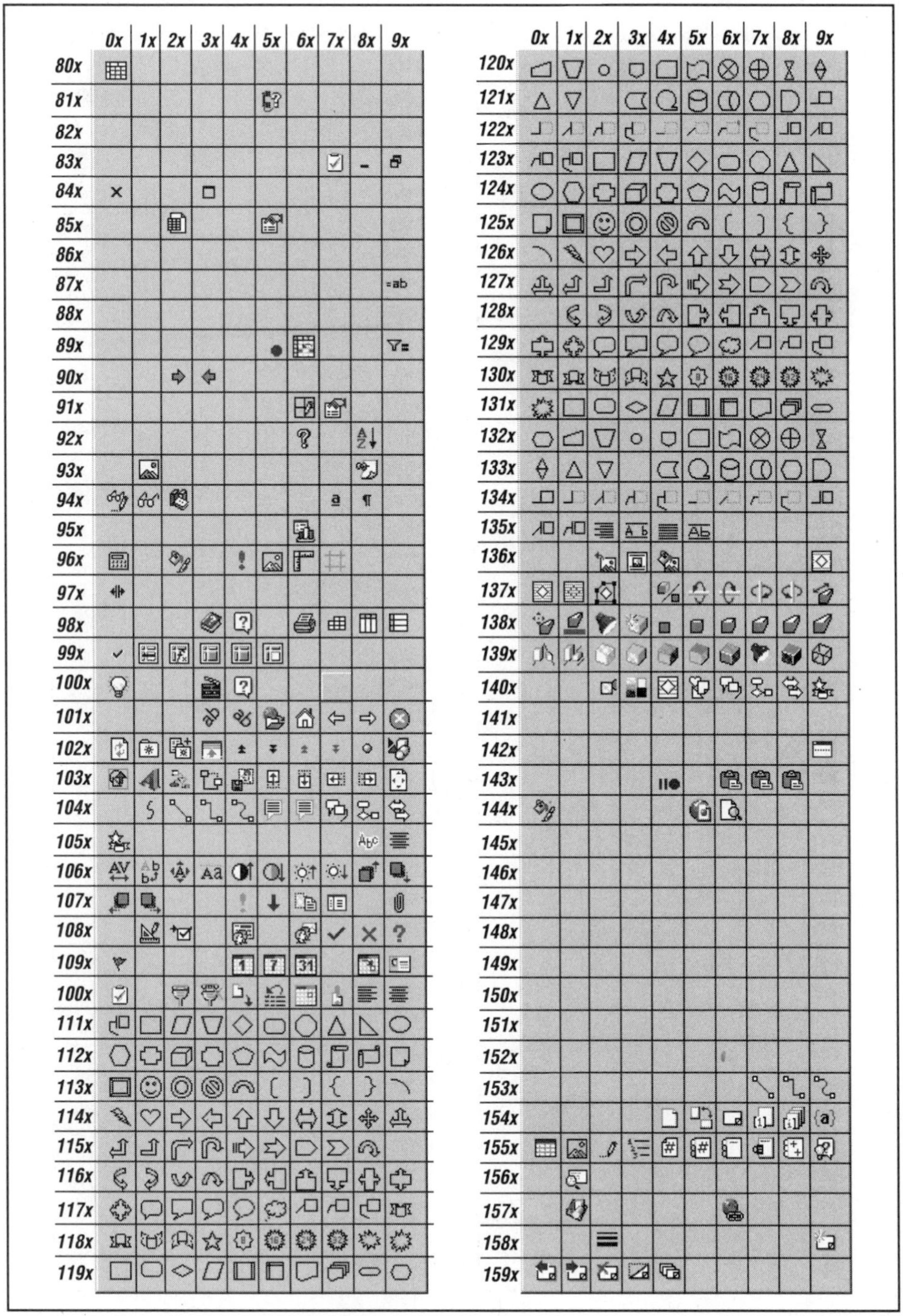

Figure D-2. FaceIDs for icons 800–1599

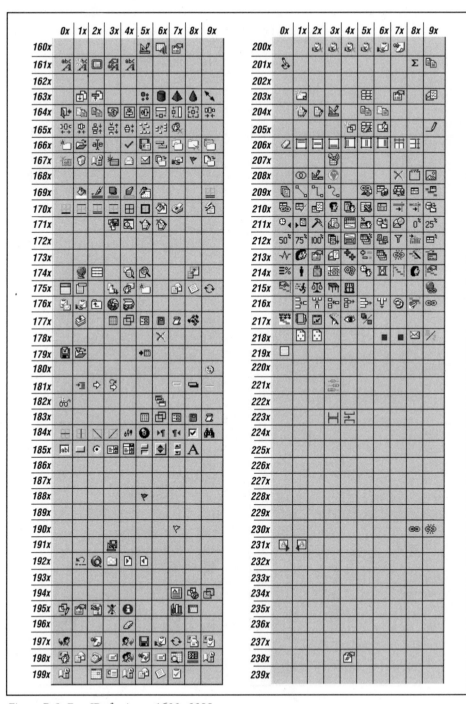

Figure D-3. FaceIDs for icons 1600–2399

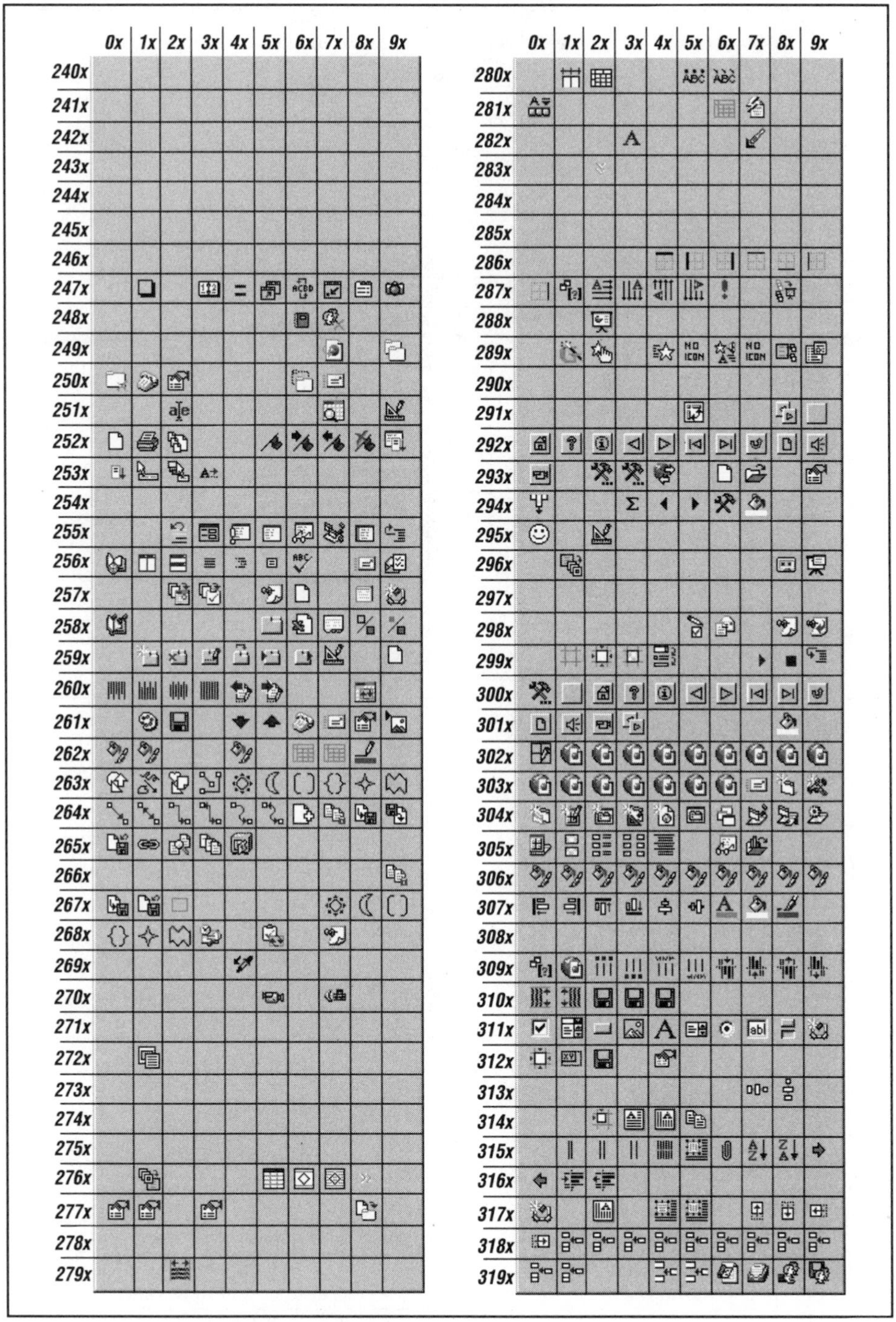

Figure D-4. *FaceIDs for icons 2400–3199*

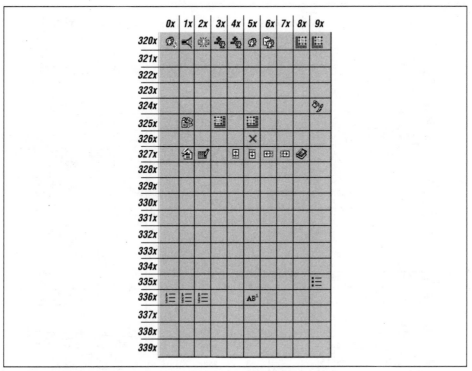

Figure D-5. FaceIDs for icons 3200–3399

E

Programming Excel from Another Application

In this appendix, we will briefly describe how the Excel object model can be programmed from within certain other applications, including Microsoft Access, Word, and PowerPoint.

Briefly put, a well-known technique that Microsoft refers to as *Automation* (formerly called OLE Automation) allows one application to gain access to the objects of another. An application that "exposes" its objects is called an *Automation server*. An application that can access the objects of an Automation server is called an *Automation controller* or *Automation client*. Since Microsoft Word, Access, Excel, and PowerPoint are Automation servers and Automation controllers, as a VBA programmer, you can program any of these applications from within any other.

Setting a Reference to the Excel Object Model

The first step in communicating with the Excel object model is to set a reference to its object library. Each of the client applications (Word, Access, Excel, and Power-Point) has a References menu item under the Tools menu. Selecting this item displays the References dialog box shown in Figure E-1. From here, we can select the object models that we want to access from within the Automation controller.

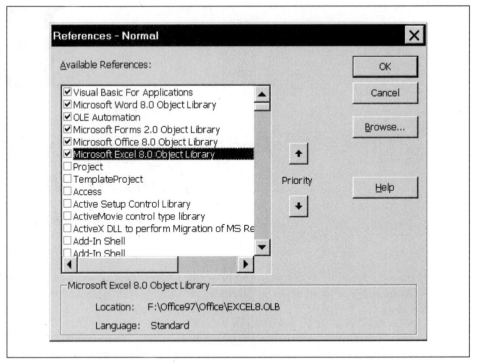

Figure E-1. The References dialog box

Getting a Reference to the Excel Application Object

Once the proper references are set, we can declare an object variable of type Application:

```
Dim XlApp As Excel.Application
```

which the Automation client will understand, because it can now check the server's object library. Note that we need to qualify the object name, since other object models have an Application object as well.

Next, we want to start the Excel Automation server, create an Excel Application object, and get a reference to that object. This is done in the following line:

```
Set XLApp = New Excel.Application
```

At this point, we have complete access to Excel's object model. It is important to note, however, that the previous line starts the Excel Automation server, but does not start Excel's graphical user interface, so Excel will be running invisibly. To make Excel visible, we just set its Visible property to **True**:

```
XLApp.Visible = True
```

We can now program as though we were within the Excel VBA IDE. For instance, the following code creates a new workbook, adds a worksheet to it, puts a value in cell A1, and then saves the workbook:

```
Sub MakeWorkbook()

Dim XlApp As Excel.Application
Dim wb As Excel.Workbook
Dim ws As Excel.Worksheet

Set XlApp = New Excel.Application
XlApp.Visible = True

Set wb = XlApp.Workbooks.Add
Set ws = wb.Worksheets.Add
ws.Name = "Sales"
ws.Range("A1").Value = 123

wb.SaveAs "d:\temp\SalesBook"

End Sub
```

Note that the Excel server will not terminate by itself, even if the *XLApp* variable is destroyed. If we have made Excel visible, then we can close it programmatically, as well as from the user interface in the usual way (choosing Exit from the File menu, for instance). But if the Excel server is invisible, it must be closed using the Quit method:

```
XlApp.Quit
```

(If we fail to terminate the Excel server, it will remain running invisibly, taking up system resources, until the PC is restarted.)

An Alternative Approach

The approach described for programming Excel from within another application is the preferred approach, since it is the most efficient. However, there is an alternative approach that you may encounter, so let us discuss it briefly. As before, we assume that a reference has been set to the Excel object library.

The CreateObject function

The *CreateObject* function can start an Automation server, create an object, and assign it to an object variable. Thus, we can write:

```
Dim XLApp as Excel.Application
Set XLApp = CreateObject("Excel.Application")
```

This approach will execute more slowly than the previous approach using the New keyword, but it is perfectly valid.

As before, we must remember to close Excel using the Quit method (or through normal means if Excel is visible).

The GetObject function

If Excel is already running, the *CreateObject* function will start a second copy of the Excel server. To use the currently running version, we can use the *GetObject* function to set a reference to the Application object of a running copy of Excel. This is done as follows:

```
Set XLApp = GetObject(, "Excel.Application")
```

(The first parameter of *GetObject* is not used here.)

One of the problems with using *GetObject* is that it will produce an error if Excel is not running. Thus, we need some code that will start Excel if it is not running or use the existing copy of Excel if it is running.

The trick to this is to know that if *GetObject* fails to find a running copy of Excel, then it issues error number 429 ("ActiveX component can't create object"). Thus, the following code does the trick:

```
Dim XLApp As Excel.Application
On Error Resume Next
' Try to get reference to running Excel
Set XLApp = GetObject(, "Excel.Application")
If Err.Number = 429 Then
    ' If error 429, then create new object
    Set XLApp = CreateObject("Excel.Application")
ElseIf Err.Number <> 0 Then
    ' If another type of error, report it
    MsgBox "Error: " & Err.Description
    Exit Sub
End If
```

No object library reference

We have been assuming that the client application has a reference to the server's object library. However, it is still possible for a client application (an Automation client) to program the objects of an Automation server (such as Excel) without such a reference. Under these circumstances, we cannot refer to objects by name in code, since the client will not understand these names. Instead, we must use the generic Object data type, as in the following code:

```
Dim XLApp As Object
Dim wb As Object
Set XLApp = CreateObject("Excel.Application")
XLApp.Visible = True
```

```
Set wb = XLApp.Workbooks.Add
wb.SaveAs "d:\temp\SalesBook"
```

This code will run even more slowly than the previous code, which, in turn, is slower than the first version.

Thus, we have three versions of Automation:

- Using the **New** keyword syntax (requires an object library reference)

- Using *CreateObject* and specific object variable declarations (requires an object library reference)

- Using *CreateObject* with generic **As Object** declarations (does not use an object library reference)

These versions of automation are sometimes referred to by the names *very early binding, early binding,* and *late binding,* respectively (although you may hear these terms used somewhat differently).

The reason for these terms has to do with the time at which VBA can associate (or *bind*) the object, property, and method names in our code to the actual addresses of these items. In very early binding, all bindings are done at compile time by VBA—that is, *before* the program runs. In early binding, some of the bindings are done at compile time and others are done at run time. In late binding, all bindings are done at run time.

The issue is now evident. The more binding that needs to be done at run time, the more slowly the program will run. Thus, very early binding is the most efficient, followed by early binding, and then late binding.

High-Level and Low-Level Languages

In this appendix, we'll examine the position of Visual Basic as a programming language by taking a somewhat closer look at high-level and low-level languages, with some examples for comparison.

A low-level language is characterized by its ability to manipulate the computer's operating system and hardware more or less directly. For instance, a programmer who is using a low-level language may be able to easily turn on the motor of a floppy drive, or check the status bits of the printer interface, or look at individual sectors on a disk, whereas these tasks may be difficult, if not impossible, with a high-level language. Another benefit of low-level languages is that they tend to perform tasks more quickly than high-level languages.

On the other hand, the power to manipulate the computer at a low level comes at a price. Low-level languages are generally more cryptic—they tend to be farther removed from ordinary spoken languages and are therefore harder to learn, remember, and use. High-level languages (and application-level languages, which many people would refer to simply as high-level languages) tend to be more user-friendly, but the price we pay for that friendliness is less control over the computer and slower running programs.

To illustrate, consider the task of printing some text. A low-level language may only be able to send individual characters to a printer. The process of printing with a low-level language might go something like the following:

1. Check the status of the printer.

2. If the printer is free, initialize the printer.

3. Send a character to the printer.

4. Check to see if this character arrived safely.

5. If not, send the character again.

6. If so, start over with the next character.

The "lowest" level language that programmers use is called *assembly language.* Indeed, assembly language has essentially complete control over the computer's hardware. To illustrate assembly language code, the following program prints the message "Happy printing." Don't worry if these instructions seem meaningless— you can just skim over them to get the feel. In fact, the very point we want to make is that low-level languages are much more cryptic than high-level languages. (Lines that begin with a semicolon are comments. We have left out error checking to save a little space.)

```
; --------------------
; Data for the program
; --------------------
; message to print
Message     DB        'Happy printing', 0Dh, 0Ah

; length of message
Msg_Len    EQU        $-Message

; --------------------
; Initialize printer 0
; --------------------
mov ah,1
mov dx,0
int 17h

; --------------------
; Printing instructions
; --------------------
; get number of characters to print
mov cx,Msg_Len

; get location of message
mov bx,offset Message

; get printer number (first printer is printer 0)
mov dx,0

Print_Loop:

; send character to printer 0
mov ah,0
mov al,[bx]
int 17h

; do next character
inc bx
loop Print_Loop
```

For comparison, let us see how this same task would be accomplished in the BASIC programming language:

```
LPRINT "Happy printing"
```

The difference is pretty obvious.

As we have discussed, high-level languages are usually designed for a specific purpose. Generally, this purpose is to write software applications of a specific type. For instance, Visual C++ and Visual Basic are used primarily to write standalone Windows applications. Indeed, Microsoft Excel itself is written in Visual C++. As another example, FORTRAN (which is a contraction of *Formula Translation*) is designed to write scientific and computational applications for various platforms (including Windows). COBOL is used to write business-related applications (generally for mainframe computers).

At the highest level in the programming language hierarchy, we find programs such as Excel VBA, whose *primary* purpose is not to manipulate the operating system or hardware, nor to write standalone Windows applications, but rather to manipulate a high-level software application (in this case Microsoft Excel).

Just for fun, let us take a brief look at a handful of the more common programming languages.

BASIC

The word BASIC is an acronym for *Beginners All-Purpose Symbolic Instruction Code*, the key word here being Beginners. BASIC was developed at Dartmouth College in 1963, by two mathematicians: John Kemeny and Thomas Kurtz. The intention was to design a programming language for liberal arts students, who made up the vast majority of the student population at Dartmouth. The goal was to create a language that would be friendly to the user and have a fast turn-around time so it could be used effectively for homework assignments. (In those days, a student would submit a program to a computer operator, who would place the program in a queue, awaiting processing by the computer. The student would simply have to wait for the results—there were no PCs in the 1960s!)

The first version of BASIC was very simple; indeed, it was primitive. For example, it had only one data type: floating-point. (Data types are discussed in Chapter 5, *Variables, Data Types, and Constants.*) Since then BASIC has made tremendous strides as a personal computer programming language, due mostly to the embrace of the language by Microsoft.

Even to this day, however, the BASIC language, and its offshoot Visual Basic, do not get much respect among computer scientists or academicians. The BASIC language gets a bad rap on two fronts. First, it is generally considered a weak language in the sense that it does not provide very much control over the computer's hardware (or operating system), at least as compared to other languages such as C. Second, BASIC has a reputation for not "forcing" (or in some cases even allowing) programmers to use good programming style.

For comparison with some other languages, here is a BASIC program that asks the user for some numbers and then returns their average. Lines beginning with an apostrophe are comment lines that are ignored by the computer.

```
' BASIC program to compute the average
' of a set of at most 100 numbers

' Ask for the number of numbers
INPUT "Enter the number of numbers: ", Num

' If Num is between 1 and 100 then proceed
' IF Num > 0 AND Num <= 100 THEN

    Sum = 0
    ' Loop to collect the numbers to average
    FOR I = 1 TO Num
        ' Ask for next number
        INPUT "Enter next number: ", NextNum
        ' Add the number to the running sum
        Sum = Sum + NextNum
    NEXT I

    ' Compute the average
    Ave = Sum / Num

    ' Display the average
    PRINT "The average is: "; Ave

END IF

END
```

Visual Basic

Microsoft took the BASIC programming language to new heights when it developed Visual Basic. In the early 1990s, Microsoft faced a dilemma. Windows was (and is) a considerably more complex operating system than DOS, so much so that only professional programmers could effectively use Microsoft's main programming tool for creating Windows-based applications—the Microsoft Windows SDK, which is based on the C language. (These days, this tool has given way to a more modern tool, Microsoft Foundation Classes, which is still not for the casual programmer.)

But Microsoft wanted more people to be able to create Windows applications, since it was good for business. So in 1991, the company introduced *Visual Basic* (VB for short), which essentially combined the BASIC language with a visual programming environment that allowed users to easily create graphical components, such as windows, command buttons, text boxes, option buttons, and menus that are required by Windows applications. The underlying language for VB is called *Visual Basic for Applications,* or VBA for short, although this term was not coined until later in the development of VB.

The first version of Visual Basic was little more than an interesting toy. It did not really have the power to create serious Windows applications. However, it provided a necessary starting point for further development of the product. Each successive version of Visual Basic has taken major steps forward in sophistication, so that now VB is by far the most widely used programming language for PCs. (Microsoft estimates that over three million people use some form of Visual Basic, about half of whom program using some form of Office VBA, the rest using the standalone VB product.)

While Visual Basic has become a very respectable tool for creating standalone Windows applications, the real popularity of Visual Basic for Applications (VBA) lies in the fact that it is the underlying programming language for the Microsoft Office application suite, which probably has closer to 100 million users, each of whom is a potential VBA programmer. Indeed, presumably the reason that you are reading this book is that you want to join the group of VBA programmers.

VBA is a high-level programming language that underlies several important Windows applications, including Microsoft Word, Excel, Access, and PowerPoint, as well as Microsoft Visual Basic. In addition, companies other than Microsoft can license VBA and use it as the underlying programming language for their applications.

Each so-called *host application* provides extensions to VBA to accommodate its own needs and idiosyncrasies. For instance, since Microsoft Word deals with documents, Word VBA needs to understand such things as headers and footers, grammar checking, page numbering, and so on. On the other hand, since Excel deals with worksheets, Excel VBA needs to understand such things as cells, formulas, charts, and so on. Finally, since Visual Basic is designed for writing standalone Windows applications, it must excel at manipulating Windows controls (text boxes, command buttons, list boxes).

C and C++

The C programming language, a descendant of several older languages (including B), was developed by Dennis Ritchie at Bell Laboratories in 1972. C is a simple language in its syntax, with relatively few instructions. However, it has been extended considerably by Microsoft (among others) for use in the PC environment.

The strength of C and its descendants, such as C++, lies in the fact that it combines the advantages of a high-level programming language, such as relative readability, with the ability to reach down to the operating system and hardware levels of the computer. Unfortunately, the power of C can sometimes be dangerous in the hands of, shall we say, programmers of only modest capability. Also, the syntax of C allows for what some programmers consider "clever" or "elegant" programming style, but which may be more accurately termed "highly unreadable."

For comparison purposes, here is the C language version of the BASIC program that computes the average of some numbers. I think you will agree that it is not quite as readable as the earlier BASIC version. Lines beginning with // are comment lines that are ignored by the computer.

```c
// C program to compute the average
// of a set of at most 100 numbers

#include <stdio.h>

void main(void)
{
    // Declare some variables
    int Num, i;
    float Sum, NextNum, Ave;

    // Ask for the number of numbers
    printf( "Enter number of numbers: " );
    scanf( "%u", &Num );

    // If Num is between 1 and 100 then proceed
    if( (Num > 0) && (Num <= 100) )
    {
        Sum = 0.0;
        // Loop to collect the numbers to average
        for( i = 1; i <= Num; i++ )
        {
            // Ask for next number
            printf( "Enter next number: " );
            scanf( "%f", &NextNum );

            // Add the number to the running sum
            Sum += NextNum;
        }

        // Compute the average
        Ave = Sum / Num;

        //Display the average
        printf ("The average is: %f\n", Ave );
    }
}
```

An object-oriented extension to C, known as C++, was developed in the early 1980s by Bjarne Stroustrup (also at Bell Labs).

Visual C++

Despite the significant strides that Visual Basic has taken, it is not, in general, the preferred language for creating complex standalone Windows applications. That role belongs to Microsoft's Visual C++.

Actually, this is a good thing. Microsoft must guard against trying to make any single language the solution for too many diverse programming needs. Such an effort can only be counterproductive. By increasing the power of Visual Basic (and VBA) in order to handle more diverse and sophisticated application programming, the language becomes more complex and difficult to learn and use. This will result in the language being used by fewer people.

Visual C++ is a marriage between the C++ programming language and the Windows graphical environment. Visual C++ is not nearly as user-friendly as Visual Basic. This is due in part to the nature of the underlying language (C is less friendly than BASIC), in part to the fact that C++ is a fully object-oriented language and therefore naturally more complicated, and in part to the fact that Visual C++ is designed to control the Windows environment at a more fundamental level than Visual Basic. For instance, Visual Basic does not provide ways to create a text box whose text can use more than one color, or set the tabs in a list box, or change the color of the caption in a command button, and so on. Simply put, when programming in VB (or VBA), we must sacrifice power in some directions in favor of power in other directions and a simpler programming environment.

Pascal

Pascal was developed by Niklaus Wirth (pronounced "Virt") in the late 1960s and early 1970s. The goal was to produce a language that could be easily implemented on a variety of computers and that would provide students with a model teaching language. That is to say, Pascal is full of features that encourage well-written and well-structured programs. Indeed, many universities teach Pascal to their computer science students as a first language. Pascal has also migrated to the personal computer arena, first with Borland's Turbo Pascal and more recently with Borland's visual programming environment called Delphi.

For contrast, here is how our program to compute the average would look in Pascal. Text contained within curly braces ({,}) are comments that are ignored by the computer.

```
{ Pascal program to compute the average
 of a set of at most 100 numbers }

program average (input, output);
   { Declare some variables }
   var
      Num, i : integer;
      Ave, Sum, NextNum : real;
   begin
      { Ask for the number of numbers }
      writeln('Enter the number of numbers');
      readln(Num);
      { If Num is between 1 and 100 then proceed }
      if ((Num > 0 ) and (Num <= 100)) then
         begin
            Sum := 0;
            { Loop to collect the numbers to average }
            for i := 1 to Num do
               begin
                  { Ask for next number }
                  writeln('Enter next number');
                  readln(NextNum);
                  { Add the number to the running sum }
                  Sum := Sum + NextNum;
               end

            { Compute the average }
            Ave := Sum / Num;

            { Display the average }
            writeln('The average is: ', Ave);
         end
   end
```

FORTRAN

FORTRAN is a contraction of *Formula Translation,* a name that comes from a technical report entitled "The IBM Mathematical FORmula TRANslating System," written by John Backus and his team at IBM in the mid-1950s. FORTRAN is primarily designed for scientific calculations and has the distinction of being the first widely used high-level programming language. Backus made some rather interesting claims about FORTRAN; for instance, it was not designed for its beauty (a reasonable statement) but it would eliminate coding errors and the consequent debugging process!

Here is the FORTRAN version of our little averaging program. (Lines that begin with a C are comments.)

```
C FORTRAN PROGRAM TO COMPUTE THE AVERAGE
C OF A SET OF AT MOST 100 NUMBERS
```

```
      Real SUM, AVE, NEXTNUM
      SUM = 0.0

C Ask for the number of numbers
      WRITE(*,*) 'Enter the number of numbers: '
      READ(*,*) NUM

C If Num is between 1 and 100 then proceed
      IF NUM .GT. 0 .AND. NUM .LE. 100 then
         C Loop to collect the numbers to average
         DO 10 I = 1, NUM
            C Ask for next number
            WRITE(*,*) 'Enter next number: '
            READ(*,*) NEXTNUM
            C Add the number to the running sum
            SUM = SUM + NEXTNUM
10       CONTINUE
         C Compute the average
         AVE = SUM/NUM
         C Display the average
         WRITE(*,*) 'The average is: '
         WRITE(*,*) AVE
      ENDIF

      STOP
      END
```

COBOL

COBOL is an acronym for *Common Business Oriented Language* and it was developed in the late 1950s by Grace Hopper for the purpose of writing business-related programs, which she felt should be written in English. However, it seems rather that the language was developed with the express purpose of avoiding all mathematical-like notation. The inevitable consequence is that conciseness and readability is also avoided.

At any rate, I could only bring myself to code a COBOL sample program that adds two numbers.

```
* COBOL PROGRAM TO ADD TWO NUMBERS

IDENTIFICATION DIVISION.
PROGRAM-ID.   ADD02.
ENVIRONMENT DIVISION.
DATA DIVISION.

WORKING-STORAGE SECTION.
01     FIRST-NUMBER     PIC IS 99.
01     SECOND-NUMBER    PIC IS 99.
01     SUM              PIC IS 999.
```

```
     PROCEDURE DIVISION.

     PROGRAM-BEGIN.

     DISPLAY "ENTER FIRST NUMBER ".
     ACCEPT FIRST-NUMBER.

     DISPLAY "ENTER SECOND NUMBER ".
     ACCEPT SECOND-NUMBER.

     COMPUTE SUM = FIRST-NUMBER + SECOND-NUMBER

     DISPLAY "THE SUM IS: " SUM.

     PROGRAM-DONE.
     STOP RUN.
```

In BASIC, the preceding program would be:

```
     INPUT "Enter first number: ", n1
     INPUT "Enter second number: ", n2
     PRINT "The sum is: ", n1 + n2
```

This clearly points out the extreme verbosity of COBOL.

LISP

BASIC, C, Pascal, and FORTRAN are in many ways quite similar. Also, programs written in these languages can be made quite readable, especially if the programmer intends to make it so. There are other languages that seem not to be readable under any circumstances. For instance, LISP was developed in the late 1950s by John McCarthy and Marvin Minsky at MIT, for the purpose of doing list processing (hence the name) in connection with artificial intelligence applications.

In LISP, everything is a list. Here is a sample:

```
; LISP sample program to define a predicate
;   that takes two lists and returns the value
; T (for true) if the lists are equal and F otherwise
(DEFINE (
    '(equal (LAMDBA (list1 list2)
        (COND
         ((ATOM list1) (EQ list1 list2))
         ((ATOM list1 NIL)
         ((equal (CAR list1) (CAR list2))
            (equal (CDR list1) (CDR list2)))
         (T NIL)
       )
    ))
))
```

This sample points out one fact. Whatever else we might think of Microsoft, we can at least thank them for choosing BASIC (VBA) as the underlying language for the Microsoft Office suite!

Index

About the Author

Steven Roman is a professor of mathematics at the California State University, Fullerton. He has taught at a number of other universities, including MIT, the University of California at Santa Barbara, and the University of South Florida. Dr. Roman received his B.A. degree from the University of California at Los Angeles and his Ph.D. from the University of Washington. Dr. Roman has authored 28 books, including a number of books on mathematics, such as *Coding and Information Theory, Advanced Linear Algebra*, and *Field Theory*, published by Springer-Verlag. He has also written *Modules in Mathematics*, a series of 15 small books designed for the general college-level liberal arts student. Dr. Roman has written *Access Database Design & Programming, Developing Visual Basic Add-ins*, and *Learning Word Programming* for O'Reilly & Associates, plus two other computer books, *Concepts of Object-Oriented Programming with Visual Basic* published by Springer-Verlag and *Understanding Personal Computer Hardware*, an in-depth look at how PC hardware works (no publisher yet). He is currently working on a book entitled *Win32 API Programming with Visual Basic* to be published by O'Reilly. Dr. Roman is interested in combinatorics, algebra, and computer science.

Colophon

Our look is the result of reader comments, our own experimentation, and feedback from distribution channels. Distinctive covers complement our distinctive approach to technical topics, breathing personality and life into potentially dry subjects.

The animal on the cover of *Writing Excel Macros* is a bluejay (*Cyanocitta cristata*), a vociferous, aggressive bird common in the eastern half of the United States and southern Canada. The blue-crested jay is also an agile flyer and occasional nest-robber. The term "bluejay" is also applied to the Steller's jay (*Cyanocitta stelleri*), a larger, darker jay common in much of the western U.S. and Canada, as well as several other species.

Bluejays eat primarily nuts, seeds, and insects, sometimes planting acorns in the ground, thus helping tree growth. Known for their loud, harsh, and easily identifiable calls, bluejays (related to crows and ravens) often spoil the hunting forays of other animals by warning potential prey.

Bluejays are bright blue, white, and black, with both sexes similar in appearance. They are about 10–12 inches in length, and build large tree nests about 25 feet off the ground, into which are laid 3–6 spotted olive-colored eggs. The male is very attentive during the nesting periods. Jays are sociable and frequently travel in groups ranging from a mating pair to a larger flock.

Clairemarie Fisher O'Leary was the production editor and copyeditor for *Writing Excel Macros*; Sheryl Avruch was the production manager; Jeffrey Liggett, Sarah Jane Shangraw, and John Files provided quality control. Robert Romano created the illustrations using Adobe Photoshop 5 and Macromedia FreeHand 8. Mike Sierra provided FrameMaker technical support. Ruth Rautenberg wrote the index.

Hanna Dyer designed the cover of this book, based on a series design by Edie Freedman. The image is a 19th-century engraving from the Dover Pictorial Archive. The cover layout was produced by Kathleen Wilson using QuarkXpress 3.3 and the ITC Garamond font. The inside layout was designed by Alicia Cech, based on a series design by Nancy Priest and implemented in FrameMaker 5.5.6 by Mike Sierra. The text and heading fonts are ITC Garamond Light and Garamond Book. This colophon was written by Nancy Kotary.

Whenever possible, our books use RepKover™, a durable and flexible lay-flat binding. If the page count exceeds RepKover's limit, perfect binding is used.

 # More Titles from O'Reilly

Windows Programming

Access Database Design & Programming

By Steven Roman
1st Edition June 1997
270 pages, ISBN 1-56592-297-2

This book provides experienced Access users who are novice programers with frequently overlooked concepts and techniques necessary to create effective database applications. It focuses on designing effective tables in a multi-table application; using the Access interface or Access SQL to construct queries; and programming using the Data Access Object (DAO) and Microsoft Access object models.

Learning VBScript

By Paul Lomax
1st Edition July 1997
616 pages, includes CD-ROM
ISBN 1-56592-247-6

This definitive guide shows web developers how to take full advantage of client-side scripting with the VBScript language. In addition to basic language features, it covers the Internet Explorer object model and discusses techniques for client-side scripting, like adding ActiveX controls to a web page or validating data before sending it to the server. Includes CD-ROM with over 170 code samples.

Win32 Multithreaded Programming

By Aaron Cohen & Mike Woodring
1st Edition December 1997
724 pages, Includes CD-ROM
ISBN 1-56592-296-4

This book clearly explains the concepts of multithreaded programs and shows developers how to construct efficient and complex applications. An important book for any developer, it illustrates all aspects of Win32 multithreaded programming, including what has previously been undocumented or poorly explained.

Learning Perl on Win32 Systems

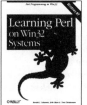

By Randal L. Schwartz,
Erik Olson & Tom Christiansen
1st Edition August 1997
306 pages, ISBN 1-56592-324-3

In this carefully paced course, leading Perl trainers and a Windows NT practitioner teach you to program in the language that promises to emerge as the scripting language of choice on NT. Based on the "llama" book, this book features tips for PC users and new, NT-specific examples, along with a foreword by Larry Wall, the creator of Perl, and Dick Hardt, the creator of Perl for Win32.

Learning Word Programming

By Steven Roman
1st Edition October 1998
408 pages, ISBN 1-56592-524-6

This no-nonsense book delves into the core aspects of VBA programming, enabling users to increase their productivity and power over Microsoft Word. It takes the reader step-by-step through writing VBA macros and programs, illustrating how to generate tables of a particular format, manage shortcut keys, create FAX cover sheets, and reformat documents.

Windows NT File System Internals

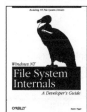

By Rajeev Nagar
1st Edition September 1997
794 pages, Includes diskette
ISBN 1-56592-249-2

Windows NT File System Internals presents the details of the NT I/O Manager, the Cache Manager, and the Memory Manager from the perspective of a software developer writing a file system driver or implementing a kernel-mode filter driver. The book provides numerous code examples included on diskette, as well as the source for a complete, usable filter driver.

Windows Programming

Developing Visual Basic Add-Ins

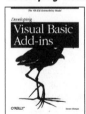

By Steven Roman
1st Edition December 1998
186 pages, ISBN 1-56592-527-0

A tutorial and reference guide in one, this book covers all the basics of creating useful VB add-ins to extend the IDE, allowing developers to work more productively with Visual Basic. Readers with even a modest acquaintance with VB will be developing add-ins in no time. Includes numerous simple code examples.

Inside the Windows 95 Registry

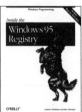

By Ron Petrusha
1st Edition August 1996
594 pages, Includes diskette
ISBN 1-56592-170-4

An in-depth examination of remote registry access, differences between the Win95 and NT registries, registry backup, undocumented registry services, and the role the registry plays in OLE. Shows programmers how to access the Win95 registry from Win32, Win16, and DOS programs in C and Visual Basic. VxD sample code is also included. Includes diskette.

Windows NT SNMP

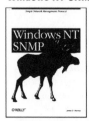

By James D. Murray
1st Edition January 1998
464 pages, Includes CD-ROM
ISBN 1-56592-338-3

This book describes the implementation of SNMP (the Simple Network Management Protocol) on Windows NT 3.51 and 4.0 (with a look ahead to NT 5.0) and Windows 95 systems. It covers SNMP and network basics and detailed information on developing SNMP management applications and extension agents. The book comes with a CD-ROM containing a wealth of additional information: standards documents, sample code from the book, and many third-party, SNMP-related software tools, libraries, and demos.

Developing Windows Error Messages

By Ben Ezzell
1st Edition March 1998
254 pages, Includes CD-ROM
ISBN 1-56592-356-1

This book teaches C, C++, and Visual Basic programmers how to write effective error messages that notify the user of an error, clearly explain the error, and most important, offer a solution. The book also discusses methods for preventing and trapping errors before they occur and tells how to create flexible input and response routines to keep unnecessary errors from happening.

Inside the Windows 95 File System

By Stan Mitchell
1st Edition May 1997
378 pages, Includes diskette
ISBN 1-56592-200-X

In this book, Stan Mitchell describes the Windows 95 File System, as well as the new opportunities and challenges it brings for developers. Its "hands-on" approach will help developers become better equipped to make design decisions using the new Win95 File System features. Includes a diskette containing MULTIMON, a general-purpose monitor for examining Windows internals.

In a Nutshell Quick References

Visual Basic Controls in a Nutshell

By Evan S. Dictor
1st Edition June 1999 (est.)
720 pages (est.), ISBN 1-56592-294-8

This quick reference covers one of the crucial elements of Visual Basic: its controls, and their numerous properties, events, and methods. It provides a step-by-step list of procedures for using each major control and contains a detailed reference to all properties, methods, and events. Written by an experienced Visual Basic programmer, it helps to make painless what can sometimes be an arduous job of programming Visual Basic.

In a Nutshell Quick References

In a Nutshell Quick References

VB & VBA in a Nutshell: The Languages

By Paul Lomax
1st Edition October 1998
656 pages, ISBN 1-56592-358-8

For Visual Basic and VBA programmers, this book boils down the essentials of the VB and VBA languages into a single volume, including undocumented and little documented areas essential to everyday programming. The convenient alphabetical reference to all functions, procedures, statements, and keywords allows VB and VBA programmers to use this book both as a standard reference guide to the language and as a tool for troubleshooting and identifying programming problems.

Windows NT in a Nutshell

By Eric Pearce
1st Edition June 1997
364 pages, ISBN 1-56592-251-4

Anyone who installs Windows NT, creates a user, or adds a printer is an NT system administrator (whether they realize it or not). This book features a new tagged callout approach to documenting the 4.0 GUI as well as real-life examples of command usage and strategies for problem solving, with an emphasis on networking. *Windows NT in a Nutshell* will be as useful to the single-system home user as it will be to the administrator of a 1,000-node corporate network.

Perl in a Nutshell

By Stephen Spainhour,
Ellen Siever & Nathan Patwardhan
1st Edition January 1999
674 pages, ISBN 1-56592-286-7

The perfect companion for working programmers, *Perl in a Nutshell* is a comprehensive reference guide to the world of Perl. It contains everything you need to know for all but the most obscure Perl questions. This wealth of information is packed into an efficient, extraordinarily usable format.

Internet in a Nutshell

By Valerie Quercia
1st Edition October 1997
450 pages, ISBN 1-56592-323-5

Internet in a Nutshell is a quick-moving guide that goes beyond the "hype" and right to the heart of the matter: how to get the Internet to work for you. This is a second-generation Internet book for readers who have already taken a spin around the Net and now want to learn the shortcuts.

ASP in a Nutshell

By A. Keyton Weissinger
1st Edition February 1999
426 pages, ISBN 1-56592-490-8

This detailed reference contains all the information Web developers need to create effective Active Server Pages (ASP) applications. It focuses on how features are used in a real application and highlights little-known or undocumented aspects, enabling even experienced developers to advance their ASP applications to new levels.

Year 2000 in a Nutshell

By Norman Shakespeare
1st Edition September 1998
330 pages, ISBN 1-56592-421-5

This reference guide addresses the awareness, the managerial aspect, and the technical issues of the Year 2000 computer dilemma, providing a compact compendium of solutions and reference information useful for addressing the problem.

Windows 95 in a Nutshell

By Tim O'Reilly & Troy Mott
1st Edition June 1998
528 pages, ISBN 1-56592-316-2

A comprehensive, compact reference that systematically unveils what serious users of Windows 95 will find interesting and useful, capturing little known details of the operating system in a consistent reference format.

How to stay in touch with O'Reilly

1. Visit Our Award-Winning Web Site

http://www.oreilly.com/

★ "Top 100 Sites on the Web" —*PC Magazine*
★ "Top 5% Web sites" —*Point Communications*
★ "3-Star site" —*The McKinley Group*

Our web site contains a library of comprehensive product information (including book excerpts and tables of contents), downloadable software, background articles, interviews with technology leaders, links to relevant sites, book cover art, and more. File us in your Bookmarks or Hotlist!

2. Join Our Email Mailing Lists

New Product Releases

To receive automatic email with brief descriptions of all new O'Reilly products as they are released, send email to:
listproc@online.oreilly.com
Put the following information in the first line of your message (*not* in the Subject field):
subscribe oreilly-news

O'Reilly Events

If you'd also like us to send information about trade show events, special promotions, and other O'Reilly events, send email to:
listproc@online.oreilly.com
Put the following information in the first line of your message (*not* in the Subject field):
subscribe oreilly-events

3. Get Examples from Our Books via FTP

There are two ways to access an archive of example files from our books:

Regular FTP

- ftp to:
  ftp.oreilly.com
  (login: anonymous
  password: your email address)
- Point your web browser to:
  ftp://ftp.oreilly.com/

FTPMAIL

- Send an email message to:
  ftpmail@online.oreilly.com
  (Write "help" in the message body)

4. Contact Us via Email

order@oreilly.com
To place a book or software order online. Good for North American and international customers.

subscriptions@oreilly.com
To place an order for any of our newsletters or periodicals.

books@oreilly.com
General questions about any of our books.

software@oreilly.com
For general questions and product information about our software. Check out O'Reilly Software Online at **http://software.oreilly.com/** for software and technical support information. Registered O'Reilly software users send your questions to: **website-support@oreilly.com**

cs@oreilly.com
For answers to problems regarding your order or our products.

booktech@oreilly.com
For book content technical questions or corrections.

proposals@oreilly.com
To submit new book or software proposals to our editors and product managers.

international@oreilly.com
For information about our international distributors or translation queries. For a list of our distributors outside of North America check out:
http://www.oreilly.com/www/order/country.html

O'Reilly & Associates, Inc.
101 Morris Street, Sebastopol, CA 95472 USA
TEL   707-829-0515 or 800-998-9938
           (6am to 5pm PST)
FAX   707-829-0104

Titles from O'Reilly

International Distributors

UK, Europe, Middle East and Africa (except France, Germany, Austria, Switzerland, Luxembourg, Liechtenstein, and Eastern Europe)

INQUIRIES
O'Reilly UK Limited
4 Castle Street
Farnham
Surrey, GU9 7HS
United Kingdom
Telephone: 44-1252-711776
Fax: 44-1252-734211
Email: josette@oreilly.com

ORDERS
Wiley Distribution Services Ltd.
1 Oldlands Way
Bognor Regis
West Sussex PO22 9SA
United Kingdom
Telephone: 44-1243-779777
Fax: 44-1243-820250
Email: cs-books@wiley.co.uk

France

ORDERS
GEODIF
61, Bd Saint-Germain
75240 Paris Cedex 05, France
Tel: 33-1-44-41-46-16 (French books)
Tel: 33-1-44-41-11-87 (English books)
Fax: 33-1-44-41-11-44
Email: distribution@eyrolles.com

INQUIRIES
Éditions O'Reilly
18 rue Séguier
75006 Paris, France
Tel: 33-1-40-51-52-30
Fax: 33-1-40-51-52-31
Email: france@editions-oreilly.fr

Germany, Switzerland, Austria, Eastern Europe, Luxembourg, and Liechtenstein

INQUIRIES & ORDERS
O'Reilly Verlag
Balthasarstr. 81
D-50670 Köln
Germany
Telephone: 49-221-973160-91
Fax: 49-221-973160-8
Email: anfragen@oreilly.de (inquiries)
Email: order@oreilly.de (orders)

Canada (French language books)

Les Éditions Flammarion ltée
375, Avenue Laurier Ouest
Montréal (Québec) H2V 2K3
Tel: 00-1-514-277-8807
Fax: 00-1-514-278-2085
Email: info@flammarion.qc.ca

Hong Kong

City Discount Subscription Service, Ltd.
Unit D, 3rd Floor, Yan's Tower
27 Wong Chuk Hang Road
Aberdeen, Hong Kong
Tel: 852-2580-3539
Fax: 852-2580-6463
Email: citydis@ppn.com.hk

Korea

Hanbit Media, Inc.
Sonyoung Bldg. 202
Yeksam-dong 736-36
Kangnam-ku
Seoul, Korea
Tel: 822-554-9610
Fax: 822-556-0363
Email: hant93@chollian.dacom.co.kr

Philippines

Mutual Books, Inc.
429-D Shaw Boulevard
Mandaluyong City, Metro
Manila, Philippines
Tel: 632-725-7538
Fax: 632-721-3056
Email: mbikikog@mnl.sequel.net

Taiwan

O'Reilly Taiwan
No. 3, Lane 131
Hang-Chow South Road
Section 1, Taipei, Taiwan
Tel: 886-2-23968990
Fax: 886-2-23968916
Email: benh@oreilly.com

China

O'Reilly Beijing
Room 2410
160, FuXingMenNeiDaJie
XiCheng District
Beijing, China PR 100031
Tel: 86-10-86631006
Fax: 86-10-86631007
Email: frederic@oreilly.com

India

Computer Bookshop (India) Pvt. Ltd.
190 Dr. D.N. Road, Fort
Bombay 400 001 India
Tel: 91-22-207-0989
Fax: 91-22-262-3551
Email: cbsbom@giasbm01.vsnl.net.in

Japan

O'Reilly Japan, Inc.
Kiyoshige Building 2F
12-Bancho, Sanei-cho
Shinjuku-ku
Tokyo 160-0008 Japan
Tel: 81-3-3356-5227
Fax: 81-3-3356-5261
Email: japan@oreilly.com

All Other Asian Countries

O'Reilly & Associates, Inc.
101 Morris Street
Sebastopol, CA 95472 USA
Tel: 707-829-0515
Fax: 707-829-0104
Email: order@oreilly.com

Australia

WoodsLane Pty., Ltd.
7/5 Vuko Place
Warriewood NSW 2102
Australia
Tel: 61-2-9970-5111
Fax: 61-2-9970-5002
Email: info@woodslane.com.au

New Zealand

Woodslane New Zealand, Ltd.
21 Cooks Street (P.O. Box 575)
Waganui, New Zealand
Tel: 64-6-347-6543
Fax: 64-6-345-4840
Email: info@woodslane.com.au

Latin America

McGraw-Hill Interamericana
Editores, S.A. de C.V.
Cedro No. 512
Col. Atlampa
06450, Mexico, D.F.
Tel: 52-5-547-6777
Fax: 52-5-547-3336
Email: mcgraw-hill@infosel.net.mx

O'Reilly & Associates, Inc.
101 Morris Street
Sebastopol, CA 95472-9902
1-800-998-9938

Visit us online at:
http://www.oreilly.com/
orders@oreilly.com

OBJECT MODEL BROWSER SOFTWARE

Many of the figures in this book are screenshots taken from the author's **Object Model Browser** software, which shows a two-dimensional tree-like view of an object model, along with a list of the properties and methods of the selected object (see the reverse side of this coupon). Some of the major features of **Object Model Browser** include the ability to: drill down an object tree using *local view*, save and recall different views, view an object's origins directly on the tree, view enums and their constants, view library statistics, search for objects by name or for all objects having a given property or method or for all parents of an object or all paths to an object, and search for constants. You can even sculpt a tree to customize the view. If you have the corresponding Microsoft help file, **Object Model Browser** will display help information on an object or member with a single mouse click. **Object Model Browser** can even be set to automatically split the screen so you can see the object model and the help information simultaneously. (The list of features is subject to change.)

Object Model Browser comes with the browser software and object libraries for *Access 8/9, DAO 3.5, Excel 8/9, Word 8/9, Outlook 8/98/9, Office 97/2000, PowerPoint 8/9, Graph 8, Binder 8, Forms 2.0, VBA Extensibility, VB5/Extensibility, VB6/Extensibility, ADO 2,* and *ASP.* (The list of object libraries is subject to change.)

Object Model Browser is priced at $99.95, but if you return this coupon with payment, you may purchase **Object Model Browser** for $79.95. Please include $5.00 shipping and handling for U.S. orders, $15.00 shipping and handling for non-U.S. orders; CA residents please add $6.20 sales tax.

To order, just send this coupon, along with payment (check or money order) in U.S. dollars, to

The Roman Press, Inc. ~ 8 Night Star ~ Irvine, CA 92612

For more information see *www.romanpress.com*; email *sroman@fullerton.edu*; or phone 949-854-5667. Please include your name, email, phone number and shipping address. Note: **Object Browser** requires Windows 95/98/NT or later and about 20 MB of disk space. Excel

O'REILLY WOULD LIKE TO HEAR FROM YOU

Which book did this card come from?

_____

Where did you buy this book?
- ❏ Bookstore
- ❏ Direct from O'Reilly
- ❏ Bundled with hardware/software
- ❏ Other _____
- ❏ Computer Store
- ❏ Class/seminar

What operating system do you use?
- ❏ Unix
- ❏ Windows NT
- ❏ Other _____
- ❏ Macintosh
- ❏ PC(Windows/DOS)

What is your job description?
- ❏ System Administrator
- ❏ Network Administrator
- ❏ Web Developer
- ❏ Other _____
- ❏ Programmer
- ❏ Educator/Teacher

❏ Please send me O'Reilly's catalog, containing a complete listing of O'Reilly books and software.

Name _____   Company/Organization _____

Address _____

City _____   State _____   Zip/Postal Code _____   Country _____

Telephone _____   Internet or other email address (specify network) _____

OBJECT MODEL BROWSER SOFTWARE

Please see the other side of this card for more information.

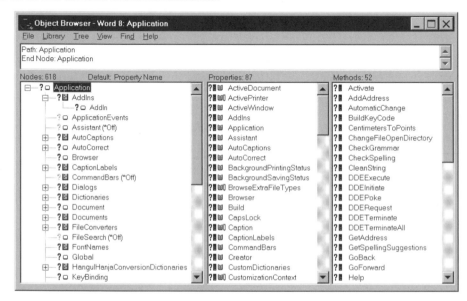

NO POSTAGE
NECESSARY IF
MAILED IN THE
UNITED STATES

BUSINESS REPLY MAIL
FIRST CLASS MAIL   PERMIT NO. 80   SEBASTOPOL, CA

Postage will be paid by addressee

O'Reilly & Associates, Inc.
101 Morris Street
Sebastopol, CA 95472-9902